Philosophical Essays

Philosophical Essays

Richard Cartwright

The MIT Press
Cambridge, Massachusetts
London, England

For permission to reprint certain of the essays that appear in this volume, I thank the editors and publishers of *Philosophy of Science, The Journal of Philosophy, Noûs,* and *Midwest Studies in Philosophy;* the Basil Blackwell Publishing Company, the D. Reidel Publishing Company, and the New York University Press. Details concerning provenance can be found at the end of each essay.

This book was set in Palatino by Datapage International Ltd., Dublin, Ireland, and printed and bound by Halliday Lithograph in the United States of America.

Library of Congress Cataloging-in-Publication Data

Cartwright, Richard.
    Philosophical essays.

    Includes bibliographies and index.
    1. Philosophy.   I. Title.
B29.C2785   1987   191   87-2608
ISBN 0-262-03130-2

To the memory of my father, Donald E. Cartwright

Contents

Introduction

It has been said, and I think it is a common view among philosophers, that philosophical theories are never refuted. A purported refutation may exact a price from advocates of the theory, but it is never a knockdown demonstration that the theory is false. The reason is that there is no clear line between unchallengeable evidence and philosophical theory. Our intuitions, so called,

> are simply opinions; our philosophical theories are the same. Some are commonsensical, some are sophisticated; some are particular, some general; some are more firmly held, some less. But they are all opinions, and a reasonable goal for a philosopher is to bring them into equilibrium. Our common task is to find out what equilibria there are that can withstand examination, but it remains for each of us to come to rest at one or another of them.[1]

From such a point of view, the job of a philosopher is to seek coherence—not only among philosophical opinions officially held but also between them and propositions which, outside the study, are irresistible objects of belief.

Consider the man who thinks he is the Emperor of the World. He is mad, of course. Or so *we* say. For, to each of our attempts to refute him, he has some response; and he is agile enough not to trip himself up more often than the next person. Eventually we leave off attempts at refutation and humor the man instead. We even buy his bonds, backed by the full faith and credit of the Emperor of the World. We pay the price: he never issues a call, and we kindly never try to redeem. His equilibrium goes undisturbed. But he *is* mad, all the same. He challenges our evidence; but that he does is only further testimony to his madness, for the evidence is unchallengeable.

To describe the situation as a mere clash of opinions will not do. For who is so to describe it? We claim to know the man is mad, and hence we cannot consistently allow that it is only our opinion that he is; and he is in the same position vis-à-vis us. But is there not someone, a metaphilosopher perhaps, who can rise above the situation and pronounce the disagreement to be at bottom a mere difference of opinion? Only at the cost of disturbing his own equilibrium, I think; for he cannot remain forever in the clouds.

Consider now a philosopher who says, "Nothing moves." He is not mad. Yet it seems we can refute him more easily than we can the man who thinks he is the Emperor of the World: it takes only a wave of the hand. How does the philosopher get off the hook? He may not. If when he says that nothing moves he means to deny, among other things, that hands move, then he is demonstrably in error—every bit as much as the vaunted emperor. If his doctrine is academic, unrelated to how he acts, he will escape confinement. He will get off that hook, but at considerable cost. Either the doctrine is not one he believes, in which case he ought not to assert it, or else he is in a severe state of disequilibrium, in which case he is bound to be in error. In neither case is our disagreement with him a mere clash of opinions.

A philosopher who says, "Nothing moves," may respond to our refutations by adding error to error. We wave our hands, and he says there are no hands. We point out that in saying what he said he moved his lips, and he replies that there are no lips. He never says anything, he says. Are we then in the helpless position of being unable to refute him? By no means, for we already have. It is one thing to refute, another to silence. Some people will *say* anything.

A philosopher who says, "Nothing moves," is more apt to respond to handwaving with a disavowal: "When I say that nothing moves, I don't mean to deny what you mean when you say that hands move. I mean only that such and such and such and such." Well, if that *is* what he meant, he should have said so in the first place. It is not a philosopher's job to shock or titillate by saying something he does not mean.

It is necessary to be on guard, here, against a curious twist the dialectic may take. For a philosopher who says, "Nothing moves," may add by way of defense that all we really mean when we say that hands move is that so and so and so and so. It is a curious twist because he implicitly concedes that so and so and so and so—whence, by his own view, that hands move, and hence, after all, that something moves. A case in point is a noisy squabble that Helen Morris and I had years ago. I said that propositions can't be written down, and she correctly pointed out that she had seen Gödel's Theorem, for instance, written on the board. I replied that to write Gödel's Theorem on the board is just to write on the board a sentence that formulates the theorem. It took me an inordinately long time to see that if it really takes no more than that, then the theorem is easily enough written down.

A philosopher more clever than I was can avoid the fallacy by saying, "Nothing *really* moves." But the problem is to understand the import of his "really," for it would be madness to deny that some things *really move*. One day we are in London, the next in Boston. Barring miracles, we surely must have moved. If we didn't really move, then, in spite of appearances, we must still be in London. "But Weierstrass, by strictly banishing all infinitesimals, has at last shown that we live in an unchanging world, and that the airplane, at every moment of its flight, is truly at rest."[2] At every moment of its *flight*, notice. Nevertheless, the advocate of a static universe can maintain his equilibrium: "Motion consists *merely* in the occupation of different places at different times, subject to continuity . . . ."[3] But now there is no need for handwaving. It has been granted that in a six-hour period we took off at Heathrow, landed at Logan, and left no point on a certain arc of a great circle untouched. Who could ask for anything more?

"Nothing moves," said by a philosopher, is not a casual remark on the passing scene. It is embedded in a text, with other parts of which it has intricate connections. In favorable cases the text as a whole coheres. But how does that help? You do not improve the truth value of a false proposition by calling attention to a coherent system of propositions of which it is one. Nor by exhibiting it as the conclusion of an argument, even a valid argument: every proposition is the conclusion of endlessly many valid arguments.

Still, how is it *possible* for the airplane to move from Heathrow to Logan? As Edmund Gettier used to say, behind every such question there lies an argument. And it is reasonable work for a philosopher to ferret out the argument and try to say where it goes wrong. Perhaps in the present case the argument is one of Zeno's: the airplane can't get off the ground, for to move from *A* to any point *Z* it must first move to some intermediate point *M*. It will not do to respond as my mother-in-law once did: "There!" she said, taking a firm step. Explanation is wanted, not refutation. The right one may be, as Russell seems to think, the one taught in orthodox courses in mathematical analysis.[4] To the very great credit of Zeno, it took (unless time is unreal) more than two thousand years for that explanation to become respectable—philosophically as well as mathematically, for this is one of a not inconsiderable number of cases in which the boundary breaks down. What then was a philosopher supposed to have thought in the meantime? That Zeno's conclusion is *true*? That, in spite of appearances, the horse never leaves the stable? There are indeed philosophers who suggest by their practice that it is incumbent on us to accept a proposition if it is the result of reasoning in which we can detect no flaw. "Well, what's wrong with my argument?" they ask us, as if to imply that we must concede their conclusion, no matter how outrageous, unless we have a satisfactory response. But we are not thus bound, any more than we are bound to accept the conclusion that $0 = 1$ unless we can expose the trick in the familiar argument. We are bound only to acknowledge perplexity and to try to pinpoint the mistake.

A philosopher who says, "Nothing moves," appears to diminish our world. A philosopher who says, "The Homeric gods *are*," appears to augment it. The rest of us cannot refute him by counterexample, any more than we can refute by counterexample the person who says there is an elephant in the breadbox. Are we up against it? Is it a matter simply of our opinion against his? Surely not. If when he says, "The Homeric gods *are*," he implies among other things that you can reasonably expect to meet one on Olympus, then he is wrong and we know he is. But of course he no more believes the myth than we do. Having said, "The Homeric gods *are*," he quickly adds, "But they don't *exist*"—from which we are to understand that he sides with us as to the inhabitants of Olympus and the explanation of lightning. We could turn away, as if from sounding brass and tinkling cymbals, were it not for a couple of special circumstances.

One is that the philosopher who says, "The Homeric gods *are*, but they don't *exist*," is likely to say also, in the same spirit, "Numbers *are*, but they don't *exist*," and thereby put the square of 3 in the same ontological boat with the husband of Hera. This should distress even avowed opponents of abstract entities; for whereas *Zeus is the husband of Hera* is backed only by a story, *9 is the square of 3* is backed by the science of arithmetic. The felt difference between the two cases is a datum. The philosopher who says that Zeus and 9 *are* makes *some* mistake, and it is up to the rest of us to say what it is.

Another is that the philosopher who says that Zeus *is* has an argument: you cannot deny that Zeus is without mentioning Zeus, and what is not is unmentionable. But even friends of the gods will become a little suspicious when they contemplate the "intolerably indiscriminate ontology"[5] that would result from application across the board of that form of argument. Perhaps, even after a good deal of effort, we are unable to nail down the mistake. We know the argument is fallacious nonetheless.

The philosopher who says, "Nothing moves," is an easy target, even if his arguments are not. Counterexamples will refute him, or at least make him show his hand. And so it is, I think, with philosophers who say, "Time is unreal," "There are no material things," "No one believes anything." But other philosophers would diminish their commitments, if not the world, in a subtler way, against which counterexamples are ineffective. Their way is not denial but eschewal, refusal to countenance; hence it is no good citing cases. In fact, it is no good attempting refutation. The philosopher who eschews does not, so far, take a position. He rather forgoes this or that, except in casual conversation; his official theories are uncommitted, one way or the other.

But merely to eschew is not yet to philosophize. The philosopher who eschews is like the person who declines dessert in the interests of some program of health and strength. The eschewal is principled, and it occurs in the context of some larger endeavor. Consider the philosopher who refuses to countenance propositions. His complaints may be that (a) there is no firm way of identifying and distinguishing them and (b) the proposition that $9 > 4$ is supposed to be distinct from the proposition that the number of major planets > 4 even though the number of major planets $= 9$. And the larger endeavor may be one in which, in spite of the eschewal, accommodations are somehow to be found for predications of truth and falsity, ascriptions of belief and doubt, assertions that this follows from that—for discovery, verification, hypothesis, and perhaps even hopes and fears. Hence it won't do just to pass up the pudding.

Equilibrium is to be preserved, of course. But I would add that a good deal of preliminary spadework is required to discern, as precisely as the subject matter admits, what there is to be accommodated. It is honest toil for a philosopher, and, in an age of high adventure, toil too often disdained. And I would add, also, that the philosopher bent on swiftly finishing the job must be wary of preserving equilibrium by dismissing, perhaps as remnants of some folk science, phenomena that prove recalcitrant. He runs the risk otherwise of sounding like the philosopher who says, "Nothing moves."

You eschew, and I do not. If your complaints are justified, and if you succeed in your endeavor, it would be irrational on my part not to applaud. But how am I to recognize success? What in fact is the endeavor? I spoke just now, vaguely, of finding accommodations for one thing and another. I could as well have spoken of saving the phenomena. The question is what this comes to. It will not do in the instance described, and it is in any case out of fashion, to say with Moore that the object is to find the correct analysis of certain propositions. Is the object rather to state the meanings of sentences of some fragment of our language? Or their truth conditions? And are these the same? Perhaps the object is instead to construct a part of an ideal language—or, if not that, to regiment everyday language in the interests of simplicity and clarity of our conceptual scheme. Perhaps it is only to chart a region of a world, relative to one or another mode of projection.

None of these suggestions gets a high mark for clarity. I think we do not know what the philosopher who eschews is up to. And in such ill-defined territory difference of opinion is premature.

The idea that philosophical theories are opinions incapable of refutation is sometimes confused with the idea that in philosophy there is no truth and no falsity, or none that goes beyond considerations of coherence. David Lewis is clear on the matter:

> Once the menu of well-worked-out theories is before us, philosophy is a matter of opinion. Is that to say that there is no truth to be had? Or that the truth is of our own making, and different ones of us can

make it differently? Not at all! ... We may each be bringing our
opinions to equilibrium in the most careful possible way, taking account of all the arguments, distinctions, and counterexamples. But one
of us, at least, is making a mistake of fact.[6]

Nevertheless, I am left uncomfortable. At least one of us is wrong, but
apparently there is simply no saying which. Or, rather, each of us *says* the
other is wrong, but our sayings are mere expressions of opinion. Neither
of us knows, neither of us has a better reason to believe than the other. A
dreary prospect, to my mind.

Fortunately, at least for those of us in the profession, matters seldom
reach the state Lewis describes. Seldom have the parties to a philosophical
disagreement taken account of all the arguments, distinctions, and counterexamples—as the history of philosophy sadly testifies. So a lot remains
to be done before some impartial umpire is in a position to call the whole
thing off. And even in those rare cases in which reason seems to have
finished its work, in which it seems that philosophers must agree to disagree, there remains the job of characterizing the disagreement. Is it always,
or ever, ultimately a clash of *opinions*?

Is it or is it not the case that, where p and q are any propositions, q follows
from p together with the negation of p? The question has been discussed on and off for centuries—never more intensely, I suppose, than in
our own.[7] Admittedly, a good deal of unnecessary dust has been raised along
the way; but when it has settled, when the various confusions and misunderstandings have been removed, a question remains about which skilled
professionals disagree and with respect to which I see no prospect of new
arguments, distinctions, or counterexamples. What is to be made of this?
Are we faced with a clash of opinions that it is beyond our powers to resolve?

From the inability of either side in the dispute to persuade the other it
does not follow that there is no fact of the matter, as we have just now
seen. Nor does it follow that neither side *knows* what the fact of the matter
is. We cannot persuade the man that he is not the Emperor of the World,
but all the same we know he is not. In the present case, however, an
impartial umpire would perhaps conclude that neither side knows something the other does not. Otherwise he would have the unpleasant job of
accounting for ignorance on the part of able logicians with respect to quite
elementary points of logic. He would be loath to call them mad, or even
blind. But then what is the impartial umpire to say? That one party is right,
the other wrong, but we shall never know which is which? That it is just
a matter of opinion? That the science of logic cannot at this point fulfill its
"important function of saying what follows from what"?[8] That it all depends on which book you read? He would do better to quote Berkeley:
"We should believe that God has dealt more bountifully with the sons of

men, than to give them a strong desire for that knowledge which he had placed quite out of their reach." But he could not go on to accept Berkeley's explanation: that philosophers "have first raised a dust, and then complain [they] cannot see."[9] For by hypothesis the dust has settled. But what then *is* the nature of the dispute?

Thus one philosophical question brings with it another, a metaphilosophical question. Such questions arise naturally in the course of primary philosophical inquiry, for we often feel uncertain as to what we are about. They become especially pressing when, as in the present case, the disputants are apparently at an ultimate impasse. If a disagreement persists even though everything that could possibly influence the intellect is already in, and known to both sides, can it be a disagreement in *opinion*? I think not. I have to concede that the menu of alternative answers is limited to a small number of ill-prepared dishes. But that means more work for the philosopher: metaphilosophy is, after all, part of philosophy. So the ultimate impasse, if that is what it is, is not an occasion for coming to rest.

I have been protesting the idea that philosophical differences are ever in the end differences in opinion, and the associated idea that to philosophize on any subject is in the end to choose from an array of theories no one of which has credentials superior to those of any other. I do not, of course, mean to disparage the quest for equilibrium. But I do not envy those who think they have reached it by coming to rest in some philosophical system. Apart from occasional tinkering, they have nothing left to do except spread the word. And why should they want to do even that? The thrill must be gone.

To the understandable distress of my parents, spinal surgery kept me on my back for nearly a year in 1941–42. For me the distress proved not unmitigated: there was time, freed up by a recess in the usual pursuits of youth. My collection of jazz records was not easily accessible, television was some years off, and radio's soap operas and ballgames occupied only part of the day. I took to reading. The family library was small; but it contained Homer, Aeschylus, Sophocles, Shakespeare, and *The Lincoln Library of Essential Information*. I read in these, with the aim of self-improvement. And I read every word of *The Complete Prose of Edgar Allan Poe*, on loan from a family friend.

Two other books, left from my mother's college days, had a greater impact: J. W. Creighton's *Introduction to Logic* and A. K. Rogers's *Student's History of Philosophy*. Not that I understood much of either. Syllogisms were easy enough, and I came to pride myself on being able to spot undistributed middles; but I had no idea what Creighton was up to in the talkier parts. Rogers took one from Thales to William James in what I remember as about three hundred pages. His story was of warring doctrines, and I had only a dim grasp of what the wars were about. Perhaps it was the challenge to understand, perhaps it was some vague sense that the subject suited me; whatever the explanation, at age sixteen I resolved to become a philosopher. Once I let the cat out of the bag in the presence of schoolmates, and there was laughter. I became more circumspect—and more determined.

In my first term at Oberlin College I bought Francis Bacon in the Modern Library Giant edition: Bacon was a philosopher, and the book was thick and cheap. I found the discussion of the Idols mildly edifying; but things went downhill thereafter, and I soon stopped reading. Could this be philosophy? I was in no position to say it was not; but I imagined that *Novum Organum* must be to the real thing what the Paul Whiteman Orchestra was to Bix Beiderbecke's Wolverines.

I got the real thing a couple of terms later, in Lucius Garvin's course in ethics. No edification, but enough ethical theory to get me through a Ph.D. prelim five years later. More to the point, Garvin required a piece of philosophical prose almost weekly for fifteen weeks. Writing those short essays, knowing they would be read with care by a professional, was my initiation into the practice of philosophy: you could read and read, but unless at some point you asked yourself whether this follows from that, whether this is true or that false, you might as well go back to Poe.

It was at Oberlin, too, that I learned that logic had gone well beyond Creighton. Browsing through the library, I came across Louis Couturat's little *Algebra of Logic*. The most recent signature on the withdrawal card was "W. V. Quine" (1928?), and I knew enough to take that as a recommendation. I think I learned from the book, but it left me vaguely puzzled as to what logic was all about. Shortly thereafter I tried, with some direction from Garvin, Quine's own *Mathematical Logic*. It was over my head, and Garvin was not a logician. But somehow I realized it was worthy of serious study; and so I returned to it many times in later years, I think with greater profit.

The essays written for Garvin were exercises in philosophical criticism. One read what some more or less eminent philosophers said about the concept of duty, or about freedom of the will, and then one responded. In spite of Garvin's good lessons in how to do it, I think what I wrote must have been pretty bad: I recall none of the content, but I do recall feeling each week that I had got things *right*.

I learned more of philosophical criticism from my teachers at Brown University—especially Ralph Blake and Roderick Chisholm, both experts. Under their tutelage I became a semipro. But Chisolm was no mere critic, and neither was his senior colleague, Curt Ducasse. From them I got some feeling for what it is like to philosophize independently of what other philosophers have said. But I did not become good at it, then or later. Like Moore, I have usually found my stimulus in what someone else has said— or what I imagine someone else might very well say, for propositions need not be asserted to be of philosophical interest. It matters to the historian whether Socrates, or anyone else, ever said that you know what virtue is only if you can say what it is. It matters to the philosopher whether you know what virtue is only if you can say what it is.

It was Blake and Chisholm who put me on to Moore's *Philosophical Studies* and to essays that later appeared in his *Philosophical Papers*. I quickly came to think of him as the Master, and to this day I am amazed at those who cannot see the philosophical subtlety behind the veneer of simple-mindedness. Not that I thought Moore always right. It went against my grain to think that of any philosopher. That attitude, I confess, sometimes turned into contempt for some great philosophers of the past. Blake and Chisholm gently rapped my knuckles, and by their own examples encouraged me to look for gems where I had tended to think there were mere stones. It was thus that I learned respect for Plato and Aristotle, for Augustine and Aquinas and Leibniz. A. K. Rogers, and others like him, had not hinted that these seeming doctrinaires were philosophical analysts of the first order. And it was thus, too, that I learned the value and pleasure of trying to understand a philosophical text.

I went to the University of Michigan in 1949, as an instructor, full of Moore and (I thought also) of Russell. My reading in Russell had been selective, and as a result I tended to think of the two together. William Frankena did his best to set me straight about their differences. And he found it odd that, with all my admiration for Moore, I would spend hours studying Quine. It was Frankena's notion that you got your rigor from logic, or else from Moore. What was I up to? I am uncertain, even now. I *still* read both Moore and Quine; and I sometimes suspect this indicates an unresolved tension, probably reflected in what I have written. But I cannot set either aside; if that is a sign of disequilibrium—well, there it is.

Frankena encouraged me nonetheless, and so did my other colleagues at Michigan. Arthur Burks aided in the publication of "Ontology and the Theory of Meaning," which he had seen as part of my dissertation. He also asked me, as someone who knew a little logic but no engineering, to pass on the readability of a paper he and Irving Copi had written on the logical design of digital computers. I was paid $50 from a contract Burks had with the Burroughs Corporation. It was the only consulting job I have ever had. Burks also got me onto the program of a meeting of the Charles S. Peirce Society, some time in the late fifties. I read a paper on Peirce's philosophy of mathematics, a subject about which Burks himself knew much more than I did. Peirce had said that the "source" of our knowledge of mathematical truths is "observation of creations of our own visual imagination, which we set down on paper in form of diagrams" (*Collected Papers*, 2.77). I covered thirteen yellow pages with an attempt to say exactly what Peirce had said in answer to exactly what question, and one more page with a Wittgenstein-like response: diagrams, even mental ones, need interpretation.

I suspect that it was at the suggestion of Burks or Frankena, or perhaps of Paul Henle, another colleague and friend, that I was invited to participate in a symposium on perception at a meeting of the American Philosophical Association (Western Division) in 1957. I called my contribution "Macbeth's Dagger," for its topic was Moore's contention that when Macbeth asked, "Is this a dagger which I see before me?" he used 'see' in the sense in which Moore used the phrase 'directly see'. I thought Moore was wrong, and I tried to show that he was. The paper is a somewhat embarrassing piece of juvenilia, and I include it (minus some introductory remarks) in this volume only after considerable hesitation. Its small point still seems to me right, however; and, toward the end, it manifests an early commitment to "essentialism," a matter on which I sided with Moore as against Quine. I am less inclined now than I was then to say that nothing that is in fact a dagger could have failed to be a dagger, but I continue to think that daggers have their limits. I pursued "essentialism" further in another APA paper, several years later, on Moore's essay, "External and Internal Relations"; and of course it is the topic of "Some Remarks on Essentialism," included in this volume.

Frankena generously saw to my being relieved of teaching duties for a term in 1959. I needed an audience, however, and so I undertook a series of lectures on Existence, which a number of graduate students and faculty were kind enough to attend. I had bitten off more than I could chew, and I managed only seven or eight, in spite of working very hard. Some of the content of those lectures can be found in "Negative Existentials."

I may be the only American philosopher who has accompanied three British philosophers to Big Ten football games: C. D. Broad and P. F. Strawson, each once, and J. O. Urmson over the course of a whole season. Broad enjoyed the half-time festivities, and Strawson thought Big Ten football superior to the Ivy League's, to which he had been exposed at Princeton. Urmson became a real fan. As he learned about American football, I learned about Oxford Philosophy, for which William Alston and I had already developed an appetite. Alston and I shared an office at Michigan, and we had organized a group of graduate students with whom we met on Monday nights to discuss the latest news from abroad. Urmson's visit brought Oxford closer, as did a year's association with Frank Sibley. And so, of course, did a one-day visit by J. L. Austin. I lamented Austin's early death—as I had, long after the event, that of Ramsey.

Alvin Plantinga has described, better than I can, life in Wayne State University's department of philosophy during the late fifties and most of the sixties.[10] I joined the department in 1961, mainly because of the character (and characters) it already had. Once there, I soon felt that Plantinga, Gettier, Robert Sleigh, and Hector Castaneda were *smarter* than I was. And I think, in retrospect, that they really were. But I think I managed for the most part to hold my own in our unending discussions. I had been around a little longer than they had, and that was a help. But my study of Moore and Quine helped more.

An instance had to do with indiscernibility principles. Some of my Wayne colleagues came to toy with the idea that *b* might be identical with *a* even though lacking some property *a* has. That was too much for me, and so I undertook to refute them. Futilely, of course, and Sleigh was always ready to show how I had begged the question. I stuck to my guns, however, and the upshot was "Identity and Substitutivity," which I delivered to a meeting of the Pacific Division of the APA in 1963, but which remained unpublished until 1971. I had become dissatisfied with the essay in the meantime, and tried to say why in an APA symposium of 1966 in which, along with Keith Donnellan, I commented on a paper by Leonard Linsky.[11] Those later thoughts appeared, finally, in "Indiscernibility Principles" (1979).

Just two more comments about Wayne. The first concerns George Nakhnikian: all of us who were there are indebted to him, not only for his virtual creation of the department but also for his wise guidance, constant encouragement, and willingness to give of himself for the sake of others. The second has to do with fun. We were in earnest, certainly, but the earnestness was never deadly. Fallacies were not all that different from pratfalls, and the atmosphere was consequently less intense than outsiders seem sometimes to have supposed. It was a healthy atmosphere, I think, both for us and for our students.

The profession of philosophy has changed much in the two decades since that little society broke up. I am enough of a moldy fig, in my tastes in philosophy as well as in jazz, to think that the changes have not all been for the better. I sometimes yearn for the good old days.

In James Thomson, who became a colleague upon my moving to MIT in 1967, I felt a soulmate: he read both Quine and Moore, and the best of Russell, and he had attended some of Austin's Saturday mornings. I remember the elegance of his thought and expression, and his delightful sense of the absurdities of our profession—indeed, of the absurdities of life.

I had met him, and also Judith Thomson and Sylvain Bromberger, prior to any association with MIT. At a meeting of the Oberlin Colloquium in 1959, Wilfrid Sellars gave the opening lecture, and in it he said that *surfaces* are at the beginning of a slippery slope that ends in *sense data*. Judy, in discussion, spoke on behalf of surfaces, and I liked what she said. Sylvain had given a paper at Wayne, another at an Oberlin Colloquium in 1961, and we had renewed our acquaintance in 1963 at Berkeley. Everyone from time to time wonders why; Sylvain wondered about "Why?" and I liked the ascent. The move to MIT was thus agreeable, and it became more so with the arrival of George Boolos a year later. Once, some years ago, I read out to him something he had written in a published paper. "George," I asked, "why do you say that's true?" Without batting an eye he replied, "It's not." I liked that, too.

In filling out IRS Form 1040, I have since 1949 written "teacher" in the little box that calls for "occupation." During too many of my years at MIT it would have been more accurate to have written "administrator." But the entry fits the spirit, and I doubt that the government will haul me in. I got my first taste of teaching as a senior in high school, when I was asked to substitute for a geometry teacher who had suddenly fallen ill. Among other things, I found myself trying to explain to a sophomore why things equal to the same thing *must* be equal to each other. It was, as Poe might have put it, a singular harbinger of future frustrations. I enjoyed the experience, however, and it started the idea that teaching was a vocation for which I was suited. What I could not have anticipated is that philosophy, of all subjects, is surely the hardest to teach. It is, at least, if you have no system to propound and you want a clear conscience. By this time I must have bored hundreds. But then, I have been blessed with a large number of able students willing to listen and unafraid to talk back. There is no way, now, in which I can adequately thank them. They are too numerous to mention, but I like to think they know who they are.

Most of what I have written derives, more or less directly, from classroom lectures. "Propositions," for example, began to take shape in a course in theory of knowledge at Michigan. It seemed appropriate to begin with the question, What is knowledge? Only what is *true* is known, I pointed out, and so there seemed to be a prior question. But how could you discuss the nature of truth without first addressing the question, What is it that is susceptible of truth or falsity? I cannot remember whether I ever got back to the nature of knowledge. Scattered objects were some of the things I talked about in a course ostensibly on Leibniz, in 1967. "Scattered Objects" emerged, more legitimately, out of a course in metaphysics given six or seven years later. "A Neglected Theory of Truth" and "On the Origins of Russell's Theory of Descriptions" derive from repeated efforts on my part to cover in a term the history of analytic philosophy from 1879 to 1929. I always had trouble getting beyond June 1905.

Students of science and engineering at MIT are required to do regularly assigned "problem sets." I thought to follow the practice in philosophy courses, and thus to revive Garvin's exercises. Mine differed from his, however, in that they presupposed little reading and were designed for advanced students. A standard "set" called for making truths from falsehoods or nonsense by using devices of quotation and quasi-quotation. Another, a spinoff, posed a problem that called for reflection on the devices themselves. It became the topic of a Special Colloquium on Problems at the Eastern Division meeting of the APA in 1971. I was proud that two of the ten solutions accepted for presentation were by students of mine. Another successful entry, by David Kaplan, was a small text on reference, with 27 homework problems of its own.[12] A reader interested in trying my problem will find it under "Problem Set 2" in the Appendix to this volume.

"Propositions of Pure Logic" and, in the main, "Implications and Entailments" are extracurricular efforts. I wrote the former, and thought a good deal about the latter, while at Clare Hall, Cambridge, to which Helen Cartwright and I were invited as visiting fellows for the first six months of 1982. My old sense of puzzlement about the nature of logic had never entirely disappeared. When a logician puts a formula on a list of "theorems," what does he assert? And why does what he asserts belong to the science that tells us what follows from what? In 1981 I had begun to think seriously about these questions. It was a pleasure to pursue them at Cambridge, even if its philosophical history was a little daunting.

I must add that I think neither paper altogether satisfactory. In fact, nothing I have written has ever seemed to me altogether satisfactory—not for more than a few months, anyhow. Perhaps the results would have been better had I more often followed the practice of distributing drafts to all and sundry in advance of delivery or publication. But though I have been ready enough to impose on students in lectures, I have been reluctant to seek criticism of first drafts. I think one reason is that my habit has been to draft and redraft paragraph by paragraph, even sentence by sentence, so that my first completed draft has had for me the aspect of a last. The thought of further revision makes me feel a little ill. I want the thing off my desk.

Talk with colleagues has been another matter. I have often sought it, others have sought it from me, and sometimes it seems just to have happened. The notion that philosophy can be done cooperatively, in the manner of scientists or engineers engaged in a research project, seems to me absurd. And yet few philosophers can survive in isolation. They need the stimulus and the caution that come from conversation with other philosophers. In my own case the benefits have been greatest when the conversation has extended over some period of time and when the interests have been shared. The danger is that one will borrow without proper acknowledgment. I cannot be sure I have not thus borrowed, especially from Helen Cartwright, with whom I have talked philosophy on and off for three decades.

Except for beginners who want to learn and who try to say what they really think, I do not like talking philosophy with nonphilosophers and avoid it whenever I can. In response to inquiries from fellow travelers on airplanes, I say I'm a mathematician. So far I've gotten away with it, for it appears that people who travel on airplanes never were any good at mathematics. I ease my conscience with the thought that, anyhow, non-philosophers would expect a philosopher to be something I'm not. I do enjoy listening to nonphilosophers talk of *their* work. When musicians, mechanics, and people in business stick to their own subjects, they give me glimpses of worlds I could never have made. They satisfy to some extent my curiosity about occupations, especially if they are themselves experts. I get satisfaction, too, from watching a good short-order cook.

Academic administration, at least at the levels in which I have been involved in it, is a chore (*American Heritage Dictionary*, sense 3). It takes you away from your proper work, especially if that work requires long periods of uninterrupted thought. Worse, it softens the intellect: on a steady diet of administrative jargon and political compromise, the muscles atrophy. When I read that NN has "stepped down" from the ——ship "to resume teaching and research," I wonder how long the recovery will take. A minimum of two years for every five, these days, I think; for those who run the academy seem unaware of the need for paperwork reduction.

In my own case, it has been a matter of trying to juggle—an art for which I have no talent. Given two responsibilities, I alternately let one or the other slide, with the result that neither gets carried out adequately. That disturbs me. But administration has had its rewards. One is the contact it has given me with professionals in other fields: I know next to nothing of science or engineering, but I think I have come to have some appreciation of the intellectual qualities of expert scientists and engineers. And I have enjoyed their humor. Seated next to a physical chemist at a dull committee meeting, I peeked at a page of equations with which he had been diverting himself. The last line read, "$0 = 0$." Pointing at it, I gave him a quizzical look. "You thought you knew it all along?" he whispered.

My own deficiencies at administration have been largely hidden from superiors by an expert administrative officer. Even as I write, Marilyn Silva and her assistants, Leigh Anne Clevenger and Concepta Siembab, protect me from interruptions and take on responsibilities that are properly mine.

To write is no longer to put pen to yellow paper. It is to enter things into a computer. ("Things?" Well, I don't know what else to say.) Were it not for that change from the good old days, this volume would never have existed. It is for the reader to judge whether, in this instance, the change is for the better.

Notes

1. David Lewis, *Philosophical Papers*, vol. 1 (New York and Oxford: Oxford University Press, 1983), p. x. I hope no reader will be led, by what I go on to say, to underestimate my respect for Lewis's own contributions to philosophy.

2. Bertrand Russell, *The Principles of Mathematics*, 2d. ed. (London: Allen & Unwin, 1937), p. 347. I have taken the liberty of putting "airplane" where the original has "arrow."

3. Russell, *Principles*, p. 473.

4. For a readable account, see Tom M. Apostol, *Calculus*, vol. 1 (Waltham, Mass.: Blaisdell, 1967), chap. 10.

5. W. V. Quine, "Russell's Ontological Development," in *Theories and Things* (Cambridge, Mass.: Harvard University Press, 1981), pp. 73–85. The phrase occurs on p. 74.

6. *Philosophical Papers*, 1, p. xi.

7. For a brief discussion of the issue, and for some references, see section 2 of "Implications and Entailments," in this volume.

8. Stephen Cole Kleene, *Mathematical Logic* (New York: Wiley, 1967), p. 3.

9. *A Treatise Concerning the Principles of Human Knowledge*, Introduction, III.

10. "Self-Profile," in James E. Tomberlin and Peter van Inwagen, eds., *Alvin Plantinga* (Dordrecht/Boston/Lancaster: Reidel, 1985), pp. 3–97. See especially pp. 22–29.

11. "Substitutivity and Descriptions," *Journal of Philosophy* 63 (1966): 673–683. Abstracts of Donnellan's paper and mine follow immediately.

12. "Bob and Carol and Ted and Alice," in K. J. J. Hintikka, J. M. E. Moravcsik, and P. Suppes, eds., *Approaches to Natural Language* (Dordrecht/Boston: Reidel, 1973), pp. 490–518.

Philosophical Essays

Ontology and the Theory of Meaning

In a number of essays published over the last decade or so, W. V. Quine has made some interesting suggestions concerning the ontology of theories.[1] If I understand him correctly, one of his principal objects has been to formulate a criterion by means of which one can correctly decide what are the ontological commitments of any given theory. My aim here is to reveal what I think are inadequacies in Quine's criterion and to indicate the direction in which a proper formulation lies.

1

It will be advisable to begin by indicating what the words 'theory' and 'ontology' are to mean.

The word 'theory' will be used throughout in a deliberately unusual way. A theory, as the word is to be used here, is a *formalized language*, in Church's sense.[2] A theory is thus a logistic system the symbols of which are provided with some fixed interpretation. To specify a theory it is therefore necessary to state the syntactical and semantical rules governing it. The syntactical rules must provide an effective characterization of the class of symbols of the theory, of those sequences of symbols which are well-formed, of those sequences of well-formed formulas which are proofs, and of those well-formed formulas which are to count as axioms. The semantical rules must provide an interpretation (in some sense) for every well-formed formula of the theory.

Among theories, some are distinguished as *elementary*. Since much of this discussion will be occupied with elementary theories, their special features will be stated in some detail. (1) The vocabulary of any elementary theory consists of symbols falling into five categories: an infinite list of variables, among which there are no distinctions as to type; a finite list of predicate constants, each of some integral degree greater than 0; existential, and perhaps also universal, quantifiers; some selection of truth-functional connectives; devices of punctuation, or grouping, such as parentheses or dots. (2) The sentences of an elementary theory consist of atomic sentences, i.e., sequences of symbols consisting of predicates of degree n

followed by *n* variables, together with such sequences of symbols as can be obtained from atomic sentences by truth-functional composition and quantification, in the usual manner. (3) Each elementary theory is provided with an effective rule for distinguishing in the usual way between free and bound occurrences of variables. (4) The axioms and rules of inference of an elementary theory are to be such as to furnish the theory with all the logical techniques of the lower functional calculus. At the same time, the theorems of an elementary theory need not be confined to such sequences of symbols as are substitution instances of theorems of the lower functional calculus. (5) In every elementary theory, the interpretation given to the quantifiers and truth-functional connectives is the normal one.

These remarks should suffice to make clear how the words 'theory' and 'elementary theory' will be used. I shall have to be less precise, at least at this point, with respect to the word 'ontology'. Many theories, perhaps all, make certain claims as to what exists and what does not exist. Such theories allege that there *are* certain entities and that there *are not* certain others. These existence claims may or may not be fulfilled: there may or may not *be* entities of the kind the theory says there are. Now if a theory claims that there are entities of a certain sort, then, whether or not that existence claim is fulfilled, the theory will be said to *presuppose* such entities; alternatively, such entities will be said to be in the *ontology* of the theory. As words are here being used, then, it does not follow from the fact that a theory presupposes certain entities, or that such entities are in the ontology of the theory, that there actually *are* such entities. To inquire into the ontological commitments of a theory is not to ask *what there is* but only to ask what that theory *says* there is.[3]

2

In the essays referred to above, Quine has set himself the problem of formulating a criterion by means of which the ontological commitments of any theory may be correctly estimated. His answer to this problem is well enough known that no lengthy exposition of it need be given here. Briefly put, Quine views the ontology of a theory as consisting of all those entities which must be regarded as falling within the range of values of the bound variables of the theory if the statements affirmed in the theory are to be true. "To be assumed by a theory," Quine has said, is "to be reckoned as the value of a variable."[4]

Now standards of clarity vary from one philosopher to another. What seems perfectly clear to one may seem fuzzy or even unintelligible to another. Quine's own standards in this connection have perhaps been more exacting than those of most philosophers. A good example of this is provided in his remarks about semantics. Within what is usually called semantics, Quine distinguishes two separate disciplines, the *theory of meaning* and the *theory of reference*.[5] The former deals with such notions as synonymy, significance, entailment, analyticity; the latter with such notions as truth, denotation, extension. Quine is apparently satisfied with the clarity of the notions dealt with in the theory of reference. But the situation is quite different when it comes to the notions dealt with in the theory of meaning. Concerning these he writes:

> The notions of synonymy, meaningfulness, analyticity, and entailment are connected in intimate ways. . . . But there is great difficulty in tying this well-knit group of concepts down to terms that we really understand. The theory of meaning . . . strikes me as in a comparable state to theology—but with the difference that its notions are blithely used in the supposedly most scientific and hard-headed brands of philosophy.[6]

Little doubt is left, then, as to the lack of clarity Quine finds in the concepts of the theory of meaning.

Given Quine's standards of clarity, a criterion of ontological commitment will be clear only if whatever semantical terms enter into its formulation are drawn exclusively from the theory of reference. To the extent that terms taken from the theory of meaning are used in formulating an ontological criterion, the criterion will, from Quine's point of view, have to be counted obscure. We are thus led to ask whether, in general, it is possible to state an adequate ontological criterion which will meet this standard of clarity, and whether, in particular, Quine has himself succeeded in doing this.

Now it seems fairly evident that the criterion Quine offers applies directly only to those theories in which devices of quantification figure as primitive.[7] The criterion becomes applicable to other theories only insofar as they prove translatable into quantified discourse. Formulated so as to be applicable to any theory whatever, the criterion would thus come to something like this: the ontology of a theory comprises all and only those entities which must be reckoned among the values of the variables *of a quantified translation of the theory,* if the affirmed statements of the theory are to be true. So stated, the criterion makes use of a term taken from the theory of meaning, namely 'translation', and inherits whatever obscurity attaches to that term. Quine has conceded this. "Insofar as we undertake to speak of ontological commitment on the part of discourse not in an explicitly quantificational form of language . . . and to rest our case on a supposed synonymy between the given statements and their translations in a quantificational language, we are of course involved in the theory of meaning."[8] Nevertheless, Quine believes that for theories in which devices of quantification *are* primitive a criterion of ontological commitment can be formulated which is both adequate and free of notions taken from the theory of meaning. "As applied to discourse in an explicitly quantificational form of language, the notion of ontological commitment belongs to the theory of reference."[9] Now elementary theories, in the sense explained above, are good examples of "discourse in an explicitly quantificational form of language." I propose, therefore, to raise the question whether Quine has succeeded in stating, without the use of terms taken from the theory of meaning, a satisfactory criterion of ontological commitment for elementary theories.

3

Let me begin by quoting four passages in which Quine has given an explicit formulation of his ontological criterion.

> . . . we are convicted of a particular ontological presupposition if, and only if, the alleged presuppositum has to be reckoned among the entities over which our variables range in order to render one of our affirmations true.[10]

> . . . an entity is assumed by a theory if and only if it must be counted among the values of the variables in order that the statements affirmed in the theory be true.[11]

> The ontology to which an (interpreted) theory is committed comprises all and only the objects over which the bound variables of the theory have to be construed as ranging in order that the statements affirmed in the theory be true.[12]

> The entities to which a discourse commits us are the entities over which our variables of quantification have to range in order that the statements affirmed in that theory be true.[13]

The differences among these formulations are minor. There is in particular one important respect in which they agree, namely, each makes use of the expression 'must be', or of some trivial variant such as 'has to be'. Each formulation specifies the ontology of a theory as consisting of just those objects over which the bound variables *must* range, if the affirmed statements of the theory are to be true. Now the use of words such as 'must be' strongly suggests that advantage is being taken of notions dealt with in the theory of meaning. To say that such-and-such objects *must be* values of variables is very much like saying that it is *necessary* that they be values of variables. And the term 'necessary' is presumably as good a candidate for the theory of meaning as the terms 'analytic' and 'entail'. Prima facie, then, Quine's formulation employs terms taken from the theory of meaning. Unless use of such terms can somehow be avoided, we shall have to conclude, given Quine's standards of clarity, that the notion of ontological commitment is fully as obscure as terms such as 'analytic' and 'necessary'.

To get a further insight into this matter, it will be profitable to look a little more closely at the notion of *values of a variable*. In stating the semantical rules of an elementary theory it is customary to provide a *rule of range* for the variables. Rules of range take some such form as the following: "The variables 'x', 'y', 'z', . . . are to be understood as ranging over the membership of such-and-such a class of objects" or "The variables 'x', 'y', 'z', . . . are to be understood as having such-and-such objects as their values." The point of stating such a rule for an elementary theory is to provide an interpretation for the quantifiers. Once the variables have been assigned a range, say the class R, we may interpret universal quantifications as assertions to the effect that *everything* in R satisfies the open sentence following the quantifier and existential quantifications as assertions to the effect that *something* in R satisfies the open sentence following the quantifier. The range of values of the variables of an elementary theory thus constitutes what is sometimes called the universe of discourse of the theory: the domain of objects about which the theory makes its affirmations.

In some elementary theories the variables have an *unrestricted* range; they are said to range over every object whatever. This is the case, for example, in the set theory of Quine's "New Foundations," where we are told that "the variables are to be regarded as taking as values any objects whatever."[14] In other elementary theories, the variables are *restricted* to some limited domain—the natural numbers, say, or physical objects, etc.

It is easy to see that we cannot simply take the rule of range for the variables as providing a statement of the ontology of an elementary theory. For this would require us to ascribe the same ontology to all elementary theories in which the variables are given an unrestricted range. Actually, any elementary theory whose variables are given a restricted range can easily be recast, through appropriate additions of primitive predicates, so as to involve only unrestricted use of variables. Assuming all elementary theories so recast, no two of them would differ ontologically. Rules of range for variables are thus uninformative as to the ontology of elementary theories.

But let us look more closely at elementary theories whose variables are given an unrestricted range. In the case of many such theories, at any rate, it seems true to say that the variables *need* not have been given so wide a range. Though the variables of "New Foundations," for example, are said to range over everything whatever, there does seem to be some sense in which a good many of the entities thereby included within the range of the variables need not have been. The truth of the theorems of "New Founda-tions" seems independent of the existence of such things as dogs, cigarettes, electrons,—indeed of any nonclasses whatever. In other words, the truth of the theorems of "New Foundations" would not be jeopardized by recognizing only classes as values of its variables; and, therefore, only classes *need* be reckoned as values of its variables. It is apparently consider-ations such as these that Quine brings to bear in estimating the ontological commitments of an elementary theory. Let us see whether we can become clearer about them and about the reasons which lead Quine to them.

Suppose we have an elementary theory, T, whose sole predicates are $P_1 \cdots P_n$. A set of objects, U, will be said to *satisfy* the axioms of T just in case these axioms turn out to be true when $P_1 \cdots P_n$ are given their intended interpretations, the variables are assigned the range U, and the quantifiers and connectives are interpreted normally. In many cases more than one set of objects satisfies the axioms of a given elementary theory. This is the case, for example, with the elementary theory—which we may call 'E'—whose sole predicate is 'L', interpreted as designating the relation *being larger in volume than*, and whose sole nonlogical axioms assert the transitivity, asymmetry, and irreflexivity of this relation. The axioms of E are in fact satisfied by any nonempty set of physical objects. In degenerate cases, as when the sole predicate is '$=$', the axioms of an elementary theory will be satisfied by any nonempty set whatever. But in more typical cases the interpretation given to the predicates, and the character of the axioms, impose limitations on the sets satisfying the axioms. This happens when the elementary theory is inconsistent, or when its axioms involve an existence claim which is not fulfilled. In still other cases, it is not known whether or not any sets of entities satisfies the axioms. This is the case with such elementary theories as that of Quine's "New Foundations."

Now it is evident that the ontology of an elementary theory cannot be equated with *the* set of objects satisfying the axioms; for in the general case, many sets will satisfy the axioms. Nor can we say that the ontology of an elementary theory is the logical product or logical sum of all such sets. Often the logical product will be null, as in the theory E. And ordinarily the logical sum will have members which, on intuitive grounds, we should hesitate to say the theory presupposes. The theory E, for example, surely does not presuppose the existence of this paper, that desk, etc. It presup-poses that some physical objects exist; but its ontological claim is no more definite than this. Any set which satisfies the axioms is a set of physical objects; but no other requirements are imposed.

Now these last remarks suggest the following criterion of ontological commitment for elementary theories:

(I)   An elementary theory, T, presupposes objects of kind K if and only if for any set of entities U, if U satisfies the axioms of T, then objects of kind K are members of U.

With respect to many elementary theories, (I) yields intuitively satisfactory results. As applied to E, for example, (I) yields the result that the theory presupposes physical objects; for every set of objects which satisfies the axioms has physical objects in its membership. Nevertheless, (I) is far from qualifying as a generally adequate criterion of ontological commitment for elementary theories. Notice that some substitution instances of 'for any set of objects U, if U satisfies the axioms of T, then objects of kind K are members of U' are trivially true, i.e., true simply because *no* set of objects happens to satisfy the axioms. And in such cases it makes no difference what specific class names are put in place of 'K'. (I) therefore has the consequence that those elementary theories the axioms of which are not satisfied presuppose objects of every kind whatever, and that the ontological commitments of all such theories are identical. With respect to those elementary theories whose axioms fail to be satisfied because of inconsistency, these results are perhaps no more than we should expect. But the axioms of consistent elementary theories sometimes fail to be satisfied; and in these cases the results are not intuitively satisfactory.

It is easy, of course, to revise (I) so as to avoid these results. One such revision is the following.

(II)   An elementary theory, T, presupposes objects of kind K if and only if there exists a set of objects satisfying the axioms of T, and for any set U, if U satisfies the axioms of T, then objects of kind K are members of U.

Though (II) does not have the odd results yielded by (I), it has peculiar results of its own. Whereas (I) exaggerates out of proportion the ontological commitments of theories whose axioms are not satisfied, (II) diminishes the commitment of such theories to zero. For according to (II), an elementary theory can make an ontological commitment only if its axioms are in fact satisfied by some set or other. (II) thus has the effect of freeing all false theories of ontological commitment. Furthermore, if (II) is taken as an explication of what is meant by saying that a given theory presupposes objects of a certain kind, then it would have the oddity that we could not say that a given theory presupposes objects of a certain kind without ourselves presupposing that there are such objects. The nominalist, for example, could accuse a theory of presupposing abstract objects only at the cost of presupposing them himself.

Though (I) and (II) are thus inadequate as criteria of ontological commitment, they do have the virtue (from Quine's point of view) of avoiding use of terms taken from the theory of meaning. The only semantical notion used in either criterion is that of *satisfaction*, which can be given an explication within the theory of reference. To say that a set of objects satisfies a group of (interpreted) axioms is simply to say that the axioms are *true of* those objects.

But this referential, or extensional, character of (I) and (II) is perhaps the very thing which causes them to be inadequate. That this is so is strongly suggested by the fact that, by using terms taken from the theory of meaning, ontological criteria can be framed which, whatever their general merits may be, at least avoid the evident defects in (I) and (II). Consider, for example, the following modification of (I).

(III)   An elementary theory T presupposes objects of kind K if and only if no set of objects, U, *could* satisfy the axioms of T unless some members of U were members of K.

This criterion frankly places the notion of ontological commitment in the theory of meaning. For it amounts to saying that an elementary theory presupposes objects of kind K if and only if the interpretation given to the predicates of the theory, and the character of the axioms, together necessitate that members of K be in any set satisfying the axioms. (III) is clearly free from the defects of (I) and (II). Even though the axioms of an elementary theory should fail to be satisfied, we might still be in a position to say that if any set of objects were to satisfy the axioms it would have to fulfill such-and-such conditions. (III) would thus enable us to ascribe ontological commitment to unfulfilled theories and at the same time keep such ascriptions within intuitively reasonable bounds.

Now (III) is presumably equivalent to those formulations of an ontological criterion quoted earlier from Quine. To say that objects of a certain sort "must be" values of the variables of a theory if the affirmed statements of the theory are to be true seems to amount to saying that objects of that sort would have to be members of any set of objects which satisfied the axioms of the theory. And it is perhaps considerations such as those raised in connection with (I) and (II) that have led Quine to formulate his criterion with the help of expressions such as 'must be' and 'have to be'. But we should not allow the similarity between (I) and (III) to obscure the fact that (III) is intensional while (I) is not. Though (I) meets Quine's standards of clarity, (III) does not. To discover, on the basis of (III), what are the ontological commitments of an elementary theory, we need to consider not what sets of objects satisfy the axioms but rather what sets *could*. We need, in other words, information concerning the nature of those conceivable, or possible, universes in which the axioms of the theory would be satisfied. But it is just such considerations of conceivability and possibility that Quine finds unintelligible.

4

I have so far argued that Quine's customary formulations of his ontological criterion, if adequate, involve essential use of terms taken from the theory of meaning. Though the point has not been demonstrated, good reasons have, I think, being offered in its favor. Further confirmation can be obtained by examining the adequacy of another formulation which Quine has presented—a formulation which does not involve use of terms taken from the theory of meaning.

This formulation reads as follows: "... to say that a given existential quantification presupposes objects of a given kind is to say simply that the open sentence which follows the quantifier is true of some objects of that kind and none not of that kind."[15] So stated, the formulation is applicable to statements rather than to theories and in particular only to statements which are existential quantifications. But it is easily revised so as to become applicable to theories which are elementary. The following seems a fair rendering of Quine's intentions.

(IV) An elementary theory, T, presupposes objects of kind K if and only if there is in T an open sentence ϕ having α as its sole free variable such that (i) $\ulcorner(\exists\alpha)\phi\urcorner$ is a theorem of T; (ii) ϕ is true of some objects of kind K and of none not of kind K.[16]

Now (IV) evidently makes no use of terms taken from the theory of meaning. Its sole semantical term is the phrase 'is true of', as applied to open sentences; and this can be explained within the theory of reference. So (IV) is satisfactory as far as Quine's requirements of clarity are concerned. But the question remains whether it is adequate.

It is not hard to see that (IV) has defects similar to those of (II). One such defect is that (IV) would require us to say that an elementary theory can be committed only to such objects as happen to exist. For the criterion informs us that a theory is committed to objects of a certain sort only if some one of its open sentences is in fact true of objects of that sort; and if there are no objects of that sort, then clearly no open sentence of any theory can possibly be true of them. On the basis of (IV) we should thus have to conclude that no theory presupposes mermaids, unicorns, phlogiston, the ether, or anything else which happens not to exist.

This consequence is enough to show the inadequacy of the criterion. But it has other oddities as well. Like (II), (IV) would require us to assert the existence of whatever objects we wish to say another theory presupposes. And like (II), (IV) has the consequences that a theory is freed of ontological commitment to the extent that its theorems are found to be false.

It is easy to alter (IV) so as to render it free from these defects. One such alteration is the following:

(V)   An elementary theory T presupposes objects of kind K if and only if there is in T an open sentence ϕ having α as its sole free variable such that (i) $\ulcorner(\exists\alpha)\phi\urcorner$ is a theorem of T; (ii) for every x, ϕ is true of x only if x is a member of K.

(V) differs from (IV) only through omission of the existential conjunct in (ii). And this omission succeeds in freeing it from the defects noted in (IV). But (V) parallels (I) and has similar inadequacies. For suppose the open sentence ϕ is in fact true of nothing whatever. Then clause (ii) of (V) will be true, no matter what class K may be. In other words, if T contains an open sentence ϕ whose existential quantification is a theorem, and if this theorem is false, then T will, on (V), presuppose objects of every kind whatever.

5

The possibility of providing an adequate criterion of ontological commitment within the theory of reference should by now seem dim indeed. In the face of this situation, two alternatives are open to us. We may, on the one hand, cling to Quine's exacting standards of clarity and write off the notion of ontological commitment as obscure. On the other hand, we may relax our standards of clarity and attempt to formulate an ontological criterion by using such terms from the theory of meaning as meet our new standards of clarity. I propose to explore briefly this latter course.

Now the oddities of (V) arose in the following way. Some elementary theories contain theorems which are existential quantifications whose open sentences are true of nothing whatever. In every such case, if in (ii) of (V) 'ϕ' is replaced by the open sentence in question and 'K' is replaced by any class name whatever, then the result is a true sentence. (V) thus convicted all such theories of presupposing objects of every kind whatever. Now perhaps the easiest way of modifying (V) so as to prevent this result is the following.

(VI)   An elementary theory, T, presupposes objects of kind K if and only if there is in T an open sentence ϕ having α as its sole free variable such that (i) $\ulcorner(\exists\alpha)\phi\urcorner$ is a theorem of T; (ii) it follows from the semantical rules of T that for every x, ϕ is true of x only if x is a member of K.

Here clause (ii) of (V) occurs in such a position as to be governed by the phrase 'it follows from the semantical rules of T that'. And this is sufficient to block the difficulties which arose in connection with (V). For, using (VI), we cannot convict a theory of presupposing objects of kind K merely on the ground that the open sentence of some one of its asserted existential quantifications is true of nothing whatever. Rather, we should have to be able to deduce from the semantical rules of the theory that the open sentence is true only of members of K.

Some clarification is needed, however, of the notion of *following from semantical rules*. In particular, information is needed concerning the nature of the semantical rules referred to in (VI). I should like to suggest that these rules may be thought of simply as those which state what Church calls the *extensional part* of the semantics of an elementary theory.[17] One way of providing the extensional part of the semantics of an elementary theory is to lay down rules of the following kinds: (i) for each atomic sentence, a rule stating under what conditions a sequence of objects satisfies that atomic sentence; (ii) a rule assigning a range of values to the variables; (iii) rules of truth for sentences involving connectives and quantifiers. If this suggestion is correct, then the situation with respect to a criterion of ontological commitment for elementary theories would seem to be as follows. Any adequate formulation of such a criterion will be intensional, in the sense that it will make essential use of some term taken from the theory of meaning. Nevertheless, application of the criterion to a given elementary theory presupposes only an extensional interpretation for the theory itself. Once in possession of this much information concerning the semantics of an elementary theory, we may proceed to investigate its ontological commitments. No further information concerning the meanings of the symbols is required.

Cases may arise in which, even though we know the syntax and the extensional part of the semantics of some elementary theory, we are still unable to decide on the basis of (VI) whether or not the theory is committed to entities of a certain sort. Suppose the question is raised, for example, whether some particular elementary theory of sets presupposes abstract entities. It would no doubt be an easy matter to find in the theory some existential quantification whose open sentence would, by the extensional rules of the theory, be true only of entities which are sets. But the semantical rules would leave us quite uninformed as to whether it follows from the fact that an entity is a set that it is an abstract entity. Are we to conclude, then, that (VI) is inadequate as an ontological criterion? I think not. For the situation as described indicates no lack of clarity in (VI) itself. The obscurity is rather in the terms 'set' and 'abstract entity'. Once these have been clarified, it should be an easy matter to decide whether sets are necessarily abstract entities.

In general, successful use of (VI) will depend upon the clarity of the expressions used in stating the extensional part of the semantics of an elementary theory. But this is no more than we should expect. Ascriptions of ontological commitment are metalinguistic. Their clarity thus depends not only on the character of our ontological criterion but equally on the extent to which the metalanguage we use has itself been made precise.

Notes

This essay was first published in *Philosophy of Science* 21, no. 4 (October 1954): 316–325.

1. W. V. Quine, "Designation and Existence," *Journal of Philosophy* 36 (1939): 701–709; "Notes on Existence and Necessity," *Journal of Philosophy* 40 (1943): 113–127; "On Universals," *Journal of Symbolic Logic* 12 (1947): 74–84; "On What There Is," *Review of Metaphysics* 2 (1948): 21–38; "Semantics and Abstract Objects," *Proceedings of the American Academy of Arts and Sciences* 80 (1951): 90–96; "Ontology and Ideology," *Philosophical Studies* 2 (1951): 11–15; "On Carnap's Views on Ontology," *Philosophical Studies* 2 (1951): 65–72. Much of the material in these essays is included in Quine's *From a Logical Point of View* (Cambridge, Mass.: Harvard University Press, 1953).

2. Alonzo Church, "The Need for Abstract Entities in Semantic Analysis," *Proceedings of the American Academy of Arts and Sciences* 80 (1951): 100–108.

3. I intend my use of 'ontology' to accord with Quine's. But I do not wish to be understood as either asserting or denying that there are good historical reasons for so using the word.

4. *From a Logical Point of View*, p. 13.

5. "Semantics and Abstract Objects," p. 91; *From a Logical Point of View*, p. 130.

6. "Semantics and Abstract Objects," p. 92.

7. Quine admits this. See, for example, *From a Logical Point of View*, p. 105.

8. *From a Logical Point of View*, p. 131.

9. *From a Logical Point of View*, p. 130.

10. "On What There Is," p. 32.

11. *From a Logical Point of View*, p. 103.

12. "Ontology and Ideology," p. 11.

13. "On Carnap's Views on Ontology," p. 67.

14. "New Foundations for Mathematical Logic," *American Mathematical Monthly* 44 (1937): 70–80.

15. *From a Logical Point of View*, p. 131.

16. Here 'ϕ' and 'α' are used as metalinguistic variables ranging over, respectively, sentences and variables of elementary theories. Corners are used as devices of quasi-quotation, in the manner of Quine. See his *Mathematical Logic*, rev. ed. (Cambridge, Mass.: Harvard University Press, 1951) pp. 33–37.

17. Church, "The Need for Abstract Entities in Semantical Analysis," pp. 105–106.

Macbeth's Dagger

In an attempt to explain what he means by the technical expression 'directly see', G. E. Moore begins by calling attention to what he takes to be "one special sense" in which the word 'see' itself is used in ordinary English, and he then introduces the expression 'directly see' as a simple substitute for the word 'see' in that special sense. And Moore believes that the only way of calling attention to the special sense of the word 'see' in question is to give examples wherein the word is used in that sense. He gives two such. "It sometimes happens," he writes,

> that if, after looking at a bright object, you close your eyes, you have, while your eyes are shut, an after-image of the object. And it is quite a correct use of 'see' to say that you *see*, though your eyes are shut, e.g., a round blue patch with a red spot in the middle, which *is* an after-image. . . . The sense in which 'see' is used here, is the sense with which I am concerned, and I will . . . use 'directly see' as a mere synonym for 'see', *when used in the sense*. . . .[1]

Moore's second example is this:

> When Macbeth says, "Is this a dagger which I *see* before me?" the sense in which he is using 'see' is that which I am now calling 'directly see'; for it is, it seems to me, obviously the same as that in which we use 'see' when we talk of "seeing" an after-image with closed eyes.[2]

It is Moore's second example that concerns me here. I want to pursue some of the consequences of taking the expression 'directly see' to mean what Macbeth meant by 'see' when he asked, "Is this a dagger which I see before me?"

Let me begin by calling attention to certain features of Macbeth's question which, though perhaps obvious enough, need to be kept in mind. To begin with, we can imagine someone asking, "Is this a dagger which I see before me?" with the intent of asking whether what he sees is a dagger *as opposed to some other material thing* such as a penknife, jackknife, or sword. Anyone who asked the question in this way would want to know *what kind* of thing it is which he sees; he would be asking, we might say, for the *proper classification* of that which he sees. He would be taking for granted that he sees a material thing of some sort or other, and his only question would be, Of what sort is it? Now it is clear from what Macbeth went on to say that his question was not of this type. He did *not* take it for granted that what he saw was a material thing, and his question was therefore *not* as to its proper classification.

It might be suggested that Macbeth was asking, "Is this a *real* dagger which I see before me?" But even this does not formulate in a perfectly unambiguous way what it was that Macbeth wanted to know. For these words might be used by someone who wants to know whether what he sees is a real dagger *as opposed to a toy one, or a replica of one, and so on*; and this was pretty clearly not Macbeth's question. He wanted to know whether what he saw was a dagger as opposed to what he called "a fatal vision, proceeding from the heat-oppressed brain." In other words, his question was, "Is this which I see before me a dagger, or is it a hallucination of a dagger?"

Another feature of Macbeth's question is of considerably greater importance for present purposes. To answer Macbeth's question affirmatively or negatively is to concede that Macbeth sees something. To answer affirmatively is in effect to say, "That which you see is a dagger"; and to answer negatively is in effect to say, "That which you see is not a dagger." So, to answer in either way is to acknowledge that Macbeth does see something. This can be put by saying that in asking his question Macbeth *presupposes* or *takes for granted* he sees something, and that anyone who answers his question affirmatively or negatively presupposes or takes for granted the same thing. Furthermore, to answer his question in the negative is surely to give a *correct* answer; had Macbeth said in answer to his own question, "This which I see before me is not a dagger," he would surely have been speaking the truth. So Macbeth was using the word 'see' in such a way that, in spite of the fact that he was having a visual hallucination, he could truly have said that he saw something.

Some writers on perception have said that there is a common use of the word 'see' in which a person suffering from a visual hallucination does not, at the time he has the hallucination, see anything at all. A. J. Ayer, for example, says that

> the fact is that in giving an account of such hallucinations we are not bound to say that anything is seen. It would be perfectly legitimate to describe Macbeth's experience by saying that he thought he was seeing a dagger, whereas he was not seeing anything. It is [a] natural way of putting it.[3]

Now even if the word 'see' is sometimes used this way (and I am not altogether sure it is), it was in any event *not* being so used by Macbeth. For, as we have seen, in the sense in which Macbeth was using the word he certainly did see something. It might be that we could, as Ayer suggests, always avoid this use of the word 'see' and still say whatever we wanted to say about visual hallucinations. But this would not affect the point that in *a* sense of the word, Macbeth did see something.

Ayer goes on to say something that I find extremely puzzling. He says that

> even if we insist on saying that [Macbeth] was seeing something, though not of course a physical object, we are not bound to infer from this that there *was* something which he saw; any more than we are bound to infer that ghosts exist from the fact that people see them. . . . One can describe someone as having seen a ghost without being committed to asserting that there was a ghost which he saw. And the same applies to Macbeth's visionary dagger or to any other example of this sort.[4]

I find this puzzling because it seems to me that the sentences 'Macbeth saw something' and 'There was something which Macbeth saw' can be correctly used to mean exactly the same thing; and, consequently, I think we *are* bound to infer that since Macbeth saw something, there was something which he saw—if, indeed, it makes sense to speak of "inference" at all in this kind of case. Ayer is right, or course, in saying that we can truly say of someone we know to be having a visual hallucination that he "sees" a dagger or "sees" a ghost without in the least implying that there are such things as ghosts or daggers. But can we say this without implying that there is *something* (not a dagger or a ghost, of course) which in some sense he *does* see? Ayer has certainly not shown that we can. And in any case he has apparently failed to notice that Macbeth was *not* using the word 'see' in that sense in which we can say of people we know to be having visual hallucinations that they "see" daggers, ghosts, and the like. For to say that one sees something in *this* sense not only does not imply that the something in question is real but also *does* imply that the something is *not* real. Macbeth could have presupposed that he saw something in this sense only if he had either known or believed that he was having a visual hallucination. And as we have seen, it is just the fact that he neither knew nor believed this that gave rise to his question in the first place.

We are now in a position to return to Moore's contention that when Macbeth asked, "Is this a dagger which I see before me?" he was using the word 'see' in such a way that it means the same as what Moore means by the phrase 'directly see'. According to Moore, Macbeth was in effect asking, "Is this which I *directly see* a dagger?" In other words, Moore interprets Macbeth as having presupposed that he directly saw something and as having asked with respect to that which he directly saw whether it was a dagger.

Now, there is a prima facie difficulty in Moore's saying this which it will be instructive to investigate. Notice, to begin with, that the question Macbeth asked himself is not one that can be settled a priori. It is a matter of empirical fact (or perhaps of empirical fiction) that what Macbeth saw was not a dagger. Had Macbeth said in answer to his own question, "This which I see is a dagger," he would have made a mistake all right, but a mistake as to a matter of fact rather than of logic. And this certainly seems to imply that in the sense in which Macbeth was using the word 'see' it is perfectly possible to see a dagger. And since daggers are material things, it seems to imply that in that sense of the word it is perfectly possible to see a material thing. If Macbeth had only not been suffering from a visual hallucination, if he had really been seeing a dagger, then he could have *truly* said, "This which I see before me is a dagger"; and in saying this he would have been using 'see' in just that sense in which he used it in his question. This surely seems to make it clear that in the sense in which Macbeth was using the word 'see' what one sees may very well be a dagger, and hence a material thing. And surely, also, we *do* from time to time *see* material things in that sense. For we are often in a position to say truly such things as "This which I see is a dagger," using those words in just the way Macbeth used them in his question. Now Moore has repeatedly said that, barring such possible exceptions as soap bubbles, no one ever directly sees a material thing. But it seems to follow from what has just been said that either Moore is wrong on this point, and people *do* sometimes directly see material things, or else he is wrong in identifying Macbeth's sense of 'see' with his own sense of 'directly see'.

For if Moore is going to identify his sense of 'directly see' with the sense in which Macbeth used the word 'see', then he must maintain both that nothing which is a dagger is seen, in Macbeth's sense, and that nevertheless people can often truly say, "This which I see is a dagger," still using 'see' in Macbeth's sense. And at first sight this looks like an impossible position, for it certainly seems contradictory to say that there is a sense of 'see' in which nothing that is a dagger is seen, and yet in which people can often truly say, "This which I see is a dagger." Nevertheless, I think it can be maintained, though at some cost. It might be argued, and perhaps Moore would argue, that it is possible to distinguish two senses of the phrase 'is a dagger' such that saying of something that it is a dagger in one of those senses does not imply that it is a dagger in the other. And Moore might then claim that it is in only *one* of these senses that a person ever sees, in Macbeth's sense, something which is a dagger, while it is in the *other* sense that nothing which is a dagger is ever, in Macbeth's sense, seen.

Is there any good reason for saying that the phrase 'is a dagger' has two such senses? Well, I think it can be argued with some plausibility that the phrase is used in ordinary English in two quite different senses, such that saying of something that it is a dagger in one of these senses does not imply that it is a dagger in the other. Suppose we were in the habit of giving proper names to daggers, in the way that some people give them to their automobiles. One dagger might be called Charlie, another Harry, and so on. We can even imagine that every dagger had a proper name of this sort. Under these circumstances we would be able to say such things as "Charlie is a dagger," "Harry is a dagger," etc. Here, then, is one use of the phrase 'is a dagger', a use which corresponds to that of the phrase 'is a man' in "Eisenhower is a man" and of the phrase 'is a horse' in "Bold Ruler is a horse." When we use these phrases in this way, we assign an individual to its kind or species.

But it can be argued that phrases like this also have a quite different use. Suppose a dagger is wedged between a bureau and the wall of a room in such a way that just an inch or so of its blade is visible from where we stand in the room. I ask, pointing to the portion of the blade that I can see from where I stand, "What's that?" and you reply, "That's a dagger." It is plausible to say that in your reply you use the phrase 'is a dagger' differently from the way it is used when we say, "Charlie is a dagger." For your statement "That's a dagger" is true even though what you refer to is not identical with Charlie, Harry, or any other dagger, but just with *part* of some one of them. Your statement is true even though in making it you were not assigning that to which you referred to its kind or species.

It might be objected that when I ask, in the situation described, "What's that?" I am in effect asking, "What's that *thing* part of which is showing above the top of the bureau?" and that consequently what I in my question and you in your answer refer to is not just part of a dagger but rather the whole of it. And hence it might be said that the phrase 'is a dagger' *is*, after all, being used in the way it is used when we say, "Charlie is a dagger." It has to be admitted, I think, that my question might have been to this effect, but surely it need not have been. I might have failed to see the silvery tip *as part* of anything at all, and if so, I surely would not have been referring to the whole dagger. Even so, the response "That's a dagger" would not have been incorrect. Perhaps such an answer is elliptical for something like "That's part of a dagger"; but if so, the phrase 'is a dagger' is being used differently from the way it is used when we say, "Charlie is a dagger."

There are many other cases in which we say, "That's a such-and-such," without thereby implying that what we refer to is itself of the kind such-and-such. At sea on a dark night we may notice a blinking light and, referring to it, say, "That's a lighthouse"; and, referring to a passing shadow, we may say, "That's an airplane." So there does seem to be justification for distinguishing two uses of such phrases, in one of which we assign an individual to a kind and in the other of which we imply only that what we refer to has some intimate relation—perhaps that of part to whole, or that of effect to cause—to something which is itself of that kind.

I have already pointed out that we are often in a position truly to say such things as "This which I see is a dagger," using those words in just the way Macbeth did. The possibility of this is, as I have said, presupposed by the very question Macbeth asked. Let us imagine, then, someone who *is* in this position, someone who really does see a dagger and knows that he does, and let us suppose that he actually says, "This which I see is a dagger." Let us suppose further, what I think Moore must suppose, that if he is to say this truly, as we are supposing him to, he must be using the phrase 'is a dagger' in such a way that it does not follow from what he says that that which he sees is identical with Charlie, Harry, or any other dagger. Then, clearly, although he is seeing a dagger, he is also seeing something which, in one sense, is not a dagger. He is seeing something which is a dagger only in the sense that it has an intimate relation to Charlie, Harry, or some other dagger. What could it be? Well, since he sees a dagger, he presumably sees part of the surface of a dagger. Perhaps we cannot say that in order to see a material thing it is always necessary to see some part of its surface: the person who sees the blinking light can perhaps be said to see the lighthouse. Still, it seems doubtful that a person could see a *dagger* without seeing some part of its surface. So the person we are imagining *does* see something which is not identical with any dagger but which does have an intimate relation to a dagger. And we might accordingly suppose that when he says, "This which I see is a dagger," he is so using the phrase 'is a dagger' that what he says amounts to, "This which I see is part of the surface of a dagger."

This suggestion does make it possible to say consistently both that nothing which is a dagger is seen, in Macbeth's sense, and also that we are sometimes in a position to say truly, using words in Macbeth's way, "This which I see is a dagger." Unfortunately, it also creates a difficulty. For the suggestion is that Macbeth was in effect asking, "Is this which I see part of the surface of a dagger?" and hence that he was using the word 'see' in a sense such that one can, in that sense, see parts of the surfaces of daggers and thus of material things. But Moore is strongly inclined to believe that no one *can* directly see a part of a surface of a material thing. So if the present suggestion is adopted, we shall apparently have to say either that Moore's inclination is misdirected—that people do directly see surfaces of material things—or else that Macbeth was not using 'see' in the sense in which Moore uses the expression 'directly see'.

By this time, however, we have learned how to handle the difficulty. What is needed is a distinction between two senses of the phrase 'is part of the surface of a dagger', in one of which to say of something that it is part of the surface of a dagger will be to say that it is *identical with* a part of the surface of a dagger, while in the other it will be to say only that the something *has an intimate relation to* something which is part of the surface of a dagger. It could then be said that it is in the first sense of the phrase that no one ever sees, in Macbeth's sense, anything which is part of the surface of a dagger, and that it is only in the second sense that what one sees, in Macbeth's sense, is ever part of the surface of a dagger.

We are to suppose, then, and I think Moore must suppose, that when our hypothetical person who really does see a dagger says, using words as Macbeth did, "This which I see is a dagger," he is using the phrase 'is a dagger' in such a way that it means what is meant by 'is part of the surface of a dagger', where that phrase in turn means *has some intimate relation to some part of the surface of a dagger.* We are to suppose that he sees something which he refers to as "this which I see" and which is a dagger *only* in the sense that it has an intimate relation to some part of the surface of a dagger. Notice, incidentally, that to say this is not to deny that in *some* sense of 'see' he sees something which is a dagger in the sense in which Charlie and Harry are. It is just to say that, in Macbeth's sense of 'see', that which he sees is a dagger only in this Pickwickian sense.

I shall not discuss the question whether the phrase 'is part of the surface of a dagger' has in English the two senses that Moore's view appears to require. I want rather to ask what reason there is—independently of the desire to say both that Macbeth's use of 'see' is the same as Moore's use of 'directly see' and that no one ever directly sees even part of the surface of a material thing—for supposing that a person who, using words as Macbeth does, says, "This which I see is a dagger," *does* refer to something which, if it is a dagger at all, is so only in the sense that it bears an intimate relation to something that is part of the surface of a dagger.

No doubt many reasons might be given, but I shall consider just one. It might be argued that a person who truly says, "This which I see is a dagger," makes a contingent statement, one which though in fact true might have been false. Hence that which he sees, what he says *is* a dagger, must be the sort of thing which *can* either be or not be a dagger. But something which is a dagger in the sense in which Charlie is a dagger is *not* the sort of thing that can either be or not be a dagger. And something which is a dagger in the sense of being literally part of the surface of a dagger could have been something other than a dagger only in the here irrelevant sense that it could have been part of the surface of another sort of material thing. So what our person sees is not a dagger in either of these senses. But nothing prevents its being a dagger in the sense of having some intimate relation to some part of the surface of a dagger; for this relation can be presumed to be external, so that what is seen might not have stood in it.

I am not altogether sure what to say about this argument, but I am inclined to think it unsound. It has to be granted, of course, that the statement "This which I see is a dagger" is contingent; and I am ready to agree that if something is a dagger in the sense in which Charlie and Harry are, then it could not have been true to say of *it* that it was not a dagger. So if the phrase 'this which I see' refers to Charlie, Harry, or some other dagger, then it refers to something of which it could not have been true to say that it was not a dagger. But I am not convinced that it follows that the phrase 'this which I see' does not refer to Charlie, Harry, or some other dagger; for I am not convinced that the contingency of the statement requires that the phrase refer to something which can either be or not be a dagger. One who truly says, "This which I see is a dagger," makes a contingent statement; but does it follow that had he been having a visual hallucination he might have seen that very thing which he does in fact refer to as 'this which I see'? I am not convinced it does. And if it does not, the argument in question is unsound.

I doubt, then, that the argument provides any reason for supposing that a person who, using words as Macbeth did, says, "This which I see is a dagger," refers to something which, if it is a dagger at all, is so only in a highly Pickwickian sense. Hence I doubt that it provides support for saying that, in Macbeth's sense of 'see', neither material things nor parts of their surfaces are ever seen.

Notes

1. G. E. Moore, "A Reply to My Critics," in P. A. Schilpp, ed., *The Philosophy of G. E. Moore*, 2d ed. (New York: Tudor, 1952), pp. 533–688. The quotation occurs on p. 629.

2. *The Philosophy of G. E. Moore*, p. 630.

3. A. J. Ayer, *The Problem of Knowledge* (Harmondsworth: Penguin Books, 1956), pp. 90–91.

4. *The Problem of Knowledge*, p. 91.

Negative Existentials

Sentences of the forms 'There is no such thing (person, place, etc.) as . . . ' and 'There are no such things (persons, places, etc.) as . . . (s)' are characteristically used to make statements which I shall call *negative existentials*. A negative existential which can be formulated in a sentence of the first form is *singular*; one which takes a sentence of the second form is *general*. Sentences of other forms can also be used to formulate negative existentials, singular or general. Instead of 'There is no such person as Santa Claus' we may have 'Santa Claus does not exist' or 'No such person as Santa Claus really exists'; and instead of 'There are no such things as unicorns' we may have 'There are no unicorns' or 'No such animal as a unicorn exists'. I will not attempt a review of the subtle differences among the various ways in which negative existentials may be formulated. For some purposes this might be desirable or even necessary; but for my purposes here it is not.

Since ancient times negative existentials have been a source of puzzlement. Although it is plain that among them some are true and some false, it has sometimes appeared on reflection that none can possibly be true. Several lines of argument have seemed to lead to this conclusion, and prominent among them is the following. To deny the existence of something—of unicorns, for example—we must indicate *what* it is the existence of which is denied; and this requires that unicorns be *referred to*, or *mentioned*: the negative existential must be *about* them. But things which do not exist cannot be referred to or mentioned; no statement can be about them. So, given that we have denied their existence, unicorns must after all exist. The apparently true negative existential is thus either false or not really a statement at all; and since the argument applies as well in any other case, we seem forced to conclude that there are no true negative existentials.

Presumably the argument tempts no one to renounce his cherished denials of existence. Nevertheless, as do other such puzzles, it focuses attention on a question of fundamental importance to logical theory. To formulate this question precisely, it is convenient first to state the argument (or rather, a slightly altered version of it) in a standard logical form. Let *S* be any negative existential, and let *a* (or *K*'s, where *S* is general) be what in *S* is said not to exist. The argument is then as follows:

(i) *S* is about *a* (or, *K*'s);

(ii) If *S* is about *a* (or, *K*'s), there is such a thing as *a* (or, there are such things as *K*'s);

(iii) If there is such a thing as *a* (or, there are such things as *K*'s), *S* is false;

therefore,

(iv) *S* is false.

Clearly, the argument is formally valid; but its conclusion is obviously false. Hence, there must be some defect in the premises—either plain falsity or the sort which gives rise to an informal fallacy. The question is, What is this defect?

Two proposed answers are by now classic. I shall begin by expounding these; then, through commenting on them, I shall make some suggestions of my own.

Proponents of the first answer, whom I shall call Inflationists,[1] regard the argument as involving a fallacy of equivocation. According to them, the words 'there is', and consequently the term 'negative existential', are ambiguous; and it is by surreptitiously trading on this ambiguity that the argument simultaneously enjoys both an appearance of soundness and an air of paradox. Inflationists contend that so-called existential statements, whether positive or negative, are of two quite different kinds. Some are affirmations or denials of *being*, others are affirmations or denials of *existence*. Taken as denials of being, "negative existentials" *are* one and all false. Thus, in a famous passage, Russell wrote:

> *Being* is that which belongs to every conceivable term, to every possible object of thought. . . . Being belongs to whatever can be counted. If *A* be any term that can be counted as one, it is plain that *A* is something, and therefore that *A* is. "*A* is not" must always be either false or meaningless. For if *A* were nothing, it could not be said not to be; "*A* is not" implies that there is a term *A* whose being is denied, and hence that *A* is. Thus unless "*A* is not" be an empty sound, it must be false—whatever *A* may be, it certainly is. . . . Thus being is a general attribute of everything, and to mention anything is to show that it is.[2]

But, taken as denials of existence, not all "negative existentials" are false; for, as Russell remarked "*existence* is the prerogative of some only amongst beings."[3] As to *how* existence is to be distinguished from being, there is apparently not much to be said; but it seems that only such things as are in some sense "concrete," or occupy some portion of space or time, enjoy existence as well as being.[4]

As applied to the argument under discussion, the Inflationist distinction between being and existence is said to have this effect. If "negative existentials" are understood as denials of being, and if the words 'there is' are correspondingly interpreted, then each of (i) through (iv) is true. But this need not be viewed as paradoxical. For "negative existentials" are more naturally taken as denials of existence; and when (i) through (iv) are interpreted accordingly, (ii)—as well as (iv)—is false. In order to be mentionable, a thing need only *be*; it need not exist.

To treat the Inflationist fairly—especially to mitigate the distressingly ad hoc character which otherwise attaches to the distinction between being and existence, it is necessary to remark that what I have presented as a solution to a problem more often appears as an independent argument for the necessity of that distinction. The argument is a familiar one: given that some denials of existence are true, that which, in any one of them, is truly said not to exist must nevertheless be; for a denial of existence is about what it says not to exist—which is possible only if what it claims not to *exist* nevertheless *is*. From this argument I have extracted, in an obvious way, the Inflationist solution to the problem before us.

Although classic, the Inflationist solution is not popular. Indeed, it has become a favorite whipping boy of metaphysical economists. They, in turn, propose an alternative which I shall call the Deflationist solution. Expositions of it vary in detail from one author to another, but the central point in each is the contention that (i) is simply false. Negative existentials are *not* about those things the existence of which they deny. They may *seem* to be; but this, Deflationists say, is mere semantic appearance, resulting from the misleading verbal form in which they are cast.

Again, this contention typically appears as the conclusion of an argument, not as an ad hoc device for avoiding a paradox. Deflationists argue that no negative existential is about that which it denies to exist; for, if true, there is no such thing for it to be about. Thus Ryle wrote:

> Suppose I assert of (apparently) the general subject 'carnivorous cows' that they 'do not exist', and my assertion is true, I cannot really be talking about carnivorous cows, for there are none. So it follows that the expression 'carnivorous cows' is not really being used, though the grammatical appearances are to the contrary, to denote the thing or things of which the predicate is being asserted.[5]

Contrary to what the quotation might suggest, Ryle does not intend to limit the conclusion to true negative existentials. It is easily extended to false ones as well by adding the premise that a false statement is about only what it would be about if true.

Deflationists characteristically proceed to tell us what negative existentials are *really* about; and here the main variations occur. Russell, once he disavowed Inflationism, regarded them as being about *propositional functions.*[6] To say there are no unicorns is, on this view, to say of the function *x is a unicorn* that it is "always false"; and to deny the existence of the present king of France is to say of *x is a present king of France* that it is not uniquely satisfied. Others[7] have said that a negative existential asserts of an *attribute* (*characteristic, property, concept*) either that it is not exemplified at all or (where the negative existential is singular) that it is not uniquely exemplified. But the variations are less important than the theme; for they would not have been fashioned were it not for the conviction that negative existentials are not about what they seem to be.

The classic answers invite obvious objections. It is a commonplace to point out that the Inflationist peoples the world not only with fictitious, mythical, and imaginary beings but also with such thoroughgoing nonexistents as carnivorous cows and such contradictions as round squares. If, in defense, it is said that he grants these "being" but not "existence," it may well be replied that he thereby parries the charge of overpopulation only by invoking an unexplained concept of being. The result is to dispel a paradox by substituting for it a mystery. The Deflationist, on the other hand, avoids mystery—but only at the cost of creating a new paradox. For if it is paradoxical to say that all negative existentials are false, it is at least disturbing to be told that when we finally tell our children that Santa Claus does not exist, we say nothing about Santa Claus. Presumably they *expect* to hear something about him—the truth about him, one way or the other; and it is scarcely believable that the hard facts of semantics force us to disappoint them. Nor is it much consolation (to us or to them) to be told that we say nothing about him *in the same sense* as that in which we say something about Caesar when we say he crossed the Rubicon; for it is not clear that 'about' has an appropriately different sense. Perhaps a Deflationist can simply *give* it one; but then it is left open whether he says anything relevant to our problem.

Perhaps these objections are too easy to be decisive. Still, they suggest a need for reexamination of the classical theories. It is convenient to begin by considering the position of the Deflationist. He says, for example, that

(1)   Carnivorous cows don't exist

is not about carnivorous cows. In so saying he intends to contrast (1) with, for example,

(2)   Barking dogs don't bite,

which obviously *is* about barking dogs.[8] Now, without denying the truth of what the Deflationist says, it may be doubted whether he thus succeeds in calling attention to the vital point of contrast between (1) and (2). He says that (1) is not about carnivorous cows because, if true, there are no carnivorous cows for it to be about. To say this is to imply that a statement can be about only such things as exist. But if we are thus led to deny that (1) is about carnivorous cows, we shall have to deny it also of

(3)   Carnivorous cows have horns;

for (1) *is* true, and there are hence no carnivorous cows for (3) to be about. So the point of contrast between (1) and (2), to which the Deflationist calls attention, obtains also—and this by his own principles—between (2) and (3). But, now, I wish to argue that there is an important respect in which (1) differs from (2), *in which respect it also differs from (3)*; and I wish to argue that it is *this* point of contrast between (1), on the one hand, and (2) and (3), on the other, which must be recognized if we are to deal adequately with the paradox of negative existentials.

A person who affirms (2) purports to refer to certain things and to say of or about them that they don't bite. More than this, he purports to *specify* which things it is he is saying don't bite. Purported references to things are not always specifying. If someone says, "*Some* dogs don't bite," he refers certainly to dogs and possibly to barking dogs; but he does not specify which dogs are those he alleges don't bite—as is shown by the fact that a hearer might ask, "Which dogs do you mean?" Of course, one who affirms (2) does not purport to mention any *individual* dogs; his purported reference is essentially *plural*, rather then *singular*—which it would not have been had he said instead that Rover, Fido, and Spot don't bite. But, though he mentions no barkers in particular, he leaves no doubt as to which things he claims to be nonbiters. Now, insofar as any proper part of his utterance can be said to carry the burden of all this, it is clearly the subject phrase which does so. Thus we may say that the grammatical subject of this formulation of (2) is so used that it there *purports to make a plural specifying reference to certain things*—namely, to barking dogs.

Exactly parallel comments can be made about (3). Its subject phrase is so used that it there purports to make a plural specifying reference to carnivorous cows. But there is an important difference. Though there are barking dogs, there are no carnivorous cows; and this may lead us to say that although one who affirms (2) refers to barking dogs, one who affirms (3) does not refer to carnivorous cows. The grammatical subject of (3) *purports* to refer, in a plural specifying way, to carnivorous cows; but, it may be said, it does not *actually* do so, since (1) is true. This contrast between (2) and (3) need not be denied, but it is more important in the present context to emphasize the respect in which they are alike; for in *this* respect, *both* stand in contrast to (1). The grammatical subject of (1) is *not* there used the way it is in (3); it does *not*, in (1), purport to refer, in a plural specifying way, to carnivorous cows. It is not that a person who affirms (1) *purports* to refer to carnivorous cows but—since there are none—fails actually to do so; rather, he does not purport to refer at all. If this is not evident in itself, it becomes so once it is recognized that any purported plural specifying reference to carnivorous cows, though plural, nevertheless presupposes the possibility of singular specifying references to particular carnivorous cows. Thus, anyone who affirms (3) must acknowledge that there is some true statement the making of which consists in actually referring in a singular specifying way to some particular carnivorous cow and saying of or about it that it has horns.[9] But it is surely evident that (1) does not require for its truth that there be a true statement the making of which consists in actually referring in a singular specifying way to some particular carnivorous cow and saying of it that it does not exist; indeed, (1) is properly taken as implying that there is no such true statement. Of course, if (1) is true, so are

(4)   The carnivorous cow does not exist

and

(5)   The cow that is carnivorous has not yet been found.

But I take it as obvious that in neither of these is the grammatical subject so used that it even purports to make a singular specifying reference to a particular cow.

The vital contrast between (1) and (2) is thus that the grammatical subject of (2), but not that of (1), is so used that it purports to refer in a plural specifying way. Now, this feature of (1) is paralleled by a feature found in certain singular negative existentials. In essentially the same way as (1) contrasts with (2), so, for example,

(6)   The man who can beat Tal does not exist

contrasts with

(7)   Botvinnik does not gamble.

The grammatical subject of (7) is so used that it there purports to refer in a singular specifying way to something. But this is obviously not true of 'the man who can beat Tal' in (6). One who affirms (6) does not purport to single out a particular man and say of him that he does not exist—as is shown by the fact that it would be absurd to respond with "To whom are you referring?" or "Who *is* the man who can beat Tal?" And to bring out *this* contrast between (6) and (7) it is not sufficient to say that whereas (7) is about Botvinnik, (6) is not about the man who can beat Tal. For neither is

(8)   The man who can beat Tal lives in Brooklyn

about the man who can beat Tal, given that (6) is true and that a statement can't be about what doesn't exist. In (8), 'the man who can beat Tal' purports to make a singular specifying reference; nor does it necessarily altogether fail to refer: it may there refer to (though mistakenly describe) Fisher. But in (6) it does not even purport to refer.

I do not really wish to insist that Deflationists are completely unaware of all this. Indeed, there is reason for thinking they are aware of it, since many of them class together (2), (3), (7), and (8), as subject-predicate statements, while withholding this status from (1) and (6). Put in these terms, all I wish to suggest is that underlying the classification is the contrast I have drawn. Again, Deflationists may be expected to say that (1) and (6) *could* not be about, respectively, carnivorous cows and the man who can beat Tal, whereas this only *happens* to be true of (3) and (8); and, with respect to this, I wish to be understood as saying only what seems to me to be the explanation of the alleged impossibility in the one case and contingency in the other.

Still, if the Deflationist recognizes that (1) and (6) are different from, respectively, (2) and (7), in the way I claim, he fails to recognize that this cannot be said of all negative existentials. He incautiously assumes that in their referential features all negative existentials are essentially alike; and he is thus led to suppose that what has been seen to be true of (1) and (6) is true of negative existentials generally. Broad, for example, asks us to consider "the two negative propositions *Cats do not bark* and *Dragons do not exist*." And concerning them he says: "It is obvious that the first is about cats. But, if the second be true, it is certain that it cannot be about dragons, for there will be no such things as dragons for it to be about."[10] Now, this is to extend Deflationist reasoning concerning (1) to

(9)   Dragons do not exist;

and it is thus to assume that (9) differs in no relevant way from (1). But the questionableness of this assumption is indicated by the linguistic outrage we feel at being told that (9) is not about dragons. Feeling this outrage, the Inflationist is led to affirm the being of dragons. And though we may hope to avoid this metaphysical conclusion, we cannot afford to ignore the semantic point upon which it is based. For behind the reluctance to concede that (9) is not about dragons is the implicit recognition that it is referentially quite different from (1).

To see this, notice first that whereas (2) is not true if there are no barking dogs, both (9) and

(10)   Dragons don't have fur

are true; to deny (10) is to exhibit an ignorance of mythology as pathetic as the ignorance of natural history displayed by denying (9). Some are led by this consideration to say that in neither (9) *nor* (10) is anything said about dragons. But to compound the paradox in this way is to overlook the referential similarity of (2) and (10). One who affirms (2) says of barking dogs that they don't bite; similarly, one who affirms (10) says of dragons that they don't have fur. In both cases a plural reference is made to those things of which something is said, and in both the reference is specifying: one who affirms (10) specifies *which* things he is claiming have no fur, just as one who affirms (2) specifies which things he alleges don't bite. Anyone who affirms (10) must, of course, grant that there is some true statement the making of which consists in actually referring in a singular specifying way to some particular dragon and saying of or about it that it has no fur. But this he may happily do, since mythology assures us of the truth of

(11)   Faffner had no fur

as much as it does of (10).

Doubtless those who say that (10) is not about dragons will also say that (11) is not about Faffner. But how is this to be understood? To the contention that in (11) 'Faffner' only *purports* to refer in a singular specifying way, it may be replied that to say this is to overlook the fact that, in just the way that (7) contrasts with (8), (11) contrasts with

(12)   Hamlet's wife was a blonde.

Hamlet had no wife; hence, (12) is not true, and one who affirms it— though perhaps he refers to Ophelia—at best purports to refer to Hamlet's wife. But (11) is not in this way defective; if it were, it would not be true. And this shows also that it will not do to say that in (11) 'Faffner' does not even purport to refer; for this would leave us with, at best, an artificial way of identifying the respect in which it succeeds and (12) fails.

Thus (10) is referentially on all fours with (2); and it differs referentially from (3) only in involving an actual rather than merely a purported, reference to certain things. Still, whereas (2) is incompatible with there being no barking dogs and (3) is in fact not true because of the truth of (1), both (9) and (10) are true. These facts taken together point to some fundamental difference between (9), on the one hand, and (1) and the denial that there are barking dogs, on the other. Now, there is in any event a striking difference between, for example, (9) and (1). Notice that although (9) is equivalent to

(13)   Dragons are not real,

it is not the case that (1) is equivalent to

(14)   Carnivorous cows are not real.

To say of certain things that they are not real is to invite the question, What are they? And although one who affirms (13) may respond by saying that dragons are mythical, legendary, imaginary, or whatever, no such answer is available to one who affirms (14). The fact is that it is not of *anything* nonexistent that unreality may be correctly predicated: given only that a person has no brothers, we can hardly say that his brothers are unreal. On the other hand, the playmates of a child whose only playmates are imaginary *are* unreal. The question whether something is real or not itself presupposes that the thing has some "status"—imaginary, fictional, or whatever.

Critical readers will have noticed that I just now spoke of "predicating" unreality. This was no parapraxis. For in one sense (philosophical as well as ordinary), to predicate is to say something of or about something to which one refers; and this, I suggest, is precisely what *is* done in affirming (13)—and hence (9). It is, indeed, in this respect that (9) fundamentally differs from (1). To assert (9) is to say of dragons that they are unreal, just as to assert (10) is to say of them that they lack fur. In both cases there is a plural reference to dragons; and in both the reference is specifying. Futhermore, if someone who asserts (9) is challenged to refer in a singular specifying way to a particular dragon, and to say truly of it that it never existed, he may easily do so; for

(15)   Faffner did not (really) exist

is among the true statements to which he may have recourse. We are apt to be told, of course, that in (15) there is not really a singular specifying reference to Faffner. But what can this mean? Surely, one who affirms (15) *purports* to refer to some one particular thing; he is (or at least should be) prepared to answer such questions as, To whom are you referring? and, Who is Faffner? In this respect he differs from one who affirms (6). And it could hardly be said that in (15) there is *only* a purported reference to Faffner. To say this would be to liken (15) to (12) and thus to overlook the fact that whereas nothing can be correctly said to have been Hamlet's wife, something *can* be correctly said to have been Faffner—namely, the dragon Siegfried slew. The familiar doctrine that existence is not a predicate, if understood as implying that *no* negative existentials are (in the sense in question) predicative, thus seems to me to be false. There is admittedly no call to regard negative existentials such as (1) as predicative; but those which, like (9) and (15), are assertions of unreality have as much claim to the subject-predicate classification as do, for example, (2) and (7).

Neither Deflationists nor Inflationists are sufficiently sensitive to the distinction between these two sorts of negative existentials. I have already argued that the former wrongly take statements like (1) and (6) as typical of negative existentials generally, and that the latter do the same with statements such as (9) and (15) is evident from their admission of such things as carnivorous cows and round squares into the realm of being. But even if the distinction should be granted, it may still be felt that the crux of the philosophical problem of negative existentials remains untouched. If some negative existentials are subject-predicate statements, then, of these, either all are false—which is absurd—or some are about what does not exist. But, it will be asked, how *can* a statement be about what does not exist?

Asked by an Inflationist, the question represents an effort to win a metaphysical consolation prize. Even if the truth of (1) does not require the being of carnivorous cows, does not what I have said about (9) require that dragons *be* even though they don't *exist*? Must not dragons have some *mode of being*, exist in some *universe of discourse*? To these rhetorical questions it is sufficient to reply with another: What, *beyond the fact that it can be referred to*, is said of something when it is said to have some mode of being or to exist in a universe of discourse? The alleged modes and universes are so admirably suited to perform their function that they are not above suspicion of having been invented for the purpose.

Put by a Deflationist, the question registers a residual fear that to give up the Bradleian dictum that "no one ever *means* to assert about anything but reality"[11] is to foster metaphysical excesses. But to remove this fear it is sufficient to recognize that discourse which is not "about reality" is "about unreality"; and unreality is just that: it is not another reality.

Notes

This essay was prepared for presentation at a symposium on "Reference and Existence" at the fifty-seventh annual meeting of the American Philosophical Association, Eastern Division, December 27, 1960. It was first published in *Journal of Philosophy* 57, nos. 20 and 21 (September 29 and October 13, 1960): 629–639.

1. I have borrowed this term, and also the term 'Deflationist', introduced below, from Isaiah Berlin. See his "Logical Translation," *Aristotelian Society Proceedings*, 1949–50.

2. *The Principles of Mathematics*, 2d ed. (London: Allen and Unwin, 1937), p. 449.

3. *The Principles of Mathematics*, p. 449.

4. In *The Principles* Russell said simply that "to exist is to have a specific relation to existence" (p. 449). In the articles on Meinong he remarked, " . . . for my part, inspection would seem to lead to the conclusion that, except space and time themselves, only those objects exist which have to particular parts of space and time the special relation of *occupying* them" ("Meinong's Theory of Complexes and Assumptions," first installment, *Mind*, n.s., 13 [1904]: 211).

5. Gilbert Ryle, "Systematically Misleading Expressions," in A. Flew, ed., *Logic and Language*, 1st series (Oxford: Blackwell, 1952), pp. 15–16.

6. See, for example, part 5 of "The Philosophy of Logical Atomism," in R. C. Marsh, ed., *Logic and Knowledge* (New York: Macmillan, 1956), pp. 228–241.

7. See, for example, Ryle, "Systematically Misleading Expressions"; C. D. Broad, *Examination of McTaggart's Philosophy* (Cambridge: Cambridge University Press, 1933), vol. 1, p. 20.

8. Some who advocate Deflationism deny that (2) is about barking dogs. But this denial enters at a deeper level than that on which I am moving.

9. Note that (3) is not to be confused with the statement that there is nothing which is both a carnivorous cow and also hornless.

10. C. D. Broad, *Religion, Philosophy, and Psychical Research* (New York: Harcourt, Brace, 1953), p. 182.

11. Francis H. Bradley, *Appearance and Reality*, 9th impression (Oxford: Clarendon Press, 1930), p. 145.

Propositions

1. What is it that is susceptible of truth or falsity? In spite of the attention given to it, this question can hardly be said to have been settled. The answers suggested constitute a bewildering variety: sentences, utterances, ideas, beliefs, judgments, propositions, statements—each has had its advocates. Perhaps variation in terminology explains some of the apparent disagreement, but it does not explain it all. And the current fashion among logicians of taking sentences to be the bearers of truth and falsity indicates less an agreement on philosophical theory than a desire for rigor and smoothness in calculative practice. Thus there is ample reason for reopening the issue.

2. Treatments of the question often proceed upon one or the other of two assumptions. Some assume that there is just one kind of thing susceptible of truth or falsity, that truths and falsehoods together comprise a single type or category of things; and accordingly we are sometimes told that it is *only* judgments or *only* utterances or *only* propositions that are, properly speaking, true or false. Others assume that there is some one category of things that are, in some sense, the "ultimate" or "primary" subjects of ascriptions of truth and falsity and that anything else which is true or false is so only "derivatively" or "secondarily." Thus we are sometimes told that although beliefs and sentences may with propriety be said to be true (or false), their truth or falsity is "derivative from" that of something else—propositions, perhaps, or statements; and to this it is added that only these latter are true "in the primary way." Perhaps it is unfair to speak of either of these as assumptions rather than as reasoned conclusions. The point need not be debated here. For I mention them only for the purpose of explaining that they are not presupposed by the question I wish to discuss. This explanation may be unnecessary in the case of the second; for perhaps we should not naturally take the question, "What is it that is susceptible of truth or falsity?" to presuppose that things of some one kind are "ultimately" true (or false). But the question is so worded that it might well be understood as the question, "What one sort (or kind or category) of things are, properly speaking, true or false?" So it

is worthwhile making it quite clear that this is *not* the question I propose to discuss. When I ask, "What is it that is true (or false)?" I intend to leave it open whether things of diverse kinds or categories may properly be said to be true (or false). And I may as well say at once that I shall not attempt to give an exhaustive answer to the question. I shall try to call attention to *one* kind of thing susceptible of truth or falsity; but I shall *not* claim that it is the *only* such kind.

3.   There is, however, another assumption often made in the present connection which cannot so easily be set aside. This is the assumption that we sometimes say of something to which we have referred that it is true (or false). Now, to say something of or about something to which one has referred is to *predicate* of it that which one says of or about it. Hence the assumption I am calling attention to is that we sometimes predicate of something to which we have referred that it is true (or false). And it will do no harm to follow the fashion of expressing this more simply, though less accurately, as the assumption that we sometimes predicate truth (or falsity) of something to which we have referred. If the question I propose to discuss is to be discussed at all, this assumption can hardly be avoided. The question presupposes that some things are true and others false. And I do not see how it could be maintained that although this is true, it is nevertheless false that we sometimes predicate truth (or falsity) of something to which we have referred. Surely, it would be absurd to suggest that although some things *are* true (or false), we never happen to say so. And surely, also, any grounds for asserting that it is in principle impossible to predicate truth (or falsity) would equally be grounds for saying that there *aren't* any things which *are* true (or false).

Perhaps it will be thought that the assumption to which I am calling attention is so plainly true that it does not need mentioning: is it not, after all, perfectly obvious that we *do* sometimes say of something to which we have referred that it is true (or false)? Are we not ordinarily doing just this when we utter such sentences as "That's true" and "What he said was false"? So we are inclined to say. But it should be noticed that there are philosophers who *apparently* wish to deny the assumption. Their position appears to be that although we often *seem* to predicate truth (or falsity), this is mere linguistic appearance; in reality, we never do what our use of the above-mentioned sentences suggests we do. This position certainly needs discussion. But I propose to set it aside and to proceed upon the assumption that sometimes we really do say of something to which we have referred either that it is true or that it is false. There is some excuse for this procedure. Even if it should emerge that we never really predicate truth (or falsity), it is of some interest to know to what sort (or sorts) of things we *seem* to refer when we *seem* to do this. Even here, I think, philosophers have not always been as diligent and careful as they might be.

4.   It will be helpful to focus attention on a particularly clear case. Let us suppose, then, that A and B are in the habit of arguing the merits of various chess openings; A, we may suppose, is a strong advocate of the French Defense, while B thinks it inadequate. In the course of one of their disputes, the following bit of dialogue occurs:

A: "Botvinnik uses it."
B: "That's true. But he lost with it against Tal."

Given the assumption that people sometimes predicate truth of something to which they have referred, there can be no doubt that this is a case in point. In uttering the words "That's true," B certainly *seemed* to predicate truth of something to which he referred. Any reason for denying that he *really* did so would be a reason for denying that we *ever* do so. Furthermore, the example is of a familiar sort; one person asserts something, and another replies, "That's true." Presumably, then, what B referred to is of a kind with what is said to be true in hosts of other cases. And presumably, also, one way of getting at that kind is to try to see, as clearly as we can, what it was to which B referred.

To what, then, did B refer? In a way the question presents no difficulty. To answer it, it is sufficient to *identify* that to which B referred; and this is easily enough done. We may say that B referred to *what A said* (asserted, stated), or to *the statement A made*, or to *the statement that Botvinnik uses the French Defense*, and so on. But the matter cannot very well be left here. For although we all know well enough how to identify what B referred to, we nevertheless find it easy to mistake other things for it. This is partly because words such as 'statement' and 'assertion', and phrases such as 'what he said', are not univocal. It is also partly because these and similar expressions, having been diverted (perhaps quite legitimately) for philosophic purposes from their customary uses, are incautiously assumed to retain, even in their new roles, their old semantic powers. In order to guard against these mistakes, it will be helpful to draw a number of distinctions. These are perhaps obvious enough in themselves and have frequently been made; but they are so often overlooked that it is worthwhile calling attention to them once again.

5.   We sometimes contrast saying (asserting, stating) with doing; but in a wider sense to say something is to do something. In this wider sense, A *did* something simply in asserting that Botvinnik uses the French Defense. Now, in general, *what is done* by someone on some given occasion is to be distinguished from *his doing it on that occasion*. The latter is a case of the former—perhaps only one among many. Thus A's asserting on the

occasion in question that Botvinnik uses the French Defense—A's asserting that p, as I shall abbreviate it—is a case of asserting that p. There may well have been previous ones, and there may well be subsequent ones. Each is a distinct case, though what is done in each is the same.

Although to assert something is to do something, what is asserted is not what is done. What is asserted is not the sort of thing that *can* be done; for what is asserted is always *that such-and-such*, and it would be nonsense to say *that such-and-such* had been done. There are two reasons why this point is apt to be overlooked. One is that the different questions "What did he do?" and "What did he say?" can both be answered by saying that he said that such-and-such; and this may be noticed without its also being noticed that while the answer to the second can be collapsed to simply 'that such-and-such', this is not possible with the first. The second reason derives from the variety of constructions of which the verb 'to say' admits. One may, of course, say (of himself or another) what he is doing (or did, or is going to do); and in this way what is said is sometimes done. But it is crucial to notice that in all such cases what is said is *that something-or-other is being (or was, or is going to be) done*; and *this* is not something that can be done.

It is equally clear that what is asserted by someone on some given occasion is not to be identified with his asserting it on that occasion. For the latter is a case of asserting whatever he asserted, while *what* he asserted is clearly not. Indeed, if what someone asserted were identical with his asserting it on some occasion, then his asserting it on that occasion would be the same as his asserting his asserting it on that occasion on that occasion. And this is absurd.

We are thus led to distinguish in the example before us: (i) what A asserted, namely, that p; (ii) A's asserting on that occasion that p; and (iii) asserting that p. Philosophers have sometimes restricted the words 'statement' and 'assertion' in such a way that (i), but not (ii) or (iii), is a statement, or an assertion. I shall follow this usage. But it is well to recognize that the words are not ordinarily so restricted. Among other things, it is to be noticed that in ordinary discourse "a statement" or "an assertion" may be *either* that which is stated, or asserted, *or* someone's stating or asserting it on some occasion. "What is said" does not have these two senses (though it has a variety of senses of its own). It does, however, partake in a further variation of usage attaching to 'statement' and 'assertion'. If A says that Botvinnik uses the French Defense and C adds that Tal does, then A and C make distinct statements—one true, the other false; what A says is not the same as what C says. Even so, A makes the same statement or assertion about Botvinnik that C makes about Tal: what A says about Botvinnik, C says about Tal. Clearly, a "statement" or "assertion," in this sense, is not itself what is asserted: it is *what is asserted of or about something*—that is, *what is predicated.* Thus (i) is not to be identified with (iv) what A predicated of Botvinnik; and that (iv) differs from (ii) and (iii) is sufficiently obvious to need no argument.

6.   Now, to say of someone that he asserted something (on some particular occasion) is never to say all that can be said as to what (on that occasion) he did. One cannot *merely* assert; in asserting one necessarily does something else in the doing of which one asserts. A, for example, *uttered certain words,* namely, the words 'Botvinnik uses it'; and in uttering those words he asserted that *p.* Had he not done *some* such thing, he could not have asserted at all. And here, as in general, what he did is to be distinguished from his doing it on that occasion. His uttering those words on that occasion is a *case* of uttering those words—just as his asserting on that occasion that *p* is a case of asserting that *p.* It is possible that those same words should be uttered by him or by others on other occasions; each such occasion provides a new case. Furthermore, *what* he uttered is not to be identified either with uttering those words or with his uttering them on that occasion; for what he uttered is not a case of the former, nor is the latter a case of it. It is accordingly necessary to distinguish: (v) what A uttered, namely the words 'Botvinnik uses it'; (vi) A's uttering those words on that occasion; and (vii) uttering those words.

A word or sequence of words admits of repeated *occurrences.* The words 'London Bridge is falling down' occur in *The Wasteland,* but of course not only there; the word 'word' has already occurred twice (at least) in this paragraph, etc. Indeed, it is often pointed out that 'word' itself is sometimes used with reference to the occurrences themselves rather than the things of which they are occurrences; and it was for the purpose of marking this distinction that Peirce introduced the expressions 'type' and 'token'. But even though words *occur,* they do not *happen* or *take place;* in this respect they are like numbers, diseases, species, and metaphors. Of course, a word cannot occur unless *something* happens: someone must utter (speak or write) the word. But although his uttering the word is something that not only occurs but also takes place, the word he utters is not. Thus a word is not to be thought of as an event—like the Kentucky Derby or the Rosenwald Tournament—which takes place via its 'instances'. This is further reason for enforcing the distinction between (v) and (vii). But it is more than that. For if a word cannot take place, then its tokens are not individual events or happenings. And so we are required to distinguish the word-token, not only from its type and from uttering that type, but also from someone's uttering that type on some given occasion. Thus (vii), as well as (v) and (vi), has to be distinguished from (viii), the token of 'Botvinnik uses it' produced by A.

7.   How are (iii), asserting that p, and (vii), uttering the words 'Botvinnik uses it', related? It is easier, I think, to say how they are *not* related. Clearly, in order to assert that p it is not *necessary* to utter exactly those words: the words 'Botvinnik uses the French Defense' and 'It is used by Botvinnik' would do as well—as would a host of others. Clearly, also, in order to assert that p, it is not *sufficient* to utter the words A uttered. One may utter them and assert nothing at all, and one may utter them and assert something other than what A asserted. On the positive side, I wish to mention only two points, neither of which, I think, takes us very far. First, (iii) and (vii) are so related that *in doing* (vii) one may (though he need not) do (iii); and, second, (iii) and (vii) are so related that *by doing* (vii) one may (though again he need not) do (iii). I say these points do not take one very far; actually, they are apt to mislead. For neither of the formulas 'In doing x one may do y' and 'By doing x one may do y' admits of just one interpretation—even where 'x' is limited to the uttering of certain words. In and by uttering the words 'Botvinnik uses it' one may (though he need not) clinch an argument, remind Botvinnik of his losses, exhibit one's knowledge of chess, and so on; and none of these stands to uttering the words in just the way that asserting that p does. To understand how (iii) and (vii) are related, we should have to isolate the relevant sense of 'in' and of 'by'. But I shall not undertake to do this.

A closely connected question is that concerning the relationship between (ii), A's asserting on that occasion that p, and (vi), A's uttering on that occasion the words 'Botvinnik uses it'. It is easy, I think, to proceed incautiously here. In particular, it is tempting to suppose that since (iii) and (vii) are distinct things to be done—(vii) being neither necessary nor sufficient to (iii)—(ii) and (vi) must be distinct (individual) events, happenings, episodes, or whatever. After all, A not only uttered the words 'Botvinnik uses it' but also asserted that p; and from this it might be inferred that his uttering those words is one event and his asserting that p another. But I doubt that this will bear examination. For, notice that although A both uttered the words and asserted that p, he did *not* do the one *and then* the other; and, in spite of this, he neither did two things *simultaneously* nor did one *in the course of* doing the other. The fact is, I think, that (vi) as well as (ii) is a case of (iii); and if it is, it is surely the same case of (iii) as is (ii). If this seems hard, notice its parallel in other areas. If Jones strikes Smith, his striking Smith may (though it need not) be a case of assault; and if it is, it is the very same case as is his assaulting Smith. And this is true even though, as we say, *striking* Smith is one thing but *assaulting* him quite another. To speak of Jones's striking Smith, on the one hand, and of his assaulting him, on the other, is not to speak of distinct happenings or events—though it *is* to imply quite different things as to what he did. Similarly with A. "His asserting that p" and "his uttering the words

'Botvinnik uses it' " are alternative ways of speaking of one and the same event; we are guided in our choice between them by considerations of what we wish to imply as to its nature.

8.   But the parallel between striking and assaulting, on the one hand, and uttering and asserting, on the other, must not be pushed too far. To begin with, one who strikes or assaults *does something to* that which he strikes or assaults. But we are presumably reluctant to say that one who utters or asserts does anything to what he utters or what he asserts. He and what he asserts (or what he utters) are not, respectively, agent and patient. Uttering something and asserting something are, with respect to this point, to be classed with, for example, building a house, making a mistake, and playing a game. This is not to say very much, however. For the principle of the classification is elusive; furthermore, among the things so classified, there are important subclassifications, and we should want to know into which of these asserting and uttering go.

There is, in any case, another point of dissimilarity which is more important for my purposes. When, in striking someone, one assaults him, what one assaults is the same as what one strikes; and one who, in killing another, murders him, murders precisely that which he kills. But it is *not* the case that when, in uttering something, one asserts something, what one utters is that which he asserts. Thus, in particular, (i) is not to be identified with (v). This point has often been made; and it has become fairly common to put it by saying that the *statement*, or *assertion*, one makes is not to be confused with the *sentence* one utters in making it. But though this distinction is often insisted upon, the reasons usually offered for making it are sufficiently abstruse to deserve some exploration.

9.   It is customary to argue that the distinction between, for example, what A asserted and what he uttered is forced upon us by what has already been said as to the relationship between asserting that p and uttering the words 'Botvinnik uses it'. We have seen that uttering those words is not a necessary condition for asserting that p. Someone might assert that p by uttering quite different words—in which event he would assert what A asserted, but what he uttered would not be what A uttered. The sentence he uttered would be different from the one uttered by A, but he and A would make the same statement. Now, it is customary to conclude immediately from this that what A asserted is not the same as what he uttered— that the statement he made is one thing and the sentence he uttered another. But the argument seems less than entirely conclusive. It *is* true, of course, that if a monolingual speaker of Russian asserts that p, what he asserts is the same as what A asserted, while what he utters is different. And this does make it impossible that *both* he and A should have asserted what they uttered. Neither uttered what the other uttered, but each

asserted the same thing; so it cannot be that *each* asserted what he uttered. But the possibility seems to be left open that *one* of them *did* assert what he uttered and that, in particular, A did. More generally, from the fact that a number of people assert the same thing, each by uttering something different, it seems not to follow that *none* of them asserts what he utters but only that if *any* of them does, *only one* of them does.

Similar remarks apply to the familiar argument which proceeds from the fact that uttering the words A uttered is not a sufficient condition for asserting that *p*. It is pointed out, quite correctly, that by uttering the words 'Botvinnik uses it' one may, even without indulging in aberrant usages, assert ever so many things other than what A asserted. From this it is concluded that the words themselves cannot be identified with any of the various statements made. But here again it seems that the only conclusion which can legitimately be drawn is that the sentence in question is at most identical with one of these statements.

Whatever is decided, finally, as to the soundness of these arguments, it has to be granted that they do at least serve to highlight an important point about the relationship between sentences and statements; and by giving some attention to this point we may be better able to assess the arguments. Given a number of cases of uttering, each of which is also a case of asserting, we may proceed to count either the things asserted (the statements made) or the things uttered (the sentences). Clearly, it is not in general true that the number of each will be the same; and this shows that the methods, or principles, of the two countings are different. If we think of each counting as a counting of the individual events of utterance *under some policy of identifying things equal in some respect*, distinct policies of identification are involved in the two cases. And this may be conveniently expressed by saying that sentences and statements *differ in their arithmetics*.

Essentially the same point can be instructively put in another way. Let R be the relation which obtains between two individual events of assertive utterance just in case what is asserted in each is the same, and let S be the relation which one such event bears to another if and only if what is uttered in each is the same. Evidently, R and S are equivalence relations: each is symmetrical, transitive, and (hence) reflexive in its field. It follows that the set of equivalence classes with respect to R and the set of equivalence classes with respect to S are partitions of the set of assertive utterances: every assertive utterance belongs to exactly one equivalence class with respect to R and to exactly one equivalence class with respect to S. It is only another way of putting this to say that there are at least two assertive utterances which belong to the same equivalence class with respect to one of the relations R and S but to different equivalence classes with respect to the other. And from this it follows that there is at least one set of assertive utterances the members of which go into *n* equivalence classes with respect to R and m equivalence classes with respect to S, where n is not the same as m. This, at bottom, is the fact upon which the arguments in question rest.

That statements and sentences differ in their arithmetics, in the sense explained, cannot be denied. But from this alone it does not follow that no one ever asserts what he utters. Consider this analogy. Given a number of boxers, each of whom has exactly one manager and exactly one trainer, we may proceed to count by identifying any two who have the same manager or by identifying any two who have the same trainer. To count in the first way is to count the number of managers, and to count in the second way is to count the number of trainers. Clearly, the numbers obtained in the two countings need not be the same; and so we may, as we did with statements and sentences, say that the arithmetic of managers is different from that of trainers. But it would obviously be wrong to conclude that no boxer's manager is also his trainer. How is it any different with statements and sentences?

Presumably those who use the arguments under discussion are tacitly supposing that there is a fundamental difference between the two situations. And perhaps the difference to which they would call attention is this: whereas there is no absurdity in supposing of two boxers who have the same manager that one is trained by his manager while the other is not, there *is* an absurdity in supposing of two individual events of assertive utterance, which coincide as to what is asserted, that while what is asserted in one is identical with what is uttered in it, what is asserted in the *other* is not identical with what is uttered in *it*. Perhaps it is being assumed, in other words, that there is an absurdity in the supposition that there should be two occasions upon which the same thing is asserted and yet that only one of these should be an occasion upon which what is asserted is what is uttered. And, clearly, *if* it is absurd to suppose this, then no one ever asserts what he utters; for, as we have seen, it is certainly true that if anyone asserts what he utters, then it is possible for others to assert what he did without uttering the words he uttered.

But is there any reason for supposing this assumption to be true? I think there is. Surely there *is* an absurdity in the supposition that one person should assert that which, in asserting it, he utters, while another should assert the very same thing but utter something different; for this could happen only if the other *asserted* certain words *without uttering them*. And even if it be granted that there is nothing intrinsically absurd in supposing that what is asserted is a sentence, it surely *is* absurd to suppose that one might assert a sentence without even uttering it. Consider A and the Russian. Whatever plausibility there is in saying that A asserted the words he uttered derives from the fact that he did, after all, utter them. But even this plausibility, minimal as it is in any case, is missing when we consider the Russian; for, on the assumption that it is A who asserts what he utters, the Russian asserts A's words only if he asserts them without uttering them. A said (i.e., asserted) that Botvinnik uses the French Defense; and in so saying he said (i.e., spoke) the words 'Botvinnik uses it'. Perhaps it is tempting to capitalize on the ambiguity by concluding that A asserted the words he spoke. But there is not even the excuse of ambiguity for saying that the Russian asserted those words. For he did not say them.

Supplemented in this way, the arguments under discussion do, then, succeed in showing that what one asserts is not that which, in asserting it, he utters. And the considerations brought to bear in them suffice to establish also the stronger conclusion that what is asserted is not a sentence at all. For if no one ever asserts what he utters, then what he asserts is a sentence only if it is some sentence other than the one he utters. But that this necessary condition should ever be fulfilled is what we have just seen to be absurd.

10.   The distinction between what a person utters and what he asserts is one to which many philosophers have called attention. But, having called attention to it, many have gone on to confuse it with another—namely, the distinction between *the words one utters* and *what those words mean*. It has been thought, in other words, that the distinction between sentences and statements coincides with that between sentences and their meanings; and this, as I shall now try to explain, is not so.

Consider, for this purpose, the words 'It's raining'. These are words in the uttering of which people often (though not always) assert something. But of course *what* is asserted varies from one occasion of their utterance to another. A person who utters them one day does not (normally) make the same statement as one who utters them the next; and one who utters them in Oberlin does not usually assert what is asserted by one who utters them in Detroit. But these variations in what is asserted are *not* accompanied by corresponding changes in meaning. The words 'It's raining' retain the same meaning throughout.

Words do sometimes undergo changes in meaning; 'deer', for example, no longer means what it once meant, for it was once properly applicable to any animal. And it *may* be that the words 'It's raining' have come to mean something other than what they once meant. We can at least imagine that they should in the future come to have a different meaning, so that (say) they come to be appropriate only for steady downpours, not for drizzles or cloudbursts. Similarly, some words mean one thing in one locality and another in another; thus 'corn' does not mean in England what it means in the United States. And we can imagine that the words 'It's raining' should be subject to some such regional variation in usage. All this is sensible enough. But it is surely ridiculous to suggest that the words 'It's raining' change in meaning from week to week, from day to day, from one moment to the next—and this only because of a change in time; and how astounding would it be were their meaning to change with *every* change in place—and this for *no* other reason than that the place had changed.

Anyone who says that the words 'It's raining' do not mean today what they meant yesterday may well be challenged to say what they *did* mean yesterday. Perhaps it will be answered that yesterday they meant what today is meant by the words 'It rained yesterday'. But this is evidently not true. For one thing that is clear about what 'It rained yesterday' means today is this: one who utters those words speaks correctly only if the day he refers to is the day before the day of his utterance. But anyone who had uttered the words 'It's raining' yesterday and conformed to *this* necessary condition would *not* have spoken correctly. Alternatively, it might be suggested that yesterday the words 'It's raining' meant that it rained yesterday, whereas today they mean that it's raining today. But it is not clear that this answer enjoys any advantage over the preceding one. If we are told that 'He speaks with the vulgar' once meant that he speaks the common language, then we are surely entitled to conclude that 'He speaks with the vulgar' once meant what is now meant by 'He speaks the common language'. Why should we not draw the analogous conclusion in the present case? But perhaps the proposed alternative is better stated thus: the difference between what the words 'It's raining' meant yesterday and what they mean today is that one who uttered them yesterday referred (if he spoke correctly) to yesterday's weather, while one who utters them today refers (if he speaks correctly) to today's weather. And a similar account might be offered of the difference in meaning which 'It's raining' is alleged to enjoy as between Oberlin and Detroit. But these suggestions, though they involve obvious truths, are hardly to the point. The facts cited about 'It's raining' are simply specifications of a quite general point concerning the meaning of those words—today *and* yesterday, in Oberlin *and* Detroit. This is that one who utters them speaks correctly only if he refers to the weather at the time of his utterance and in his (more or less) immediate vicinity. It is this general fact about what the words mean which makes it possible for distinct utterances of them to vary as to statement made. And it is surely odd to use this general fact about what they mean to explain the contention that in no two places, and at no two times, do they have the same meaning.

The fundamental point is this. It is perfectly possible to know what the words 'It's raining' mean. Any speaker of English knows what they mean. Probably many Russians do not know; but they can easily enough find out by consulting dictionaries, grammars, and speakers of English. But it is *not* possible to know what (one and only one) statement is made by assertively uttering those words. There is no such statement. They are used, without any alteration in meaning, to assert now one thing, now another. And the same is true of hosts of other sentences—for example, the sentence 'Botvinnik uses it'. With no change in meaning, those words may be used to make the statement A made, or the statement that Botvinnik uses the Caro-Kann Defense, or the statement that he uses the Queen's Gambit, etc.

Perhaps it will be thought that although sameness of meaning of sentence uttered is not a sufficient condition of sameness of statement made, it is nevertheless a necessary condition. That is, it might be supposed that if two people assert the same thing, the words uttered by the one must mean the same as the words uttered by the other. But even this seems to me not to be true. Fifty years from now someone might assert what A asserted by uttering the words 'Botvinnik used it'. Such a person asserts exactly what A asserts, but the words he utters do not mean the same as A's words. To tell someone learning the language that 'Botvinnik uses it' and 'Botvinnik used it' have the same meaning would lead him to suppose that they can be used interchangeably; and this is clearly not true.

I trust it will be understood that I am not suggesting that, given any and every sequence of words, it is appropriate to speak without qualification of "what they mean." Some such sequences make no sense, and others have no single meaning. This latter consideration leads us to speak of what some sequence of words means in this or that context of utterance—of what they mean *here* in contrast with what they mean *there*. Also, words are sometimes used idiosyncratically, through downright misuse or through deliberate innovation. In such cases we distinguish what so-and-so means by such-and-such words from what they usually or customarily or ordinarily mean. All this is evident enough. My point is simply this: to determine what certain words mean—always, or in this or that sort of context, or as used by someone on some occasion—is not in general to determine what (one and only one) statement is made by someone who uses them in that way. What tends to obscure this point is, I think, the ease with which we interchange "what so-and-so meant by such-and-such words (on some particular occasion)" with "what, as used by so-and-so (on that occasion), such-and-such words mean"—this coupled with the fact that what a *person* means by the words he utters *may* be a statement. It is appropriate in some circumstances to say that what so-and-so means (meant) by such-and-such words is some statement or other. It may be the statement he actually made; in other cases it may be a statement only implied, suggested, or hinted at, or it may be the statement he would have made had he spoken strictly, or with sufficient forethought, or with no verbal slip—and so on, through a variety of cases we need not bother to detail. But from the fact that, in one or another of these ways, what a *person* means may be a statement, it by no means follows that the statement is what his *words* meant—even as used by him on that occasion. If someone utters 'It's waning', he may thereby assert that it's raining (at that time and in that place). But this statement is *not* what the words 'It's waning' mean as used by him on that occasion; for he used them synonymously with 'It's raining', and hence anyone else might use them as he did to make a different statement. The fact is that phrases of the form 'what so-and-so means (meant) by such-and-such words (on this or that occasion)' are ambiguous as between, on the one hand, what those words mean as used by him on the occasion in question and, on the other, the statement which (in one or another sense) he means (meant) to make. It is by overlooking this ambiguity that we are so easily led to confuse the distinction between sentences and statements with the distinction between sentences and their meanings.

11.   The line of argument just presented does, I think, establish conclusively that the distinction between what one utters and what he asserts is not the same as the distinction between the sentence uttered and its meaning. It shows, that is, that what one asserts cannot in general be identified with the meaning of one's words: sometimes, at least, what is asserted in the uttering of a sentence is not what that sentence means. But I think the argument has sometimes been thought to establish more than this; it has, I believe, been thought to prove the stronger conclusion that *in no case whatever* does one assert that which the words he utters mean. I wish now to raise the question whether this stronger conclusion really does follow.

The argument appeals at bottom to the fact that statements differ in arithmetic not only from the sentences used to make them but also from the meanings of those sentences. Given a set of individual events of assertive utterances, we may proceed to count by identifying any two which are so related that what is meant (on that occasion of its utterance) by what is uttered in the one is the same as what is meant (on that occasion of *its* utterance) by what is uttered in the other. Clearly, the number thus obtained will not necessarily be the same as the number of sentences uttered; and what we have just seen in addition is that neither will it necessarily be the same as the number of statements made. This may be put somewhat more formally, as follows: Let T be the relation which one individual event of assertive utterance bears to another if and only if what is meant (on that occasion of its utterance) by what is uttered in the one is the same as what is meant (on that occasion of *its* utterance) by what is uttered in the other. Evidently, T is an equivalent relation having the set of assertive utterances as its field. Hence, like R and S, T yields a partition of the set of assertive utterances; but this partition is identical neither with that yielded by S nor with that yielded by R: the set of T equivalence classes is not identical with the set of S equivalence classes nor is it identical with the set of R equivalence classes.

Still, from this alone it simply does not follow that no one ever asserts that which the sentence he utters means—any more than it followed, from the mere fact that sentences and statements differ in arithmetic, that what is asserted is *never* what is uttered. Why should there not be *some* assertive utterances with respect to which what is asserted coincides with what is meant by the words uttered? The fact of arithmetical difference between statements and meanings does indeed preclude the possibility that this should be true of all assertive utterances; but it *is* compatible with its being true of *some*. Thus an argument from the arithmetical difference between statements and "meanings" to the conclusion that in *no* case is what is asserted the meaning of the words uttered, is at best enthymematic; and we are accordingly led to look for satisfactory missing premises.

Recall, to begin with, the procedure used in the case of the argument for distinguishing statements from sentences. There it was pointed out that any statement made on some occasion by uttering certain words can, on another occasion, be asserted by uttering different words. No statement, we might have said, is so "tied to" a given sentence that it cannot be made by uttering some other sentence. From this it was seen to follow that if anyone were ever to assert the words he uttered, he or someone else might assert those words without uttering them; and this consequence was said to be absurd. Now, it is tempting to proceed analogously in the present case. Thus it might be suggested that any statement, asserted on one occasion by uttering words which there have a certain meaning, *can*, on another occasion, be asserted by uttering words which, on this second occasion, have a different meaning. Statements, it might be said, are no more tied to the meaning of sentences than they are to the sentences themselves. From this it would follow that if what someone asserts, on some occasion, is the meaning which the words he utters have on that occasion of their utterance, then it is possible that he or someone else should, on another occasion, *assert* that meaning by uttering words which, on that occasion of their utterance, don't *have* it; and this consequence, it might be said, is absurd.

Although this procedure is tempting, its effectiveness in the present connection is less than entirely clear. It does have to be acknowledged, I think, that every statement whatever is such that there is no one meaning which any sentence used to assert it must have. The only serious candidates for counterinstances are the statements of pure mathematics and some (at least) of the statements of the sciences. But even these are not really exceptions. In order to assert, for example, that 2 is a prime, it is not necessary to utter a sentence having the same meaning as the sentence '2 is a prime'. The sentence 'It's prime' will, in the right context, do perfectly well. And a similar move will take care of any other alleged counterexample. If the meaning of a sentence is such as to permit utterances of the sentence to vary as to statement made, let us call the sentence *incomplete*.

The sentence 'It's prime' is, in this sense, incomplete—as are 'It's raining' and 'Botvinnik uses it'. In contrast, the sentence '2 is prime' is (we may presume) *complete*: its meaning is such that assertive utterances of it coincide as to statement made. Now, it should be obvious that an incomplete sentence cannot have the same meaning as a complete one. And any statement which can be made by uttering a complete sentence can also be made by uttering an incomplete one. It follows that no statement is such that every pair of sentences used to make it must agree in meaning.

It has to be acknowledged, also, that the meaning of an incomplete sentence cannot be identified with any of the various statements it can be used to assert. We could not, for example, identify the meaning of the incomplete sentence 'Botvinnik uses it' with the statement that *p*. To do so would leave it a mystery how it is that the sentence can be used, without alteration of meaning, to make other statements. And for the same reason we must avoid identifying the meaning of an incomplete sentence with any statement at all.

But to acknowledge these points is not in itself to preclude the possibility that the statement made by someone who utters an incomplete sentence should itself be the meaning of some sentence or other. It cannot, as we have seen, be the meaning of an incomplete sentence; and thus it cannot be the meaning of the incomplete sentence uttered in the making of it. But why should it not be the meaning of some complete sentence? The statement A made, for example, is not the meaning of the sentence he uttered, nor is it the meaning of any other incomplete sentence; but we have yet to be given any reason for denying that it is the meaning of some complete sentence. If it is, then A asserted that meaning, even though he uttered words which don't have it; and it is not clear that in this there is any absurdity—unless, of course, the whole idea of asserting meanings is absurd. It does, indeed, sometimes appear to be held that for each statement that can be made by uttering some given incomplete sentence, there is (or in theory could be) a complete sentence having that statement as its meaning. And this view, though perhaps false, is not absurd. It is not absurd, that is, unless there is some absurdity in supposing a meaning to be asserted *at all*. And an appeal to this absurdity (if it is such) would evidently be inappropriate in the present context.

That what is asserted is never what is meant (by what is uttered) can thus *not* be established by arguing in a way analogous to that in which it was earlier argued that what is asserted is never what is uttered. And it is worthwhile calling attention, also, to the inadequacy in the present case of another move which might with some plausibility have been made in the earlier discussion of the relationship between statements and sentences. In that discussion it was pointed out that the set of sentences which can be used to assert a given statement is in no case a unit set—even when aberrant usages are neglected. And we may now add that this holds even if incomplete sentences are disregarded: in no case is the set of complete sentences which can be used to make a given statement a unit set. Now, it might well have been pointed out that if we sought to identify the statement made with one of these complete sentences, we should have absolutely no reason for picking one of them rather than any other. None is in any way a more natural or reasonable choice than any other. I take it that this consideration by itself will appear to some to be sufficient reason for refusing to identify the statement made with any of the (complete) sentences which can be used to assert it. It cannot be a perfectly arbitrary matter, they will say, which, if any, of a number of *distinct* things is identical with some *one* thing.

This move is one of a kind which is familiar in philosophy and with which I feel a good deal of sympathy. Yet I doubt whether *by themselves* arguments of this sort ever accomplish much; and, what is more important for present purposes, none such is available as a means for protesting against a proposed identification of (even some) statements with the meanings of complete sentences. Let me explain, in turn, each of these points.

Russell has often remarked on our tendency to assume that for every equivalence relation E there exists a many-one relation F such that one thing bears E to another if and only if both bear F to some third thing. Now, if our *only* aim were to provide such a many-one relation in the case of the equivalence relation R, it would suffice to take as converse domain any set of sentences in one-one correspondence with the set of R equivalence classes. And among the available candidates the most natural choices are perhaps sets made up by selecting some one complete sentence (assuming there to be one) from every set which has as members just those sentences uttered in the members of some R equivalence class. In other words, if we demanded of statements *only* that, for each set of assertively equivalent individual events of assertive utterance, there be a unique statement, then what might be called "representative sentences" would do quite well. So, too, would the R equivalence classes themselves, or representative members of them, and so, for that matter, would an infinity of other things. And it *would* be quite arbitrary, so far, which of these were to be designated "statements"—unless, of course, grounds for choice are somehow to be found in those very general considerations at best vaguely indicated by words like 'convenience' and 'simplicity'. Our position with respect to statements would, in fact, be not unlike what it is sometimes claimed to be with respect to natural numbers. Peano's axioms evidently do embody at least some of the features of the natural numbers; and they are in addition categorical, that is, any two models are isomorphic. Some have accordingly been led to say that the concept of a natural number is adequately represented by those axioms; and they have gone on to conclude that the concept is insufficiently determinate to permit a reasonable identification of the system of natural numbers with one rather than another of the various distinct (but isomorphic) models. Each, they say, may quite legitimately be "taken as" the system of natural numbers. The concept of a natural number might, on this view, be said to be *open*, in the sense that distinct sets of things may equally legitimately be identified as the set of natural numbers. Now, anyone who proposes to identify statements with some set of representative sentences is presumably prepared to say that the concept of a statement is, similarly, open. Perhaps his preference for representative sentences as against, say, the R equivalence classes reveals that he expects more of statements than simply that they form the converse domain of such a many-one relation as was just described. And a justification of this preference would involve at the least an explicit statement of these further requirements. But whatever they are, they are presumably not such as to give preferential status to one set of representative sentences as against another. Hence, to object to the proposed identification *as arbitrary* is, so far, only to beg a question. It is to assume that the concept of a statement is not open—at least not open in the respect the opposition claims it to be.

It seems to me, then, that the charge of arbitrariness is ineffective—even in relatively unproblematic cases like that of statements and sentences. But it should be recognized, apart from this, that no such objection can reasonably be made to a proposed identification of statements with sentential meanings. It could not be objected that it would be an arbitrary matter with which of several distinct sentential meanings a given statement is to be identified; for there is in this case no plurality from which an arbitrary selection could be made. It is, in the first place, incredible that a statement should be the meaning of some sentence which could not be used to assert it; and, in the second place, we have already seen that the meaning of an incomplete sentence is not a statement. Hence, if a statement is the meaning of *any* sentence, it must be the meaning of some complete sentence which can be used to assert it; and it is surely plausible to suppose that no two of these could differ in meaning.

12.   These considerations, coupled with the previous failure, lead me to suspect that in order to show that no one ever asserts the meaning of the words he utters, it is necessary to employ arguments which bypass altogether the fact of arithmetical difference between statements and the meanings of sentences. Arguments to this purpose are in any case readily available; they have indeed been difficult to suppress in earlier phases of discussion.

If what someone asserts, on some occasion, is itself the meaning which the words he utters have, on that occasion of their utterance, then anything predicable of what he asserts must also be predicable of the meaning of his words. But it is obvious on very little reflection that ever so many things predicable of what is asserted cannot (on pain of nonsense) be predicated of the meaning of a sentence. And the fundamental point to be noticed in this connection is that although we may predicate of something asserted that it is (or was) asserted, this cannot be predicated of the meaning of a sentence. It simply makes no sense to say that someone asserted the meaning of a sentence—any more than it makes sense to say he *said* it. Of course, we *can* say of someone that he asserted what certain words mean. But this is not to the point. To assert what certain words mean is to assert that they mean such-and-such; but one who asserts that 2 is a prime by uttering the words '2 is prime' does not *assert* anything whatever as to what those words mean—as is evident once we reflect that he asserts nothing that could not also be asserted by someone totally unfamiliar with their meaning. Along with this fundamental point there go many others. Just as the meanings of sentences cannot be asserted, neither can they be affirmed, denied, contradicted, questioned, challenged, discounted, confirmed, supported, verified, withdrawn, repudiated; and whereas what is asserted can be said to be accurate, exaggerated, unfounded, overdrawn, probable, improbable, plausible, true, or false, none of these can be said of the meaning of a sentence.

We could easily lengthen these lists, and we could explore in other directions the ways in which what is predicable of statements fails to be predicable of sentential meanings. But to do either of these would serve no purpose here. Those who are convinced by what has already been said would find further elaboration tedious—at least for the project in hand. And, no matter how much detail were piled up, those who are unconvinced would still be ready with a familiar sort of objection. They will grant that we never in fact speak of sentential meanings in the ways just mentioned; but they will claim that this is, somehow, only a point of usage—a linguistic accident which could well be avoided in languages specifically designed for philosophical clarification. But in spite of its familiarity, this objection is not easily understood. One wonders, in the first place, how it could be a mere fact of usage that, for example, meanings cannot be asserted. Usage of what? The fact that meanings cannot be asserted, if it *is* a fact, is *not* a fact about particular words in some particular language; it pertains no more to English than it does to Navajo or to some applied functional calculus—though it has implications (in some sense) for all three. And one wonders, in the second place, how to tell those points of usage which are *merely* that from those which are something more. Here, perhaps, recourse will be had to the possibilities of artificially constructed languages: significant distinctions, as opposed to superficial linguistic oddities, are those preserved in philosophically adequate formalized languages. I should hardly wish to deny this; but I am at a loss to understand, then, how it could be maintained that the distinction between statements and sentential meanings is *not* worth preserving. If what has already been said does not show that it *is* worth preserving, what would? And what would show this in the case of any other distinction we might see fit to make? Moore is reported to have once had a nightmare in which he was unable to distinguish propositions from tables. It is well to ask ourselves how we might show *this* distinction to be worth preserving.

13.   We may distinguish, then, what A asserted from (ix), the meaning of the words 'Botvinnik uses it'. And this distinction, it should be noted, does not depend upon the legitimacy of distinguishing in *every* case what is asserted from what is meant by what is uttered. For A uttered an incomplete sentence; and we have seen that what is asserted coincides with the meaning of what is uttered in, at best, those rare cases in which what is uttered is complete.

And with this we may return, finally, to the question which generated these technicalities—the question, What was that to which B referred and of which he predicated truth? The answer is surely obvious: the subject of B's predication of truth was (i), the statement that A made. This, indeed, was evident enough at the outset; and nothing subsequently said should be taken as an effort to *prove* it. The advantage gained, so far as that question is concerned, is simply the protection we now have against confusing (i) with any of (ii) through (ix).

But I think we are thereby better equipped, also, to deal with the general question as to the proper subjects of predications of truth and of falsity. Statements, or assertions, are surely to be counted as at least *some* amongst these. This, too, might well have been said at the outset. For what could be more obvious than that something asserted—something put forward as true—can properly be *said* to be true? Still, the frequency with which sentences—or their meanings, or their utterances—are claimed to be the *sole* bearers of truth and falsity suggests that, unless the obvious is often overlooked, statements are all too easily misidentified.

Still, protection against these misidentifications is by no means the whole story so far as this general question is concerned. For one thing, there may well be things other than statements that can equally qualify as truths or falsehoods. And, more importantly perhaps, to say what statements are *not* is not to say what they *are*. To distinguish them from other things is not by itself to provide either means for their detection or rules for distinguishing one of them from another. There is thus an important sense in which it remains to be said *what* it is that is susceptible of truth or falsity.

Addenda (1986)

1. In section 12 of the above essay one reads: "If what someone asserts, on some occasion, is itself the meaning which the words he utters have, on that occasion of their utterance, then anything predicable of what he asserts must also be predicable of the meaning of his words. But it is obvious on very little reflection that ever so many things predicable of what is asserted cannot (on pain of nonsense) be predicated of the meaning of a sentence." This is said, one gathers, in the interest of showing that "no one ever asserts the meaning of the words he utters"—that, for example, the meaning of the sentence '2 is prime' is not identical with what is asserted by someone who assertively utters that sentence.

It is predicable of 2 that it is prime. In other words, it is possible to say of 2 that it is prime. That, notice, is a fact about 2, and hence anything of which it is not possible to say that it is prime must be other than 2. And so we *seem* to have a way of establishing the nonidentity of 2 with, for example, the man playing third base: surely, we might argue, it is obvious on very little reflection that

(1)   It is possible to say of 2 that it is prime

and

(2)   It is not possible to say of the man playing third base that he is prime,

whence

(3)   2 is not identical with the man playing third base.

But hold! If there is such a proposition as (3), there must also be such a proposition as

(4)   2 is identical with the man playing third base

and hence such a proposition as

(5)   The sole even prime is identical with the man playing third base.

But then there must be such a proposition as

(6)   The man playing third base is prime,

for surely (6) is among the propositions that follow from (5). And if there is such a proposition as (6), we can hardly deny that there is also such a proposition as

(7)   Boggs is prime,

for Boggs is in fact the man playing third base. How, then, can (2) be true? It is not, I think; for I do not see how it can be denied that there is such a proposition as (3), and I see no way to break the chain that follows. In fact, I think there is no counterexample to any proposition expressed by an instance of the schema

(8)   For every x and y, if it is possible to say of x that it is . . . , then it is possible to say of y that it is . . . .

For an argument like that just now given for the existence of (7) seems always available. Hence I think we never succeed in establishing the non-identity of x with y by an argument like that from (1) and (2) to (3). And hence I think that the arguments of that kind given in section 12 do not establish that—for example—the meaning of the sentence '2 is prime' is not identical with what is asserted by someone who assertively utters that sentence.

I continue to think, however, that the meaning of '2 is prime' is not the proposition (or "statement") that 2 is prime. And to establish the noniden-tity it is of course enough to point out something true of the proposition that 2 is prime that is not true of the meaning of '2 is prime'. In doing so one will bank on a nose for the absurd. But I confused absurdity with nonsense. In effect I went from the absurdity of (7) to (2)—thinking, apparently, that the absurdity of (7) carried with it the meaninglessness of 'Boggs is prime'. But it does not. Perhaps the absurdity in (7) is not the same as the absurdity in *2 is not prime* or in *Boggs is not identical with Boggs*. Still, 'Boggs is prime' contrasts with 'toves are slithy'.

2. In section 6 it is implied that an "occurrence" of a word is a "token" of it, in Peirce's sense. But consider. There is, we may suppose, exactly one occurrence of the word 'etherized' in the whole of English poetry. Exactly one *token*? An occurrence of a word, in this sense at least, is to be likened rather to an occurrence of a number in a sequence.

3. Contrary to what is said in section 10, it is not true that "one who utters [It's raining'] speaks correctly only if he refers to the weather at the time of his utterance and in his (more or less) immediate vicinity." "It's raining," the reporter in Boston says, referring to the weather in Seattle. And what is to be made of "It's raining" said by someone gazing into a crystal ball?

Note

This essay, other than the addenda, was first published in R. J. Butler, ed., *Analytical Philosophy*, 1st series (Oxford: Basil Blackwell, 1962), pp. 81–103.

Propositions Again

1. Avrum Stroll has recently published an article[1] in which he gives a good deal of attention to my paper, "Propositions."[2] That paper had as its point of departure the question, What is it that is susceptible of truth or falsity? In it I took the position that it is obvious enough that statements, in a certain sense of that word, are at any rate among the things that are true or false; and the bulk of the paper was given over to distinguishing statements, in that sense, from other things with which I thought they had sometimes been confused: in particular from acts of assertion, from sentences, and from the meanings of sentences. Now Stroll sees in my paper evidence of a philosophical hang-up. I am, in his words, gripped by the vehicle-content model; I am held captive by a picture: of coal cars and the coal they contain, of automobiles and their passengers. When I first read this diagnosis, I wanted to issue a vigorous denial: I am not now, and was not when I wrote my paper, suffering from any such malady. But in a cooler moment I realized the protest would be taken as mere resistance, perhaps even as confirmation of the diagnosis. When responding to analysts it is better to proceed more cautiously.

There is reason for special caution in the present case. If a patient is told that he thinks his wife is intent on destroying his masculinity, there is a well-known obscurity. What the patient is told is supposed to be true even though the thought that his wife is intent on destroying his masculinity has never crossed his mind and even though he is prepared quite sincerely to deny that he thinks this of her. The obscurity is in the sense of 'think' in which he is supposed to think this awful thing of her. Still, there is no very serious obscurity as to *what* in this obscure sense he is supposed to think. But if someone is told that he is gripped by the vehicle-content model (or, to make the thing more specific, the automobile-passenger model), there is a double obscurity: he is accused of thinking (obscure sense) *something* about automobiles and passengers (and, in my case, sentences and statements), but it is pretty obscure what this *is*. So, a vigorous denial would be premature. We had better see first what has been affirmed.

2. A patient who thinks his wife is intent on destroying his masculinity

might be said, by a therapist with a flair, to be gripped by the Samson-Delilah model. The therapist would not mean that the patient thought himself to *be* Samson or his wife to *be* Delilah. The patient is not gripped by a psychotic delusion. Nor would the therapist mean that the patient is afraid his wife is going to cut his hair. It is rather that the patient thinks his situation vis-à-vis his wife is in a certain respect like that of Samson vis-à-vis Delilah: just as Delilah was out to get Samson, so (the patient thinks) his wife is out to get him. This can be put in a way that has the air of mathematical precision. There is a relation that an object x bears to an object y if and only if x is a man and y is the wife of x and y is intent on destroying the masculinity of x. And a patient is gripped by the Samson-Delilah model if and only if he thinks (obscure sense and irrationally) that he bears this relation to his wife.

I should suppose the situation ought to be similar in the case of someone gripped by the automobile-passenger model. He does not think that sentences *are* automobiles or that statements *are* passengers. Nor does he think statements quite literally go riding about in sentences. It is rather that he thinks the situation vis-à-vis the sentence uttered on a certain occasion and the statement thereby made is in a certain respect *like* that of the automobile vis-à-vis its passengers. But in *what* respect? Here is where I find Stroll obscure. Apparently he thinks there is some particular relation that an automobile bears to its passengers, which relation *I* think the sentence uttered bears to the statement made. But what *is* this relation? There are ever so many relations that automobiles bear to their passengers. But none of the most "natural" of these can be the one Stroll has in mind—unless, indeed, he really *does* think I'm psychotic. He can't suppose, at least not justifiably on the evidence available to him, that I think the sentence uttered bears to the statement made that relation we are inclined to refer to as *the* relation of an automobile to its passengers: the relation that x bears to y if and only if x is an automobile and y is a passenger in x. For then he would be supposing that I think sentences are automobiles and statements their passengers. Nor can he suppose I think statements occupy the interior of sentences, or are separated from the surface of the earth by sentences; and so on. But then what *does* he think I think? The therapist can cash his "Samson-Delilah" metaphor. How would Stroll cash *his*?

Clearly, Stroll thinks it is a bad thing to be gripped by the automobile-passenger model. And presumably it is. It is a bad thing to be gripped by *any* model. One held captive by a picture fails to see things as they are; worse, he sees them distortedly. He attributes to things—to his wife or to statements—properties they don't really have. From innocent facts he draws suspect conclusions. Indeed, it is from the character of these irrationalities that we infer the character of the malady. *Which* picture holds him captive is determined by *how* he distorts the facts. So perhaps in the effort to cash Stroll's metaphor we ought to inquire into what distortions one gripped by the automobile-passenger model is likely to be led. What properties will he be apt to attribute to statements that statements don't really have? What mistakes in inference can he be expected to make?

3.   On page 194 of Stroll's article we find the following passage:

> It seems natural enough to distinguish between the words a German utters when he says "Es regnet" and the words an Englishman utters when he says (on the same occasion) "It is raining." Obviously the words they use are different; therefore, the vehicles they use are different; yet both vehicles have been employed in those circumstances to make the same statement. Accordingly, it seems to follow that the statement the speakers make in using the vehicles they do must be different from the vehicles they employ. Cartwright describes this situation by saying that the "arithmetics of statements and sentences are different," and therefore that the entities in question must be different from one another.

Apparently it is Stroll's intent here to call attention to a certain bad inference apt to be made by one who is, as I am supposed to be, gripped by the vehicle-content model. I say "apparently" because Stroll never says in so many words that the inference *is* a bad one. He says "it seems to follow" that the statement the speakers make is different from the sentences they utter. I shall suppose he means that it doesn't *really* follow. After all, it really *doesn't*. From

(1)   The sentence uttered by Heinrich is not identical with the sentence uttered by Maynard

and

(2)   The statement made by Heinrich is identical with the statement made by Maynard

one simply cannot validly deduce

(3)   The statement made by Maynard is not identical with the sentence uttered by Maynard.

But what I find odd—in fact, annoying—is Stroll's suggestion that I think, or thought when I wrote my paper, that (3) *does* follow from (1) and (2). On the contrary: in the paper I made quite a point of the fact that (3) does not follow from (1) and (2). Indeed, I labored it to the point of tedium. Still, there's some consolation for me. *If* being gripped by the vehicle-content model manifests itself in readiness to infer (3) from (1) and (2), then so far Stroll can't put a glove on me. At least that's *one* symptom I haven't got.

There is, however, good evidence that the argument from (1) and (2) to (3) is *persuasive*. I, and I expect others as well, have a good deal of success in persuading students that the statement made is to be distinguished from the sentence uttered by citing such facts as (1) and (2). It is usually helpful to point out, also, such obvious possibilities as that

(4)   The sentence uttered by Bertrand is identical with the sentence uttered by Ludwig

and yet that

(5)   The statement made by Bertrand is not identical with the statement made by Ludwig,

from which the students will happily conclude that

(6)   The sentence uttered by Bertrand is not identical with the statement made by Bertrand.

And it is not just students who are thus persuaded. Strawson once wrote: "What these examples [such as (4) and (5)] show is that we cannot identify that which is true or false (the statement) with the sentence used in making it; for the same sentence may be used to make quite different statements, some of them true and some of them false."[3] And in a recent article G. Nerlich remarks that Strawson's argument is "decisive."[4] How are we to account for this? How are we to account for the fact that not only beginning students but trained professionals are persuaded by such obviously fallacious arguments?

No doubt Stroll is ready with an answer: these persons are gripped by the vehicle-content model. But I can't believe we need go to such depths. I suggest that people are persuaded of the truth of (3) on the strength of (1) and (2) simply because they take for granted a proposition which, when conjoined with (1) and (2), yields (3), namely,

(7)   If the statement made by Maynard is identical with the sentence uttered by Maynard, then the statement made by Heinrich is identical with the sentence uttered by Heinrich.

Similarly in the other case. There it is tacitly assumed that

(8)   If the sentence uttered by Bertrand is identical with the statement made by Bertrand, then the sentence uttered by Ludwig is identical with the statement made by Ludwig.

Of course, the arguments from (1), (2), and (7) to (3) and from (3), (4), and (8) to (6) are sound only if (7) and (8) are true; and they are proofs only if there is independent reason for thinking (7) and (8) to be true—independent, that is, of the alleged truth of (3) and (6). And I suppose Stroll might contend that (7) and (8) are false and that only someone gripped by the vehicle-content model could think them true. But then I think the burden would fall on him to make out a case. For (7) and (8) have a good deal of plausibility. They have the plausibility of such propositions as

(9)   If the number denoted by the arabic numeral '7' is identical with the arabic numeral '7', then the number denoted by the roman numeral 'VII' is identical with the roman numeral 'VII',

(10) If the class having as members Caesar's nose and the state of Utah is identical with its fusion, then the class having as members Caesar's nose and the counties of Utah is identical with *its* fusion,

(11) If the sense of 'the author of *Waverley*' is identical with the denotation of 'the author of *Waverley*', then the sense of 'the author of *Marmion*' is identical with the denotation of 'the author of *Marmion*',

and

(12) If the property of being a marine mammal alive in 1940 is identical with the class it determines, then the property of being a whale or porpoise alive in 1940 is identical with the class *it* determines.

Each of these is apt to be taken for granted in an argument formally similar to that from (1) and (2) to (3). One wants to explain that the arabic numeral '7' is not to be confused with the natural number 7. And so he points out that the roman numeral 'VII', though not identical with the arabic, nevertheless denotes the same natural number. Of course, all that follows so far is that the number is not identical with *both* numerals. But this is never noticed. And the reason is, I suggest, that everyone unhesitatingly takes (9) for granted. Or consider this passage from Nelson Goodman:

> . . . even assuming that classes exist, we cannot identify an individual with a certain class of its parts, for there will be many such classes. The class having as members Caesar's nose and the state of Utah is different from the class having as members Caesar's nose and the counties of Utah, yet the individual that exactly exhausts the members of the first class is the same as the individual that exactly exhausts the members of the second. If the classes are different, they clearly cannot be identified with the same individual.[5]

The conditional with which the passage ends is true. And so is its antecedent. But all that follows is that at most one of the classes is identical with the individual. What is missing is (10). And I suppose Goodman was simply taking it for granted.

4.   So much for bad inferences. What of false attributions of properties? In this connection Stroll relies heavily on the last paragraph of my paper. Having made my effort to distinguish statements from things with which I thought they had sometimes been confused, I there wrote:

> Still, protection against these misidentifications is by no means the whole story so far as this general question [as to the proper subjects of predications of truth and of falsity] is concerned. For one thing, there may well be things other than statements that can equally qualify as truths or falsehoods. And, more importantly perhaps, to say what statements are *not* is not to say what they *are*. To distinguish them from other things is not by itself to provide either means for their detection or rules for distinguishing one of them from another. There is thus an important sense in which it remains to be said *what* it is that is susceptible of truth or falsity.

Stroll quotes this paragraph twice and infers from it that I think of statements as "mysterious, hidden things," as "esoteric entities not immediately discernible to the ordinary eye."[6] My remarks are, he says,

> characteristically philosophical. They exude an air of mystery about things not easily identifiable—but unmistakably there, even if hidden from the ordinary eye by a welter of items (sentences, utterances and the rest) with which they are only too readily confused. Such things must be "detected" by "means" not available to the native speaker, or even to the intelligent, reflective nonspecialist. They must be uncovered and distinguished from one another by "rules" which the philosopher must devise.[7]

Well, that last paragraph of mine must have been pretty opaque. It was intended as a disclaimer. Friends of statements are sometimes challenged by hard-heads to state a precise criterion of identity for statements; and they are sometimes challenged, also, to give a criterion for deciding with respect to any given individual event of utterance whether or not it is assertive. I wanted to make it clear that I hadn't even attempted to state such criteria; hence my talk (which seemed innocent at the time) of not having given "means for their detection" or "rules for distinguishing one of them from another." I wanted to make it clear, too, that I thought that in the absence of such criteria someone might reasonably feel he didn't know *what* a statement *is*. Hence my concluding sentence. It seems to me now that this last sentence was unfortunate. For it's now not clear to me that there is a sense of 'know what a statement is' in which to know what a statement is it is necessary to have such criteria. But the challenges are good ones all the same and ones that I don't know how to meet.

I do not, however, regret having said that statements are all too easily confused with other things. Evidently they are, for examples of such confusion are to be found in Stroll's own paper. Consider this passage:

> When we translate from a foreign language into English, or into another foreign language, there is something we translate and which, when the translation is correct, remains invariant under such transformations. This something is the content to be translated, to be rendered from one language into another. Not all such contents are statements, of course (we translate things other than statements), but it is commonly held that statements are among such contents; that they are among the things we render from one body of discourse into another. The picture here is thus like transferring a load of coal from one car into another. And since it is the same content which is thus transferred, while the vehicles which convey it are different, it seems to follow that the statemental content in such cases differs from the vehicles used to carry (convey, transfer, express) it.[8]

A variety of things get translated: Wittgenstein, his *Philosophical Investigations*, the sentence 'Es ist ein Hase', the word 'Hase'. For present purposes it is appropriate to concentrate on the sentence 'Es ist ein Hase'. As Stroll points out, something remains invariant under any correct translation of this into English. But it is simply a howler to say, as he does, that what remains invariant is what is translated. It is the *sentence* that is translated; and were *that* to remain invariant we should have no translation at all. Now, it is undeniable that there *is* a correct translation of 'Es ist ein Hase' into English, namely, the sentence 'It's a rabbit'. Of course, what Heinrich says when he utters the sentence might, for some purposes, be better rendered in some other English sentence. Perhaps Heinrich used the sentence idiosyncratically, or perhaps he was looking at Jastrow's picture, or perhaps through some slip he said "ein Hase" and meant 'eine Hosen'. Even so, the *sentence* 'Est ist ein Hase' is correctly translated into English as 'It's a rabbit'. What, then, remains invariant? It is not clear to me that there is anything better to say than this: the *meaning* of the sentence 'Es ist ein Hase'. But whether or not this is the right thing to say or even a very clear thing to say, it is certainly dead wrong to say (as Stroll seems to suggest) that what remains invariant is a *statement*. What statement would it be? The statement that it's a rabbit? But what statement is *that*? Is it the statement Ludwig made on the occasion in Austria in 1920 when, noticing a rabbit in the yard, he uttered the sentence 'Es ist ein Hase'? Or is it rather the statement he made in Ithaca in 1949 when, looking out Norman's window and seeing a squirrel, he uttered the very same sentence? *Which* of the many statements that have been and will be and might be made by uttering that sentence is that which remains invariant under translation into English? It is absurd to suggest we have to choose. The meaning of the sentence 'Es ist ein Hase'—that which remains invariant under translation into 'It's a rabbit'—is simply not a statement.

Stroll says "we translate things other than statements." We certainly do. But do we translate statements at all? Perhaps it is correct to say we do. I don't propose to argue the point. And *if* we do, then I suppose the statement itself remains invariant under the translation. But then what changes? Presumably the answer is: the *formulation* of the statement. A statement formulated in one sentence receives formulation in another. But even if it is correct to call this translation, there is danger in doing so: we are apt to be led into thinking that the process is successful just in case the new sentence is a correct translation of the old and hence that the statement itself is the common meaning of both. The fact is that it is neither necessary nor sufficient for success in reformulation that the new sentence be a correct translation of the old. If Ludwig looks at Jastrow's picture and says, "Es ist ein Hase," any of the following *might* do as formulations of the statement he makes: 'Das ist einen Bildhasen', 'It's a picture of a rabbit', 'It looks like a rabbit', 'It's a rabbit'; but only the last is a correct translation of the sentence Ludwig uttered. And although 'It's a rabbit' is a correct translation of the sentence Ludwig uttered when he looked out Norman's window, it's not a formulation of the statement he made.

Thus sentence uttered, meaning of sentence uttered, and statement made are almost inextricably confused in the passage under discussion. Perhaps Stroll will respond that he was there speaking not for himself but for one in the grip of the vehicle-content model. Well, that lets him off the hook. But then notice: it lets me off too. If *that's* the way people gripped by the vehicle-content model talk, then so far there's no reason to think I'm gripped. After all, a good two-thirds of my paper was devoted to making the very distinctions that are ignored in Stroll's paragraph.

5.   I doubt very much that anything I've said so far would convince Stroll that I'm not held captive by a picture. Don't I *really* think of statements as esoteric, mysterious, hidden things, discernible only to the eye of a philosopher? I think it is better not to answer this question. So let me ask another: Apart from what I said in that opaque last paragraph of my paper, about which enough has already been said, why is Stroll led to think I *do* think of statements this way? There is some indication that at bottom it is just because I made such a point of distinguishing statements from sentences. I argued for

(13)   No statement is a sentence;

and the fact that I was so intent upon arguing for it is perhaps what indicates to Stroll that I'm gripped by the vehicle-content model. It's not that Stroll thinks (13) is false; on the contrary, he seems to think it's true. It's rather that in coming down so very hard in favor of (13) I gave every indication of being prepared to deny another proposition that *apparently* Stroll thinks is also true, namely,

(14)   Every statement is a sentence.

I distorted reality, not so much by affirming (13) as by affirming it *and then neglecting* to affirm (14) as well. This, perhaps, is what Stroll takes to be the real symptom of my disease.

I've spoken hesitantly here, because I can't be sure; Stroll never puts it the way I have. What I'm relying on is this passage: "But if statements are not identical with sentences or with the utterances of sentences, and if they are not mysterious, ineluctable entities different from sentences and utterances, then what are they? The answer is that they are both identical with sentences (utterances, words, etc.) and yet different from them. . . ."[9] This certainly does suggest that he thinks my error consists in having affirmed (13) without having added immediately that (14) is true too.

Let me at once enter a plea of guilty. I did assert (13), and I neglected to assert (14). But given that I didn't think (13) was just vacuously true, this neglect seemed entirely rational: otherwise, I thought, I would be involved in an inconsistency. If there *are* any statements, how *can* (13) and (14) both be true?

Stroll sees there is a problem here. The problem he says, "is to provide an explanation showing how these apparently incompatible things can be so."[10] He seems to think, you see, that (13) and (14) are not *really* incompatible; that there is an explanation of how both can be true. Let's see what his explanation is.

The heart of it is to be found in the following passage:

> Sentences per se, or the utterances of sentences or words, do not automatically "count as" statements. But when something does "count as" a statement nothing more happens than that a person has uttered a sentence or a string of words. A statement is thus nothing more than a sentence or a string of words uttered in certain circumstances. But what then makes such a sentence or string of words "count as" a statement? The answer is that it will depend on what the circumstances are.[11]

One gathers from this that the "apparently incompatible" propositions (13) and (14) can be seen to be really compatible by recognizing that, although a statement is not a "sentence per se," it is nevertheless "nothing more than a sentence . . . uttered in certain circumstances."

What is a "sentence per se"? Well, I suppose it is just a sentence. What is the sentence 'Es ist ein Hase' per se if not just the sentence 'Est ist ein Hase'? A rabbit per se is just a rabbit, a number per se is just a number; everything is per se just what it is, and not another thing. Let us recognize, then, with Stroll, that a statement is not a sentence per se; that is, a statement is not a sentence; that is, (13) is true. But then let us recognize also that it is *not* the case that every statement *is* a sentence per se; that is, it is not the case that every statement is a sentence; that is, (14) is false. It's clear now that Stroll knew this all along. When he seemed to assert (14), he was just asserting

(15)   A statement is nothing more than a sentence uttered in certain circumstances.

He didn't really think (13) and (14) are compatible; he thought (13) and (15) are compatible.

But what about (15)? Is *it*, as Stroll thinks, compatible with (13)? At first sight it would seem not. It would seem that anything that is a sentence uttered in certain circumstances is at any rate a sentence, just as a rabbit noticed by Ludwig is at any rate a rabbit and a philosopher gripped by the vehicle-content model is at any rate a philosopher. But if so, and if (15) is true, then statements are sentences after all and (13) is false. Evidently we have not yet managed to see clearly *what* proposition (15) is supposed to be. We have not properly understood Stroll's phrase 'a sentence uttered in certain circumstances'.

Mathematicians sometimes speak of "ordered sets"; and a curious thing about this is that an ordered set is not a set, or at least it's not the set you'd think it would be. To anyone perplexed by this, the mathematician can offer one or another of several explanations. He can point out that the expression 'ordered set' can simply be dropped: to say something about an ordered set is only to say something (though of course not quite the same thing) about a set and some given ordering of it. Or, since all that really matters is the ordering relation itself (perhaps appropriately restricted), he can suggest instead that we talk simply about *it*. Or he can point out that for his purposes an ordered set can be taken to be a pair whose first term is a set and whose second term is some ordering of that set. The paradoxical air of "An ordered set is not a set" is thus explained away. Can we explain away the air of paradox in "A sentence uttered in certain circumstances is not a sentence"?

Perhaps the thing to do is to try to see what considerations lead Stroll to the assertion of (15). They are to be found, I think, in the passage quoted above and also in his discussion of strokes and swings. Let me explain what I take them to be. Suppose a man makes a statement. Without loss of generality, we may suppose he does so by uttering some sentence. He makes the statement that snow is white and does so by uttering the sentence 'snow is white'. Now, his making the statement is not *just* a matter of his uttering the sentence; that is to say, uttering the sentence is not sufficient unto making the statement. Someone might utter the sentence without making the statement—indeed, without making any statement at all. Still, it is not as though in making the statement that snow is white our man does something *in addition to* uttering the sentence 'snow is white'. He doesn't utter the sentence *and then* make the statement, nor does he do two things at once in the way that someone does who sings "Careless Love" while strumming a guitar. It's rather that he utters the sentence in circumstances such that to utter that sentence in those circumstances *is* to make the statement.

Such considerations do, I think, influence the intellect. They give some plausibility to

(16)   Making a statement is nothing more than uttering a sentence in certain circumstances.

Of course, making the statement that snow is white and uttering the sentence 'snow is white' are distinct acts: some cases of the one are not cases of the other, and some cases of the other are not cases of the one. But if someone makes the statement that snow is white by uttering the sentence 'snow is white', then *his* uttering that sentence *is* a case of making that statement. Taking candy from a child and stealing candy from a child are distinct acts, but some cases of the one are cases of the other. Or, to switch to Stroll's analogy, some swings are strokes even though to take a swing is one thing and to take a stroke another. But we should not want to put this by saying that the stroker both swings *and* strokes. For, as we might say, to stroke is just to swing in the right circumstances. Similarly, there is some plausibility, if not much precision, in the suggestion that to make a statement is nothing more than to utter a sentence in certain circumstances.

I think we can now see which proposition (15) is supposed to be. It is supposed to be (16). When Stroll speaks of "a sentence uttered in certain circumstances" he means an *utterance* of a sentence in certain circumstances. That's why there's no real paradox in "A sentence uttered in certain circumstances is not a sentence." Obviously, no *utterance* of a sentence is itself the sentence uttered, no matter *what* the circumstances are in which the utterance occurs. Similarly, when Stroll speaks of "a statement" he means an *assertion* of a statement, or (if you'll allow the barbarism) a *making* of a statement: what in my paper I referred to as "an individual event of assertive utterance." He wants to say that an assertion of a statement is nothing more than an utterance of a sentence in certain circumstances. It is thus (16) Stroll thinks is compatible with (13). And quite obviously it is.

But then where is my error? In my paper I asserted (13), but Stroll asserts it too. And as far as I can see, there's not a thing in my paper to suggest that I then thought (13) and (16) incompatible. It's true that I didn't come right out and assert (16). I was tempted to, but held off—partly because it is a pretty uninformative proposition in any case, partly because I suspected some readers would see in it signs of behaviorism and hence be diverted from my main concerns. Now does Stroll really find in any of this evidence of my being held captive by a picture? I can't believe he does. It's just too innocent.

6.   If I'm gripped by the vehicle-content model, then there must be some point with respect to which Stroll and I disagree; otherwise, he's gripped too. What is it? A hint is perhaps to be found in one of his footnotes—the seventh. This is a note on a passage in which Stroll is explaining what he refers to as the "apparent universal applicability to a wide range of things"[12] of the vehicle-content model. The note reads as follows:

> The form this may take in philosophy may consist in attempting to distinguish between the act of stating something and that which is stated. Cartwright says, for instance, "It is equally clear that what is asserted by someone on some given occasion is not to be identified with his asserting it on that occasion."[13]

I "attempted" to distinguish what is asserted by someone on some given occasion from his asserting it on that occasion. That, if not my only symptom, is apparently at least one.

I certainly did make the attempt. But why is that bad? If it's a bad thing to attempt to make a distinction, it must be because there's no such distinction to be made. Otherwise, one tries and fails but then gets "A" for effort, or else one succeeds—which is a pleasant symptom of rationality. So apparently Stroll thinks there simply is no distinction to be made between what is asserted by someone on some given occasion and his asserting it on that occasion. My mistake was to have supposed there is.

If someone says there's no distinction between A's and B's, he can be understood to mean that every A is a B and every B an A. Is this the way to understand Stroll? Are we to understand him as holding that, on *every* occasion on which a person asserts something, what he asserts is identical with his asserting it on that occasion? If so, there's nothing to say except that he's wrong. Here's a proof: sometimes, what someone asserts on one occasion is identical with what he asserts on another; but his asserting it on the one occasion is not identical with his asserting it on the other; and hence either what he asserts is not identical with his asserting it on the one occasion or it is not identical with his asserting it on the other.

Of course, the proof leaves it open that *sometimes* what someone asserts on a given occasion is identical with his asserting it on that occasion. And perhaps it is only this weaker proposition that Stroll wants to assert. But then what about the arguments I gave in my paper against this very proposition? In section 5 I argued that

> what is asserted by someone on some given occasion is not to be identified with his asserting it on that occasion. For the latter is a case of asserting whatever he asserted, while *what* he asserted is clearly not. Indeed, if what someone asserted were identical with his asserting it on some occasion, then his asserting it on that occasion would be the same as his asserting his asserting it on that occasion on that occasion. And this is absurd.

Stroll simply ignores these arguments. But if he wants to deny their conclusion, it would seem he ought to say what's wrong with them. It's just not possible that the *only* mistake in an argument should be that its conclusion is false.

7.   I think we must conclude that Stroll is *not* concerned to claim that what someone asserts on a given occasion is always or even sometimes identical with his asserting it on that occasion. But then where is the error in attempting to distinguish what someone asserts on a given occasion from his asserting it on that occasion? Well, suppose one philosopher says somewhat scathingly of another, "He attempts to distinguish souls from bodies." It's unlikely that his point is that souls *are* bodies; it's rather that there *aren't* any souls at all, and hence none to be distinguished from bodies. And that, I think, is how we have to understand Stroll. He thinks there aren't any such things as statements in that dictionary sense of the word in which "a statement" is that which is asserted. There are sentences and utterances of sentences, and among these latter some are statements in the sense in which "a statement" is a particular event of assertive utterance. But statements in the other sense are myths. Stroll in fact agrees with what Benson Mates meant when he said that statements have "a rather serious drawback, which, to put it in the most severe manner, is this: they do not exist."[14]

It has to be conceded that Stroll is not completely unequivocal on the point. He is apparently not ready to give unqualified approval to Mates's forthright negative existential. The relevant paragraph is this:

> Mates, of course, does not believe that the word 'statement' has no use (or uses) in English. Nor does he believe that its uses are the same as those of sentences. And therefore he does not really believe that statements do not exist. What he does not believe, as he says, is that there are entities of the sort described by those who accept the vehicle-content model. What he wishes to emphasize by putting his

point in so paradoxical a way is that it is impossible to give an independent description of statements, to identify them independently of the vehicles which presumably convey them. His remarks thus stem from a temper of mind which is on the whole admirable—
· tough-minded and antimetaphysical.[15]

Now, I have some doubt that Mates would welcome the interpretation here placed upon his words. I suspect he meant just what he said: statements do not exist; there are no such things. But, however that may be, it seems that Stroll himself is not prepared to go so far. Indeed, he implies that he thinks statements *do* exist. That, he seems to think, follows from the fact that the word 'statement' has uses in English, uses different from those of the word 'sentence'. But notice that he *is* ready to deny the existence of *something*, namely, of "entities of the sort described by those who accept the vehicle-content model." And what sort of entity is that? As one who is supposedly gripped by the model, I think I am qualified to answer: it is just the sort of thing that is a statement in that dictionary sense of the word in which "a statement" is that which is asserted. And thus, as it seems to me, Stroll *does* agree with Mates: statements, in *that* sense of the word, do not exist.

Stroll says this is a paradoxical way of putting a point. And it certainly seems to be. After all, it seems so very easy to give *examples* of statements: the statement that snow is white, the statement that there are infinitely many primes—indeed, the statement that there are no statements. Would Stroll say these *aren't* statements? And if they *are*, then how can it be true that there are no statements?

Here, I suppose, Stroll would remind us of something he said in the paragraph quoted above, namely, "that it is impossible to give an independent description of statements, to identify them independently of the vehicles which presumably convey them." It is in fact Stroll's view that the vehicle-content model "breaks down" at precisely this point.

The model requires that there must be an independent way of characterizing both the vehicle and its content. It is clearly possible to do this for the vehicle. It is invariably a word or group of words belonging to some given language, and is easily describable. But how is one to characterize the statement which a person uses these words to make if the statement is different from them? It seems that any attempt to do so only leads to the production or description of another vehicle belonging to a given language. We thus seem to be in the position of attempting to characterize the content conveyed by the vehicle by either describing the vehicle itself or some other vehicle belonging to a different language—something which *ex hypothesi* is different from its statemental component. The model thus differs importantly from its prototypes. I can give independent descriptions of the coal car and the coal it carries; I can give independent descriptions of the automobile and its passengers; but I cannot give independent descriptions of the vehicles which convey statements and the statements they convey.[16]

Superficially at least, there is confusion here. Stroll seems to think that if one is asked to identify or describe or characterize, for example, the last statement made by Stalin, then one must identify or describe or characterize some sentence or other. But this is surely false. Perhaps Stalin's last statement was the statement that there are infinitely many primes. Then, to identify or describe or characterize his last statement I suppose it is sufficient to say, "It was the statement that there are infinitely many primes." And in saying this one does not identify or describe or characterize any sentence whatever. Of course, one *utters* a sentence that formulates the statement. But an utterance of a sentence need not be an identification or description or characterization of it.

This confusion aside, Stroll will no doubt insist that a point remains: In giving an example of a statement one can do no better than produce some sentence that formulates a statement; the statement itself cannot be presented "neat," independently of one or another sentence that formulates it. But, granting this, what is supposed to follow? It hardly follows that examples of statements cannot be given, nor does it follow that the sentence uttered is itself an example of a statement, and least of all does it follow that there are no statements. If asked to give an example of a prime number between 9 and 13, one can do no better than produce some numeral—the arabic numeral '11', say; the number itself cannot be presented "neat," independently of one or another numeral that designates it. But it does not follow that an example of a prime number between 9 and 13 cannot be given, nor does it follow that the numeral is the number, and least of all does it follow that there are no prime numbers between 9 and 13.

But doesn't the vehicle-content model require that it be possible to present the statement itself, independently of any of its formulations? Perhaps so. But we have yet to see any evidence that friends of statements are inevitably gripped by that model. A man who thinks his wife is intent on destroying his masculinity is not necessarily gripped by the Samson-Delilah model: he may have excellent reasons; he may even be right.

Notes

This essay was first published in *Noûs* 2, no. 3 (August 1968): 229–246.

1. "Statements," in Avrum Stroll, ed., *Epistemology* (New York: Harper and Row, 1967), pp. 179–203.

2. In R. J. Butler, ed., *Analytical Philosophy*, 1st series (Oxford: Basil Blackwell, 1962), pp. 81–103.

3. P. F. Strawson, *Introduction to Logical Theory* (London: Methuen, 1952), p. 4.

4. "Presupposition and Entailment," *American Philosophical Quarterly* 2 (1965): 34.

5. *The Structure of Appearance* (Cambridge, Mass.: Harvard University Press, 1951), pp. 46–47.

6. "Statements," p. 192.

7. "Statements," p. 191.

8. "Statements," p. 194.

9. "Statements," p. 199.

10. "Statements," p. 199.

11. "Statements," p. 200.

12. "Statements," p. 193.

13. "Statements," p. 202.

14. *Elementary Logic* (New York: Oxford University Press, 1965), p. 8.

15. "Statements," p. 197.

16. "Statements," pp. 195–196.

A Neglected Theory of Truth

If I am asked "What is good?" my answer is that good is good, and that is the end of the matter. Or if I am asked "How is good to be defined?" my answer is that it cannot be defined, and that is all I have to say about it. . . . My point is that "good" is a simple notion, just as "yellow" is a simple notion; that, just as you cannot, by any manner of means, explain to anyone who does not already know it, what yellow is, so you cannot explain what good is. Definitions . . . which describe the real nature of the object or notion denoted by a word . . . are only possible when the object or notion in question is something complex. . . . But yellow and good, we say, are not complex: they are notions of that simple kind, out of which definitions are composed and with which the power of further defining ceases.

G. E. Moore, *Principia Ethica*

Moore's doctrine that "good," as he curiously calls it, is a simple unanalyzable quality is well known and much discussed. I shall here add nothing to its discussion. Less well known is a parallel doctrine that Moore, and Russell too, held about truth; like "good," truth was said to be a simple unanalyzable quality. In contrast with the doctrine concerning "good," that concerning truth has received little attention in the literature. This relative neglect is perhaps understandable: on the surface at least, the doctrine seems to have little to recommend it; neither Moore nor Russell held to it for very long; and its place in their published writings is hardly conspicuous.

Primary sources are in fact not easy to come by. Moore defends the doctrine briefly in his early paper "The Nature of Judgment" (1899),[1] and it is close to the surface in his entry on truth in Baldwin's *Dictionary* (1901);[2] but he advocates it nowhere else in his published writings. It receives a short exposition and defense in the third installment of Russell's article "Meinong's Theory of Complexes and Assumptions" (1904),[3] and in *The Principles of Mathematics* (1903)[4] truth is counted among the "indefinable logical constants"; but except for brief remarks in an essay of 1906 and heavy criticism in "On the Nature of Truth and Falsehood" (1910),[5] the doctrine goes unmentioned in the rest of Russell's published works.

A welcome addition to this meager fare is Moore's *Some Main Problems of Philosophy*,[6] especially the chapter called "Beliefs and Propositions." Although written at a time (1911) when Moore no longer held truth to be a simple unanalyzable quality, the chapter contains a lengthy discussion of the doctrine and is a reasonably good guide to the nature of the theory he had earlier held. Later in this paper I shall argue, in effect, that the chapter must be read in the light of the Baldwin's *Dictionary* article, if a certain error of interpretation is to be avoided. Even so, *Some Main Problems of Philosophy* can serve as a principal source.

1

In that book Moore describes the theory we are concerned with as follows:

> It is a theory which I myself formerly held, and which certainly has the advantage that it is very simple. It is simply this. It adopts the supposition that in the case of every belief, true or false, there is a proposition which is what is believed, and which certainly is. But the difference between a true and a false belief it says, consists simply in this, that where the belief is true the proposition, which is believed, besides the fact that it *is* or "has being" also has another simple unanalysable property which is possessed by some propositions and not by others. The propositions which don't possess it, and which therefore we call false, *are* or "have being"—just as much as those which *do*; only they just have *not* got this additional property of being "true." (p. 261)

Consider a particular case. Brown, we may suppose, believes there are subways in Boston. Given this, the theory requires that we recognize that there is something, a certain "proposition," which Brown believes and which "is" or "has being" whether or not there are subways in Boston. After all, if Brown believes there are subways in Boston, he certainly believes *something*; and from this it appears to follow that there *is* something he believes.[7] Now, the proposition which Brown believes, the proposition that there are subways in Boston, must be distinguished from his belief in it. This is not to deny that in ordinary discourse a "belief" is often something believed—that is, a proposition. It is in this sense that we may speak of *the* belief that there are subways in Boston. But in another sense Brown's belief that there are subways in Boston is one thing and Smith's belief that there are subways in Boston another: Brown's belief may have been acquired earlier than Smith's, be better gounded, and so on. Neither Brown's belief nor Smith's belief is *the* belief that there are subways in Boston. In the Baldwin's *Dictionary* article Moore says that 'true' and 'false' are ambiguous according as they are applied, on the one hand, to *beliefs*—

in the sense in which Brown's belief is not the same as Smith's—and, on the other hand, to *propositions*, to *what* is believed. Brown's belief that there are subways in Boston is true in the sense that its "object," the proposition that there are subways in Boston, is true; and if someone happens to believe that there are no subways in Boston, then his belief is false in the sense that *its* object, the proposition that there are no subways in Boston, is false. But no proposition is true in the sense of having a true object, or false in the sense of having a false object; for propositions do not have objects at all. Rather, a true proposition is one that has a certain simple unanalyzable property, and a false proposition is one that lacks the property.[8]

The theory invites a response of which notice must be taken at once. I think we are all inclined toward some form of "correspondence" theory of truth. If asked what is the difference between a true proposition and a false one (or between a true belief and a false one, or a true sentence and a false one), we are likely to say that the difference is that the former, but not the latter, "corresponds to fact" or "agrees with reality." It seems virtually undeniable that whether it is true that there are subways in Boston depends upon how things are in the world—not just anywhere in the world, of course, but in Boston, underground Boston. The proposition is true if it is a *fact* that there are subways in Boston, and is false otherwise. It is precisely this dependence on reality, this agreement with fact, which the theory that truth is a simple unanalyzable property seems altogether to ignore.

Moore and Russell were aware that the theory invites this sort of response. As Russell remarked, the theory "*seems* to leave our preference for truth a mere unaccountable prejudice, and in no way to answer to the feeling of truth and falsehood."[9] They nonetheless felt driven to it because of their view that correspondence theories, though plausible at first sight, cannot survive closer scrutiny.

Presumably an essential feature of any correspondence theory is that the *proposition* that there are subways in Boston is one thing and the *fact* that there are subways in Boston quite another. The proposition is supposed to correspond to or agree with the fact, and this would appear to require that it not be identical with the fact. But distinct entities must differ; and neither Moore nor Russell could think of any way in which the true proposition differs from the fact to which it allegedly only corresponds. Thus Russell wrote:

> The fundamental objection [to the theory that truth is a simple unanalyzable property] may be expressed by saying that true propositions express *fact*, while false ones do not. This at once raises the problem: What is a fact? And the difficulty of the problem is this, that a fact

appears to be merely a true proposition, so that what seemed a significant assertion becomes a tautology.[10]

In the Baldwin's *Dictionary* article Moore wrote similarly:

> It is commonly supposed that the truth of a proposition consists in some relation which it bears to reality; and falsehood in the absence of this relation. The relation in question is generally called a "correspondence" or "agreement"; and it seems to be generally conceived as one of partial similarity to something else, and hence it is essential to the theory that a truth should differ in some specific way from the reality, in relation to which its truth is to consist. . . . It is the impossibility of finding any such difference between a truth and the reality to which it is supposed to correspond which refutes the theory.

Moore went on to suggest that those who think there is a difference are very likely confusing the proposition either with belief in it or with some sentence commonly used to express it. And so he concluded that "once it is definitely recognized that the proposition is . . . not a belief or form of words, but an *object* of a belief, it seems plain that a truth differs in no respect from the reality to which it was supposed merely to correspond."

Let me leave exposition long enough to call attention to a curious feature of the view to which Moore and Russell thus felt themselves driven: it eludes proper formulation. The true proposition that there are subways in Boston is identical with the fact that there are subways in Boston; the true proposition that Scott wrote *Waverley* is identical with the fact that Scott wrote *Waverley*; the true proposition that the sum of 7 and 5 is 12 is identical with the fact that the sum of 7 and 5 is 12. So far, so good; but what is the generalization of which these are intended to be instances? It is not the proposition that every true proposition is a fact and every fact a true proposition; for that proposition requires for its truth only that each true proposition be identical with some fact or other and each fact with some true proposition or other, and hence it does not preclude the identity of the true proposition that there are subways in Boston with, say, the fact that Scott wrote *Waverley*. Given a particular true proposition, it is easy enough to specify the fact with which the proposition is supposed to be identical. But a generalizing formula seems unavailable. Thus

(1)   For every proposition p, if p is true then p is identical with the fact that p

is ill formed, in that the final occurrence of 'p' does not occupy a variable-accessible position. Semantic ascent yields

(2)   Every result of putting a sentence for 'S' in 'If the proposition that S is true then the proposition that S is identical with the fact that S' expresses a true proposition.

But this does not formulate the desired generalization, because the proposition it expresses speaks directly of sentences rather than propositions. In addition, (2) takes no account even obliquely of propositions unexpressed by any sentences—of which I am sure Moore and Russell would have thought there are ever so many.

We grasp the thought nonetheless. At any rate I hope we do, for I intend to go on to say a good deal about it.

2

It is on this matter of the identification of facts with true propositions that Moore himself, in *Some Main Problems of Philosophy*, appears to have misrepresented his earlier theory. Recall that in that book the theory is no longer defended; indeed, it is in the course of an objection to the theory that the apparent misrepresentation occurs. Moore argues, against his earlier theory, that a fact

> does not, if you think of it, seem to consist merely in the possession of some simple property by a proposition—that is to say, by something which has being equally whether the belief be true or false. For instance, the fact that lions really do exist does not seem to consist in the possession of some simple property by the proposition which we believe, when we believe that they exist, even if we grant that there is such a thing as this proposition. The relation of the proposition to the fact doesn't seem to consist simply in the fact that the proposition is a constituent of the fact—one of the elements of which it is composed. (pp. 262–263)

We can concede to Moore that the fact that lions exist does not consist in the possession of some simple property by the proposition that lions exist and that the proposition is not related to the fact in such a way as to be a constituent of it. Otherwise we should presumably have to say that the fact that lions exist is a fact *about* the proposition that lions exist, and that seems hard. But how is this relevant to Moore's earlier theory? It was no part of that theory to claim that the fact that lions exist *does* consist in the possession of some simple property by the proposition that lions exist or that the proposition *is* related to the fact in such a way as to be a constituent of it. On the contrary, according to that theory the fact that lions exist simply *is* the proposition that lions exist. It is the fact itself—that is, the true proposition—that possesses the simple property in question. The theory will of course allow that *some* facts consist in the possession by propositions of the simple unanalyzable property of being true. Anyone who believes that the proposition that lions exist is true believes a proposition which is itself true and which is, therefore, according to the theory, a fact; and an advocate of the theory will take the position that this fact does consist in the possession by the proposition that lions exist of the property of being true. But not so in the case of the fact that lions exist or the fact that there are subways in Boston. According to the theory, the proposition that there are subways in Boston, since it is true, is identical with the fact that there are subways in Boston. But if, as suggested in *Some Main Problems of Philosophy*, the fact that there are subways in Boston consists in the possession by the proposition that there are subways in Boston of the simple unanalyzable property of being true, then the identity fails. For surely the *proposition* does not consist in the possession by *it* of any property at all.[11]

One wonders how Moore could have come thus to misrepresent a theory he himself had formerly held. I suspect it is really less a case of misrepresentation than of attempted refurbishing. By the time he wrote *Some Main Problems of Philosophy* Moore had come to the conclusion that the doctrine that every belief has an "object"—the proposition believed, which "is" or "has being" whether the belief is true or false—is incompatible with the identification of facts with true propositions. He had concluded that *if* there are such things as propositions at all, those among them that are true cannot be correctly identified with facts. So when he came to expound and criticize the doctrine that truth is a simple unanalyzable property, he attempted to do the best he could for it by looking for an alternative relation that a true proposition might bear to a fact. Hence he imported into the theory the idea that a fact *consists in* the possession by a proposition of the simple unanalyzable property of being true.

The refurbishing is not very successful. Moore himself notes, as we just now saw, that there are facts that do not seem to consist in a proposition's having a certain simple property. But I think the situation is worse than this. Once facts and true propositions are distinguished, there would seem to be no need for the simple property. If a fact is available as correspondent, why invoke the simple property? It was, after all, through inability to see any difference between a true proposition and the fact to which allegedly it merely corresponds that Moore and Russell were *led* to the simple-property view.

The doctrine that a fact is identical with the proposition that would, on other theories, be said merely to correspond to it is thus central to the early Moore-Russell theory. What, then, led Moore to conclude that even if there are such things as propositions, the true ones among them cannot be correctly identified with facts? His argument is best understood when formulated with reference to a particular case. So let us suppose again that Brown believes that there are subways in Boston; and let us assume, in keeping with the early Moore-Russell theory, that this implies that there is something—namely, the proposition that there are subways in Boston—which Brown believes. Now, Brown's belief happens to be true; but of course it is crucial to the theory that even had it been false it would have had the same proposition as its object. What someone believes, what the object of his belief is, cannot depend on the truth value of his belief. Hence the proposition Brown believes, the proposition that there are subways in Boston, would have been present in the universe—there really would have been such a proposition—even if Brown's belief had been false. But consider the *fact* that there are subways in Boston. Since Brown's belief is true, there certainly is such a fact. But had his belief been false, there surely would not have been. This fact, which, as things stand, certainly is present in the universe, would simply have been missing from the universe had Brown's belief been false. Thus there is something true of the *proposition* that there are subways in Boston which is not true of the *fact* that there are subways in Boston. The proposition would have been in the universe even if Brown's belief had been false; but not so the fact. Hence the proposition is not identical with the fact.

Ayer finds the argument "entirely cogent."[12] To me it appears simply to beg the question against the early Moore-Russell theory. In one respect, certainly, the argument is unexceptionable: *if* something is true of the proposition that there are subways in Boston that is not true of the fact that there are subways in Boston, then the proposition and the fact are not identical. But *is* something true of the proposition that is not true of the fact? According to the early Moore-Russell theory, the proposition that there are subways in Boston would have been present in the universe even if Brown's belief had been false. Without questioning that, let us ask whether Moore is right in contending that the same is not true of the fact that there are subways in Boston. Evidently it does have to be conceded that had Brown's belief been false, it would not have been a fact that there are subways in Boston. Had his belief been false, nothing that would then have been in the universe could have been correctly described as the fact that there are subways in Boston. All this seems reasonably clear. But what is not clear, I think, is that in order for Brown's belief to have been false it is necessary that something which *is* in the universe and *is* correctly described as the fact that there are subways in Boston should simply have been missing from the universe. Although it is clear that had Brown's belief been false, it would not have been a fact that there are subways in Boston, it is not clear that there is in the universe a certain entity which can be correctly described as the fact that there are subways in Boston and which simply would not have been present in the universe had Brown's belief been false.

For consider. There is in the universe someone who can in fact be correctly described as the author of *Word and Object*. Presumably there might very well not have been. But in order for there not to have been, it is not necessary that any person who is in fact present in the universe should simply have been missing from it. All that is required is that no one person should have written *Word and Object*. If that book had never been written at all, or if it had been the joint production of two or more persons, then no one could have been correctly described as the author of *Word and Object*; and yet all the persons who are in fact present in the universe might nonetheless still have been in it. Why should the situation not be the same with the fact that there are subways in Boston? Why should we not say that there is something present in the universe which is in fact correctly described as the fact that there are subways in Boston but which, though it would have been present in the universe even if there had been no subways in Boston, would not in such an event have been a fact? I think this is precisely what can and should be said by an advocate of the early Moore-Russell theory. His position is that there is in the universe a certain proposition which is true and hence a fact; that if there had been no subways in Boston, this proposition would have been false and hence not a fact; but that it would have *been* all the same.

An advocate of the early Moore-Russell theory will hold that the sentence

(3)   The fact that there are subways in Boston might not have been the fact that there are subways in Boston

has a reading on which it expresses a true proposition, just as does the sentence

(4)   The author of *Word and Object* might not have been the author of *Word and Object*.

He will thus hold that the phrase 'the fact that there are subways in Boston', like the phrase 'the author of *Word and Object*', is not a "rigid designator," in one sense of that phrase.[13] In criticizing his earlier theory, Moore assumes in effect that 'the fact that there are subways in Boston' *is* a rigid designator, in that sense. As to the question whether Moore's later self knew better than his younger, my point here is only that the answer appears to depend upon whether the fact that there are subways in Boston is identical with the true proposition that there are subways in Boston.

3

I have already remarked that Moore and Russell soon came to abandon the view that truth is a simple unanalyzable property. And I have considered one of Moore's objections to the view—a misguided objection, if I am right. But he had another. It is an objection, not against the specific contention that truth is a simple unanalyzable property, but against the associated theory of belief, the theory that every belief has an "object" which "is" or "has being" whether the belief is true or false. Moore came to doubt that there are such things as false propositions and hence to doubt that false beliefs have objects. But if a false belief has no object, then "since there seems plainly no difference, in mere analysis, between false belief and true belief, we should have to say of all belief . . . generally, that [it] *never* [consists] in a relation between the believer and something else which *is* what is believed."[14] Moore goes on to characterize his new position as one according to which "there simply are no such things as *propositions.*" But we must take care not to misunderstand. Moore's intention is to deny that there are any entities that serve as "objects of belief." But he does not intend to deny the reality of the entities he had earlier called "true propositions" and identified with facts. Though no longer conceived as "objects of belief," these entities remain in his ontology. Nothing remains answering to false propositions, however; and their exclusion requires, by parity of analysis, that facts no longer be taken as "objects" of true beliefs.

Russell shared Moore's aversion to false propositions. He found it "almost incredible" that there should be "entities . . . which can be described as objective falsehoods."[15] This explains in part his rejection of the view that "every judgment, whether true or false, consists in a certain relation . . . to a single object." But only in part, as is clear from his saying that

> it is difficult to believe that there are such objects as 'that Charles I died in his bed', or even 'that Charles I died on the scaffold'. It seems evident that the phrase 'that so and so' has no complete meaning by itself, which would enable it to denote a definite object as (e.g.) the word 'Socrates' does. We feel that the phrase 'that so and so' is essentially incomplete, and only acquires full significance when words are added so as to express a judgment, e.g. 'I believe that so and so'. . . . Thus, if we can avoid regarding 'that so and so' as an independent entity, we shall escape a paradox.[16]

Apparently the true proposition that Charles I died on the scaffold is as objectionable as the false proposition that Charles I died in his bed. But here, as with Moore's declaration that there are no such things as propositions, we must guard against a misunderstanding. Russell's intent is not to reject *all* the entities he had called "propositions"; for facts, earlier identified with true propositions, remained in his ontology for years to come. His intent is rather to claim that the "single-object" theory of belief, or judgment, has an implausible consequence: that in such a sentence as 'Brown believes that Charles I died on the scaffold' the clause 'that Charles I died on the scaffold' is a name, on all fours with 'Brown'. The *fact* that Charles I died on the scaffold remains, but it is no longer a *proposition*.

I do not find Russell's claim obviously true. But to discuss it would take me too far afield. Of greater relevance here is the question, What were the objections to false propositions?

In the essay "On the Nature of Truth and Falsehood" Russell says merely that "we feel that there could be no falsehood if there were no minds to make mistakes" (p. 152). He surely cannot mean that it could be false that there are no subways in Boston only if someone believed that there are no subways in Boston: it *is* false that there are no subways in Boston, and yet for all that it is possible that no one believes that there are no subways in Boston. Perhaps he means rather that it could be false that there are no subways in Boston only if there were someone who *could* mistakenly think that there are no subways in Boston. But from

(5)   There are subways in Boston

there surely follows

(6)   It is false that there are no subways in Boston.

Hence if

(7)   There is someone who can think that there are no subways in Boston

were a consequence of (6), it would be a consequence of (5) as well. And I take it to be obvious that (7) is not a consequence of (5). The "feeling" we are alleged to have seems nothing more than a mistake.

I think Russell had a deeper objection to false propositions. That he did is suggested in a passage written a few years later:

> Time was when I thought there were propositions, but it does not seem to me very plausible to say that in addition to facts there are also these curious shadowy things going about such as 'That today is Wednesday' when in fact it is Tuesday. I cannot believe they go about the real world. It is more than one can manage to believe, and I do think no person with a vivid sense of reality can imagine it. . . . To suppose that in the actual world of nature there is a whole set of false propositions going about is to my mind monstrous. I cannot bring myself to suppose it.[17]

We are left wondering, nevertheless, precisely what the objection to false propositions was. How is it that they violate "a vivid sense of reality"?

Here it will be helpful, I think, to return to *Some Main Problems of Philosophy*. It is quite true that there Moore's official objection to false propositions is obscurely expressed:

> [The objection] is that, if you consider what happens when a man entertains a false belief, it doesn't seem as if his belief consisted merely in his having a relation to some object which certainly *is*. It seems rather as if the thing he was believing, the *object* of his belief, were just *the* fact which certainly is *not*—which certainly is not, because his belief is false. (p. 263)

In an effort to elucidate Ayer writes:

> But to say that the fact is not is only a clumsy way of saying that there is no such fact: and if there is no such fact, then no belief can have it for an object. Moore is therefore led to the conclusion that beliefs do not . . . have any objects at all.[18]

Perhaps this removes the obscurity, but what remains seems just a bad argument: one cannot conclude that since a false belief has no *fact* as object, it has no object at all. A clue to what Moore meant is to be found, I think, earlier in *Some Main Problems of Philosophy*, in a passage in which he is expounding the view that beliefs have propositions as objects.

> And what I want you to notice is that according to this view, *what* is believed—the *object*—the proposition, is something which *is*— there really *is* such a thing in the universe, *equally* whether the belief be true or false. If, for instance, we believe that lions exist, then whether this belief be true or false, there is such a thing as 'that lions exist', there is such a thing as 'the existence of lions'; because these phrases 'that lions exist', or 'the existence of lions' are a name for what is believed—for the proposition that is believed. (p. 260)

It comes as something of a surprise to find Moore saying that according to the view he is expounding, the phrase 'the existence of lions' is a name of the proposition that lions exist. But no slip is involved. For it does seem to have been his view, and Russell's too, that if beliefs have propositions as objects, then, considerations of linguistic complexity aside, what is believed can always be named by a so-called "verbal noun." What, for instance, is believed by someone who believes that God exists? "It is," Moore says, "that God exists, or, turning it another way, we may say that it is 'God's existence'; since to say that a man believes in God's existence is plainly merely another way of saying that he believes that God exists." Admittedly, what is believed is sometimes so complex that we cannot easily devise a verbal noun to name it. "But this is, I think, plainly only a question of words: in every case what is believed is equivalent to what could be expressed by some verbal noun, if only it were not too complex so to express it" (p. 250).

We thus appear to have at hand a demonstration that there is no such thing as the proposition that there are no subways in Boston: if there is, then there is such a thing as the nonexistence of subways in Boston; and there is such a thing as the nonexistence of subways in Boston only if there are no subways in Boston; but there *are* subways in Boston.

It would be pleasant to be able to report unqualifiedly that this was Moore's and Russell's objection to false propositions. Unfortunately, things are not that clear-cut. Moore does say at one point that "it is *only if* the belief [that lions exist] be true, that there is such a thing as the existence of lions" (p. 260); and this, in conjunction with what he has already said, suggests that he would have approved of the argument. But what, in effect, he says about it is only that it "creates a difficulty" for the theory that beliefs, whether true or false, always have objects and "suggests a suspicion that the theory is false." Nevertheless, I think it *was* his objection to false propositions. I see no other way of understanding his obscure remark that in the case of a false belief it seems as if the object believed is "just *the* fact which certainly is *not*." I take this to imply that if we say that someone's belief that there are no subways in Boston has an object at all, we must say that its object is the nonexistence of subways in Boston; but of course there is no such thing as the nonexistence of subways in Boston.

But what about the assumption on which the argument is based, the assumption that, at least in linguistically simple cases, what is believed can be named by a "verbal noun"? Moore's argument for the assumption is unconvincing, to say the least. Perhaps the sentence 'Brown believes that God exists' is synonymous with the sentence 'Brown believes in the existence of God'. But it hardly follows that *what* Brown believes is the existence of God. Indeed, 'what Brown believes is the existence of God' is not a sentence of English. In general, one cannot correctly use a phrase of the sort Moore and Russell call a "verbal noun" to designate what someone believes.[19] How could they have come to think otherwise?

The answer is to be found, I suggest, in a particular view of the nature of propositions—a view to which both Moore and Russell subscribed, but for an exposition of which one must rely mainly on Russell.

A proposition was thought to be a *complex* entity, of which various entities are *constituents*. For example, the proposition

(8)   Brown is taller than Smith

would be said to have three constituents: Brown, the relation *is taller than*, and Smith. It is like the proposition

(9)   Robinson is taller than Smith

except that it has an occurrence of Brown where (9) has an occurrence of Robinson. The proposition

(10)   Smith is shorter than Brown,

though no doubt in some sense equivalent to (8), differs from (8) in three respects: where (8) has an occurrence of Brown, (10) has an occurrence of Smith; where (8) has an occurrence of *is taller than*, (10) has an occurrence of *is shorter than*; and where (8) has an occurrence of Smith, (10) has an occurrence of Brown.

Consideration of more complicated cases is unnecessary at this point,[20] but I need to stress one feature of the proposed analysis of even these simple cases. Brown and Smith themselves, those very men, occur in (8) and (10); similarly, the men Robinson and Smith are constituents of (9). As Russell wrote to Frege, it is Mont Blanc itself which, "in spite of all its snowfields," is a "component part" of the proposition that Mont Blanc is more than 4,000 meters high.[21] And it needs equal emphasis that the very relations *is taller than* and *is shorter than* occur in the above propositions, not "senses" expressed by 'is taller than' and 'is shorter than' that merely determine those relations. Russell's propositions are not Frege's thoughts.

A proposition is a complex entity; but, as Russell emphasized, it is no mere collection of its constituents. "A proposition," he wrote, "is essentially a unity, and when analysis has destroyed the unity, no enumeration of constituents will restore the proposition."[22] The identity of a proposition depends not only on its constituents but also on the mode of connection those constituents have in the proposition. We cannot specify (8) by saying that it is the proposition of which the constituents are Brown, the relation *is taller than*, and Smith; for the different proposition *Smith is taller than Brown* has exactly the same constituents. We must also say how the constituents are there united so as to constitute the proposition. And how *are* they there united? Well, someone who believes the proposition believes that Brown *is* taller than Smith. Hence we seem required to say that in (8) Brown, the relation *is taller than*, and Smith are so united that the first bears the second to the third. And thus it appears that the proposition is the complex object, Brown's being taller than Smith.

Such an account of the complexity of propositions helps to explain Moore's and Russell's inability to detect any difference between a true proposition and the fact to which it might be thought only to correspond. If it is true that Brown is taller than Smith, then it is a fact that Brown is taller than Smith—or, as we might equally well say, Brown's being taller than Smith is a fact. And we easily fall into thinking of the fact as consisting of Brown, *is taller than*, and Smith so united that the first bears the second to the third. It is indeed difficult to see how, thus construed, the fact and the proposition could differ.

Unfortunately, it becomes equally difficult to see how the proposition can fail to be true.[23] If in (8) Brown is related to Smith by *is taller than*, how can Brown fail to be taller than Smith? "Consider," Russell says,

> the proposition "*A* differs from *B*." The constituents of this proposition, if we analyze it, appear to be only *A*, difference, *B*. Yet these constituents, thus placed side by side, do not reconstitute the proposition. The difference which occurs in the proposition actually relates *A* and *B*, whereas the difference after analysis is a notion which has no connection with *A* and *B*.[24]

But if the difference that occurs in the proposition actually relates *A* and *B*, then surely *A* really does differ from *B*—in which event it cannot be false that *A* differs from *B*. The very subsistence of (8) thus appears to require that (8) be true: if there is such a proposition as (8), then Brown is taller than Smith.

Even in *The Principles of Mathematics* Russell seemed aware that there is *some* difficulty. But as a way out he was able to suggest only that

> there is [a] sense of assertion, very difficult to bring clearly before the mind, and yet quite undeniable, in which only true propositions are asserted. True and false propositions alike are in some sense entities . . . ; but when a proposition happens to be true, it has a further quality, over and above that which it shares with false propositions, and it is this further quality which is what I mean by assertion in a logical as opposed to a psychological sense. (p. 49)

Doubtless the further quality is the simple unanalyzable quality of being true. But its invocation comes too late. Either the constituents of the proposition are appropriately united, in which case the proposition is inevitably true; or they are not, and then we have no proposition at all.

4

Moore and Russell did not give the doctrine that truth is a simple unanalyzable quality a run for its money. They coupled it with a certain theory of the nature of propositions; and once the incoherence of that theory became evident, they virtually ignored the doctrine about truth. Having abandoned propositions, Moore and Russell took the further step of identifying the primary bearers of truth with beliefs, or judgments. Some form of correspondence theory then came to seem inevitable: any adequate theory of the nature of truth must fulfill the requirement that "the truth or falsehood of a belief always depends upon something which lies outside the belief itself," and fulfillment of the requirement seemed to require the view "that truth consists in some form of correspondence between belief and fact."[25]

The question remains, however, whether the doctrine that truth is a simple unanalyzable property *must* be combined with so vulnerable a theory of the nature of "objects of belief." Need propositions be so conceived that none can be false?

If we are to think of (8), for example, as a complex entity of which the constituents are Brown, *is taller than*, and Smith, then we must agree with Russell that (8) is not the *set* of which those entities are the members. Otherwise we should be at a loss to distinguish (8) from the proposition that Smith is taller than Brown. We must also agree that no mere augmentation of {Brown, *is taller than*, Smith} would result in something that could reasonably be identified with (8). It might be suggested, however, that (8) can be identified with the ordered triple ⟨Brown, *is taller than*, Smith⟩; that, in general, a proposition can be identified with some ordered n-tuple of its constituents. But if 'can be identified with' is to be understood in the sense of 'is identical with', I feel sure Russell would have rejected the suggestion. For one thing, he would have raised the curious question why (8) should be identical with ⟨Brown, *is taller than*, Smith⟩ rather than with, say, ⟨Smith, Brown, *is taller than*⟩. For another, I think he would have regarded the ordered triple as "still merely a list of terms," though admittedly one in which order matters. We may, and do, say that *is taller than* "occurs in" ⟨Brown, *is taller than*, Smith⟩; but Russell would have said that it does not there "occur as a verb" and hence something essential to (8) is missing. "The verb, when used as a verb, embodies the unity of the proposition, and is thus distinguishable from the verb considered as a term, though I do not know how to give a clear account of the distinction."[26]

I am no more able to give a clear account than was Russell. But I can say how he would have illustrated the distinction. In (8) the relation *is taller than* occurs as a verb. In the equivalent, but distinct, proposition

(11)   Brown bears *is taller than* to Smith

it does not. Although *is taller than* is a constituent of (11), it does not there occur as a verb. The relation that occurs as a verb in (11) is rather that answering to 'bears . . . to'. In the terminology of *The Principles*, *is taller than* is a "term of" (11), but not of (8): it is a constituent of both propositions, but of the two only (11) is *about* it.

One is reminded of Frege's doctrine that "not all the parts of a thought can be complete; at least one must be 'unsaturated,' or predicative; otherwise they would not hold together."[27] No doubt Russell would have been willing to say that the "parts" of (8) "hold together" because the relation *is taller than* there occurs as a verb. But one must bear in mind two respects in which Russell's analysis of (8) diverges from Frege's. First, it is the relation *is taller than* itself, not a "sense" that determines that relation, which is supposed to prevent the proposition from degenerating into a mere "list." Second, the relation is *not* unsaturated, in Frege's sense: it occurs as a term of (11), on all fours with Brown and Smith. To deny this, Russell thought, would bring on paradox. We should find ourselves saying that *is taller than* is not a term of (11), thereby asserting a proposition of which that very relation is a term.[28]

It is thus understandable that Russell should have felt himself unable to explicate the distinction between the two sorts of occurrences of which relations are susceptible. Worse, it appears a mystery how relations succeed in performing their function: how can an entity that is simply one of the terms of (11) bring together Brown and Smith in such a way as to yield (8)? Perhaps it is understandable, too, that Russell should have felt compelled to say that in (8) *is taller than* actually *relates* Brown to Smith.

I intend to offer Russell a way out. It will not in the end prove entirely satisfactory, but I think it worth exploring nonetheless. To explain it, and make it as plausible as I can, I shall begin by considering a proposition more complicated than any so far considered, namely:

(12)   Brown is taller than Smith and Robinson is taller than Smith.

What is the relation that here "occurs as a verb" and "embodies the unity of the proposition"? The relation *is taller than* is supposed to do the trick for the two conjuncts, but surely not for their conjunction. The proposition is to have among its constituents a relation that occurs in it as a verb and thereby provides the unity indispensable to the proposition. But what can this constituent be?

As far as I know, Russell nowhere gives an answer. Indeed, *The Principles* is curiously silent on the question how compound propositions such as (12) are constituted.[29] But the most obvious style of analysis, one suggested by remarks about conditionals in an unpublished manuscript of 1905,[30] would take propositions (8) and (9) to be *immediate* constituents of (12)—that is, constituents of (12) that are not themselves constituents of constituents of (12); and the constituents of (8) and (9) would be taken to be *ultimate* constituents of (12)—that is, constituents of (12) of which no constituents of (12) are in turn constituents. Now, if we can take (8) and (9) to be themselves already possessed of the unity required of propositions, we might seek to uncover an additional constituent of (12) that would so relate (8) to (9) as to constitute (12). Let K be the operation of conjunction—that is, the operation which has as arguments all ordered pairs of propositions and which, upon application to an ordered pair $\langle p, q \rangle$ of propositions, yields the conjunction of p with q. Taking K to be a constituent of (12), we can distinguish (12) from

(13)   Brown is taller than Smith or Robinson is taller than Smith

in Russellian fashion thus: (12) is like (13) except for having an occurrence of K where (13) has an occurrence of the disjunction function, A. But notice that K cannot be the required relation. It is an operation, and so we may conceive it to be a relation. But so conceived it relates *ordered pairs* of propositions to propositions—in particular, $\langle (8), (9) \rangle$ to (12). It does not relate (8) to (9).

I see no hope of teasing further constituents out of (12). To find a relation that unifies (8), (9), and K in such a way as to yield (12), we must thus look beyond its constituents. And in fact it is not hard to find what would appear to be exactly the relation wanted: it is the triadic relation that holds among entities O, p, and q (in that order) just in case O is a binary propositional operation and p and q are propositions. (A binary propositional operation is a function on ordered pairs of propositions, having propositions as values.) Evidently K, (8), and (9) stand in that relation; and *that* they do is sufficient and necessary for there to be such a proposition as (12). Similarly with (13): there is such a proposition just in case A, (8), and (9) stand in the triadic relation in question—which of course they do.

Some readers will feel let down. An analogy may serve to articulate their sense of dissatisfaction. There is a triadic relation that holds among entities h, n, and m just in case h is a binary arithmetic operation and n and m are numbers. Addition, 2, and 3 stand in that relation, and *that* they do is necessary and sufficient for there to be such a thing as $2 + 3$. But there is no reasonable sense in which addition, 2, and 3 could be said to be "constituents" of $2 + 3$. The case is one of functionality: $2 + 3$ is a certain function of addition, 2, and 3—that function the arguments to which are the ordered triples that stand in the above relation and the value of which for an arbitrary such triple $\langle h, n, m \rangle$ as argument is $h(n, m)$. But it is not a case of compositionality in any stronger sense. Just so in the propositional case, as treated above. Associated with the triadic relation in which we have seen K, (8), and (9) to stand is a function the arguments to which are the ordered triples that stand in the relation and the value of which for an arbitrary such triple $\langle O, p, q \rangle$ as argument is $O(p, q)$. But the fact that (12) is thus a function of K, p, and q does not justify taking those entities to be, in Russell's phrase, "component parts" of (12).

I think Russell and Moore would have voiced some such objection. They would have insisted that a proposition is a special kind of *whole*, or *unity*, which has *parts* in a straightforward, if indefinable, sense.[31] They would have added that it is one thing for (12) to be a function of K, (8), and (9), and another for those entities to be parts of (12); and on this point they would no doubt have been right. But why the demand for more than functionality?

Perhaps the thought was that functionality is cheap: (12) is *some* function of any objects you choose, and it is the value of any number of functions for $\langle K, (8), (9) \rangle$ as argument. One feels that K, (8), and (9) are somehow more intimately related to (12) than mere functionality would imply. But the alternative to compositionality, in a strong sense, is not *mere* functionality. It is indeed pointless to remark that (12) is some function of, among other things, K, (8), and (9). But if F is the function the arguments to which are all the ordered triples of the form $\langle O, p, q \rangle$ and the value of which for such a triple as argument is $O(p, q)$, then to specify (12) as $F(K, (8), (9))$ is by no means pointless. It is to describe (12) in such a way as to exhibit what is required of anyone who is to entertain that proposition: the proposition must be seen as the conjunction of (8) with (9). And the description prepares the way for comparisons of (12) with other propositions. Thus (12) is the same function of K, (8), and (9) that (13) is of A, (8), and (9). And this, I should suppose, is the best sense to be made of saying that (12) is like (13) "except for having K where (13) has A."

5

I have been urging that Russell and Moore should have been content with a view according to which a proposition is a function of what they would have taken to be its constituents. So far, however, (12) has been seen to be a function only of its immediate constituents. To push on, we must consider how things stand with (8) and (9). It is here, I believe, that we come upon what Russell was wont to call "grave logical problems."

We know that the constituents of (8) are supposed to be Brown, *is taller than*, and Smith. And it is easy enough to specify a relation that "unites" the three in such a way as to yield (8): it is the triadic relation that holds among x, R, and y if and only if x and y are any entities and R is a dyadic relation. It is evident that Brown, *is taller than*, and Smith stand in that relation; and, granted Russell's liberal stance with respect to propositional subsistence, *that* they do is sufficient and necessary for there to be such a proposition as (8).[32]

But to say all this is not yet to exhibit (8) as a function of Brown, *is taller than*, and Smith. What is wanted is a function G such that (i) the arguments to G are precisely those ordered triples $\langle x, R, y \rangle$ such that x and y are any entities and R is a dyadic relation, and (ii) $G(\text{Brown}, \textit{is taller than}, \text{Smith})$ is (8), $G(\text{Robinson}, \textit{is taller than}, \text{Smith})$ is (9), $G(\text{Smith}, \textit{is shorter than}, \text{Brown})$ is (10), and so on. But to specify the desired function, it is necessary to do more than wave a hand in the direction of its values for other arguments. One must say what the value of the function is for an arbitrarily chosen argument. And how is this to be done?

The idea that comes immediately to mind is this: the value of G for

$\langle x, R, y \rangle$ as argument is the proposition that x bears R to y. But a difficulty arises at once, even granted the existence of G, as thus allegedly specified. For $G(\text{Brown}, \textit{is taller than}, \text{Smith})$ becomes (11), rather than what we have been told is the equivalent but distinct proposition (8). Some philosophers will be inclined to dismiss the difficulty, on the ground that (11) is really the same proposition as (8). Without taking a stand on the question of identity versus equivalence (in some sense), let me suggest that there is in any case a function H that takes (11) to (8) and that similarly takes the propositions

(14)   Robinson bears *is taller than* to Smith

and

(15)   Smith bears *is shorter than* to Brown

to, respectively, (9) and (10). In general, H takes values of the alleged function G to their *deflated counterparts*. Note that associated with each dyadic relation R is a function R^* which, applied to an ordered pair $\langle x, y \rangle$ as argument, yields the deflated counterpart of $G(x, R, y)$ as value; that is,

$$R^*(x, y) = H(G(x, R, y)).$$

And R^* appears to qualify as a "propositional function," at any rate in one of the senses in which Russell used that expression.

Although I would not undertake to specify H, I think we see well enough for present purposes what function it is supposed to be. But I fear that matters are otherwise in the case of G. Its proposed specification is problematic, because of peculiarities of the phrase 'the proposition that'.

That phrase plays two very different roles in English sentences, both of which can be detected in the syntactically ambiguous sentence 'The proposition that Brown wrote on the board yesterday is true'. Taken in one way, it has the sense of 'That Brown wrote on the board yesterday is a true proposition'; taken in another way, it has the sense rather of 'The proposition which Brown wrote on the board yesterday is true'. On both readings the phrase 'the proposition that Brown wrote on the board yesterday' is a singular term that results from prefixing 'the proposition that' to 'Brown wrote on the board yesterday'. But whereas on the second reading the singular term is a definite description, on the first it is not.[33] No doubt there are problems connected with the use of 'the proposition that' thus to form definite descriptions, problems that arise from uncertainties as to how propositions are to be identified and distinguished. But the problems alluded to above concern rather the use of 'the proposition that' to form singular terms that are not definite descriptions. How are they to be understood?

For sentences that formulate exactly one proposition, the answer appears to be contained in the following rule:

> Every result of putting a sentence that formulates a proposition for '*S*' in 'the proposition that *S*' designates the proposition formulated by that sentence.

But this is of no help in trying to understand the proposed specification of *G*; for there 'the proposition that' is prefixed to an *open* sentence, and the result designates no proposition at all. Moreover, difficulties stand in the way of supplementing the rule so as to cover the sorts of cases that arise in the effort to specify such functions as *G*.

The proposed specification of *G* is successful only if it has the consequence that whenever *x* is identical with *z*, *H(G(x, R, y))* is identical with *H(G(z, R, y))*. Or, to keep matters simple, identity of *x* with *z* always requires identity of *H(G(x, is taller than, Smith))* with *H(G(z, is taller than, Smith))*. Hence, the proposed specification requires that whenever *x* is identical with *z*, the proposition that *x* is taller than Smith be identical with the proposition that *z* is taller than Smith. It is thus required that if Brown happens to be Smith's employee, then the proposition that Brown is taller than Smith is identical with the proposition that Smith's employee is taller than Smith. And yet we seem here to have distinct propositions, whatever the working relationship between Brown and Smith.

I say we *seem* to have distinct propositions, in anticipation of an objection to a categorical denial of identity. The objection is that the phrases 'the proposition that Brown is taller than Smith' and 'the proposition that Smith's employee is taller than Smith' are ambiguous: taken in accordance with the rule stated above, they do designate distinct propositions; but they may also be understood in such a way that if Brown is Smith's employee, they designate one and the same proposition, namely, the proposition with respect to Brown—i.e., Smith's employee—that *he* is taller than Smith. And recognition of the ambiguity paves the way to understanding the results of prefixing 'the proposition that' to open sentences. Thus, for any object *x*, the proposition that *x* is taller than Smith is the proposition with respect to *x* that *it* is taller than Smith. And the proposed specification of *G* is to be understood accordingly: *G(x, R, y)* is the proposition with respect to *x*, *R*, and *y* (whatever they may be) that the first bears the second to the third.

Neither Moore nor Russell would have hesitated to speak of the proposition with respect to some given object that it is taller than Smith. Such expressions, or their equivalents, are frequent in Moore's writings.[34] And how without use of such expressions are Russellian propositional functions to be specified? The expressions are nonetheless not altogether unproblematic. Given some object x, which proposition *is* the proposition with respect to x that it is taller than Smith?

If x is Brown, then the proposition that Smith's employee is taller than Smith is not a likely candidate. But (8), the proposition that Brown is taller than Smith, *is*. For it is plausible to say that in asserting (8) we simply refer to Brown and say of him that he is taller than Smith. We do not describe him as Smith's employee, or as anything else: we refer to him neat. Hence the proposition requires for its truth merely that a certain object, the one denoted by 'Brown', be taller than Smith. 'Brown', as Russell put it, "merely indicates without meaning."[35]

But of course there is a problem. Suppose that, when not at work for Smith, Brown writes detective fiction under the name Roger Greene. Smith, a devotee of Greene's stories, knows well enough that (8) is true, but sincerely professes ignorance as to Greene's height relative to his own. It is not an unlikely supposition. But it appears to require that *Brown is taller than Smith* be one proposition and *Greene is taller than Smith* another; for, apparently, Smith believes the one but not the other. But then which is *the* proposition with respect to Brown—i.e., Greene—that *he* is taller than Smith?

The difficulty of the question is that no answer to it saves the appearances. We may say, with Frege, that, in spite of appearances, neither proposition is one the truth of which requires merely that the denotation of 'Brown' be taller than Smith—that, indeed, there is *no* such proposition and hence no such thing as *the* proposition with respect to Brown that he is taller than Smith. We may say, as Russell himself was soon to say,[36] that there is such a function as G but that, in spite of appearances, its value for Brown as argument is a proposition that Brown alone can entertain: *our* access to Brown, and hence to the proposition, is indirect, via some description for which our use of 'Brown' is a substitute. Or we may say, clinging to *The Principles*, that, in spite of appearances, *Brown is taller than Smith* and *Greene is taller than Smith* are one and the same proposition.[37] I have no firm conviction as to which of these positions is the least unattractive.

Notes

Sections 1–3 of this essay are substantially the content of a paper presented to the Department of Philosophy at Princeton University in 1971, and to the Departments of Philosophy at Tufts University and the University of Rochester some years later.

1. *Mind*, n.s., 8 (1899): 176–193.

2. "Truth," in J. Mark Baldwin, ed., *Dictionary of Philosophy and Psychology* (London: Macmillan, 1902), vol. 2, pp. 716–718.

3. In Douglas Lackey, ed., *Essays in Analysis* (New York: Braziller, 1973), pp. 21–76. Originally published in *Mind*, n.s., 13 (1904): 204–219, 336–354, 509–524.

4. Bertrand Russell, *The Principles of Mathematics*, 1st ed. (Cambridge: Cambridge University Press, 1903).

5. Bertrand Russell, "On the Nature of Truth and Falsehood," essay 7 of *Philosophical Essays* (New York: Simon and Schuster, 1966). This is a drastic revision of the third section of his "On the Nature of Truth," *Proceedings of the Aristotelian Society*, n.s., 7 (1906–1907): 28–49, in which he had said that he was unable to decide between the theory that truth is a simple quality and a certain form of the correspondence theory.

6. (London: Allen and Unwin, 1953.) Lectures delivered in 1910–1911.

7. Thus Russell: "Direct inspection seems to leave no room whatever for doubt that, in all presentations and judgments, there is necessarily an object. If I believe that A is the father of B, I believe something; the subsistence of the something, if not directly obvious, seems to follow from the fact that, if it did not subsist, I should be believing nothing, and therefore not believing" ("Meinong's Theory," *Essays in Analysis*, p. 61).

8. Moore thus took falsity to be definable in terms of truth. But not so Russell. "What is truth, and what falsehood, we must merely apprehend, for both seem incapable of analysis" ("Meinong's Theory," p. 76).

9. "Meinong's Theory," p. 75

10. "Meinong's Theory," p. 75.

11. In "Meinong's Theory" Russell remarked that "truth does not seem to be a constituent of most asserted propositions even when they are true" (p. 75).

12. A. J. Ayer, *Russell and Moore: The Analytical Heritage* (Cambridge, Mass.: Harvard University Press, 1971), p. 211.

13. See Saul Kripke, *Naming and Necessity* (Cambridge, Mass.: Harvard University Press, 1980), p. 49; and "Identity and Necessity," in M. K. Munitz, ed., *Identity and Necessity* (New York: New York University Press, 1971), pp. 148–149. Of course, an advocate of the early Moore-Russell theory would *not* hold that, just as 'the author of *Word and Object* is such that something other than it might have been the author of *Word and Object*' has a reading on which it expresses a true proposition, so 'the fact that there are subways in Boston is such that something other than it might have been the fact that there are subways in Boston' has a parallel reading on which it expresses a true proposition.

14. *Some Main Problems of Philosophy*, p. 265.

15. "On the Nature of Truth and Falsehood," p. 152.

16. "On the Nature of Truth and Falsehood," p. 151.

17. Bertrand Russell, *Logic and Knowledge*, ed. R. C. Marsh (London: Allen and Unwin, 1956), p. 223.

18. *Russell and Moore*, p. 210.

19. Similarly for 'think', 'disbelieve', 'know', 'opine', and 'say'. But not for 'assert', 'affirm', 'doubt', 'assume', 'deny', and 'prove'. I have no theory to offer, nor do I know whether the data are of any significance.

20. For a fuller exposition of Russell's views on the constitution of propositions, see "On the Origins of Russell's Theory of Descriptions," in this volume.

21. Russell to Frege, 12 December 1904. In *Gottlob Frege: Philosophical and Mathematical Correspondence*, edited by G. Gabriel et al., abridged from the German edition by B. McGuiness, translated by H. Kaal (Chicago: University of Chicago Press, 1980), p. 169.

22. *Principles*, p. 50.

23. The difficulty was first pointed out to me by Edmund Gettier.

24. *Principles*, p. 49.

25. Bertrand Russell, *The Problems of Philosophy* (London: Oxford University Press, 1912), p. 121.

26. *Principles*, p. 50. The reader must simply tolerate Russell's habit of using names of parts of speech in application to nonlinguistic entities.

27. Peter Geach and Max Black, eds., *Translations from the Philosophical Writings of Gottlob Frege*, 3d ed. (Totowa, N.J.: Rowman and Littlefield, 1980), p. 54.

28. See *Principles*, p. 48.

29. The treatment there of the propositional calculus (pp. 13–18) is uninformative. In particular, Russell's definition of conjunction is, by his own admission, "highly artificial, and illustrates the great distinction between mathematical and philosophical definitions" (p. 16).

30. "On Fundamentals," begun 7 June 1905, Russell Archives. The relevant portions of this document are briefly discussed in section 8 of "On the Origins of Russell's Theory of Descriptions."

31. See *Principles*, chap. 16.

32. It was Russell's view in *The Principles* that for all terms x and y, and for every dyadic relation R, there is a proposition like (8) except for having respectively x, y, and R where (8) has Brown, Smith, and *is taller than*. See p. 45.

33. I do not mean to deny that in a regimented language such singular terms can be replaced systematically by definite descriptions. See Quine, *Word and Object* (Cambridge, Mass.: MIT Press, 1960), p. 185.

34. See especially his "External and Internal Relations," in *Philosophical Studies* (London: Routledge and Kegan Paul, 1922), pp. 276–309.

35. *Principles*, p. 502.

36. See "On the Origins of Russell's Theory of Descriptions" for an account of the transition.

37. See, for example, Nathan Salmon, *Frege's Puzzle* (Cambridge, Mass.: MIT Press, 1986); Joseph Almog, "Naming without Necessity," *Journal of Philosophy* 83 (1986): 210–241, and "Form and Content," *Noûs* 19 (1985): 603–616. Their work derives in part from David Kaplan, "Demonstratives" (unpublished manuscript, 1977), and John Perry, "Frege on Demonstratives," *Philosophical Review* 86 (1977): 474–497. Ruth Marcus was an earlier champion: see her "Modalities and Intensional Languages," *Synthese* 13 (1961): 303–330. For an informed discussion of the issues involved, see Howard Wettstein, "Has Semantics Rested on a Mistake?" *Journal of Philosophy* 83 (1986): 185–209.

On the Origins of Russell's Theory
of Descriptions

Russell's initial break with the ontology of *The Principles of Mathematics*[1] is often associated with his discovery of the theory of descriptions. The nature of the association is apt to be left somewhat vague, but one is led to think that until the discovery Russell had subscribed to an ontology that included Homeric gods, chimeras, and perhaps even round squares—either because he did not think to question their subsistence or because he did not see how to avoid denying full referential status to expressions that seem to designate them. Thus, after remarking on the "intolerably indiscriminate ontology" of *The Principles*, Quine writes:

> Russell's long article on Meinong[2] came out in *Mind* in installments [in 1904]. In it he . . . protested none against the exuberance of Meinong's realm of being. In the same quarterly three issues later, however, a reformed Russell emerges: the Russell of "On Denoting"[3] . . . , fed up with Meinong's impossible objects. The reform was no simple change of heart; it hinged on the discovery of a means of dispensing with the unwelcome objects. The device was Russell's theory of singular descriptions. . . . It involved defining a term not by presenting a direct equivalent of it, but by what Bentham called *paraphrasis*: by providing equivalents of all desired sentences containing the term. In this way, reference to fictitious objects can be simulated in meaningful sentences without our being committed to the objects.[4]

Russell himself encouraged such an understanding of his ontological development, remarking that it was "the desire to avoid Meinong's unduly populous realm of being [that] led me to the theory of descriptions."[5] But the facts, as I shall try to show, are quite otherwise: Russell had repudiated Homeric gods and the rest before he hit upon the theory of descriptions; the repudiation was grounded on a theory of denoting developed out of that presented in *The Principles*; and it was the "inextricable tangle" to which Russell soon came to think that theory led, and which he attempted to set out in "On Denoting," that immediately occasioned the theory of descriptions.[6]

1

The facts are clear from certain of Russell's unpublished manuscripts. But examination of two of his published writings from the period in question already undermines the idea that he saw his way clear to renouncing the extravagant ontology of *The Principles* only upon discovery of the theory of descriptions. One, called "The Existential Import of Propositions," appeared in *Mind* for April 1905 and is a response to a piece by Hugh MacColl that had appeared in the preceding issue. The other was published in *Mind* for October of the same year and is a review of a volume of essays, one by Meinong and the others by his students, bearing the title *Untersuchungen zur Gegenstandstheorie und Psychologie.*

MacColl had contended that an adequate treatment of traditional categorical propositions requires a universe of discourse comprising not only *"real existences"* but also *"non-existences, that is to say, . . . unrealities* such as *centaurs, nectar, ambrosia, fairies,* [along] with self-contradictions, such as *round squares, square circles, flat spheres,* etc."[7] Russell responded that "the members of every class are among realities," and of MacColl's unrealities he had this to say:

> Concerning all these we shall simply have to say that they are classes which have no members, so that each of them is identical with the null class. There are no Centaurs; '*x* is a Centaur' is false whatever value we give to *x*. . . . Similarly, there are no round squares. The case of nectar and ambrosia is more difficult, since these seem to be individuals, not classes. But here we must presuppose definitions of nectar and ambrosia: they are substances having such and such properties, which, as a matter of fact, no substances do have. We have thus merely a defining concept for each, without any entity to which the concept applies. In this case, the concept is an entity, but it does not denote anything. To take a simpler case: 'The present King of England' is a complex concept denoting an individual; 'the present King of France' is a similar complex concept denoting nothing. The phrase intends to point out an individual, but fails to do so: it does not point out an unreal individual, but no individual at all. The same explanation applies to mythical personages, Apollo, Priam, etc. These words have a *meaning*, which can be found by looking them up in a classical dictionary; but they have not a *denotation*: there is no entity, real or imaginary, which they point out.[8]

This is hardly the Russell of *The Principles*; for whether or not the ontology of that book included round squares and the present king of France, it does appear to have included Apollo and Priam. But neither is it the Russell of "On Denoting"; for the ontology of *The Principles* is cut back, not by paraphrasing away seeming references to the objectionable entities, but by invoking a distinction between meaning and denotation that comes under heavy attack in that later essay.

The review of *Untersuchungen* appeared in the same issue of *Mind* as "On Denoting." It is therefore natural to think that when Russell remarks in the review that "the difficulties of excluding such objects [as the round square] can, I think, be avoided by the theory of denoting,"[9] the reference is to the theory defended in "On Denoting." There is, however, a puzzling footnote in which *both* "On Denoting" and "Frege's distinction of *Sinn* and *Bedeutung*" are cited, as if by way of explanation. And that the theory Russell means is in fact *not* that of "On Denoting" is clear from his mention, just three paragraphs later, of "a sharp distinction of meaning and denotation such as we *require* for the denial of denotation in the case of impossible objects."[10] Again, this is hardly the Russell of "On Denoting."

In spite of its publication date, and that curious footnote, the review must thus have been written during a period in which Russell had abandoned the more bizarre features of the ontology of *The Principles* but had not yet hit upon the theory of descriptions. Can the limits of the period be more precisely determined? And can anything more definite be said about the "distinction of meaning and denotation" that appears to buttress the change in ontology?

2

The discovery of the theory of descriptions can be dated with considerable accuracy. Russell himself places it in the spring of 1905.[11] We can be more precise. A letter to Lucy Donnelly dated 13 June 1905 refers to the discovery,[12] and that it did not occur much earlier is confirmed by an unpublished manuscript in the Russell Archives bearing the title "On Fundamentals" and the annotation "1905 (begun June 7)." There, suddenly, after nearly forty tortuous pages on meaning and denotation, appears the theory of descriptions. And with it the distinction between meaning and denotation is swept aside. "On this view," Russell writes, " 'the author of *Waverley*' has no significance at all by itself, but propositions in which it occurs have significance. Thus in regard to denoting phrases of this sort, the question of meaning and denotation ceases to exist" (p. 38).

Russell's initial disenchantment with the ontology of *The Principles* is less easily pinpointed. The difficulty stems in part from uncertainties as to what the ontology of the book is. Just how extravagant is it? Two famous passages appear to tell us:

> Whatever may be an object of thought, or may occur in any true or false proposition, or can be counted as *one*, I call a *term*. This, then, is

the widest word in the philosophical vocabulary. I shall use as synonymous with it the words unit, individual, and entity. The first two emphasize the fact that every term is *one*, while the third is derived from the fact that every term has being, i.e. *is* in some sense. A man, a moment, a number, a class, a relation, a chimera, or anything else that can be mentioned, is sure to be a term; and to deny that such and such a thing is a term must always be false. (p. 43)

Being is that which belongs to every conceivable term, to every possible object of thought—in short to everything that can possibly occur in any proposition, true or false, and to all such propositions themselves. Being belongs to whatever can be counted. If *A* be any term that can be counted as one, it is plain that *A* is something, and therefore that *A* is. "*A* is not" must always be either false or meaningless. For if *A* were nothing, it could not be said not to be; "*A* is not" implies that there is a term *A* whose being is denied, and hence that *A* is. Thus unless "*A* is not" be an empty sound, it must be false— whatever *A* may be, it certainly is. Numbers, the Homeric gods, relations, chimeras and four-dimensional spaces all have being, for if they were not entities of a kind, we could make no propositions about them. Thus being is a general attribute of everything, and to mention anything is to show that it is. (p. 449)

These passages leave it unclear, however, which of two doctrines Russell means to affirm. Some of what he says suggests

(I)   Any result of putting a singular term for 'A' in 'there is no such thing as A' expresses a false proposition.

But he can also be read as affirming rather

(II)   Anything that can be mentioned has being.

Now, (I) and (II) would appear to be very different doctrines: whereas (I) is easily refutable, (II) is not. To refute (I), suppose it true. Then, in particular, the sentence 'There is no such thing as the false proposition identical with (I)' expresses a false proposition. But if so, then surely there is such a thing as the false proposition identical with (I), from which it follows that (I) is false. Thus (I) is false even if true, and hence it is false. No such easy refutation is available in the case of (II), however. Any effort to cite a counterexample could be written off as a failure to mention anything at all. Thus (II) has ontological clout only when coupled with one or another doctrine concerning mentionability.

   Now, I think there is no doubt that Russell subscribed to (II). And no doubt either that in *The Principles* he took a liberal view of what can be mentioned: witness the Homeric gods. But what about (I)? What, in particular, about impossible objects such as the greatest prime number and the round square cupola on Berkeley College? And, for that matter, what about the present king of France? I see no clear answers to these questions in *The Principles*. On the one hand, we are told that '*A* is not' must always be either false or meaningless. On the other hand, we are told that there is no such thing as the null class (p. 75), no such thing as the class (as one) of those classes (as ones) that are not members of themselves (p. 102), no such thing as the immediate predecessor of the first limit ordinal (p. 361), and so on. And of course *some* such denials of being were inevitable in a work on the principles of mathematics: there is no such thing as the greatest prime number, else Euclid's theorem is false; and there is no such thing as the class of all those classes that are not members of themselves, else Russell's own paradox is false. And no sound principle of *ontology* can have the consequence that there is such a thing as the least odd perfect number, or the least even number greater than 4 which is not the sum of two primes.

But do not the Homeric gods and the present king of France remain? The Homeric gods, apparently—though even here it is disconcerting to find chimeras cited along with them, for we are told in another place that there are no chimeras, that the propositional function *x is a chimera* is false for all values of *x* (pp. 73–74). Matters are even less clear when it comes to the present king of France. No such case is explicitly discussed in *The Principles*, as far as I have been able to discover. One is forced to try on, as best one can, Russell's intuitions. And, speaking for myself anyhow, Zeus fares better as a "possible object of thought," as something "that can be mentioned." One can make some progress counting Homeric gods; but not present kings of France.[13]

The ontology of *The Principles* is thus less firm than one would like: no doubt anything that can be mentioned has being, but the sphere of the mentionable is ill defined. Still, the impression of a bloated realm of being remains. And as for its unequivocal renunciation, no evidence known to me suggests a date earlier than late 1904. The criticism of MacColl must have been written early in 1905. Three unpublished manuscripts develop in some detail the views on meaning and denotation mentioned in that essay.[14] Two bear the annotation "early 1905," and the third is dated "before 18 January 1905." An earlier date is clearly possible, but not one so early as to conflict with the writing of the three-part essay on Meinong; for there, as Quine notices, Russell's ontology seems thoroughly unrestrained.[15]

3

Were it not for the unpublished manuscripts just now mentioned, it would be reasonable to suppose that "the theory of denoting" alluded to in the review of *Untersuchungen* is Frege's; that the "sharp distinction of meaning and denotation such as we require for the denial of denotation in the case of impossible objects" is Frege's distinction between *Sinn* and *Bedeutung*. After all, there is the footnote reference to Frege; and the very choice of terminology suggests Frege's distinction. The unpublished manuscripts make it plain, however, that the theory in question has only a little in common with Frege's and much more with the theory of denoting presented in *The Principles*.

The less mathematical portions of that book are given over in good part to what Russell calls the "philosophical analysis" of one or another proposition: the determination of the "constituents" of the proposition and their manner of "occurrence" in it. "Grammar" is supposed to guide the analysis:

> Although a grammatical distinction cannot be uncritically assumed to correspond to a genuine philosophical difference, yet the one is *prima facie* evidence of the other, and may often be most usefully employed as a source of discovery. Moreover, it must be admitted, I think, that every word occurring in a sentence must have *some* meaning: a perfectly meaningless sound could not be employed in the more or less fixed way in which language employs words. The correctness of our philosophical analysis of a proposition may therefore usefully be checked by the exercise of assigning the meaning of each word in the sentence expressing the proposition. (p. 42)

Words have meaning "in the simple sense that they are symbols which stand for something other than themselves," and "a proposition contains the entities indicated by words" (p. 47).

The picture called up is that of a one-one correspondence between occurrences of words in a sentence and occurrences in the proposition expressed of the entities for which the words stand. One wants to point out at once the apparently devastating consequence that sentences of different verbal complexity will never express the same proposition. But it is clear that Russell was not prepared to insist on the accuracy of the picture across the board. "Grammar" is not, after all, to be our master: "[its] excellence . . . as a guide is proportional to the paucity of inflexions, i.e. to the degree of analysis effected by the language considered" (p. 42, n.), and even relatively uninflected languages sometimes mislead.[16] Still, over a large class of cases Russell seems ready to preserve the picture by making unusually fine distinctions among propositions. An extreme example is his willingness to distinguish

(1)   9 exceeds 7

from

(2)   9 is greater than 7.

The constituents of (1) are the numbers 9 and 7 and the relation *exceeds*. But (2) has in addition constituents answering to the words 'is' and 'than'. "The *is* seems to state that [9] has to *greater* the relation of referent, while the *than* states similarly that [7] has to *greater* the relation of relatum."[17]

It is a good deal more plausible to distinguish, as Russell would, (1) from

(3)   9 bears *exceeds* to 7.

If 9, 7, and *exceeds* are constituents of (1), then presumably they are also constituents of (3). But it is natural to suggest that (3) has an additional constituent, namely, a triadic relation answering to 'bears . . . to'. This suggestion would sacrifice the one-one correspondence between occurrences of words in the sentence and occurrences in the proposition of entities for which the words stand. If, alternatively, we try to preserve the one-one correspondence by ignoring the triadic relation and assigning to the proposition constituents answering to the words 'bears' and 'to', we lose the proposition itself: (3) is not equivalent to, though it does imply, the conjunction of the propositions that 9 bears *exceeds* to something and that something bears *exceeds* to 7.

A compromise might be suggested: assign to the proposition constituents answering to each of 'bears', 'to', and 'bears . . . to', taking the last to be itself (somehow) composed of the other two. A one-one correspondence could then be claimed to hold between occurrences of words in the sentence and occurrences in the proposition of *ultimate* constituents, where a constituent is ultimate if and only if it is a constituent of no constituent. Propositions would take on the structure of trees. But I think there is no saying whether Russell would have welcomed the suggestion or whether instead he would have seen in (3) a case in which verbal and propositional complexity fail to go hand in hand.

In any case, the example serves nicely to illustrate a distinction, which Russell takes to be of the first importance, among the constituents of a proposition. He takes it as evident that (1) is *about* the numbers 9 and 7, and nothing else. The relation *exceeds* occurs in (1), but not in such a way that (1) is *about* it. In contrast, (3) *is* about *exceeds*, as well as 9 and 7. Russell puts the point by saying that *exceeds*, though a constituent of both propositions, is a "term of" (3) but not of (1). Similarly, although Socrates and humanity are constituents of

(4)   Socrates is human,

(4) is about Socrates, and not humanity; hence Socrates is its only term.[18] But both Socrates and humanity are terms of

(5)   Socrates has humanity,

for (5) is about both. In general: the *terms of* a proposition are those of its constituents that the proposition is about.

If Russell is conservative about propositional identity, he is liberal when it comes to propositional subsistence. "It is," he says, "a characteristic of the terms of a proposition that any one of them may be replaced by any other entity without our ceasing to have a proposition" (p. 45). We can go some way toward cashing the metaphor: x is a term of a proposition p if and only if x is a constituent of p and, for every y, there is a proposition q which is like p except for having an occurrence of y where p has an occurrence of x. Thus, given any term y, there is a proposition which is like (4) save for having y where (4) has Socrates: 'humanity is human', '9 is human', 'exceeds is human'—all express propositions; their defect is that they express false propositions. Still, it is only the *terms* of a proposition that are thus universally "replaceable." There is no proposition which is like (4) except for having (say) 9, or 7, or Socrates where (4) has humanity; nor any proposition which is like (1) except for having something other than a dyadic relation where (1) has *exceeds*.

Anything that is a term of at least one proposition Russell calls a "term," *tout court*. One can as well say that a term is anything that is a constituent of at least one proposition. For anything that is a constituent but not a term of one proposition is sure to be a term of some other proposition: to say, as we have, that *exceeds* is a constituent but not a term of (1) is to assert a proposition of which *exceeds* is a term. Similarly, there is nothing that is a constituent of no proposition: to say of x that it is a constituent of no proposition is to assert a proposition of which x is a constituent. Thus it is that 'term' is "the widest word in the philosophical vocabulary."[19]

Terms divide into *things* and *concepts*. The former are terms of all propositions of which they are constituents; the latter are constituents of some propositions of which they are not terms. Humanity is a concept, because it is a constituent but not a term of (4). Socrates is a thing, because he is a term of every proposition of which he is a constituent: "Socrates is not capable of that curious twofold use which is involved in *human* and *humanity*" (p. 45). The distinction is reminiscent of Frege's distinction between objects and functions. But of course we have in effect already seen that Russell's concepts, unlike Frege's functions, are not "unsaturated."

I come, finally, to denoting. Russell introduces the subject with what appears to be a definition. "A concept *denotes*," he writes, "when, if it occurs in a proposition, the proposition is not about the concept, but about a term connected in a certain peculiar way with the concept" (p. 53). Whether or not intended as a definition, what Russell says is carelessly worded. It obscures a distinction between two notions, the notion of a *denoting concept* and the more fundamental notion of a *denotative occurrence* of a concept in a proposition; and it wrongly suggests that to explain these notions it is necessary, or at any rate useful, to invoke a peculiar connection that certain concepts have with certain terms.

The right approach to the subject is, I think, through examples. For, although we may say that a *denoting* concept is one susceptible of denotative occurrences in propositions, the notion of denotative occurrence is best regarded as primitive. Consider then

(6)   Some number exceeds 7.

This proposition, Russell would say, is like (1) except for having an occurrence of the concept *some number* where (1) has an occurrence of 9. Since 9 is a term of (1), it will be convenient to say that its position in (1) is *term-accessible*.[20] Thus the concept *some number* occupies a term-accessible position in (6). Nevertheless, (6) is not *about* the concept *some number*: whereas (6) is true,

(7)   *Some number* exceeds 7

is false. Hence *some number* is not a term of (6), even though it occupies a term-accessible position in (6); and it is by virtue of this that the occurrence of *some number* in (6) is denotative.[21]

We may say, in general, that an occurrence of a concept in a given proposition is denotative if it is at a term-accessible position in the proposition and yet the concept is not a term of the proposition. Without too much strain, this can be made to yield many of the cases Russell wants. Thus *every number* can with some plausibility be said to have a denotative occurrence in *Every number exceeds* 7; likewise *any number* in *Any number exceeds* 7. But certain sorts of cases prove recalcitrant. One such is exemplified in the proposition *All the generations from Abraham to David are fourteen generations*. Here the occurrence of the concept *all the generations from Abraham to David* is supposed to be denotative; but I do not see how to make out that the concept occupies a term-accessible position in the proposition. Another sort of difficulty is presented by, for example, the second occurrence (if one may so speak) of *some number* in the (false) proposition

(8)   *Some number* exceeds some number.

That occurrence is presumably denotative; yet, by virtue of its first occurrence, *some number* is a term of (8). To handle this and like cases, one appears to need the notion of a term's being a term of a proposition *at such-and-such a position in* the proposition. But I see no way of explaining this with the conceptual apparatus available.

For my purposes here, the most important examples of denoting concepts are those represented linguistically by definite descriptions, or equivalents of definite descriptions. Russell takes the proposition

(9)   The teacher of Plato is human

to be like (1) except for having the concept *the teacher of Plato* where (1) has Socrates. *The teacher of Plato* thus occupies a term-accessible position in (9). But of course (9) is not about the concept: we can suppose, following custom, that (9) is true; but

(10)   *The teacher of Plato* is human

is absurd. Hence *the teacher of Plato* is not a term of (9), and its occurrence in that proposition is denotative.

Russell claims that the theory of denoting explains why it is sometimes worthwhile to affirm an identity:

> If we say "Edward VII is the King," we assert an identity; the reason why this assertion is worth making is, that in the one case the actual term occurs, while in the other a denoting concept takes its place. . . . Often two denoting concepts occur, and the term itself is not mentioned, as in the proposition "the Present Pope is the last survivor of his generation." (p. 64)

Russell remarks parenthetically that 'Edward VII', in the first example, is to be taken as a proper name. The implication is that proper names are not to be construed as disguised definite descriptions. The question how, then, it can be worthwhile to affirm such a proposition as that Twain is Clemens is not addressed.

It remains to say something, if only a little, about the *relation* of denoting, i.e., the peculiar connection that denoting concepts may have with terms. Much of what is said in *The Principles* about this relation is exceedingly obscure. It is fortunate for present purposes, however, that the relation is at its clearest in the case of denoting concepts represented linguistically by definite descriptions. Such cases are governed by the following simple principle:

(III)   Every result of putting a definite description for 'C' in 'If there is such a term as C then C denotes C' is true.

Thus *the successor of 8* denotes the successor of 8, i.e., 9; for there is such a term as the successor of 8, and it is 9. If there is such a term as the teacher of Plato, then *the teacher of Plato* denotes the teacher of Plato; and if in addition Socrates is the teacher of Plato, *the teacher of Plato* denotes Socrates. A second principle is equally straightforward:

(IV)   Every result of putting a definite description for 'C' and a singular term for 'A' in 'If *C* denotes A then A = C' is true.

Thus *the successor of 8* denotes 9 and nothing else; and if *the teacher of Plato* denotes anything at all, it denotes the teacher of Plato.

Notice that (III) is so worded as to be noncommittal on the question whether such denoting concepts as *the present king of France* and *the round square cupola on Berkeley College* in fact denote. In the light of uncertainties about the ontology of *The Principles*, this is as it should be.

The relation of denoting becomes obscure when one turns to denoting concepts that cannot be represented linguistically by definite descriptions. It will suffice here to consider what Russell says about *some man*:

> . . . *some man* must not be regarded as actually denoting Smith and actually denoting Brown, and so on: the whole procession of human beings throughout the ages is always relevant to every proposition in which *some man* occurs, and what is denoted is essentially not each separate man, but a kind of combination of all men. (p. 62)

Russell concedes that the required combination is a "very paradoxical object." Fortunately, it can be ignored here, as can the equally paradoxical objects allegedly denoted by such concepts as *every man, any man,* and *a man.*[22]

4

In appendix A of *The Principles*, titled "The Logical and Arithmetical Doctrines of Frege," Russell writes, "The distinction between meaning (*Sinn*) and indication (*Bedeutung*) is roughly, though not exactly, equivalent to my distinction between a concept as such and what the concept denotes" (p. 502). But in fact the two distinctions are not even in the same ballpark. Russell's is a distinction between a denoting concept and what (if anything) the concept denotes. But Frege's is not a distinction between *Sinne* as such and their *Bedeutungen*, for the simple reason that it is not *Sinne* but linguistic expressions that have *Bedeutungen*. Of course, there is for Frege the relation of *Sinn* to *Bedeutung*,[23] and it need not be considered merely derivative from the relation that a *Sinn* bears to an expression that has that *Sinn* and the relation that an expression bears to its *Bedeutung*.[24] Nevertheless, in Frege's hands properties of that relation are used to elucidate a distinction within the general notion of the meaning of an expression—a use to which, in the text of *The Principles*, Russell never puts his distinction. There, as I have already noted, words have meaning in "the simple sense" that they stand for entities other than themselves; no differentiations within this sense are contemplated.

In appendix A, then, Russell at most borrows from Frege a semantic distinction unrecognized in the text, and attempts to graft it onto an already developed metaphysics of propositions: denoting phrases (as we may now say) *mean* denoting concepts and *indicate* what (if anything) those concepts denote. But the fit with Frege's views on *Sinn* and *Bedeutung* is far from comfortable. First, there is no hint that Russell would extend the distinction of meaning and indication to predicate-expressions like 'exceeds' and 'is human', or to functional expressions like 'the father of'. Second, if the distinction obtains in the case of sentences, and Russell seems at least doubtful that it does, Frege's view that sentences are proper names of truth values is "untenable" (p. 504). Third, Frege would have thought it retrograde to recognize as syntactical units any of Russell's denoting phrases save definite descriptions. Fourth, Russell explicitly denies that proper names, in a sense narrow enough to exclude definite descriptions, have meaning as well as indication: "such words as *John* merely indicate without meaning" (p. 502).

Comparisons with Frege are, I think, best set aside. The importance of appendix A is that it exhibits a willingness to pull apart two strands within a previously undifferentiated notion of "meaning." And separating the two strands makes possible a certain unification: a single relation of "indication" can now be seen to carry not only proper names to their bearers but also denoting phrases to the terms, or combinations of terms, denoted by the denoting concepts which the denoting phrases "mean." If this is implicit in the text of *The Principles*, it is surely no more than that. And if the distinction of "meaning" and "indication" receives little more than passing mention in appendix A, it becomes a principal topic in the unpublished manuscripts of early 1905.[25]

A terminological change occurs: as a technical term, 'indicate' disappears. In one of the manuscripts 'designate' is officially substituted, its sense carefully distinguished from that of 'denote':

> There are phrases which have to do with denotation only, others which have to do with meaning only, and yet others which have to do with both. The phrases which have to do with both have a different relation to the two: the denotation is what they designate . . . , and the meaning may be said to be what they *express*. But both designating and expressing have to do with language: the logically important matter is the relation between what is expressed and

what is designated. For when one name both designates and expresses, this is not arbitrary, but is due to a relation between the objects designated and expressed. This relation is what I shall call *denoting*. Thus it is the meaning, not the name, which denotes the denotation; and denoting is a fact which concerns logic, not the theory of language or naming.[26]

But even in this manuscript Russell cannot stick to his terminological resolution. And in another, the threefold distinction with which the above passage begins is put this way: "Words and phrases are of three kinds: (1) those that denote without meaning; (2) those that mean without denoting; (3) those that both mean and denote."[27] Ambiguity threatens, and it cannot be said that Russell is altogether successful in avoiding it. But I shall try to make do simply with 'denote', trusting to context to make clear the intended sense. The important thing in any case is the threefold distinction itself, however labeled.

In the manuscripts under discussion, the distinction is brought to bear primarily on the category of singular terms. And within that category Russell is especially concerned to contrast definite descriptions with what he calls "names in the narrow sense."

[Descriptive] phrases may be regarded as names for that which they describe; but they differ from names in the narrow sense by the fact that they do *describe* that which they name. A name in the narrow sense is merely a symbol arbitrarily selected to designate some object.[28]

Names in the narrow sense are thus "destitute of meaning,"[29] and hence appear in the class of expressions that denote without meaning. In contrast, if a description denotes an object, it does so by virtue of expressing a meaning which (in another sense, of course) denotes the object. So a description will either mean and denote, or else merely mean.

That some descriptions *do* merely mean is now quite unproblematic. "It is impossible to deny *meaning* to ['the present King of France']; it has just as distinct a meaning as 'the present King of England'. But unlike this latter phrase, it denotes nothing."[30] Similarly with 'the even prime other than 2', 'the rational square root of 2', 'the bed in which Charles I died', and 'the difference between Mr. Arthur Balfour and the present prime minister of England'.[31] If Russell was once tempted by (I), he is no longer.

This suggests a "reformed Russell." A surer indication is his denial of denotation in the case of such seeming proper names as 'Apollo' and 'Odysseus'. Such expressions are in reality "substitutes for descriptions."[32]

These appear to be proper names, but as a matter of fact they are not so. "Odysseus" may be taken to *mean* "the hero of the *Odyssey*," where the meaning of this phrase is involved, and not the imagined object designated. If the *Odyssey* were history, and not fiction, it would be the designation that would be in question: "Odysseus" would then not express a meaning, but would designate a person, and "the hero of the *Odyssey*" would not be identical in *meaning* with Odysseus [*sic*], but would be identical in designation.[33]

It is natural at this point to think that "names in the narrow sense" can be characterized as those expressions that denote actual objects and are, from the point of view of grammar, proper names. And we are encouraged to think thus by many of Russell's examples: 'Arthur Balfour', 'Aeschylus', 'Mr. Chamberlain', 'M. Combes'. But the characterization will not do. For one thing, it would exclude numerals and abstract singular terms: '2', 'diversity', 'whiteness' are said to denote but not mean,[34] and at one point 'blackness' is said to be, like 'Arthur Balfour', "a proper name, . . . destitute of meaning."[35] For another, in one of the manuscripts Russell allows that "even genuine proper names, when they belong to interesting people, tend to become names which have meaning"; 'Homer', for example, is said to be synonymous with 'the author of the *Iliad* and the *Odyssey*'.[36] But given this, "names in the narrow sense" become an ill-defined lot indeed. One wonders why Russell failed to find Aeschylus and Arthur Balfour interesting.

There are indications, however, that the category of names that denote but do not mean is a good deal narrower than mere considerations of interestingness would require. I use the word 'indications' advisedly: Russell is not explicit on the matter, and some reading between the lines, even some judicious resolution of ambiguities and inconsistencies, is necessary. Nevertheless, I detect in these manuscripts steps in the direction of two theories—one a compositional theory of meaning, the other a theory of understanding, or thought—the combined effect of which would reduce drastically the extent of "names in the narrow sense."

5

It is commonly held that the meaning of a complex syntactical unit is, as a rule, a function of the meanings of its immediate constituents; exceptions count as idioms. Frege went a step further: the sense of a complex name is itself complex, having the senses of its surbordinate names as *parts*.[37] Now, Russell agrees that compositionality is not in general a mere matter of functionality.[38] He does not agree, however, that it is always the *meanings* of words and phrases that are constituents of the meanings of larger syntactical units. Indeed, he could not. Imagine 'A' and 'B' to be names that merely denote, and suppose their denotations to be distinct. The descriptions 'the term identical with A' and 'the term identical with B' will then differ in denotation. But they denote what they do because their *meanings* denote what *they* do. Hence the descriptions must differ in meaning. And the only way to account for the difference, given that 'A' and 'B' do not mean, is to take the denotation of 'A' and the denotation of 'B' to be constituents of the meanings of, respectively, 'the term identical with A' and 'the term identical with B'. But of course neither is it always the *denotations* of words and phrases that are constituents of the meanings of larger syntactical units. Imagine that 'the F' is a definite description which denotes A. The phrases 'the term identical with A' and 'the term identical with the F' will agree in denotation but differ in meaning. Hence the meaning of the second phrase must contain the meaning, not the denotation, of 'the F'.

Compositionality thus becomes a little complicated. Insofar as one is concerned only with what I shall call *names*—i.e., proper names in the grammar book sense, definite descriptions, and such abstract singular terms as Russell would count as "names in the narrow sense"—the following rule appears to obtain:

(V)   If E is a complex name in which the name N is embedded, then E has a meaning; and according as N means or merely denotes, its meaning or its denotation is a constituent of the meaning of E.

Thus the meaning of 'the even prime' is a constituent of the meaning of 'the positive square root of the even prime', whereas the denotation of '2' is a constituent of the meaning of 'the positive square root of 2'.

The principle just enunciated is only a small step toward a full-blown compositional theory. How is it to be extended? The natural thought is that one should take to be true of syntactical units generally what (V) affirms of names. Thus:

(VI)   If E is a syntactical unit in which the syntactical unit N is embedded, E has a meaning; and according as N means or merely denotes, its meaning or its denotation is a constituent of the meaning of E.

Now, 'syntactical unit' presupposes a reader who, in Frege's phrase, "does not begrudge a pinch of salt"—especially in view of Russell's virtual silence on matters of syntax; a similar comment applies to 'embedded'. But even with this apology, we had better not attribute (VI) to Russell before considering how he would treat meaning and denotation in cases other than names.

The case to which he gives greatest attention is that of sentences. He takes for granted, naturally enough, that sentences mean. The issue is whether they denote. It is discussed in each of the three manuscripts, but with no single outcome. In "Points about Denoting" and "On the Meaning and Denotation of Phrases" Russell inclines to the position that sentences have both meaning and denotation. In the first we are told that if Triphena is Smith's wife, the sentences 'Triphena has blue eyes' and 'Smith's wife has blue eyes' differ in meaning but agree in denotation; but, except that it is preserved under substitution for 'Triphena' of any co-designative name, we are not told what the denotation is. It is unclear, too, whether a suppressed assumption is that Triphena indeed has blue eyes. In "On the Meaning and Denotation of Phrases" the second uncertainty is addressed, inconclusively: the question whether (say) 'Shakespeare was blind' denotes is said to be difficult, and is left open. But again nothing is said as to what the denotation of 'Shakespeare was not blind' might be.

This cluster of questions is dealt with at length in "On Meaning and Denotation," Russell's conclusion there being that "it seems to me impossible to establish . . . that a [sentence] has denotation as well as meaning."[39] With one exception, his arguments are tangential to the concerns of this essay. The exception, as I reconstruct it, goes as follows. Let 'A' and 'B' be as above. The sentence 'A exceeds B' will then express a proposition of which the constituents are A, B, and *exceeds*; and this proposition will be the meaning of the sentence, since there is nothing else to fill that role. But what is to fill the role of denotation? If there is a denotation, it is presumably something of which A, B, and *exceeds* are again constituents: the *fact*, perhaps, that A exceeds B. But then, if meaning and denotation are to differ, we must suppose A, B, and *exceeds* to be combined in one way in the meaning and in another in the denotation. "But inspection reveals, at least to me, no such twofold combination: the combination involved in the meaning appears to be the only one."[40]

Even if Russell is sometimes inclined to ascribe denotation as well as meaning to sentences, it is the meanings that occur in the meanings of syntactical units of which the sentences are parts. If 'Triphena has blue eyes' and 'Smith's wife has blue eyes' agree in denotation, they nonetheless differ in meaning; and thus it is that 'the proposition that Triphena has blue eyes' and 'the proposition that Smith's wife has blue eyes' can differ in denotation. Moreover, though he does not bring the matter up, Russell is thereby enabled to distinguish in meaning 'Jones thinks that Triphena has blue eyes' and 'Jones thinks that Smith's wife has blue eyes'.

Considered in relation to syntactical units in which they are contained, sentences constitute no departure from (VI). Neither do verbs, adjectives, and common nouns (in predicative position); for these go into Russell's class of words that mean but do not denote. But two categories give trouble. One consists of demonstratives and, more generally, of phrases the meanings of which are constant but the denotations of which vary in accordance with some rule. The other consists of the determiners that figure in denoting phrases: 'all', 'every', 'any', 'some', 'a', and 'the'.

Russell says that words like 'I', 'here', and 'now', and phrases like 'the present time', "have obviously a clear and constant meaning"; but "their denotation varies," not in a "perfectly unfettered" way, but "subject to laws."[41] The idea of course is that 'I' varies in denotation as the speaker varies, 'the present time' as the time varies, and so on. It would be better, I think, to forgo denotation altogether in the case of the words and phrases themselves. It is their utterances that may vary in denotation, one from another. It nonetheless seems right to say that 'I', for example, has a clear and constant meaning. By virtue of its meaning variations in denotation of its utterances are systematic: roughly, the meaning of 'I' is such that an utterance of it denotes the utterer. And there would seem to be no special barrier to supposing its meaning to be a constituent of the clear and constant meaning of, for instance, 'I have blue eyes'. Still no departure from (VI).

But consider. When Triphena and I assertively utter 'I have blue eyes', we assert distinct propositions. And it is beyond belief that either of our propositions is the constant meaning of that sentence.[42] Indeed, no proposition is the meaning of 'I have blue eyes'. We can retain (VI). But we must recognize that it does not entail

(VII)   If E is a sentence in which the syntactical unit N is embedded, then, according as N means or denotes, its meaning or denotation is a constituent of the proposition expressed by E.

And we must also recognize that it is no improvement to substitute 'sentence token' for 'sentence' in (VII). Barring aberrations or mistakes, the meaning of a token of 'I have blue eyes' is the meaning of 'I have blue eyes'. The substitution would confound Triphena's proposition and mine.

In contrast with demonstratives, the determiners mentioned above pose a direct threat to (VI). The denoting phrases of which they are parts, considered in relation to larger syntactical units, are indeed no problem: they have meaning, and their meanings are evidently to be taken as constituents of the meanings of containing syntactical units. It is rather that, in their relation to contained syntactical units, denoting phrases appear not to conform to (VI). The matter was discussed briefly in *The Principles*:

> The word *all* has certainly some definite meaning, but it seems highly doubtful whether it means more than the indication of a relation. "All men" and "all numbers" have in common the fact that they both have a certain relation to a class-concept, namely to *man* and *number* respectively. But it is very difficult to isolate any further element of *all-ness* which both share. . . . It would seem, then, that "all *u*'s" is not validly analyzable into *all* and *u*, and that language, in this case as in

some others, is a misleading guide. The same remark will apply to
every, any, some, a, and *the.* (pp. 72–73)

Russell is silent on the matter in early 1905. Perhaps he thought it of no
great significance. As he seemed aware in *The Principles,* however, what is
there said about 'all' and the rest is at variance with (VI): there is a function
semantically associated with 'all' which, applied to the meanings of 'men'
and 'numbers', yields respectively the meanings of 'all men' and 'all numbers', but the meanings of these phrases are not complexes of which the
meaning of 'all' is a constituent. Similarly with the other determiners. Here
at least compositionality is mere functionality.

6

A compositional theory of meaning is naturally joined with a theory as to
the understanding of complex syntactical units: one understands such a
complex by understanding its subordinate syntactical units and their syntactical connections within the complex. If the compositional theory is not
merely functional, such understanding is apt to be seen as a matter of
grasping a complex whole by grasping its parts and their form of connection within the whole. The graspings are themselves acts of thought, and
their objects therefore double as objects of thought. Whether or not the
limits of thought are the limits of language, the theory of understanding
thus naturally develops into a parallel theory of thought. The object of a
thought, if complex, is apprehended by apprehending its elements and their
mode of union.

Although sympathetic with these generalities, Russell would have
thought that to speak thus of apprehending objects is to threaten a distinction. Provisionally formulated, the distinction is that between a proposition's being *about* some given object and its having that object as a
constituent. Not that the two never coincide: as we have seen, this is
precisely what happens when the object is a *term* of the proposition. But
they often diverge:

> If we say, for instance, "Arthur Balfour advocates retaliation," that
> expresses a thought which has for its object a complex containing as
> a constituent the man himself; no one who does not know what is the
> designation of the name "Arthur Balfour" can understand what we
> *mean:* the object of our thought cannot, by our statement, be commu-
> nicated to him. But when we say "the present Prime Minister of
> England believes in retaliation," it is possible for a person to under-
> stand completely what we mean without his knowing that Mr. Arthur
> Balfour is Prime Minister, and indeed without his even having heard
> of Mr. Arthur Balfour.[43]

Admittedly, this is no more than we should expect given what has already been said—at least if we can assume that Arthur Balfour is sufficiently uninteresting that his name denotes but does not mean. But Russell goes on to make a point not yet noted, namely, that there is a sense in which the proposition that the present prime minister of England favors retaliation is *about* Arthur Balfour.

> For the proposition is certainly *about* the present Prime Minister of England; and the present Prime Minister of England *is* Mr. Arthur Balfour. The *is* here expresses absolute identity; and if *a* and *b* are identical, whatever holds of *a* holds of *b*. Hence, since the proposition is about the present Prime Minister of England, it plainly must be also about Mr. Arthur Balfour.[44]

Russell grants that this conclusion has the further "strange consequence" that someone might assert the proposition that the present prime minister of England favors retaliation, and thereby assert a proposition about Arthur Balfour, and yet think that Mr. Chamberlain is the present prime minister— or, indeed, never have heard of Arthur Balfour. Still, the conclusion is one "from which there is no escape."

A general principle is involved:

(VIII)   If *C* is a concept which has a denotative occurrence in a proposition *p*, then, if and only if *C* denotes, *p* is about anything identical with the denotation of *C*.

This principle explains how it is possible for us to speak of, and have knowledge about, objects that we are not able to designate directly. A favorite example, here and later, is the center of mass of the solar system at the beginning of the twentieth century. It is a point of space about which we know many propositions. And yet "we do not know *what* point it was, i.e. we know it only through denoting complexes, and not directly by an idea designating it."[45]

Those familiar with Russell's later writings will be reminded at this point of his distinction between "knowledge by acquaintance" and "knowledge by description."[46] And I think that this is the distinction here intended. It is in fact introduced as such in another of the early 1905 manuscripts:

> Generally speaking, we may know ... that *every* term of the class *a* has the relation R to one and only one term, as e.g. we know that every human being now living has one and only one father. Thus given any term of class *a*, say *x*, we know that "the term to which *x* has the relation R" has a perfectly definite denotation. Nevertheless, it's a wise child etc. *This shows that to be known by description is not the same thing as to be known by acquaintance,* for "the father of *x*" is an

adequate description in the sense that, as a matter of fact, there is only one person to whom it applies.[47]

It has long been recognized that the choice of terminology is poor. Judging from the example, the rationale seems to be that it is one thing to know, for example, that there is such a thing as the denotation of a concept C and another to know with respect to something that *it* is the denotation of C. But of what in the first case does one have knowledge? Perhaps the answer is that, in accordance with (VIII), one who has mere "knowledge by description" is at any rate in a position to entertain propositions which are as a matter of fact about the denotation of C. He is thus able, in a weak sense, to think about the denotation of C. But it is not an object of thought for such a person in the direct way in which it is for someone who is able to entertain propositions of which the denotation of C is a constituent.

   We are now in a position to see in Russell's discussion of Arthur Balfour not only a distinction but also a doctrine. We were told in effect that the proposition expressed by 'Arthur Balfour favors retaliation' has the man himself as a term and that consequently one can entertain that proposition only if possessed of "knowledge by acquaintance" of Arthur Balfour. Thus, in general,

(IX)   In order to entertain a proposition, it is necessary to have knowledge by acquaintance of each of its terms.

Now this will be recognized by fans of Russell as a corollary of the Principle of Acquaintance. It is therefore not surprising to find that principle enunciated in the document in which, as far as I know, the distinction between "knowledge by acquaintance" and "knowledge by description" was first drawn. The formulation is more than a little garbled, and evidently presupposes some distinction of meaning and denotation in the case of sentences: "It is necessary, for the understanding of a prop[osition], to have *acquaintance* with the *meaning* of every constituent of the meaning, and of the whole; it is not necessary to have acquaintance with such constituents of the denotation as are not constituents of the meaning."[48] Yet it is a recognizable ancestor of the version given in "On Denoting":

(X)   In every proposition that we can apprehend, all the constituents are really entities with which we have immediate acquaintance.

Both (X) and its garbled ancestor go beyond (IX) in applying generally to the constituents of propositions, not just their terms. But there is another noteworthy difference: where (IX) requires "knowledge by acquaintance of" the terms of a proposition, the more general principle requires "(immediate) acquaintance with" them. The difference could be taken to represent only a terminological simplification. But I suspect more is involved.

We saw the distinction between knowledge by acquaintance and knowledge by description at work first in Russell's discussion of the propositions *Arthur Balfour favors retaliation* and *The present prime minister of England favors retaliation,* where the point appeared to be that to entertain the latter proposition one need have no idea who Arthur Balfour is, whereas to entertain the former one's thought must zero in on the man himself. This has a certain persuasiveness, I think; but only so long as it is understood to be compatible with *our* being able (ignoring tense) to entertain the proposition that Arthur Balfour favors retaliation—and some of us, at least, cannot have set eyes on the man. But there is nothing persuasive in the suggestion that to entertain the proposition it is necessary to have *acquaintance* with Arthur Balfour. After all, *we* appear to have been entertaining the proposition. How else could we have come to acknowledge that it is distinct from the proposition (again ignoring tense) that the present prime minister of England favors retaliation?

It is one thing to require that, in order to grasp a proposition, one have "knowledge by acquaintance" of its terms, in the sense that we were originally led to attach to the phrase; it is another, and stronger, to require *acquaintance* with the terms. Hence the transition from (IX) to (X) causes considerable shrinkage in Russell's category of "names in the narrow sense." 'Aeschylus' is out, and has been for centuries; and for most of those among the living so are 'Arthur Balfour', 'Mr. Chamberlain', and 'M. Combe'. And the shrinkage must somehow be squared with the fact that many of us can entertain the propositions expressed by such sentences as 'Arthur Balfour was once prime minister of England' and 'Aeschylus wrote tragedies'. Russell was later to explain that the names in question are, like 'Homer', substitutes for descriptions. But if we can go by the manuscripts under discussion, in early 1905 he was unaware that an explanation was called for, unaware how the Principle of Acquaintance would cut back his category of names that merely denote.

Innocence soon ended.

7

"On Fundamentals" divides into two parts: the first 37 pages, and the rest. It is the first part that is of primary interest here; for in the second Russell launches his "new theory of denoting," with only occasional looks back, while in the first he puts the old theory to new tests, until finally convinced that it fails. The document as a whole represents work in progress—work on the philosophical underpinnings of mathematical logic, apparently intended for Whitehead's eyes only. Its first part contains a rush of fresh insights interspersed with false starts, abrupt reversals, inconsistencies, and obscurities. A summary is out of the question. All that I can attempt here is a brief discussion of those parts of it that I find relatively clear and that bear on the origins of the "new theory" finally expounded in "On Denoting."

There is to begin with the matter of lost innocence alluded to above. "On Fundamentals" contains no extended discussion of the Principle of Acquaintance. But some brief remarks, described as a "digression," reveal that Russell had by no means forgotten it, that he had given thought to the bounds of acquaintance, and that he had set the stage for what has been called "the hunt for the 'logically proper name.' "[49] Almost casually he remarks that "most things are only known to us by denoting concepts," and proceeds to illustrate the point as follows:

> Thus Jones = the person who inhabits Jones's body. We don't have *acquaintance* with Jones himself, but only with his sensible manifestations. Thus if we think we know prop[osition]s about Jones, this is not quite right; we only know propositional functions which he satisfies, unless indeed we *are* Jones. (p. 17)

It would be a digression on my part to take up here Russell's views on persons or on the limits of acquaintance. But two relevant generalizations can be extracted from the passage:

(XI)   One cannot entertain propositions about an entity with which one lacks acquaintance.

(XII)   One can entertain propositions in which there are denotative occurrences of concepts that denote entities with which one lacks acquaintance.

Of course (XII) is no news: it has never been in question that, for example, someone to whom Arthur Balfour is utterly unknown can entertain the proposition that the present prime minister of England favors retaliation. But earlier we saw Russell holding that the proposition is *about* Arthur Balfour. And evidently (XI) rules that out, independently of any special views about persons or the limits of acquaintance. Indeed, in the face of (XI) and (XII), (VIII) will have to go.

I think this is no loss. Recall that in saying that *The present prime minister of England favors retaliation* is about Arthur Balfour, Russell implied nothing as to the beliefs of one who entertains the proposition or the intentions of one who asserts it. It was enough that Arthur Balfour *be* the present prime minister. This suggests a weak sense of 'about', one in which a proposition *p* is about an entity *x* if and only if some concept that has a denotative occurrence in p denotes x. If 'about' is given that sense, (VIII) becomes a trivial truth. But that was not Russell's intent. He contemplated a single, unconcocted sense in which both *The present prime minister of England favors retaliation* and *Arthur Balfour favors retaliation* are about Arthur Balfour.[50] But I doubt that there is such a sense. Russell was led to say that *The present prime minister of England favors retaliation* is about Arthur Balfour because he thought the proposition is "certainly" about the present prime minister— and because of the undeniable general truth that if p is about x and x is identical with y then p is about y. But how firm really is that initial intuition? I suppose we have some inclination to say that *The present president of the United States is a Republican* is about the present president of the United States and hence about Ronald Reagan. But I think we hesitate to say that *The next president of the United States will be a Republican* is about the next president of the United States, even if we are without doubt that there will be one. And I think the hesitation is attributable in part to a desire to avoid the "strange consequence" that, unbeknownst to anyone, the proposition is about George Bush, or Robert Dole, or someone now politically unheard of. I do not mean to deny that someone who asserts the proposition may refer to, and therefore say something about, Bush or Dole or even Mario Cuomo. But he need not; and if he does, that by itself is no guarantee that he refers to and says something about the next president of the United States. And even if *he* is sufficiently prescient or lucky to say something about the next president of the United States, it does not follow that the *proposition* is about the next president.

Many will feel a loss, however, on being told that not even *Ronald Reagan is a Republican* is about the present president of the United States. And the sense of loss will not be limited to those who have shaken his hand. Admittedly, it was already a consequence of the Principle of Acquaintance that most of us are unable to entertain a proposition of which Reagan is a constituent. But some of us will have hoped that we might at least entertain propositions *about* him. With (XI), the hope is dashed. Moreover, Russell's view about the possibility of acquaintance with persons puts Reagan's intimates in the same boat with the rest of us; for they are acquainted not with him but with his "sensible manifestations." Only Reagan can entertain propositions about Reagan. As Russell would later put it, the propositional function *x is a Republican* has a value of which Reagan is a term; but that value is a proposition which Reagan alone can entertain. Others can *describe* the proposition; it is, for example, the value of the function *x is a Republican* for Reagan as argument. To revert to the older terminology, others can entertain propositions in which concepts that denote the proposition have denotative occurrences. But they can no more entertain propositions *about* the proposition than they can about Reagan himself.

What then *is* the proposition that Ronald Reagan is a Republican? Nothing said in "On Fundamentals" bears directly on the question, and hence one is forced to speculate. I hazard, in the light of things Russell said later, that there really is no such proposition—no *one* proposition, that is, that the sentence 'Ronald Reagan is a Republican' expresses. What is expressed will vary with variations in the denoting concepts associated with 'Ronald Reagan'. Of course it is useful for purposes of philosophical exposition to ignore the variation and to feign that there is *the* proposition that Reagan is a Republican. But even if the fiction were fact, it would remain that 'Ronald Reagan' is not a "name in the narrow sense." It is a name that both means and denotes. Hence, in accordance with (VI), what it contributes to the meanings of sentences in which it occurs is its meaning, not its denotation.

Insofar as they are thought of as common coin, the conclusion extends to all grammatical proper names. Thus among descriptions, grammatical proper names, and abstract singular terms, only the last remain as candidates for "names in the narrow sense"; and in this connection abstract singular terms go undiscussed in "On Fundamentals." Perhaps Russell would have counted 'I' and 'this' in, as he did six years later.[51] If so, he gives no hint how their inclusion might be reconciled with their apparently having "clear and constant" meanings.

8

The first part of "On Fundamentals" is devoted primarily to a discussion of "modes of occurrence" of entities in propositions—or, as Russell would also say, to "positions" in propositions. The subject had been broached in *The Principles*; but there Russell had gone no further than to distinguish term-accessible positions, in my terminology, from the rest. That distinction is retained in "On Fundamentals," but within it others are drawn. The more intricate theory that results is in the end deemed open to "fatal" objections. Of interest nonetheless is Russell's effort to make an extended theory of propositional positions accommodate data not noticed in *The Principles*.

Complications caused by the Principle of Acquaintance, and associated principles, are ignored throughout: for purposes of exposition 'Socrates', 'Scott', and the like are treated as if "names in the narrow sense," and 'about' is used with consonant latitude. The practice is no more troublesome here than in Russell's later expositions of the new theory of denoting. It is perhaps significant, however, that the explanation of *term-accessible position—entity-position*, in contrast with *meaning-position*, in the terminology of "On Fundamentals"—proceeds by way of what in *The Principles* had been only "a characteristic,"[52] and thereby avoids reliance on 'about':

An entity A may occur in a complex B in such a way that any entity, simple or complex, may be substituted for A in B without loss of significance; or A may occur in such a way that it can only be significantly replaced by an entity of a certain sort, e.g. a proposition . . . or a relation. This is the most fundamental division of modes of occurrence. We will call the two modes concerned occurrence as *entity* & occurrence as *meaning* respectively. (p. 24)

Upon resolution of certain ambiguities, correction of careless wording, and limitation to the case of propositions, the explanation comes to this: an occurrence of an entity x in a proposition p is an *entity-occurrence* if and only if for every entity y there is a proposition which is like p save for having y where p has that occurrence of x; otherwise the occurrence of x is a *meaning-occurrence*. Succinctly, in terms of propositional positions: an *entity-position* in a proposition is a position accessible to any entity, *salva propositionalitate*; any other is a *meaning-position*.

The explanation has the virtue of avoiding a hard word. And if the notion of propositional position is taken as fundamental, one may proceed to define certain other notions used in *The Principles*. Thus a *constituent* of a proposition is any entity that has a position in it; *things* are those entities that are limited to entity-positions, *concepts* those that are not. But 'about' cannot be altogether avoided. Presumably it is now a thesis that a necessary condition for a proposition to be about one of its constituents is that the constituent have an entity-position in the proposition. More importantly, the condition is not sufficient: denotative occurrences of denoting concepts must be counted exceptions.

The apparatus available in *The Principles* for philosophical analysis of propositions is thus retained in the first part of "On Fundamentals." And its application to simple cases—such as (1), (3), (4), and (5) of section 1, above—is the same as in *The Principles*. "On Fundamentals" becomes interesting when Russell explores new ground and makes new finds in ground already covered.

Russell said surprisingly little in *The Principles* about occurrences of *propositions* in propositions.[53] The subject is a major one in "On Fundamentals." We may begin with a distinction regrettably lost in Russell's later writings—that between, for example,

(11)   If 9 exceeds 7 then some number exceeds 7

and

(12)   The proposition that 9 exceeds 7 implies the proposition that some number exceeds 7.

Russell recognizes that the antecedent and consequent of (11) occupy meaning-positions therein. And, consistently with his liberal stance on propositional subsistence, he holds that they occupy entity-positions in (12). Hence (11) and (12) are distinct, even if equivalent.

I can cite no firm evidence, but I think Russell took *Scott was the author of Waverley* to occur at an entity-position in

(13)   People were surprised that Scott was the author of *Waverley*.

In any case that position is "non-implicational": not every proposition is true which is like (13) save for having a true proposition where (13) has the (true) proposition that Scott was the author of *Waverley*. Evidently a position is "implicational" if and only if, as Russell would later say, "truth-functional." Russell takes it that the positions of antecedent and consequent in (11) *are* implicational; and since his 'implies' means *materially implies*, the same is true of their positions in (12).

Scott and *the author of Waverley* of course occupy entity-positions in the proposition that Scott was the author of *Waverley*. But what about their positions in (13)? Early in "On Fundamentals" Russell writes:

> The manner of occurrence of "the author of *Waverley*" in [(13)] is peculiar. It has one of the marks of occurrence as entity, namely that any other entity can be substituted without loss of significance; but it has not the other mark, that a complex with the same denotation can be substituted without altering the truth or falsehood of the proposition concerned. Thus there would seem to be a third mode of occurrence of a complex, in which the occurrence is an entity-occurrence as regards significance, & a meaning-occurrence as regards truth. (p. 19)

Now, "the other mark" had not previously appeared in "On Fundamentals," and we have in effect seen it discarded five pages later. I conjecture that it had never really functioned as a "mark" but had been implicitly supposed to be consequent upon universal replaceability *salva propositionalitate*. Generalizing a bit, I take it to have been Russell's expectation that

(XIII)   If C is a concept that has a denotative occurrence at a certain position in a proposition p, and if q is a proposition like p except that at the corresponding position in it there occurs the denotation of C, or a concept that denotes the denotation of C, then q has the same truth value as p.

The expectation may have originated from nothing other than inattention to cases such as (13). But whatever the origin, (XIII) would legitimize the move from (13) to

(14)   People were surprised that Scott was Scott.

But (13) is true, and (14) false; hence (XIII) must be abandoned.

The falsity of (XIII) leads Russell to distinguish two modes of occurrence within the general category of entity-occurrences:

> When a *denoting* complex A occurs in a complex B, it may occur in such a way that the truth-value of B is unchanged by the substitution for A of anything having the same denotation. [For the sake of brevity, it is convenient to regard anything which is *not* a denoting complex as denoting itself.] This is the case with "the author of *Waverley*" in "Scott was the author of *Waverley*," but not in "people were surprised that Scott was the author of *Waverley*." ... We will call A a *primary constitutent* of B when only the denotation of A is relevant to the truth-value of B, & we will call the occurrence of A a *primary occurrence* in this case; otherwise we will speak of A as a *secondary constitutent*, & of its occurrence as a *secondary occurrence*. (p. 25)

The intent is apparently to recast (XIII) in such a way that it becomes a definition: a denotative occurrence of a concept *C* in a proposition *p* is *primary* if and only if for every proposition *q*, if *q* is like *p* save for having the denotation of *C*, or a concept that denotes the denotation of *C*, where *p* has the occurrence of *C* in question, then *q* has the same truth value as *p*; otherwise the occurrence is *secondary*. Thus the occurrence of *the author of Waverley* in *Scott was the author of Waverley* is primary; but its occurrence in (13) is secondary.

So far, however, the distinction between primary and secondary occurrences has not been drawn within the category of entity-occurrences generally; for the definition just given speaks only to denotative occurrences of (denoting) concepts. What is to be said of entity-occurrences of "things," in Russell's technical sense, and of nondenoting concepts?

Russell does not address the question in "On Fundamentals." I think the explanation for this omission is that he took for granted the following principles:

(XIV) If a thing *x* has an occurrence in a proposition *p*, and if *q* is like *p* except that, where *p* has that occurrence of *x*, *q* has a denotative and primary occurrence of a concept the denotation of which is *x*, then *q* has the same truth value as *p*.

(XV) If a nondenoting concept *C* has an entity-occurrence in a proposition *p*, and if *q* is like *p* except that, where *p* has that occurrence of *C*, *q* has a denotative and primary occurrence of a concept the denotation of which is *C*, then *q* has the same truth value as *p*.

The two principles are sufficiently similar in their workings that it will be enough here to limit attention to (XIV). For that purpose consider the occurrence of Scott in (13). If (XIV) is true, then in particular every proposition is true which is like (13) except for having a denotative and primary occurrence of *the author of Waverley* where (13) has Scott. Now there are two propositions which are like (13) except for having a *denotative* occurrence of *the author of Waverley* where (13) has Scott, and both can be formulated in the sentence 'People were surprised that the author of *Waverley* was the author of *Waverley*'. One is a proposition equivalent to

(15)   The author of *Waverley* is such that people were surprised that he was the author of *Waverley*.

The other is equivalent rather to

(16)   *The author of Waverley is the author of Waverley* is a proposition the truth of which surprised people.

Though the first of these propositions is presumably true, the second is surely false. But this says nothing against (XIV). For neither occurrence of *the author of Waverley* in (16) is primary: "substitution" of Scott for (say) the first occurrence takes one from a truth to a falsehood. The same must surely hold for any proposition equivalent to (16).

We can now see how to extend the use of 'primary' and 'secondary' so as to cover occurrences of things in propositions: an occurrence of a thing x in a proposition p is *primary* just in case for every proposition q, if q is like p save that, where p has that occurrence of x, q has a denotative and primary occurrence of a concept the denotation of which is x, then q has the same truth value as p. Thus the occurrence of Scott in (13) is primary, but his occurrence in

(17)   *Scott was the author of Waverley* is a proposition the truth of which surprised people

is secondary. The extension to entity-occurrences of nondenoting concepts proceeds analogously.

The occurrence of Scott in *Scott was the author of Waverley* is of course primary. But we have just seen that his occurrence in (17) is secondary. This pair of facts leads Russell to call the occurrence of *Scott was the author of Waverley* in (17) "unanalyzable," in the sense that it is not an occurrence that preserves as primary all contained primary occurrences. In contrast, the occurrence of the proposition that 9 exceeds 7 in (12) is "analyzable": 9 and 7 have primary occurrences in (12) as well as in the contained proposition.

Russell hazards some generalizations:

An occurrence of A in B is *primary* (1) when A does not occur in any proposition which occurs in B (except B itself), (2) when any proposition in which A occurs & which occurs in B has an *implicational* occurrence in B, (3) when, if A occurs in C & C occurs in B, then the occurrence of C in B is analyzable. (p. 31)

On the understanding that Russell's 'when' has the sense of 'if', the second and third are unexceptionable. But the first will not do, as is shown by the occurrence of *the site of Troy* in the proposition that Schliemann sought the site of Troy.[54]

The attentive reader will have long since wanted to protest that in all the preceding discussion of modes of occurrence of entities in propositions, nothing has been said of nondenotative occurrences of denoting concepts. The omission is not the result of oversight. Explanation of it will in fact take us to the "inextricable tangle" Russell thought to be involved in the distinction of meaning and denotation.

9

Recall to begin with that the occurrence of *the author of Waverley* in

(18)   Scott was the author of *Waverley*

is supposed to be primary, in the sense that if q is any proposition like (18) save for having the denotation of *the author of Waverley*, or a concept that denotes the denotation of *the author of Waverley*, where (18) has *the author of Waverley*, then q has the same truth value as (18). But consider

(19)   Scott was *the author of Waverley*.

This proposition is surely false, and yet it appears to be like the true proposition (18) save for having a concept that denotes the denotation of *the author of Waverley* where (18) has *the author of Waverley*. The obvious repair, as far as the present example is concerned, is to require agreement in truth value with (18) only on the part of those propositions which are like (18) except for having the denotation of *the author of Waverley*, or *a denotative occurrence of* a concept that denotes the denotation of *the author of Waverley*, where (18) has *the author of Waverley*.

But recognition that a repair is necessary only serves to bring into focus a question that should have been raised pages back: how do (18) and (19) differ? In *The Principles* the story had been that whereas (19) is *about* the denoting concept *the author of Waverley*, (18) is not. But even if the story is true, it needs an explanation. Russell is committed to the position that the identity of a proposition is determined by its constituents, together with the way in which they are united in the proposition. The two propositions appear to have exactly the same constituents; ignoring tense, they are Scott, identity, and *the author of Waverley*. And the mode of union is the same in each; for "the constituent occurring as meaning . . . gives form and unity to the complex,"[55] and in the present case the only such constituent is identity. How *can* (18) and (19) differ?

Early in "On Fundamentals" there occurs a passage that appears to provide an answer:

> It seems that if we wish to put a denoting meaning in an entity-pos[i-tion], & say something about the meaning itself, we can only do so by means of a denoting concept; for if, instead of a denoting concept, we put the meaning in question, we shall be talking unintentionally about the denotation of the meaning instead of about the meaning. Thus a denoting meaning can only be spoken of by means of denoting concepts which denote the meaning in question. This is what inverted commas do: they give a denoting concept which denotes the meaning of what is between the inverted commas. (p. 7)

Here I see two principles enunciated:

(XVI)   If a denoting concept occurs in an entity-position in a proposition, then the proposition is not about the denoting concept.

(XVII)   A proposition is about a denoting concept C only if it contains an occurrence of a denoting concept the denotation of which is C.

Their combined effect with respect to (19) is this: if (19) is about *the author of Waverley*, then it contains no occurrence of that concept but instead an occurrence of a denoting concept the denotation of which is *the author of Waverley*. Hence, if (19) is about *the author of Waverley*, (18) and (19) can be said to differ in that where (18) has an occurrence of *the author of Waverley*, (19) has instead an occurrence of a concept the denotation of which is *the author of Waverley*.

So far, so good. For there may seem to be no denying that (19) is about *the author of Waverley*. Yet it is precisely in (XVI) and (XVII) that Russell thinks he sees the Achilles heel of the theory of meaning and denotation. Thus, a good deal further on, he reflects on the consequences of assuming that theory to hold in the case of the denoting concept *everything*:

> We shall have to distinguish between "everything" and every-thing, i.e. we shall have: "everything" is not everything, but one thing. Also we shall find that if we attempt to say anything about . . . "everything," we must do so by means of a denoting concept which denotes that meaning, & which must not contain that meaning occurring as entity, since when it occurs as entity it stands for its denotation, which is not what we want. These objections, to all

appearance, are as fatal here as they were in regard to *the*. Thus it is better to find some other theory. (p. 41)

The problem for the commentator is to figure out what the Achilles heel is really supposed to be. It is not clear what defect is supposed to be present in the proposition that *everything* is not everything. Nor is it clear what problem is supposed to be created by the inability to say something about a denoting concept except by means of a denoting concept that denotes the concept. What *are* the fatal objections Russell takes himself to have exhibited in the case of *the*?

I may as well say at once that I do not know how to answer the question. The relevant pages of "On Fundamentals" seem to me to rival in obscurity the corresponding pages of "On Denoting," those in which Russell attempts to expound the "inextricable tangle." It is clear, however, that the problem Russell sees, or thinks he sees, has somehow to do with the effort to say something about a denoting concept. And it is clear, too, that the problem is at least a part of the "inextricable tangle" itself. Let me say what I can about it.

At first sight there may seem to be no problem in formulating propositions about denoting concepts. We appear to have been doing just that for some little time—most recently, in distinguishing (18) from (19). It may well seem, moreover, that Russell's (XVI) is plainly false. For

(20)   *The author of Waverley* denotes the author of *Waverley*

appears to be an obvious truth about *the author of Waverley* in which that concept nevertheless has an entity-occurrence. But whatever in the end is to be said about (20), I think it is reasonably clear that Russell's intention in enunciating (XVI) was to state a proposition to this effect: it is not by virtue of *entity*-occurrences of a denoting concept in a proposition that the proposition is about the concept. But how is this to be put at all clearly? I suggest the following:

(XVIII)   If *q* is a proposition which is not about a denoting concept *C*, and if *p* is like *q* except for having *C* at any number of positions corresponding to entity-positions in *q*, then *p* is not about *C*.

Roughly, one cannot obtain a proposition about a denoting concept *C* by substituting *C* for entities that occur at entity-positions in a proposition that is not already about *C*. If (20) is a counterexample to (XVI), it is at any rate not a counterexample to (XVIII); for it cannot be generated in the way required by the antecedent of (XVIII).

Although Russell never explicitly says so, I think he takes for granted that all propositions in which denoting concepts occur can be generated in the manner contemplated in the antecedent of (XVIII). That is, I believe he subscribed to

(XIX)   If a denoting concept C occurs in a proposition p, then there is a proposition q which is not about C and which is such that p is like q except for having C at one or more positions corresponding to entity-positions in q.

From (XVIII) and (XIX) together it follows that denoting concepts are never *terms of* propositions: no proposition is about any of the denoting concepts that are constituents of it. It does not follow that no proposition is about a denoting concept. It does follow, however, that no denoting concept is a term *simpliciter*—a circumstance that presumably still "raises grave logical problems."[56]

Since denoting concepts are not terms, they cannot be given "names in the narrow sense." For a sentence in which there occurs a "name in the narrow sense" inevitably expresses a proposition of which the named entity is a term. Any designation of a denoting concept must therefore be a denoting phrase, a phrase that means a concept that denotes the denoting concept designated by the phrase. Thus it must be with '*the author of Waverley*' as used in the formulation above of (20). And at the corresponding position in the proposition there occurs, not *the author of Waverley*, but the denoting concept meant by '*the author of Waverley*'. In these respects '*the author of Waverley*' is like '*the denoting concept that occurs in* (18)', as used in the formulation of

(21)   The denoting concept that occurs in (18) denotes the author of *Waverley*.

But surely (20) and (21) are distinct propositions, even though the denoting concept that occurs in (18) is *the author of Waverley*; for the denoting concept which occurs in (20) and which denotes *the author of Waverley* is surely not *the denoting concept that occurs in* (18). But what denoting concept is it? Of the endlessly many denoting concepts that denote *the author of Waverley*, which one is a constituent of (20)? Without an answer to the question, we do not know which proposition (20) is supposed to be.

The denoting phrase that occurs in the formulation of (21) is in particular a definite description. Now, '*the author of Waverley*' is not a definite description, but is it perhaps a substitute for one? I doubt that Russell would have found comfort in an affirmative answer, for we have already noticed his abandonment of (VIII): he no longer holds that *The present prime minister of England favors retaliation* is about Arthur Balfour.[57] Surely, then, (21) is not about *the author of Waverley*; for one can grasp (21) without having the least idea which concept *is* the denoting concept that occurs in (18). And if '*the author of Waverley*' is an equivalent of a definite description no more intimately connected with *the author of Waverley* than 'the denoting concept that occurs in (18)', the same will hold of (20). I think it will be worthwhile even so to explore the suggestion that '*the author of Waverley*' is a disguised description, for it is not clear to me that the difficulty Russell sees in trying to say something about a denoting concept is simply that "we can only do so by means of a denoting concept."

Italicization converts a graphemic representation of a word or phrase into italics. Associated with its use here is the convention that words and phrases in italics denote their meanings. Russell uses quotation marks to the same effect. This suggests that '*the author of Waverley*' is a substitute for 'the meaning of 'the author of *Waverley*' '. But that would have a consequence unacceptable to Russell, namely, that (20) is identical with

(22)   The meaning of 'the author of *Waverley*' denotes the author of *Waverley*.

No doubt (20) and (22) agree in truth value, but it is doubtful that they are equivalent in any stronger sense. What is wanted is a description in which 'the author of *Waverley*' is not mentioned.

A more flexible notation will allow us to see the problem in greater generality. For italicization quickly gives out: there is no further italicizing of an already italicized word or phrase. Let us therefore use asterisks instead, and reserve italics for other conventional purposes. Thus (20) is to be reexpressed as

(23)   *The author of *Waverley** denotes the author of *Waverley*.

The convention again is that a word or phrase embedded in a pair of asterisks denotes the meaning of the word or phrase. It allows us to write as well:

(24)   **The author of *Waverley*** denotes *the author of *Waverley**,

and so on up. Now, this convention is a rule of designation for asterisked expressions. What is wanted is a rule of meaning—more specifically, a rule that assigns to each asterisked expression a synonymous definite description.

The notation just introduced looks functional. But of course it is not: the author of *Waverley* is identical with the author of *Ivanhoe*, but *the author of *Waverley** is not identical with *the author of *Ivanhoe**. In this respect our use of asterisks is like a standard use of single quotation marks. In analogy with (23) and (24) one writes:

'Twain' designates Twain and ' 'Twain' ' designates 'Twain'.

Again the notation looks functional, and again it is not: Twain is identical with Clemens, but 'Twain' is not identical with 'Clemens'.[58] This is not to deny that there is a function that might be called the quotation function. Applied to a word or phrase as argument, it yields as value that very word or phrase: quot('Twain') is 'Twain'. We can grant, similarly, that there is a function—*h*, say—which, upon application to a given denoting concept, gives back that very denoting concept as value: *h*(*the author of *Waverley**) is *the author of *Waverley**. And thus *the author of *Waverley** can be described as the value of *h* for *the author of *Waverley** as argument, just as 'Twain' can be described as the value of quot for 'Twain' as argument. But I trust no one will find explanatory value in either quot or *h*. Each is simply an identity function, the former on words and phrases, the latter on denoting concepts.

The problem has to do with the meaning of '*the author of *Waverley*'— that is, with the identity of **the author of *Waverley***. Presumably it is complex, and hence to be grasped by grasping its constituents and their mode of connection. And the natural thought is that a grasp of **the author of *Waverley*** involves a grasp of *the author of *Waverley**. But granted that this latter feat has somehow been accomplished, how is the move to **the author of *Waverley*** to be made? As Russell was soon to point out, "there is no backward road from denotations to meanings."[59]

10

To unravel the tangle, if one can, is not yet to explain how Russell hit upon the theory of descriptions. And if "On Fundamentals" provides little light on the nature of the tangle, it provides even less on the process of discovery. The transition to something now recognizable as the theory of descriptions occupies no more than a manuscript page, and it is a page that raises more questions than it answers.

Writing with reference to the tangle, Russell begins the page as follows:

> It might be supposed that the whole matter could be simplified by introducing a relation of denoting: instead of all the complications about "C" & C, we might try to put "x denotes y." But we want to be able to speak of what *x* denotes, & unfortunately "what *x* denotes" is a denoting complex. (p. 38)

One might rather have supposed that a relation of denoting had been present all along, for surely the idea had been that a denoting phrase designates an entity by virtue of meaning a concept that *denotes* the entity. And one wonders how the fact that, for example, *what *the author of *Waverley** denotes* is a denoting concept makes for some special difficulty with the "introduction" of a relation of denoting. Russell does not pause to explain, but instead suggests a way in which "we might avoid this."

Schematic instructions are given which Russell says have the effect that, for example, (18) "becomes"

(25)   For some y: *the author of *Waverley** denotes y and, for every z, if *the author of *Waverley** denotes z then $z = y$, and Scott $= y$.[60]

And Russell adds, "This, then, was what surprised people, as well it might." With the hindsight provided by the theory of descriptions, (25) can be seen to be identical with

(26)   Scott is the denotation of *the author of *Waverley**.

But it takes more than that to see (18) as identical with (26): **the author of *Waverley** occurs in (26), but not in (18). Russell appears to have confused a proposition that might be asserted in the course of giving a "philosophical analysis" of (18) with (18) itself. Still, a small advance has been made. In spite of appearances, (26) has been seen to contain no occurrence of *the denotation of *the author of *Waverley**. But of course it does not contain occurrences of **the author of *Waverley**. And (18) still appears to contain an occurrence of *the author of *Waverley*. We remain very far from the general theory of descriptions.

A mere three lines later, however, and without explanation, the relation of denoting altogether disappears. Russell gives a schematic definition which has the effect of identifying

(27)   Scott is the sole member of W,

where 'W' abbreviates 'the class of authors of *Waverley*', with

(28)   For some y: y is a member of W and, for every z, if z is a member of W then $z = y$, and Scott $= y$.

It may be doubted whether (27) is the same proposition as (18), and in any case (28) contains occurrences of a denoting concept. But Russell immediately notices the second point, and in dealing with it is led by the middle of the next page to a schematic definition that would equate (18) with

(29)   For some y: y wrote *Waverley* and, for every z, if z wrote *Waverley* then $z = y$, and Scott $= y$,

in the now classic fashion.[61]

Since "On Fundamentals" does not address questions having to do with scope, its theory of descriptions remains incomplete. But Russell does attempt to extend the new theory to denoting phrases other than definite descriptions. Their treatment is less than conclusive, and raises problems that surface again in the discussion of general propositions in *Principia Mathematica*. These are problems well beyond the bounds of the present essay.

Notes

1. Bertrand Russell, *The Principles of Mathematics*, 1st ed. (Cambridge: Cambridge University Press, 1903).

2. Bertrand Russell, "Meinong's Theory of Complexes and Assumptions," *Mind*, n.s., 13 (1904): 204–219, 336–354, 509–524. Reprinted in Douglas Lackey, ed., *Essays in Analysis* (New York: Braziller, 1973), pp. 21–76. (Note added by me.)

3. Bertrand Russell, "On Denoting," *Mind*, n.s., 14 (1905): 479–493. Reprinted in (of many places) *Essays in Analysis*, pp. 103–119. References are to that reprinting. (Note added by me.)

4. "Russell's Ontological Development," *Journal of Philosophy* 63 (1966): 657–667. Reprinted in *Theories and Things* (Cambridge, Mass.: Harvard University Press, 1981), pp. 73–85, where the quotation is to be found on p. 75. See also Ronald W. Clark, *The Life of Bertrand Russell* (New York: Knopf, 1976), pp. 111–112; Michael Dummett, *Frege: Philosophy of Language* (London: Duckworth, 1973), pp. 160–161; J. O. Urmson, *Philosophical Analysis: Its Development between the Two World Wars* (Oxford: Clarendon Press, 1956), pp. 23–24; Alan Wood, *Bertrand Russell: The Passionate Skeptic* (New York: Simon and Schuster, 1958), pp. 63–64.

5. Bertrand Russell, "My Mental Development," in P. A. Schillp, *The Philosophy of Bertrand Russell* (Evanston: Northwestern University Press, 1944), p. 13. See also his *My Philosophical Development* (London: Allen and Unwin, 1959), p. 84. And in a letter to Quine dated 6 June 1935, Russell wrote: "In reading [your *A System of Logistic*] I was struck by the fact that, in my work, I was always being influenced by extraneous philosophical considerations. Take e.g. descriptions. I was interested in 'Scott is the author of *Waverley*', and not only in the descriptive functions of PM. *If you look up Meinong's work, you will see the sort of fallacies I wanted to avoid*; the same applies to the ontological argument." Quoted from Russell's *Autobiography* (London: Allen and Unwin, 1967), vol. 1, p. 324. Emphasis mine.

6. For a brief statement of the facts see Peter Hylton, "Russell's Substitutional Theory," *Synthese* 45 (1980): 1–31, esp. pp. 14–15.

7. Hugh MacColl, "Symbolic Reasoning," *Mind*, n.s., 14 (1905): 74–81. Reprinted in *Essays in Analysis*, pp. 308–316, where the quoted phrases appear on p. 308.

8. Bertrand Russell, "The Existential Import of Propositions," *Mind*, n.s. 14 (1905): 398–401. Reprinted in *Essays in Analysis*, pp. 98–102. There the quotation appears on p. 100.

9. Bertrand Russell, review of Meinong et al., *Untersuchungen zur Gegenstandstheorie und Psychologie* (Leipzig, 1904), *Mind*, n.s., 14 (1905): 503–508. Reprinted in *Essays in Analysis*, pp. 77–88. The quotation is from p. 81.

10. *Essays in Analysis*, p. 83. Emphasis mine.

11. See *Autobiography*, vol. 1, p. 229, and "My Mental Development," p. 13.

12. See *Autobiography*, vol. 1, pp. 269–270.

13. For more along these lines, see my "Negative Existentials," in this volume.

14. "On the Meaning and Denotation of Phrases," "On Meaning and Denotation," and "Points about Denoting"—all in the Russell Archives.

15. Hence I take issue with David Pears, who sees "the decisive step" as already having been taken in *The Principles*. See *Bertrand Russell and the British Tradition* (New York: Random House, 1967), p. 25.

16. English provides an important class of examples: count nouns, or phrases with a count noun as head, preceded by one of the words 'all', 'every', 'any', 'some', 'a', and 'the'. These are taken up below, in section 5.

17. *Principles*, p. 100. (An entity x bears the relation of referent to an entity R if and only if R is a relation that x bears to something; and x bears the relation of relatum to R if and only if R is a relation that something bears to x.) It must be acknowledged that Russell says only that propositions such as (1) and (2) *may* be distinguished, while allowing that "it would be absurd to deny" that "people usually mean the same thing" by the sentence in question. I do not know how he would reconcile this with "the principle, from which I see no escape, that every genuine word must have some meaning."

18. Socrates and humanity are not the only constituents of (4). There is also a constituent corresponding to 'is'. Russell seems uncertain how to categorize it. It "cannot [be] a relation in the ordinary sense," because (4) has only one term; yet "it is very difficult to conceive the proposition as [involving] no relation at all" (*Principles*, p. 49). (I try here and elsewhere to observe, more carefully than does Russell, his official distinction between propositions and sentences. But to avoid circumlocution, I sometimes allow numbered displays to do double duty—as the sentences used to express propositions and as the propositions themselves. Hence my reference to "a constituent corresponding to 'is'.") For more on Russell's views as to the constitution of "subject-predicate propositions," see *Principles*, pp. 45, 54, 77, 96.

19. But see below, note 22.

20. The terminology is not Russell's. The best I can do by way of a definition is this: the position of an occurrence of x in a proposition p is *term-accessible* if and only if, for some y and q, y is a term of q and q is like p save for having y where p has that occurrence of x.

21. Again the terminology is not Russell's. I introduce it in order not to overwork 'denoting': *some number* is a denoting concept; its occurrence in (6) is denotative, but its occurrence in (7) is not.

22. From Russell's point of view they are paradoxical at least in part because they are not terms: some are not "one," and it is open to question whether any can be constituents of propositions. 'Object' thus has a wider sense than 'term', a circumstance which "raises grave logical problems" (p. 55, n.).

23. Peter Geach and Max Black, eds., *Translations from the Philosophical Writings of Gottlob Frege*, 3d ed. (Totowa, N.J.: Rowman and Littlefield, 1980), p. 64.

24. As Russell would later put it, the relation of *Sinn* to *Bedeutung* need not be regarded as "merely linguistic through the phrase" ("On Denoting," p. 111).

25. Again I refer to "On Meaning and Denotation," "On the Meaning and Denotation of Phrases," and "Points about Denoting." It would be of some interest to know the order of their composition, but I hesitate to make a conjecture. "On Meaning and Denotation" is the lengthiest and most polished, and it is therefore tempting to rely most on it. Note that I reserve "On Fundamentals" (June 1905) for later discussion.

26. "On Meaning and Denotation," p. 7.

27. "On the Meaning and Denotation of Phrases," p. 5

28. "On Meaning and Denotation," p. 1.

29. "On the Meaning and Denotation of Phrases," p. 1.

30. "On the Meaning and Denotation of Phrases," p. 3.

31. "On Meaning and Denotation," p. 9.

32. "On the Meaning and Denotation of Phrases," p. 3.

33. "On Meaning and Denotation," pp. 9–10.

34. "On Meaning and Denotation," p. 8.

35. "On the Meaning and Denotation of Phrases," p. 1.

36. "On the Meaning and Denotation of Phrases," p. 3.

37. Thus "not all the parts of a thought can be complete; at least one must be 'unsaturated,' or predicative; otherwise they would not hold together" (Geach and Black, p. 54).

38. I say "in general" because I have found no evidence that Russell withdrew exceptions to which he called attention in *The Principles*. See above, note 16. And see the discussion below of the meanings of denoting phrases.

39. For the entire discussion, see pp. 10–29. The quotation is at p. 29. I have put "[sentence]" where the manuscripts has "proposition." See note 18, above.

40. "On Meaning and Denotation," p. 12. One is reminded of Russell's and Moore's inability to detect any difference between a true proposition and the fact to which it is supposed to correspond. See my "A Neglected Theory of Truth," in this volume.

41. "On Meaning and Denotation," p. 34.

42. For arguments to this effect—some bad, some not so bad—see my "Propositions," in this volume.

43. "On Meaning and Denotation," p. 3.

44. "On Meaning and Denotation," p. 4.

45. "On Meaning and Denotation," p. 19.

46. See especially "Knowledge by Acquaintance and Knowledge by Description," *Proceedings of the Aristotelian Society*, n.s., 10 (1910–1911): 108–128. Reprinted in *Mysticism and Logic* (New York: Norton, 1929), pp. 209–232. Subsequent references are to this reprinting. See also *Problems of Philosophy* (London: Oxford University Press, 1912), chap. 5.

47. "Points about Denoting," p. 2. Emphasis mine.

48. "Points about Denoting," p. 6.

49. Dummett, *Frege*, p. 163. But, as we shall shortly see, it is at best misleading for Dummett to say that it was the theory of descriptions that "set in motion" the hunt.

50. In "On Meaning and Denotation" Russell says that 'Arthur Balfour' and 'the present prime minister of England' stand in "exactly the same" relation to Arthur Balfour. Each is "a symbol for the object" (pp. 1–2).

51. See "Knowledge by Acquaintance and Knowledge by Description," p. 224.

52. P. 45.

53. One remark might even be taken to rule them out: "One verb, and one only, must occur as verb in every proposition" (p. 52). But presumably it was not so intended.

54. I take the example from Alonzo Church, *Introduction to Mathematical Logic* (Princeton: Princeton University Press, 1956), p. 8, n. 20.

55. "On Fundamentals," p. 33.

56. See note 22.

57. And we saw that there are good reasons for the abandonment, independent of the fact that Arthur Balfour is not a constituent of *The present prime minister of England favors retaliation*. Thus I cannot accept John Searle's suggestion, in "Russell's Objections to Frege's Theory of Sense and Reference," *Analysis* 18 (1958): 137–143, that Russell inexplicably forgot his earlier distinction between the constituents of a proposition and the entities the proposition is about.

58. Both devices thus contrast with Quine's quasi-quotation. For example, if A = B then ⌜A & A⌝ = ⌜A & B⌝. See W. V. Quine, *Mathematical Logic*, rev. ed. (New York and Evanston: Harper and Row, 1951), pp. 33–37.

59. "On Denoting," p. 112. There is by this time a large literature on the "inextricable tangle." I have not tried to canvass it here; but I must remark that I have benefited especially from Simon Blackburn and Alan Code, "The Power of Russell's Criticism of Frege," *Analysis* 37 (1978): 65–77.

60. I think that in fact the instructions do not have the effect Russell intended. But they are easily enough amended. And once again I have ignored tense.

61. I here neglect Moore's point that Scott might have been the author of *Waverley* without having *written* it. More importantly as far as exegesis of Russell is concerned, I have avoided not only the notation of "On Fundamentals" but also fine points concerning its interpretation. In particular, my 'for some y' and 'for every z' are to be regarded as no more than typographical variants of Russell's quantificational notation (which is that of *Principia Mathematica*).

Identity and Substitutivity

Since the publication of Frege's "Über Sinn und Bedeutung,"[1] there has been a good deal of discussion of something variously referred to as Leibniz's Law, Leibniz's Principle, Leibniz's Rule, or—in what one is led to suppose is a reference to the same thing—the Principle of Substitutivity. Much of the discussion has, I think, been interesting and valuable, but I think also that some of it has been marred by a failure to be perfectly clear what the law or principle in question is. Evidently it is something in connection with which it is somehow relevant to talk about 9 and the number of the planets, the Evening Star and the Morning Star, and Giorgione and Barbarelli. But it is not always sufficiently appreciated that whether and how these are relevant to Leibniz's Law depends upon which of several distinct propositions that Law is taken to be.

Let us begin at the beginning, namely, with the passage from Leibniz's writings to which the name 'Leibniz's Law' presumably alludes. In C. I. Lewis's translation this reads as follows:

> Two terms are the *same* if one can be substituted for the other without altering the truth of any statement. If we have A and B and A enters into some true proposition, and the substitution of B for A wherever it appears, results in a new proposition which is likewise true, and if this can be done for every such proposition, then A and B are said to be the *same*; and conversely, if A and B are the same, they can be substituted for one another as I have said.[2]

It is doubtful that Leibniz here succeeded in saying what he wanted to say. For one thing, the passage contains an unfortunate confusion of use and mention: words, or expressions, are substituted for one another and not, as Leibniz suggests, the things to which the words refer. For another, his use of the word 'proposition' appears to me to obscure an important distinction. Substitution is an operation performed upon sentences and yielding sentences as values; but, as Leibniz himself urged in other places,[3] it is what is expressed, or formulated, in sentences that is properly said to be true.

Allowing, then, for these deficiencies of exposition, we may take Leibniz to have been enunciating the following:

(A)   For all expressions α and β, $\ulcorner \alpha = \beta \urcorner$ expresses a true proposition if and only if, for all sentences S and S', if S' is like S save for containing an occurrence of β where S contains an occurrence of α, then S expresses a true proposition only if S' does also.

Even this does not have all the accuracy and precision one might hope for, but I think it will do for present purposes.

Let us agree to use the words 'substitution of β for α is truth preserving' to express the condition which, according to (A), is both necessary and sufficient for $\ulcorner \alpha = \beta \urcorner$ to express a true proposition. Then we may say that (A) is the conjuction of

(B)   For all expressions α and β, $\ulcorner \alpha = \beta \urcorner$ expresses a true proposition if substitution of β for α is truth preserving

with

(C)   For all expressions α and β, $\ulcorner \alpha = \beta \urcorner$ expresses a true proposition only if substitution of β for α is truth preserving.

Now it should be remarked at once that recent references to "the Principle of Substitutivity" are references to (C) rather than (A). Thus Quine formulates what he calls "the principle of substitutivity" in these words: "given a true statement of identity, one of its two terms may be substituted for the other in any true statement and the result will be true."[4] And, making allowances for what I should regard as an equivocal use of the word 'statement', this amounts to (C) rather than (A). Though historical purists will perhaps regret that (C) is sometimes referred to as "Leibniz's Law," it could hardly be claimed that departing in this way from Leibniz's formulation is of any great consequence: the logical relationships among (A), (B), and (C) are simply too transparent.

There is, however, another departure from Leibniz that is apt to seem a good deal more radical. Frequently what is put forward as "Leibniz's Law" is

(D)   If $x = y$, then every property of x is a property of y.

Here, notice, there is no talk of substitution, indeed no talk of expressions at all. We are given instead a necessary condition for an *object* x to be identical with an *object* y. And there would thus appear to be all the difference between (C) and (D) that there is between the world and discourse about it. Yet I think it is often supposed that (D) somehow comes to the same thing as (C), that (D) is only a "material mode" version of (C). So at any rate we might infer, given that either is apt to be called "Leibniz's

Law." But is this view correct? Only if (D) implies (C). But *does* (D) imply (C)?

Let us agree to call (C) *the Principle of Substitutivity* and (D) *the Principle of Identity*. My question is, Does the Principle of Identity imply the Principle of Substitutivity? The question can be sharpened with the help of some further terminological conventions. Let S and S' be any sentences. I shall say that the pair (S, S') *is a counterexample to the Principle of Substitutivity* if and only if there are expression α and β such that (1) $\ulcorner \alpha = \beta \urcorner$ expresses a true proposition, (2) S' is like S save for containing an occurrence of β where S contains an occurrence of α, (3) S expresses a true proposition, and (4) S' expresses a false proposition; and if, in addition, $\ulcorner S \cdot \sim S' \cdot \alpha = \beta \urcorner$ expresses a proposition from which the negation of the Principle of Identity follows, then (and only then) I shall say that the pair (S, S') *falsifies the Principle of Identity*. Now, the Principle of Substitutivity is false if and only if there is a counterexample to it, and the Principle of Identity implies the Principle of Substitutivity if and only if the falsity of the Principle of Substitutivity implies the falsity of the Principle of Identity. So to ask whether the Principle of Identity implies the Principle of Substitutivity is to ask whether from the proposition that there is a counterexample to the Principle of Substitutivity one can legitimately infer the falsity of the Principle of Identity. But surely such an inference would be legitimate only if any counterexample to the Principle of Substitutivity itself falsified the Principle of Identity. Thus we may appropriately ask, Does every counterexample to the Principle of Substitutivity falsify the Principle of Identity?

In discussing this question it is important to recognize once and for all that there *are* counterexamples to the Principle of Substitutivity. The Principle is simply false. Let S_1 and S_2 be, respectively, 'Giorgione was so called because of his size' and 'Barbarelli was so called because of his size'. These are alike, save that S_2 contains the name 'Barbarelli' where S_1 contains the name 'Giorgione'; the sentence 'Giorgione = Barbarelli' expresses a true proposition; and S_1 expresses a true proposition and S_2 a false proposition. It follows that the pair (S_1, S_2) is a counterexample to the Principle of Substitutivity and hence that the Principle is false.[5]

Some respond to this by pointing out that the proposition expressed by S_1 is also expressed by the different sentence, "Giorgione was called 'Giorgione' because of his size," and that here substitution of 'Barbarelli' for the first occurrence of 'Giorgione' yields a sentence which, in contrast with S_2, expresses a true proposition. But the proper response to this is: true but irrelevant. For, however it may be with other pairs of sentences, the fact remains that the pair (S_1, S_2) is a counterexample. Again, it is sometimes said that the occurrence of 'Giorgione' in S_1 is not purely referential (not purely designative, oblique). But far from saving the Principle of

Substitutivity, this only acknowledges that the pair (S_1, S_2) is indeed a counterexample to it. For we are also told that an occurrence of a name in a sentence counts as purely referential only if substitution for that occurrence of any and every co-designative expression preserves truth value. And, even if accompanied by an independent criterion of purely referential occurrence, this second response is really no more relevant than the first. For the Principle of Substitutivity, as formulated above, contains no qualifications; it purports to cover *all* occurrences of *all* expressions.

The question remains, however, whether the pair (S_1, S_2) falsifies the Principle of Identity. If it does, then from the propositions expressed by S_1 and S_2 it must follow that Giorgione has some property that Barbarelli lacks. What could that property be? Evidently it is not the property of being called 'Giorgione' because of one's size, since Giorgione and Barbarelli share that property. Nor will it do to say that it is the property of being so called because of one's size, for this only invites the question, Being called *what* because of one's size? A more likely suggestion is that the property in question is that which a given object has if and only if the proposition that the object in question is so called because of its size is a true proposition. Thus it might be suggested that if we let P be the property which a thing x has just in case the proposition that x is so called because of its size is true, then since the proposition that Giorgione was so called because of his size is true, Giorgione has P, and since the proposition that Barbarelli was so-called because of his size is false, Barbarelli lacks P; and from this, together with the identity of Giorgione with Barbarelli, it might be concluded that the pair (S_1, S_2) falsifies the Principle of Identity.

But the contention that there is such a property as P, possessed by Giorgione though not by Barbarelli, can be seen to be incoherent. The defender of P affirms

(1)   Giorgione has P

and can scarcely deny

(2)   Giorgione is called 'Barbarelli'.

From (1) and (2) it follows by existential generalization that

(3)   There is someone called 'Barbarelli' and he has P;

and, by the proposed definition of P, this is equivalent to

(4)   There is someone called 'Barbarelli' and the proposition that he is so called because of his size is true.

But if we can make sense of (4) at all, we shall have to count it false: no one called 'Barbarelli' is so called because of his size.

What is the advocate of P to say? He cannot object to the inference from

(1) and (2) to (3). Existential generalization on (2) is surely permissible. And to contend that it is not permissible in the case of (1) is in effect to concede that there is no such property as P, for it is absurd to suggest that it is possible that Giorgione should have a certain property and yet that there should not be something that has that property. And, in any case, existential generalization on (1) is essential to the project of deducing the negation of the Principle of Identity. For that was to be accomplished by arguing that from the propositions that Giorgione has P, that Barbarelli does not, and that Giorgione is identical with Barbarelli, it follows that *there is* something x and something y such that x has P, y does not, and yet x is identical with y.

Perhaps, then, the advocate of P will contend that the English sentence just now used to express (4) is simply not an accurate formulation of the proposition obtained by properly expanding (3) in accordance with the definition of P. He will point out that the expression 'so called', as it occurs in that sentence, inevitably picks up 'Barbarelli' as antecedent and that accordingly the sentence is naturally read as expressing a proposition from which it follows that someone is called 'Barbarelli' because of his size. Of course, it is unlikely that there is an appropriate English sentence without this defect. So perhaps it will be suggested that we retain the sentence already used but assiduously avert our eyes from the reference back to 'Barbarelli'. Otherwise put, we shall perhaps be told that the proposition obtained by proper definitional expansion of (3) is one from which it follows that

(5)   there is someone such that the proposition that he is so called because of his size is true,

where now 'so called' stands on its own, free from the misleading suggestions of a surrounding linguistic environment.

But obviously the expression 'so called' is just the kind of expression that *cannot* thus stand on its own. To make sense of sentences in which it occurs, to determine what propositions they express, it is necessary to look to the environment—linguistic or otherwise—of the expression 'so called'. And if this fails to reveal a referent, no proposition has as yet been formulated. It was, in part, the failure to recognize this that led to the proposed definition of P. According to that definition, a given object has P just in case the proposition that it is so called because of its size is true. But how is this to be understood? If we take the expression 'so called' to have a *fixed* referent—the name 'Giorgione', say—then P will not serve to falsify the Principle of Identity; and if we are to understand that the referent of 'so called' changes with each difference in choice of name for the given object, then the definition presupposes what is false, namely, that there is such a thing as *the* proposition that the object in question is so called because of its size.

I suspect I have in a way been attacking a strawman. Perhaps no one would suppose that there is such a property as the alleged P or that the pair (S_1, S_2) falsifies the Principle of Identity. Nevertheless the attack is not without point. It shows that not every counterexample to the Principle of Substitutivity is a counterexample to the Principle of Identity and therefore that the Principle of Identity does not imply the Principle of Substitutivity. And this, it seems to me, is something that ought to be recognized once and for all.

But of course, for all that has been said so far, it remains possible that *some* counterexamples to the Principle of Substitutivity *do* falsify the Principle of Identity and hence that the Principle of Identity is, like the Principle of Substitutivity, simply false. This view has had its proponents. One of them, the late E. J. Lemmon, wrote as follows:

> ... '$x = y$' may be true, even though x has an attribute (for example, that of necessarily being x) which y has not got. Thus the morning star, though it *is* the evening star, has the attribute of being necessarily the morning star, which the evening star does not have. This ... will be unpalatable to many, but I believe it to be a paradox of intensionality that should be accepted on a par with the paradoxes of infinity that we have now come to accept (for example, that a totality may be equinumerous with a proper part of itself). ... The paradoxes of the infinite are paradoxical only because we normally think in terms of finite classes; this paradox of intensionality is paradoxical only because we normally think, with Leibniz, in extensional terms.[6]

Lemmon's alleged exception to the Principle of Identity at once suggests hosts of others. We can agree that whereas it is a necessary truth that 9 is greater than 7, it is only contingently true that the number of planets is greater than 7; and from this I suppose Lemmon and others of his persuasion would say it follows that 9 has a property the number of the planets lacks; and this in spite of the astronomical fact that 9 *is* the number of the planets. Again, though 9 is identical with 3^2, we may suppose Herbert knows that 9 is greater than 7 but is ignorant of the fact that 3^2 is greater than 7. And from this it will perhaps be concluded that although 9 has the property of being known by Herbert to be greater than 7, 3^2 does not.

Lemmon anticipated—correctly, I think—that many would find his position unpalatable. If y lacks a property x has, then to most people it will seem evident and undeniable that y cannot be the very same object as x. But what is one to say to those few who see the matter differently? I think it wise to concede at once that demonstration is out of the question. To *prove* there are no counterexamples to the Principle of Identity would require appeal to some more fundamental principle, and it is doubtful that any such is available. Still, there are strategies open to the Leibnizian. He may try to exhibit disturbing consequences of the negation of the Principle of Identity, hoping thereby to present considerations that will at least influence the intellect of the non-Leibnizian. He may try to show that one or another alleged counterexample is not really such. And he may seek to show that the non-Leibnizian is led to his position through bad arguments and intellectual confusions.

Demonstration of the nonequivalence of the Principle of Identity and the Principle of Substitutivity is itself an effort in this direction, for I suspect some have rejected the Principle of Identity only because they have confused it with the Principle of Substitutivity. In what follows I shall attempt further efforts, though of a quite limited nature. What I have to say concerns a single example; and although my discussion of it is somewhat detailed, I doubt that it is exhaustive.

Consider, then, the pair (S_3, S_4), where S_3 is the sentence '9 is necessarily greater than 7' and S_4 the sentence 'The number of planets is necessarily greater than 7'. Now of course my main concern is to determine whether this pair falsifies the Principle of Identity. But I think it will be of some value to attend first to the question whether it really is, as it is usually thought to be, a counterexample to the Principle of Substitutivity. There is a straightforward enough argument: from the premises

(6) S_3 expresses a true proposition if and only if '9 is greater than 7' expresses a necessary proposition,

(7) S_4 expresses a true proposition if and only if 'the number of planets is greater than 7' expresses a necessary proposition,

(8) '9 is greater than 7' expresses a necessary proposition,

and

(9) 'The number of planets is greater than 7' does not express a necessary proposition

it is inferred that

(10) S_3 expresses a true proposition, while S_4 expresses a false proposition;

and this coupled with

(11) '9 = the number of planets' expresses a true proposition

yields the desired conclusion.

The argument is clearly valid, and I shall suppose there is no doubt that

(6), (8), (9) and (11) are true. Hence, if (7) is true, the conclusion will have to be granted. But is (7) true?

Those who think it is would perhaps invoke the following general principle:

(E)   If α is any singular term and φ any predicate expression, ⌜α is necessarily φ⌝ expresses a true proposition if and only if ⌜α is φ⌝ expresses a necessary proposition.

And certainly *if* (E) is unexceptionable, (7) has to be counted true. But is (E) unexceptionable? Consider in this connection the sentence S_5, 'The proposition at the top of page 210 of *Word and Object* is necessarily true'. Does this express a true proposition or not? Notice that, given (E), we can answer without knowing *what* proposition *is* at the top of page 210 of *Word and Object*—indeed, without knowing whether there is any proposition at all at the top of that page. For according to (E), S_5 expresses a true proposition if and only if the sentence 'The proposition at the top of page 210 of *Word and Object* is true' expresses a necessary proposition. And clearly this last sentence does not express a necessary proposition; that is, the proposition

(12)   The proposition at the top of page 210 of *Word and Object* is true

is not a necessary truth. But this shows that something is wrong with (E). Asked whether S_5 expresses a true proposition, we surely have some inclination to suppose that we cannot answer unless we *do* know what proposition appears at the top of page 210 of *Word and Object*. That is, it is altogether natural to take S_5 to express a proposition which is true if and only if

(13)   There is exactly one proposition at the top of page 210 of *Word and Object*, which proposition is necessarily true.

And so understood, S_5 expresses a true proposition, for the proposition at the top of page 210 of *Word and Object* is the proposition that for every positive integer x, the class of positive integers less than or equal to x has x members, and this is necessarily true.

There is no need to insist that S_5 *has* to be read in such a way that it expresses a true proposition if and only if (13) is true. No doubt it can also be read in such a way that it expresses a true proposition if and only if (12) is necessary. But then S_5 will have to be counted ambiguous, and it is precisely this ambiguity that is not taken account of in (E).

Now, I think the same sort of ambiguity is present in S_4. No doubt that sentence can be so understood that it expresses a true proposition if and only if the sentence 'The number of planets is greater than 7' expresses a necessary proposition. And, so understood, it does not express a true proposition since

(14)   The number of planets is greater than 7

is not a necessary truth. But I should suppose that S_4 can just as easily be understood in such a way that it expresses a proposition which is true if and only if it is true that

(15)   There is a unique number of planets, which number is necessarily greater than 7.

This is the way it would be understood by someone who supposed—what it is perfectly natural to suppose—that one cannot say whether S_4 expresses a true proposition unless one knows *which* number *is* the number of the planets. And understood in this way S_4 expresses a true proposition: There is a unique number of planets and it is necessarily greater than 7.

So, read in one way S_4 expresses a false proposition, and read in another, equally natural way it expresses a true proposition. Is there a similar ambiguity in S_3? I think there is, though I think it occasions no disparity in truth value. S_3 can be understood *de dicto*, that is, as expressing the proposition that

(16)   9 is greater than 7

is a necessary truth. But it can also be understood *de re*, that is, as asserting of the number 9 that it is necessarily greater than 7. Under either interpretation it seems to me to express a true proposition.

What, then, is to be said of the pair (S_3, S_4)? Is it or is it not a counterexample to the Principle of Substitutivity? The fact is that in the formulation of that principle cases of sentential ambiguity were simply not anticipated. The principle was formulated under the useful fiction that a sentence expresses at most one proposition. The fiction *is* a useful one. Let us preserve it by leaving the Principle of Substitutivity undisturbed and ruling that S_3 and S_4 are to be understood *de re*, while the new sentences S_6, 'Necessarily, 9 is greater than 7', and S_7, 'Necessarily, the number of the planets is greater than 7', are to be understood *de dicto*. I suspect there is some sanction in English usage for these rulings, but whether there is or not is of little importance once the propositions in question have been distinguished. And thus we may say that whereas the pair (S_6, S_7) is a counterexample to the Principle of Substitutivity, the pair (S_3, S_4) is not.

But the question remains whether the pair (S_6, S_7) falsifies the Principle of Identity. If it does, then from

(17)   Necessarily, 9 is greater than 7,

(18)   9 = the number of planets,

and

(19)   Not (necessarily the number of planets is greater than 7)

it must follow that 9 has a property that the number of planets lacks. What might this property be? The quick answer is: the property of being necessarily greater than 7. But exactly what property is this? The question is urgent, for we might have supposed that the property of being necessarily greater than 7 is the property which in S_3 and S_4 is *correctly* attributed to *both* 9 and the number of planets; and what is presently needed is a property which in S_6 is correctly attributed to 9 but which in S_7 is *in*correctly attributed to the number of the planets. Perhaps we should ask how, in the light of (17) and (19), 9 is supposed to differ from the number of the planets. What is supposed to be true of 9 that is not true of the number of the planets? It might be suggested that in view of (17) it is true of 9 that necessarily it is greater than 7, while in view of (19) it is not true of the number of the planets that necessarily it is greater than 7. Given our conventions concerning the word 'necessarily', the suggestion comes to this: It is true of 9 that the proposition that it is greater than 7 is necessary, but it is not true of the number of planets that the proposition that *it* is greater than 7 is necessary. And so it will perhaps be suggested that if we define Q as the property which a thing x has if and only if the proposition that x is greater than 7 is necessary, then from (17) it will follow that 9 has Q and from (19) it will follow that the number of planets does not have Q.

The suggestion is worth some exploration. The advocate of Q will of course agree that there is a unique number of planets. This is an immediate consequence of

(20) $(m)(m$ is a number of the planets iff $m = 9)$,

which is simply a fact of astronomy. Something, then, and one thing only, is a number of the planets. Does it have Q or not? This question, which I suppose certainly ought to have an answer, is bound to embarrass the advocate of Q. From (20) and

(21)   9 has Q

it follows that

(22) $(\exists n)((m)(m$ is a number of the planets iff $m = n)$ and n has $Q)$.

But equally, from the undeniable

(23) $(m)(m$ is a number of the planets iff $m = $ the number of planets)

and the non-Leibnizian's

(24)   The number of planets lacks Q

it follows that

(25) (∃n)((m)(m is a number of the planets iff m = n) and n lacks Q).

The advocate of Q is thus committed to both (22) and (25): to the proposition that there is a unique number of planets and it has Q, and to the proposition that there is a unique number of planets and it lacks Q. But anyone who affirms both these is surely ill-equipped to answer the question whether, given that there is a unique number of planets, it has Q or not.

The point is not that (22) and (25) are incompatible. I think they are, but to invoke this would beg the question; for a contradiction follows from the conjuction of (22) and (25) only on the assumption of the Principle of Identity. Nor is the point that on Russell's theory of descriptions (22) is the expansion of

(26) The number of the planets has Q

and thus that the advocate of Q is committed to the very thing he wishes to deny. I suppose it is open to someone simply to reject Russell's theory. The point is rather this: If I am told that exactly one thing numbers the planets, I expect to be able to ask whether it—that number—has Q; and I expect my question to have a determinate answer. But no answer can be given by one who affirms both (22) and (25).

I suspect it will be suggested that my words 'There is a unique number of planets. Does it have Q?' amount to 'Does the number of planets have Q?' and that this is a question the advocate of Q is quite prepared to answer. After all, one of his claims is that the number of planets lacks Q. Now, I myself do not object to this rephrasing of my question. But I should like it noted that it is just the possibility of this sort of paraphrase that lends credence to Russell's theory—a theory that we have seen the advocate of Q must reject. And in any case, it seems to me that the question needs no paraphrase and that a friend of Q ought himself to find its original formulation perfectly intelligible. Recall that Q is supposed to be the property that an object has just in case the proposition that it is greater than 7 is a necessary truth. Well, there is an object—and one only—that numbers the planets. Can we not consider, then, the proposition that *it* is greater than 7? And should not reflection reveal whether this proposition is a necessary truth? I submit that reflection can reveal nothing better than *both* (22) and (25).

The difficulty originates in what seems to me to be an illegitimate form of definition. We are invited to speak of the property which an object x has if and only if the proposition that x is greater than 7 is a necessary truth. But it ought to be clear by now that it is simply a mistake to suppose that in the case of any given object there is such a thing as *the* proposition that it is greater than 7. Ever so many propositions will qualify as propositions that it, the object in question, is greater than 7. The point is obvious but often overlooked. There is an unfortunate temptation to suppose that it is possible to specify a function, in the mathematical sense, by stipulating that its domain is a particular well-defined class of objects and by stipulating further that, for any element x of that class, the value of the function for the argument x is the proposition that x is such-and-such—greater than 7, or whatever. But the fact is that these stipulations simply do not succeed in specifying a function. Suppose, for example, the domain of the alleged function is to be the class having 9 as sole member and suppose the value for x as argument is to be the proposition that x is greater than 7. What is the value for 9 as argument? If the proposition that 9 is greater than 7 qualifies, so too does the different proposition that the number of planets is greater than 7; for the number of the planets is the only member of the class whose sole member is 9. Thus the alleged function is not single-valued and hence not properly a function at all.

Let me put the point another way. Consider the propositions

(27)   9 is greater than 7

and

(28)   8 is greater than 7.

In (27) it is said of 9 that it is greater than 7, and in (28) it is said of 8 that *it* is greater than 7. Thus (27) and (28) are alike in that in each it is said of something that it is greater than 7. But that of which this is said in (27) is not the same as that of which this is said in (28). This is how the propositions differ. It is what makes them *two*. In the light of this it is tempting to go on to suppose that (27) can be fully identified by saying that it is the proposition in which it is said of 9 that it is greater than 7: we specify the object concerning which something is said and specify further what is said of it. But the supposition that this succeeds in distinguishing (27) from all other propositions is not true. That of which in (27) something is said is the number 9, that is, the number of the planets; hence (27) has not yet been distinguished from the proposition that the number of planets is greater than 7.

What strikes me as especially odd in the case of the definition of Q is that those who would use it to show the falsity of the Principle of Identity must implicitly recognize its illegitimacy. They speak, on the one hand, of *the* proposition that x is greater than 7, for arbitrary but unspecified choice of x; yet, on the other hand, it is crucial to their argument that for one and the same object x there be distinct propositions to the effect that x is greater than 7: after all, one such proposition is to be necessarily true, another only contingently so. Were there not such distinct propositions, it could hardly emerge that 9 has Q while something identical with it does not.

Of course, a really determined proponent of Q will not waver in the face of what I have been saying. He will insist that, given any object x, there *is* such a thing as *the* proposition that x is greater than 7. He will insist, in particular, that the necessary truth that 9 is greater than 7 really is identical with the contingent truth that the number of the planets is greater than 7. And he will see in this only another exception to the Principle of Identity. Now frankly this strikes me as a desperation move. But how is one to reply? To show that two things—propositions or any other things—really *are* two, nothing will suffice short of mentioning something true of one of them that is not true of the other. Perhaps in the end all that can be said is that the Principle of Identity is a self-evident truth.

Notes

This essay was first published in Milton K. Munitz, ed., *Identity and Individuation* (New York: New York University Press, 1971), pp. 119–133.

1. *Zeitschrift für Philosophie und philosophische Kritik* 100 (1892): 25–50.

2. Clarence I. Lewis, *A Survey of Symbolic Logic* (New York: Dover, 1960), p. 291.

3. E. g., *New Essays Concerning Human Understanding*, trans. A. G. Langley (La Salle, Ill.: Open Court, 1949), pp. 450–451.

4. W. V. Quine, *From a Logical Point of View*, 2d ed. (New York: Harper and Row, 1963), p. 139.

5. Cf. Quine, *From a Logical Point of View*, p. 139.

6. "A Theory of Attributes Based on Modal Logic," *Acta Philosophica Fennica* (1963): 98.

Some Remarks on Essentialism

Essentialism, as I shall understand it, is the doctrine that among the attributes of a thing some are essential, others merely accidental. Its essential attributes are those it has necessarily, those it could not have lacked. Its accidental attributes are those it has only contingently, those it might not have had. Some attributes are essential to everything whatever—the attribute of being self-identical, for example, or perhaps the attribute of having some attribute or other. Others—for example, the attribute of being greater than 7—are essential to all things that have them. Still others are essential only to some of the things that have them. Thus truth is essential to the proposition that 9 is greater than 7 but not to the proposition that the number of the planets is greater than 7. Advocates of the doctrine can be expected to disagree over particular cases. What are the essential attributes of, say, Dancer's Image? No doubt it will be counted essential that he is a horse and accidental that he was disqualified in this year's Kentucky Derby. But what of the attribute of being male, or of being a thoroughbred, or of not being a Clydesdale stallion? Here, I suppose, essentialists may disagree. Indeed, a reasonable essentialist might well take the position that these are hard cases that admit of no clear decision.

When the essentialist says, for example, that 9 is necessarily greater than 7, he of course intends to say something about the number 9. If he succeeds and if what he says is true, then what he says of 9 will thus be true of that number quite independently of the way in which it is designated. If it is true of 9 that it is necessarily greater than 7, then that is true of the number of the planets, the number of players on a baseball team, and the number designated by the Arabic numeral '9'; for each of these *is* 9. It is no part of the essentialist's program to deny the principle of the indiscernibility of identicals: that if x is identical with y, then everything true of x is true of y. It is precisely here, however, that some philosophers seem to think essentialism is in difficulty; for, they say, 9 is necessarily greater than 7 but the number of the planets is not. Their point is not that identicals are not always indiscernible. It is rather that "to be necessarily greater than 7 is not a trait of a number, but depends on the manner of referring to the number."[1] Otherwise 9 would exhibit the trait, but the number of the planets would not.

If this objection is to be more than a simple denial of something the essentialist asserts, it must be accompanied by support for the contention that the number of the planets is not necessarily greater than 7. And it is not hard to see what support would be offered. It would be pointed out that whereas

(1)   9 is greater than 7

is a necessary truth,

(2)   The number of the planets is greater than 7

is not. But how is this relevant? Apparently it is simply taken for granted that if the number of the planets is necessarily greater than 7, then (2) is a necessary truth. But this conditional is one the essentialist could have been expected to deny. After all, his claim purports to be about the number 9, however specified; and he knows as well as anyone that the modal value of a statement about 9 is not, in general, thus indifferent to the way in which that number is designated. Certainly, there is no attribute which, in virtue of the necessity of (1) and the contingency of (2), is present in 9 but not in the number of the planets. But then the essentialist never claimed there was. His claim concerned 9, the number that happens to be the number of the planets.

It has to be conceded that the sentence 'the number of the planets is necessarily greater than 7' admits of a reading under which it formulates a proposition that is true only if (2) is a necessary truth. I suppose the same holds for alternatives such as 'the number of the planets could not have failed to be greater than 7' and 'it is impossible that the number of the planets should not have been greater than 7'. Following a medieval usage, we may say that these sentences can be understood *de dicto*. But there can be no real doubt that they admit also of a *de re* reading, a reading under which the proposition formulated is true or false depending upon which number is in fact the number of the planets. I doubt that any English sentence invariably carries the latter rather than the former sense, although 'the number of the planets is such that it is necessarily greater than 7' and 'that number which is in fact the number of the planets is necessarily greater than 7' are sometimes suggested as candidates. And in any event I do not wish to urge that it is altogether clear what proposition is then formulated. But it is surely clear that when the essentialist says the number of the planets is necessarily greater than 7, he is to be understood in this second way; and once he is, it is also clear that his claim is unaffected by the contingency of (2).

The ambiguity in 'the number of the planets is necessarily greater than

7′ does not arise from the possibility of placing alternative interpretations on some word or phrase that occurs in the sentence. It is syntactic in nature and is recognizable also in sentences containing such adverbs as 'probably', 'obviously', 'demonstrably', and 'certainly'. It is especially easy to detect when the adverb modifies 'true' or 'false'. Thus, 'what the policeman said is obviously false' can be understood in the sense of 'that what the policeman said is false is obvious', but it is perhaps more naturally understood as formulating a proposition in which obvious falsehood is attributed rather to the statement the policeman made. Again, 'the proposition at the top of page 210 of *Word and Object* is demonstrably true' can be understood in the sense of 'that the proposition at the top of page 210 of *Word and Object* is true is demonstrable', though it is more naturally taken to formulate a proposition in which demonstrability is attributed to the proposition that actually appears at the top of page 210 of *Word and Object*.

The ambiguity in question has been noticed by others, but some who have seen it have gone on to characterize it inadequately. Arthur Smullyan saw it as having to do with the scope of definite descriptions, and he accordingly proposed to treat it by means of an extended version of Russell's theory.[2] But though this may serve the purposes of disambiguation in some cases, it does not in all. For '9 is necessarily greater than 7' would appear to admit of both *de dicto* and *de re* readings. Of course, it is open to Smullyan to argue that '9' is in reality a disguised definite description; but he countenances names that are not, and, with these, sentences exhibiting the ambiguity will surely be constructible. More recently, B. Rundle has suggested that the ambiguity arises through the fact that one who says "The number of the planets is necessarily greater than 7" may or may not be using the definite description "referentially," that is, in such a way as simply to single out a certain number.[3] Now, that it is necessary to distinguish "referential" from "attributive" uses of definite descriptions has been persuasively argued of late by Donnellan.[4] And no doubt the possibility of this variation in use is present in the case of 'the number of the planets is necessarily greater than 7'. But I see no reason to think (nor does Donnellan suggest) that one who uses the sentence *de re* inevitably uses 'the number of the planets' referentially; in fact, there is reason to think the contrary, in view of such a sentence as 'the number of the planets, whatever it may be, is necessarily greater than 7'.

Recognition of the ambiguity cannot, however, be expected to convert opponents of essentialism. They will urge that presence of a syntactic ambiguity means only that the sentence in question is subject to alternative structural descriptions; it does not mean that under each of these it makes coherent sense. They will agree that the essentialist intends to say *something* about 9 when he says that 9 is necessarily greater than 7, but they will profess to be in the dark as to what this is. More specifically, opponents of essentialism are apt to take the position that 'necessary', 'contingent', and the rest are intelligible when applied to propositions (or to whatever other entities are deemed to be bearers of truth value); hence the intelligibility of 'necessarily true', 'contingently true', and the like. But, they will say, such compounds as 'necessarily a horse' and 'contingently a male' are baffling.

Quine has attempted "to evoke the appropriate sense of bewilderment" in the following passage:

> Mathematicians may conceivably be said to be necessarily rational and not necessarily two-legged; and cyclists necessarily two-legged and not necessarily rational. But what of an individual who counts among his eccentricities both mathematics and cycling? Is this concrete individual necessarily rational and contingently two-legged or vice versa? Just insofar as we are talking referentially of the object, with no special bias toward a background grouping of mathematicians as against cyclists or vice versa, there is no semblance of sense in rating some of his attributes as necessary and others as contingent.[5]

Viewed as an attempt to refute essentialism, this is a failure. The sentences 'mathematicians are necessarily rational and not necessarily two-legged' and 'cyclists are necessarily two-legged and not necessarily rational' are ambiguous. Understood *de dicto*, they formulate propositions to the effect that *Mathematicians are rational* and *Cyclists are two-legged* are necessary truths whereas *Mathematicians are two-legged* and *Cyclists are rational* are not. But all that follows is that any given mathematical cyclist is in fact both rational and two-legged. Understood *de re*, they formulate propositions to the effect that every mathematician is such that he is necessarily rational and not necessarily two-legged and that every cyclist is such that he is necessarily two-legged and not necessarily rational; and there is surely no reason to suppose the essentialist is committed to both these.[6]

But refutation was not Quine's aim. He intended rather to produce in us the sense of bewilderment that essentialism occasions in him. Faced with Wilson, a mathematical cyclist, how *are* we to decide whether he—Wilson himself—is or is not necessarily rational? For although it is a necessary truth that mathematicians are rational, it is not a necessary truth that cyclists are rational. And so to come down, in Wilson's case, on either side seems to Quine indicative of nothing more than bias in favor of one way of classifying Wilson over another. Substantially the same point could have been made with respect to the number 9. Given that (1) is necessary but (2) is not, how can it be determined whether 9 is or is not necessarily greater than 7? A decision either way would appear to Quine to manifest only favoritism toward one way of designating the number over another.

This line of criticism does not as such find anything problematic in *de dicto* readings of modal sentences.[7] Hence the essentialist is in a position to look for defense by attempting to explain the *de re* via the *de dicto*. Of course, no direct reduction of the former to the latter will do; that, in effect, we have already seen. Still, it might be thought that, by some more or less complicated device of paraphrase, the essentialist's characteristic assertions can be expressed in sentences in which such otherwise suspect adjectives as 'necessary' and 'contingent' appear only in application to bearers of truth value.

A suggestion along these lines has recently been put forward, albeit somewhat tentatively, by Plantinga.[8] His proposed explanation is a two-staged affair, consisting of a definition of what it is for an object to have a property "necessarily," followed by an explanation of what it is for a property to be "essential" to an object.[9] The definitions are as follows:

(3)   *x* has *P necessarily* if and only if *x* has *P* and the proposition that *x* lacks *P* is necessarily false (where the domain of the variable '*x*' is unlimited but its substituend set contains only proper names, and where the domain of the variable '*P*' is the set of properties and its substituend set contains no definite description or expressions definitionally equivalent to definite descriptions).

(4)   *P* is an *essential property* of *x* if and only if *x* has *P* and there is something *y* identical with *x* and a property *P'* identical with *P* such that *y* has *P'* necessarily (in the sense of (3)).[10]

Now, it might appear at first sight that in these definitions we have one definition too many, for it might appear that the definiens of (4) is logically equivalent to the definiendum of (3). Thus, if *x* has *P* necessarily, then *x* surely qualifies as something *y* identical with *x* and *P* as a property *P'* identical with *P* such that *y* has *P'* necessarily; conversely, if there is something *y* identical with *x* and a property *P'* identical with *P* such that *y* has *P'* necessarily, then by the indiscernibility of identicals *x* has *P* necessarily. We shall soon see that this appearance is deceptive, but for the moment let us focus on (3).

Here, attention must be called at once to the very great importance of the parenthesized material. Notice the effect of its deletion: what results is scarcely intelligible, since it presupposes that for each object *x* and each property *P* there is such a thing as *the* proposition that *x* lacks *P*. This is dubious, to say the least. Of the two propositions

(5)   Dancer's Image lacks the property of being a horse

and

(6)   The horse that was disqualified in the 1968 Kentucky Derby lacks the property of being a horse

which is *the* proposition that Dancer's Image—that is, the horse that was disqualified in the 1968 Kentucky Derby—lacks the property of being a horse?[11] It might be suggested that the difficulty can be avoided by a technical maneuver: switch from the *predicate* 'is necessarily false' to the *sentence operator* 'it is necessarily false that', understanding the result of prefixing this to a sentence S to formulate a truth just in case S itself formulates a necessary falsehood, and supplant (3) with

(7)   *x* has *P necessarily* if and only if it is necessarily false that *x lacks P.*

But this remains unintelligible in the absence of some supplementary convention for interpreting 'it is necessarily false that' when, as in (7), it precedes an *open* sentence. What is needed is a rule of satisfaction for the condition expressed by the definiens of (7). But it is by no means clear that such a rule is obtainable without violation of the principle of the indiscernibility of identicals. For, by the convention governing 'it is necessarily false that' when prefixed to closed sentences, it is necessarily false that 9 lacks the property of being greater than 7 but not necessarily false that the number of the planets lacks the property of being greater than 7. Or, to put the burden on '*P*' rather than '*x*', it is necessarily false that 9 lacks the property of being greater than 7 but not necessarily false that 9 lacks the property just now mentioned.

It was apparently Plantinga's thought that this difficulty can be handled by placing suitable restrictions on the substituends of the variables '*x*' and '*P*': hence the parenthesized material in (3). But the effect of the restriction is that we are given a good deal less than we seem to have been promised. Instead of an explanation of what it is for an object to have a property necessarily, we are given an explication of a quite limited range of sentences involving the construction 'has . . . necessarily'. The definition in fact comes to just this:

(8)   Where α is a proper name and ϕ is a canonical designation of a property,[12] $\ulcorner\alpha$ has ϕ necessarily$\urcorner$ means the same as $\ulcorner\alpha$ has ϕ and the proposition that α lacks ϕ is necessarily false$\urcorner$.

Now this, I suppose, enables us to say with confidence that 9 has the property of being greater than 7 necessarily. But what of the number of the planets? Here (8) is silent, for 'the number of the planets' is not a proper name.

It is at this point that we need to restore the second of Plantinga's definitions. And the following appears to accord with his intentions:

(9) $\ulcorner\psi$ is an essential property of $\beta\urcorner$ formulates a truth if and only if there is a proper name α and a canonical property-designation ϕ such that each of $\ulcorner\alpha = \beta\urcorner$, $\ulcorner\phi = \psi\urcorner$, and $\ulcorner\alpha$ has ϕ necessarily$\urcorner$ formulates a truth.

And the combined effect of (8) and (9) is to enable us to say that the property of being greater than 7 is an essential property of the number of the planets, as well as of 9.

But there are difficulties even so. To begin with, there is the problem of unnamed objects. Taking (9) at its word, we shall be forced to say that the property of being a horse is not essential to the horse in the barn unless the beast is lucky enough to have a name. Similarly for properties that have no canonical designations. And this surely accords ill with the spirit of essentialism. Plantinga is of course not unaware of the difficulty. Speaking of (3) he remarks: "Here we must recognize that the domains of the variables 'x' and 'P' are not really unlimited; they must contain only objects for which there are proper names, and properties denoted by expressions other than definite descriptions" (p. 179). In (9), then, we are to understand ψ to be a designation of a property for which there is some canonical designation and β to be a singular term that denotes something having a proper name. It is apt to be suggested that this severely limits the applicability of (9). But, Plantinga says, "this limitation really comes to very little; for it is always open to us to *name* individuals and to furnish the appropriate sort of denoting expressions for properties" (p. 179). This is a more sanguine view of the situation than I think is justified. No matter how furiously we go in for naming things, there will always remain a nondenumerable infinity of things that lack names but which the essentialist will suppose have some properties essentially. And, aside from this, I am not convinced that naming an object is as easy a matter as Plantinga appears to think. Suppose I tell you there is exactly one domesticated animal in the barn, and suppose the animal to be so far unnamed. Are you, without further ado, in a position to name it? I suppose you might proceed to refer to it as "Charlie." But I suspect that then 'Charlie' is a disguised description, short for 'the sole domesticated animal in the barn'. And if it is said that this counts nothing against its being a name, then it will have to be agreed at once that the property of being a horse is not essential to Charlie; for the proposition that the sole domesticated animal in the barn lacks the property of being a horse is evidently not a necessary falsehood.

The difficulty arises from the form in which (8) and (9) are cast. Their yield is significantly less than what (7) seemed anyway to promise; for, as they stand, they do not even purport to provide a condition necessary and sufficient for an object to have a property essentially. Equipped solely with them, we do not know how to complete the formula 'an object x has a property P essentially if and only if . . .'. We might hazard that what is intended is

(10)   An object x has a property P essentially if and only if there is a proper name α of x and a canonical designation ϕ of P such that $\ulcorner \alpha$ has ϕ and the proposition that α lacks ϕ is necessarily false$\urcorner$ is true.

But the implausibility of this as an interpretation of essentialism has already been noticed. We might, then, on Plantinga's advice, take (8) and (9) as providing only a condition necessary and sufficient for named objects to have canonically designated properties essentially. But if essentialism is to be understood, we need more. According to that doctrine, the property of being a horse is essential not only to Dancer's Image and his sire but to horses generally; and we have yet to be given a way to understand this.

There is in any case another objection to (8) and (9), one the opponent of essentialism is sure to raise and one the essentialist himself is wise to heed. Suppose an essentialist says, as he presumably would, "The horse that was disqualified in the 1968 Kentucky Derby has the property of being a horse essentially." This is a case in which (8) and (9) are applicable, since the horse that was disqualified in the 1968 Kentucky Derby bears the proper name 'Dancer's Image'. And according to (8) and (9) our essentialist speaks the truth only if (5) is necessarily false. But is it? I cannot see that it is. Argument on such a matter is always difficult, but in the present case the burden seems to me to fall on one who says that (5) *is* necessarily false. After all, it would seem to be a matter for empirical investigation whether Dancer's Image really is a horse. And so I propose to ask what considerations could be brought to bear on the other side.

Some will say that the name 'Dancer's Image', like proper names generally, has a sense, or meaning, which is the sense of some definite description—the horse that was disqualified in the 1968 Kentucky Derby', say, or 'the horse entered by Peter Fuller in this year's Kentucky Derby', or even 'the horse named "Dancer's Image" '. If so, (5) is the proposition that the horse that was disqualified in the 1968 Kentucky Derby lacks the property of being a horse, or the proposition that the horse named 'Dancer's Image' lacks the property of being a horse; and each of these is an obvious contradiction. Now, I find this view of proper names implausible. But what needs emphasis here is that it gives the essentialist more than he is likely to want. The proposition that the horse that was disqualified in the 1968 Kentucky Derby lacks the property of having been disqualified in the 1968 Kentucky Derby is also an obvious contradiction, but I cannot think an essentialist would suppose that having been disqualified in the 1968 Kentucky Derby is an essential property of Dancer's Image. Similarly for the property of having been entered by Peter Fuller in this year's Kentucky Derby and the property of being named 'Dancer's Image'. And it is difficult to think of any very likely candidate for the "sense" of the name 'Dancer's Image' that does not exhibit the same sort of defect.

A suggestion that falls short of taking proper names as disguised definite descriptions, but nevertheless accords them a sense, is one according to which a proper name expresses or conveys a "nominal essence," the sense of some common noun such as 'horse' or 'cat' or 'man', by reference to which sense is given to the question whether the object designated by the name on one occasion is or is not the same as that designated by it on some other occasion. Advocates of the view see support for it in the alleged fact that recognition of an object as the *same* as some previously presented one requires recognition of it as the *same such-and-such*, where 'such-and-such' stands in for some count noun of a rather restricted applicability.[13]

This view deserves a more extended discussion than is possible here. I shall restrict myself to arguing that there is in it no real support for the contention that (5) is a necessary falsehood. Suppose I am first introduced to the name 'Dancer's Image' ostensively. You point to the animal and say, "That's Dancer's Image." For your act of ostension to succeed, it is necessary that I gather *which* thing your demonstrative indicates. And there are various ways in which I may fail. I may not take your act as one of ostension at all but rather as one of asserting that the indicated object is the image of Native Dancer. Or, I may take you to be giving me the name of a species, or a horse stage, or an undetached horse part. But, for your ostension to be successful, it is surely not necessary that I gather *what sort* of object it is you have indicated—not, at least, if that is taken to mean that I must gather that it is a horse and not an ass or a mule or a zebra. Indeed, we need not stay this specific. I may gather which thing you have indicated without knowing that it is a mammal or even that it is alive. No doubt I grasp the assignment of name to object only if I am able to understand subsequent applications of the name as being or not being applications of it to the same object. And perhaps there is plausibility in the suggestion that this requires that I somehow associate with the name the sense of some count noun that is more narrowly applicable than 'object' or 'thing'. But there is no plausibility in the suggestion that it must be a noun with such restricted applicability as 'horse'. So the view that 'Dancer's Image' somehow conveys or expresses that the thing so called is a horse seems to me wrong. Consequently, we have yet to see any support for the contention that (5) is necessarily false.

What has been at stake is not the truth of essentialism but its intelligibility: the meaningfulness of rating some attributes of a thing as essential, others as merely accidental. Now, a charge of unintelligibility is always hard to answer: *proof* of intelligibility cannot be expected. Of course, the opposition can sometimes be mollified by explanation of the allegedly unintelligible in terms it finds intelligible. It was for this reason that we just now examined an effort—unsuccessful, I have argued—to reduce modalities *de re* to modalities *de dicto*. But the opposition cannot insist on such explanation unless prepared to give presumptive evidence against the locutions in question. Where, as in the present case, these are not outright gibberish, those who see in them no semblance of sense owe us an argument.

But the fact is that arguments to the point are hard to find and, once found, hard to construe. Thus, it is apparently supposed to be an obstacle to understanding modalities *de re* that the modal value of a statement about an object is not in general independent of the way in which the object is designated: (1) is necessarily true, but (2) is not; and (6) is necessarily false, but (5) is not. But what I find exceedingly difficult to understand is how precisely this is supposed to be an obstacle. Perhaps I can convey *my* sense of bewilderment as follows.

Tom, we may suppose, is well enough up on Roman history to agree that Cicero denounced Catiline, but, not knowing that Tully was Cicero, he is unwilling to agree that Tully denounced Catiline. It is surely clear, and it appears to be agreed on all sides, that this is no insuperable obstacle to *understanding* the claim that there is someone—namely, Cicero—whom Tom believes to have denounced Catiline. Again, it is true that Oedipus wanted to marry Jocasta but not true that he wanted to marry his mother. Even so, we should all understand well enough someone who said that Jocasta, the mother of Oedipus, was such that Oedipus wanted to marry her. In these cases, and in hosts of others, "transparent" readings of otherwise "opaque" constructions are readily intelligible. Why is the situation any different in the case of modalities? There is apparently supposed to be some quite special circumstance which, given the necessity of (1) and the contingency of (2), renders unintelligible the claim that 9—the number itself—is necessarily greater than 7. But I for one have no idea what this special circumstance could be.

Apparently, also, those who think essentialism unintelligible see support for their position in the doctrine that necessary truths are one and all analytic. The idea is, I take it, that this doctrine somehow implies that only relative to some mode of designation does it make sense to speak of an object as necessarily this or that. The meaning of '9' involves the attribute of being greater than 7, but the meaning of 'the number of the planets' does not. Hence, if necessity is analyticity, there is no sense in speaking of the number itself as necessarily or contingently greater than 7.

It is difficult to see anything but a howler here. The doctrine in question identifies necessity with analyticity just insofar as necessity itself is taken to be a property of bearers of truth value. That is, it concerns modalities *de dicto*. How, then, can it have any consequences at all with respect to essentialism? To suppose it somehow implies the meaninglessness of essentialism is to confound at the outset modalities *de re* with modalities *de dicto*.

I see no reason, then, for thinking essentialism unintelligible. At the same time, I do not mean to suggest that it is without its perplexities. Chief among these is the obscurity of the grounds on which ratings of attributes as essential or accidental are to be made. Apparently, in any particular case, one is simply to reflect on the question whether the object in question could or could not have lacked the attribute in question. Now, such reflection perhaps assures us that every object is necessarily self-identical and that 9 is necessarily greater than 7. But the criteria to which one appeals in such reflection are sufficiently obscure to leave me, at least, with an embarrassingly large number of undecided cases. Is Dancer's Image necessarily or contingently a male? Necessarily or contingently a thoroughbred? And, for that matter, necessarily or contingently not a philosopher? The existence of such cases, even in such large number, does not show that there simply is no distinction between essential and accidental attributes of an object. But it does show that the distinction is a good deal less clear than essentialists are wont to suppose.

Notes

This essay was prepared for presentation at a symposium on "Essentialism" at the sixty-fifth annual meeting of the American Philosophical Association, Eastern Division, December 27, 1968. It was first published in *Journal of Philosophy* 65, no. 20 (October 24, 1968): 615–626.

1. W. V. Quine, *From a Logical Point of View*, 2d ed. (New York: Harper and Row, 1963), p. 148.

2. Arthur F. Smullyan, "Modality and Description," *Journal of Symbolic Logic* 13, no. 1 (March 1948): 31–37. See also Frederick B. Fitch, "The Problem of the Morning Star and the Evening Star," *Philosophy of Science* 16, no. 2 (April 1949): 137–141.

3. B. Rundle, "Modality and Quantification," in R. J. Butler, ed., *Analytical Philosophy*, 2d series (Oxford: Basil Blackwell, 1965), pp. 27–39.

4. Keith S. Donnellan, "Reference and Definite Descriptions," *Philosophical Review* 75, no. 3 (July 1966): 281–304.

5. W. V. Quine, *Word and Object* (Cambridge, Mass.: MIT Press, 1960), p. 199.

6. Substantially this is pointed out by Ruth Barcan Marcus in "Essentialism in Modal Logic," *Noûs* 1, no. 1 (March 1967): 91–96.

7. Of course Quine looks with suspicion on modalities generally.

8. Alvin Plantinga, *God and Other Minds* (Ithaca, N.Y.: Cornell University Press, 1967); see pp. 175–180.

9. No significance is to be read into this terminological convention.

10. Quoted, almost verbatim, from Plantinga, *God and Other Minds*, pp. 179–180.

11. Compare Hilary Putnam, "The Thesis That Mathematics Is Logic," in Ralph Schoenman, ed., *Bertrand Russell: Philosopher of the Century* (Boston: Little, Brown, 1967), pp. 273–303.

12. A "canonical" designation of a property is one which, in Plantinga's words, is neither a definite description nor definitionally equivalent to a definite description.

13. Some such view as this is suggested by Peter Geach in *Reference and Generality* (Ithaca, N.Y.: Cornell University Press, 1962), pp. 43–44. See also G. E. M. Anscombe and P. T Geach, *Three Philosophers* (Ithaca, N.Y.: Cornell University Press, 1961), pp. 10–11.

Classes and Attributes

1.   How are attributes and classes to be distinguished? No doubt some will take the position that there is really no problem here: attributes and classes are so very different, they will say, that the question how to distinguish them need not arise. Perhaps so. But some philosophers have raised the question and given answers to it. My aim in this paper is not to defend their question but to attack certain of their answers.

2.   A standard answer to the question appears at first sight straightforward enough: whereas no two classes coincide in membership, there are, or at any rate are commonly supposed to be, distinct but coextensive attributes. Indeed, Quine has said that this is the *only* respect in which attributes and classes differ. Thus in *From a Logical Point of View* he writes:

> ... what sets attributes apart from classes is merely that whereas classes are identical when they have the same members, attributes may be distinct even though present in all and only the same things.[1]

This passage is anticipated by one that occurs in his *Mathematical Logic*:

> If there is any difference between classes and properties, it is merely this: classes are the same when their members are the same, whereas it is not universally conceded that properties are the same when possessed by the same objects. The class of all marine mammals living in 1940 is the same as the class of all whales and porpoises living in 1940, whereas the property of being a marine mammal alive in 1940 might be regarded as differing from the property of being a whale or porpoise alive in 1940.[2]

And the point is rather neatly summarized in *Word and Object* with the remark that "classes are like attributes except for their identity condition."[3]

Now, a difference between two sorts of things is a respect in which each and every thing of the one sort differs from each and every thing of the other. And to say *how* two sorts of things differ it is necessary to mention such a difference. It is necessary to point out something that is true of all things of the one sort and of none of the other. It is necessary to say something true of the form, Whereas it is true of all C's that . . . , it is true of no A's that. . . . Of course, for some choices of 'C' and 'A' no such true statement is available, even though we are prepared to count C's and A's as "different sorts of things": the distinction between C's and A's is simply not all that sharp. But I should suppose this situation need not be anticipated in the case of classes and attributes. Presumably it is a plain truth, without need of qualification, that no attribute is a class.

What, then, according to Quine is the difference between classes and attributes? What is it that is supposed to be true of all classes but of no attributes? We are told two things: that "classes are identical when they have the same members" and that "attributes may be distinct even though present in all and only the same things." Here, certainly, we are given something true of every class x, namely, that if y is any class having the same members as x, then y is identical with x. And I shall take for granted that we are also given something true of no attribute x, namely, that if y is any attribute present in the same things as x, then y is identical with x. But the oddity is that to be given these is *not* to be given a *difference* between classes and attributes; for what is said to be true of every class is simply not what is said to be false of every attribute.

To see the point clearly, view Quine as presenting an argument for the conclusion that no attribute is a class. One premise is that every class satisfies the open sentence

(1)   If y is any class having the same members as x, then y is identical with x.

And the other is that no attribute satisfies the open sentence

(2)   If y is any attribute present in the same things as x, then y is identical with x.

Though the premises are true, it is obvious they do not yield the desired conclusion.

3.   Some simple repairs are apt to be proposed. First off, it will perhaps be pointed out that whereas every class satisfies (1), no attribute does. This, it will be said, qualifies as a difference between classes and attributes and is perhaps the one to which Quine meant to direct attention. I very much doubt this. I suppose we do have here a respect in which classes and attributes differ, but I cannot believe it is the one Quine intended. No doubt attributes—indeed, non-classes generally—fail to satisfy (1). But notice that the failure is quite independent of their "condition of identity." If no attribute is a class, then no attribute satisfies (1) even if *every* attribute satisfies (2). But Quine's intentions aside, the proposal can in any case hardly be said to provide a way of distinguishing classes from attributes.

Wherein lies the confidence that no attribute satisfies (1)? Well, if some attribute were to satisfy (1), its membership—empty or otherwise—would presumably coincide with that of some class and hence it would be identical with that class; but no attribute is a class. Thus, we agree that no attribute satisfies (1) only because we are antecedently prepared to agree that no attribute is a class. To cite a difference is not always to draw a distinction. Otherwise, it would suffice in the present connection to point out that although classes are classes, attributes are not.

Perhaps it will be thought that this deficiency can be remedied simply by deleting from (1) the condition that y be a class, thereby obtaining the open sentence

(3) If y is anything having the same members as x, then y is identical with x.

Here, it might be said, is an open sentence satisfied by all classes and by no attributes; and to point this out is genuinely to distinguish classes from attributes. But I do not see how it can be maintained that all classes satisfy (3) and yet that no attribute does. Attributes have members or they do not. As already noted, their membership is in either case the membership of some class: some non-empty class in the former case, the empty class in the latter. So if every class satisfies (3), every attribute is identical with some class and thus after all itself satisfies (3). The fact is that it is curious to resort to (3) in the attempt to distinguish classes from objects of *any* sort. For if every class satisfies (3), there simply are no non-classes at all; hence no objects from which classes need to be distinguished.

The repairs so far considered have pretty much overlooked the fact that no attribute satisfies (2); and herein, perhaps, lies the source of their inadequacy. An alternative seems to remedy this. Suppose we say that an object x is *congruent* with an object y if and only if either x and y are classes having the same members or x and y are attributes present in the same things.[4] It is then easily seen to be true of every class, but of no attribute, that anything congruent with it is identical with it. That is, the open sentence

(4) If y is anything congruent with x, then y is identical with x.

is satisfied by every class but by no attribute. Certainly this is a difference between classes and attributes. But I doubt that it is the one to which Quine meant to call attention, and I doubt also that mention of it suffices to distinguish classes from attributes. Notice, in the first place, that this respect in which classes differ from attributes is one in which non-attributes generally differ from attributes. For suppose x to be any non-attribute. Then x is a class or not. If the former, then x evidently satisfies (4); and if the latter, nothing is congruent with x and consequently x vacuously satisfies (4). So (4) is satisfied by every non-attribute whatever. But then it seems odd to cite satisfaction of (4) as the way in which *classes* are to be distinguished from attributes. In the second place, and more importantly, the efficacy of (4) in distinguishing attributes from non-attributes depends upon the suppressed occurrence in it of the notions of class and attribute. This can be seen by comparing (4) with

(5)   If y is anything having the same members or present in the same things as x, then y is identical with x.

If we suppose every class to satisfy (5), then by reasoning like that used in connection with (3) we shall be forced to say that (5) is satisfied by all objects whatever, attributes included; for the membership of every object is that of some class.

4.   Classes are extensional, attributes are not. That, briefly stated, is what Quine would have us believe is the sole difference between classes and attributes. The difficulty has been to see in what extensionality is supposed to consist. It is true that no two classes have the same members and no doubt false that no two attributes are present in the same things. But from this we have been unable to extract the desired property.

In the introduction to his recent *Set Theory and Its Logic,* Quine presents what seems a promising picture.

> Imagine a sentence about something. Put a blank or variable where the thing is referred to. You have no longer a sentence about that particular thing, but an open sentence, so called, that may hold true of each of various things and be false of others. Now the notion of class is such that there is supposed to be, in addition to the various things of which that sentence is true, also a further thing which is the *class* having each of those things and no others as member. It is the class *determined* by the open sentence. Much the same characterization would serve to characterize the notion of attribute; for the notion of attribute is such that there is supposed to be, in addition to the various things of which a given open sentence is true, a further thing which is an *attribute* of each of those things and of no others. . . . But the difference, the only intelligible difference, between class and attribute emerges when to the above characterization of the notion of class we adjoin this needed supplement: classes are identical when their members are identical. This, the *law of extensionality,* is not considered to extend to attributes.[5]

Let us agree not to disturb this picture by any doubts we may have that to each open sentence (in a single free variable) there corresponds a class and an attribute. That is, let us agree that there is a many-one correspondence, f, whereby with each open sentence ϕ there is associated the class determined by ϕ—the class of things satisfying ϕ. Similarly, let us agree that there is a many-one correspondence, g, that associates with each such ϕ an attribute—the *at*tribute, as Quine says, that ϕ at*trib*utes. Now, f and g are distinct correspondences. For if ϕ and ψ are open sentences satisfied by precisely the same things, $f(\phi)$ will be identical with $f(\psi)$, whereas $g(\phi)$ may well be distinct from $g(\psi)$. But from this it does not follow that no attribute is a class. It does not even follow that *some* attributes are not classes. The picture requires that f and g diverge in values for some arguments, but not for all; and it does not preclude the possibility that the range of values of f is the same as that of g. We can improve matters somewhat by supposing that a given attribute is identical at best with the class of things in which it is present—by supposing, that is, that $g(\phi)$ is a class only if $g(\phi)$ is identical with $f(\phi)$. This guarantees that not *all* attributes are classes. It guarantees that of the various attributes common and peculiar to the members of some given class, at most one is a class. But the conclusion that *no* attribute is a class is still not forthcoming.

The point is a perfectly general one. Let K be any collection, let R be an equivalence relation on K, and suppose h and i to be functions with domain K such that for all x and y in K

$$xRy \leftrightarrow h(x) = h(y)$$

but for some u and v in K

$$uRv \cdot i(u) \neq i(v).$$

Then of course h and i are distinct functions. But they may nevertheless have the same range. This can be precluded by imposing the further conditions that $i(x)$ is in the range of h only if in fact $i(x)$ is identical with $h(x)$. But even then it obviously remains possible that there are elements y in K for which $i(y)$ *is* identical with $h(y)$.

What emerges from the picture, then, is simply that *class* abstraction differs from *attribute* abstraction. The schema

(6) $(x)(Fx \leftrightarrow Gx) \rightarrow \hat{x}Fx = \hat{x}Gx$

comes out true for all choices of 'Fx' and 'Gx' provided the circumflex is understood to indicate class abstraction, but not so if it represents attribute abstraction. In view of this it is perhaps not inappropriate to call the one abstractive operation "extensional," the other "intensional." But so conceived extensionality is not a property of classes, nor intensionality one of attributes. The contrast is thus not one whereby classes can be distinguished from attributes.

5.   At the end of the passage from *Set Theory and Its Logic* quoted above, Quine remarks that the law of extensionality "is not considered to extend to attributes." What can this mean? The law of extensionality is simply the

true statement that no two classes agree in membership. What can it mean to say that this does or does not "extend to" attributes? That it is false that no two attributes have the same members? Presumably it *is* false, for the trivial reason that no attribute has *any* members. But it is surely not in this that the alleged intensionality of attributes is supposed to consist; otherwise *all* non-classes would be equally intensional. Is it rather that it is false that no two attributes are present in the same things? If so, it is difficult to see what in the one case fails to "extend to" the other. There is a shift not only in objects talked about but also in what is said about them. And it is of no help to think of the law of extensionality as being about the membership relation itself. What it truly affirms of membership is no doubt false of exemplification: distinct classes may (vacuously) be present in the same things. But this could hardly be taken to qualify exemplification as intensional, since it is compatible with their being no two attributes exemplified by the same things.

Matters would be simpler if the law of extensionality could be taken to be the statement that no two *objects* have the same members. Then at least we would have a difference between membership and exemplification: the former but not the latter would satisfy

(7) $(x)(y)((z)(zRx \leftrightarrow zRy) \rightarrow x = y)$.

but of course doubt can be raised whether membership *does* satisfy (7). It does not if there is more than one memberless object. And, incidentally, it will not do to adopt at this point a device used by Quine in other contexts: that of taking all purported nonclasses to be identical with their unit-classes.[6] Under such a ruling, what were non-classes become classes with the peculiar property of being their own sole members. Accordingly, every object whatever—in particular, every attribute—comes to satisfy (3); and thus in a quite straightforward sense the law of extensionality *does* extend to attributes.

There is, however, something to be rescued here. Suppose the variables 'x' and 'y' of (7) to be restricted to such objects as are in the converse domain of whatever relation R is taken to be. Consider, that is, the open sentence

(8) $(x)(y)(((Ez)(zRx) \cdot (Ez)(zRy)) \rightarrow ((z)(zRx \leftrightarrow zRy) \rightarrow x = y))$.

It can safely be assumed that only classes appear in the converse domain of the membership relation; and since no two have the same members, that relation satisfies (8). But presumably in the converse domain of the relation of exemplification there are to be found distinct attributes present in the same things. Hence that relation does not satisfy (8). It is true, of course, that not all classes are in the converse domain of the membership relation: the empty class is the exception. And I suppose some attributes fail to be exemplified. Even so, we have here an important difference between membership and exemplification, one that perhaps justifies calling the former "extensional," the latter "intensional." But notice that it is a difference between the two *relations*, and one that is compatible with any amount of overlap in their converse domains. It thus provides no basis for distinguishing classes from attributes on the point of extensionality.

Perhaps it will be suggested that we count as "extensional" any object that appears in the converse domain of *some* relation that satisfies (8). But then every object becomes extensional; for every object has something identical with it, and identity satisfies (8). If this move is declared unfair, then to show some given object x to be extensional according to the proposal, take as R some many-one relation having x in its converse domain. It is always easy enough to concoct one. If again this is counted as trickery, take R to be an appropriate reflexive and antisymmetric relation. And so on. The fact is that there is no hope of distinguishing so-called "intensions" from "extensions" *via* formal properties of relations. Given any formal property of relations possessed by at least one non-empty relation, every object appears in the converse domain of at least one relation that possesses the property.[7]

6.   Sense has been made of contrasting class abstraction and attribute abstraction with respect to extensionality. Similarly with membership and exemplification. Sense can be made also of a like contrast between class theory and attribute theory. It is convenient to think of a pure theory of classes as a theory with standard formalization[8] in which the sole nonlogical symbol is the two-place predicate 'ϵ', interpreted in the sense of 'is a member of'. So also in the case of a pure theory of attributes, though here of course 'ϵ' will have the sense rather of 'exemplifies'. But a pure attribute theory will part company with a pure class theory over the formula

(9) $(x)(y)((z)(z \in x \leftrightarrow z \in y) \to x = y)$.

This will be a theorem of any pure theory of classes but presumably of no pure theory of attributes. Perhaps attribute theory and class theory will naturally diverge in other ways as well. Even so, we have a significant difference between the two, one for which there is perhaps no better word than 'extensionality'. But it is a difference between *theories*, and I know of no coherent way in which it can be supposed to carry over to the objects dealt with in the theories.

It does, of course, reflect a difference between the *concepts* class and attribute: it is true of the one, but not of the other, that no two things falling under it have the same members. Indeed, it is perhaps only this that Quine intended to point out in the passage from *Set Theory and Its Logic*. He there speaks, after all, of "the difference . . . between class and attribute" rather than of the difference between classes and attributes. Still, there are two points to be borne in mind. In the first place, the mentioned respect in which class differs from attribute is a respect in which it differs also from hosts of other concepts: dog, novel, person, and so on. Hence it seems inappropriate to take the difference to consist in divergence with respect to some presumed property of "extensionality." In the second place, that there is this difference between the two concepts does not imply that nothing falls under both. Put abstractly, the situation is this. Associated with a certain concept C is a sufficient condition for identity of things falling under C, that is, a condition satisfied by a pair (x, y) of things falling under C only if x is identical with y. But the condition is not thus associated with a certain concept A. It follows that C and A are distinct concepts. But it does not follow that nothing falls under both C and A. This is easily seen by taking C to be the concept father and A the concept parent. If x is a father and y is a father and something z is a child of x and of y, then x is identical with y. But this does not carry over to parent, even though all fathers are parents.[9]

7.   Intensionality is apparently sometimes thought to consist not in the failure of some sufficient condition of identity but in the presence of a certain necessary condition. On this view, an object x is intensional just in case it is such that

(10) $(y)(y = x \rightarrow \Box y = x)$.

Extensional objects are, in contrast, those that may be identical without being necessarily so. Now, we may suppose no class satisfies (10). But it is difficult to see that this distinguishes classes from attributes—or, for that matter, from objects of any sort whatever. For, as Quine has pointed out, every object "is specifiable in contingently coincident ways if specifiable at all."[10] Hence every object, or at any rate every specifiable object, appears to satisfy (10). Consider, for example, the attribute of being a marine mammal alive in 1940. This, as it happens, is the first attribute mentioned on page 120 of the revised edition of Quine's *Mathematical Logic*. But only as it happens. The identity is contingent, and it appears to follow that the attribute in question does not satisfy (10).

I say "appears" because it might be argued that the attribute of being a marine mammal alive in 1940 *is* necessarily identical with the attribute mentioned on page 120 of the revised edition of Quine's *Mathematical Logic*, not on the ground that the statement of identity is a necessary truth, but on the ground that otherwise we should have to allow that the attribute in question might have been some other attribute, which is surely absurd. Implied here is the view that being identical with the attribute of being a marine mamal alive in 1940 is *essential* to that attribute—and this no matter how the attribute is designated. Perhaps so. But if this is good reason for saying the attribute satisfies (10), there is equally good reason for saying that every object satisfies (10). If it is absurd to suppose that the attribute in question could have been some other attribute, it is equally absurd to suppose of *any* object that it could have been some other object.

Suppose now the universal quantifier '(y)' to be deleted from (10) and view the result as a schema in which the schematic letters 'x' and 'y' are understood to be replaceable by class designations and attribute designations. What has just been noticed is that given any attribute designation α there is some attribute designation α' such that, if α is put for 'x' and α' for 'y' in the thus obtained schema, the result will be false. The same holds, of course, for class designations. But suppose the replacements for 'x' and 'y' to be limited to attribute abstracts (as we might call them), that is, to expressions of the form 'the attribute of being . . .'. It is then not unplausible to suppose that the schema will without exception yield truths. Not so, however, in the case of class abstracts, that is, expressions of the form 'the class of all objects x such that . . . x . . .'. If a particular class abstract is put for 'x', it will be an easy matter to find another such that, if it is put for 'y', the resulting statement will be false. There is thus a difference between class abstracts and attribute abstracts, and recognition of this is perhaps what underlies efforts to distinguish classes from attributes *via* the open sentence (10).

The difference is, however, a difference between two sorts of singular terms; and it remains to be demonstrated that it reflects a difference in the designated objects. Perhaps it will be claimed that every class x is such that

(11)   if α is a class abstract designating x, then some class abstract α' designates x even though $\ulcorner \sim \Box (\alpha = \alpha') \urcorner$ is true

whereas no attribute x is such that

(12)   if α is an attribute abstract designating x, then some attribute abstract α' designates x even though $\ulcorner \sim \Box (\alpha = \alpha') \urcorner$ is true.

Granting this claim, we still do not have a difference between classes and attributes—and this for a reason that should by now be familiar: what is said to be true of all classes is simply not what is said to be false of all attributes.

8.   The adjectives 'extensional' and 'intensional' are, I believe, overworked. Still, as I have tried to indicate, they can be intelligibly used to mark significant contrasts. But I doubt that one of these is a contrast between classes and attributes.

Notes

This essay was first published in *Noûs* 2 (1968): 229–246.

1. W. V. Quine, *From a Logical Point of View*, 2d ed., rev. (New York: Harper and Row, 1963), p. 107.

2. W. V. Quine, *Mathematical Logic*, rev. ed. (Cambridge, Mass.: Harvard University Press, 1951), p. 120.

3. W. V. Quine, *Word and Object* (Cambridge, Mass.: MIT Press, 1960), p. 209.

4. The terminology and concept were suggested to me by Richard Sharvy.

5. W. V. Quine, *Set Theory and Its Logic* (Cambridge, Mass.: Harvard University Press, 1963), pp. 1–2.

6. See, for example, *Mathematical Logic*, rev. ed., p. 135.

7. I call a property of relations *formal* just in case it is present in any given relation only if it is present in all relations ordinally similar to the given relation. And two relations R and S are *ordinally similar* just in case there is a one-one function f from the field of R onto the field of S such that, for all x and y in the field of R, xRy if and only if $f(x)Sf(y)$.

8. In the sense of Alfred Tarski, Andrzej Mostowski, and Raphael M. Robinson, *Undecidable Theories* (Amsterdam: North-Holland, 1953), pp. 5–6.

9. The example was suggested to me by George Landrum.

10. W. V. Quine, *The Ways of Paradox* (New York: Random House, 1966), p. 182.

Scattered Objects

According to Hobbes, "a body is that, which having no dependence on our thought, is coincident or coextended with some part of space."[1] Bodies in Hobbes's sense are material objects in ours; so at any rate I shall assume. And I shall assume also that his definition is correct at least in its implication that coincidence with some part of space is required of anything that is to count as a material object. But what is to count as a part of space?

By a *region of space*, or simply a *region*, let us agree to understand any set of points of space. And by a *receptacle* let us understand a region of space with which it is possible some material object should be, in Hobbes's phrase, coincident or coextended. Plainly, not every region is a receptacle. The null region is not; neither is any region that consists of a single point or, for that matter, of any finite number of points. Nor are higher cardinalities by themselves sufficient: no region exceeds a straight line in sheer number of members;[2] yet straight lines, along with curves and surfaces, are not receptacles. How, then, are receptacles to be characterized?

Let p be any point of space. By an *open sphere about p* is meant a region the members of which are all and only those points that are less than some fixed distance from p. In other words, a region A is an open sphere about the point p if and only if there is a positive real number r such that A is the set of all those points whose distance from p is less than r. A region that is an open sphere about some point or other is called simply an *open sphere*.

Every open sphere is, I suggest, a receptacle. There are of course neither minimal nor maximal open spheres: given any open sphere, no matter how large or small, there is a larger and a smaller. My suggestion will thus disturb those for whom material objects are "moderate-sized specimens of dry goods."[3] But surely not all material objects *are* moderate-sized. Heavenly bodies are bodies, some of them very large; and antibodies are bodies, extremely small ones. Given these actualities, why impose bounds on the possibilities?

Others will be disturbed because they think of receptacles as closed. Let me explain. A point p is said to be a *boundary point* of a region A if and only if every open sphere about p has a non-null intersection with both A and the complement of A (where the *complement* of a region is the set of points of space not in the region). Otherwise put, p is a boundary point of A just in case every open sphere about p has in it points of A and points of the complement of A. To illustrate, let S be the open sphere of radius r about p and let q be a point whose distance from p is exactly r. Then, every open sphere about q will intersect both S and the complement of S; and hence q is a boundary point of S. In fact, the boundary points of S are precisely those points that are like q in that their distance from p is exactly r. A point whose distance from p is less than r will be the center of an open sphere included in S; and a point whose distance from p is greater than r will be the center of an open sphere included in the complement of S. Now, a region, spherical or otherwise, is said to be *open* just in case none of its boundary points is a member of it and *closed* just in case all its boundary points are members of it. We have just seen that an open sphere is, appropriately enough, an open region: an open sphere and its surface have no points in common. And it is precisely this that will cause some to resist the suggestion that every open sphere is a receptacle. Their intuitions tell them that a receptacle should be closed. Descartes's told him otherwise. After explaining that what he calls the "external place" of a body is "the superficies of the surrounding body," he remarks that "by superficies we do not here mean any portion of the surrounding body, but merely the extremity which is between the surrounding body and that surrounded."[4] I shall follow Descartes, though I should have no idea how to defend my choice; indeed, the issue seems hardly worthy of serious dispute. There is, however, a possible misconception that needs to be cleared away, a misconception perhaps latent in Descartes's use of 'between'. If receptacles are open, it might seem that bodies never touch, since something—if only a very fine something—is always in between. But this *is* a misconception. On either view body x touches body y when and only when at least one boundary point of the region occupied by x is also a boundary point of the region occupied by y. The only issue is whether such a boundary point must belong to the regions occupied by x and y. And it is this issue that seems hardly worthy of serious dispute.

I shall assume, then, that every receptacle is an open region. But not every receptacle is an open sphere; bodies do, after all, come in other shapes. To allow for the endless possibilities, it will perhaps be suggested that an open region be counted a receptacle provided only that it is non-null. Receptacles would thus come to be identified with non-null open regions, spherical or otherwise. A good many unwanted regions would thereby be excluded; regions with only a finite number of points, curves, and surfaces, for example. But the suggestion will not do. Consider a region the members of which are all the points of an open sphere S save for a single point p. Consider, that is, $S - \{p\}$, where S is an open sphere and p is a point in S. We are reluctant, I think, to suppose this a receptacle.

Surely no material object could occupy all the points of an open sphere save one. It is not that objects never have holes; it is rather that holes are never so small. Yet $S - \{p\}$ is open, for it contains none of its boundary points.

Only some, then, among open regions are receptacles. Which ones? To investigate the question we shall need the notions of the interior and the closure of a region. By the *interior* of a region is meant the set of all points in the region that are not boundary points of the region. Note that a region is open if and only if it is identical with its interior, for no boundary point of an open region is a member of the region and interiors themselves are always open. The *closure* of a region is the union of the region with the set of all its boundary points. Just as a region is open if and only if it is identical with its interior, so a region is closed if and only if it is identical with its closure; for a closed region includes the set of its boundary points and closures themselves are always closed. Now consider again the region $S - \{p\}$. The point p is a boundary point of the region, for every open sphere about p intersects both $S - \{p\}$ and its complement. But as boundary points go, p is peculiarly situated, for it is also a member of the interior of the closure of $S - \{p\}$. Close $S - \{p\}$ and you pick up p along with the points on the surface of S; take the interior of the resulting region and you keep p, though you lose the points on the surface of S. In view of this peculiarity of situation, let us say that p is an 'inner' boundary point of $S - \{p\}$, where in general an *inner boundary point* of a region is a boundary point of the region that is also a member of the interior of the closure of the region. It is possession of an inner boundary point that leads us to exclude the region $S - \{p\}$ from the class of receptacles; and, accordingly, I suggest that at least a necessary condition for a non-null open region to qualify as a receptacle is that it have no inner boundary points.

It is easily shown that open regions having no inner boundary points are precisely those regions that are identical with the interiors of their closures. And a region that is identical with the interior of its closure is known as an *open domain*.[5] So the present suggestion comes to this: a region of space is a receptacle only if it is a non-null open domain. Another example may serve to clarify the suggestion. Imagine an open sphere cut by a plane. Let the open region on one side of the plane be A and that on the other be B. Both A and B are open domains, but their union is not; for the points on the plane other than those on the surface of the sphere are inner boundary points of $A \cup B$. Otherwise put, since the points on the plane that are not on the surface of the sphere are members of the interior of the closure of $A \cup B$ but not of $A \cup B$, $A \cup B$ is not identical with the interior of its closure and is therefore not an open domain.[6] Thus $A \cup B$ is not a receptacle: no object can be coincident or coextended with it. This is not to exclude the possibility of cracks; it is simply to insist that cracks are never so fine. Of course, the interior of the closure of $A \cup B$ is a receptacle. It is in fact the open sphere with which we began. Thus a body can occupy a region that *includes* $A \cup B$. But such a region must include as well the set of inner boundary points of $A \cup B$.

The proposition that every receptacle is a non-null open domain is not apt to meet with serious opposition. But what of its converse? Is every non-null open domain a receptacle? Here there is likely to be controversy. The issue turns on the notion of connectedness, and we therefore need to see exactly what this notion is.

It is customary to say that two regions are *separated* if and only if the intersection of either with the closure of the other is null. Thus, in the example just discussed, the regions A and B are separated: take the closure of either and you pick up no points of the other. That is, no point or boundary point of either is a member of the other. Obviously, if two regions are separated, their intersection is null. But two regions with a null intersection need not be separated. Thus the intersection of A with the closure of B is null; yet A and the closure of B are not separated, for there are boundary points of A in the closure of B. Now, a region is said to be *disconnected* if and only if it is the union of two non-null separated regions; and a region is *connected* if and only if it is not disconnected. Thus, keeping to the same example, $A \cup B$ is disconnected. In contrast, the interior of the closure of $A \cup B$ is connected, for there do not exist two non-null separated regions of which it is the union. It is a connected open domain. But it is by no means the case that all open domains are connected. Consider, for example, two open spheres that touch at a single point. The closure of either intersected with the other is null, and the two are therefore separated. Hence their union is disconnected. But it is an open domain: none of its boundary points is inner, even the point of contact. Or consider two open spheres situated at some distance from each other. Their union is evidently a disconnected open domain.

Connected open domains, as long as they are non-null, presumably present no problems. Each is a receptacle. But disconnected open domains are another matter. Are they receptacles? I shall defend the position that they are, though admittedly I have no conclusive argument.

Let us say that a material object is *scattered* just in case the region of space it occupies is disconnected. That there are scattered material objects seems to me beyond reasonable doubt. If natural scientists are to be taken at their word, all the familiar objects of everyday life are scattered. But I have in mind nothing so esoteric. Rather, it seems to me a matter of simple observation that among material objects some are scattered. Consider, for example, my copy of McTaggart's *The Nature of Existence*. There surely *is* such a thing; and it is a *material* thing, even a moderate-sized specimen of dry goods. After all, it is made of paper and certain other materials; it weighs roughly three and a quarter pounds; it is bound in a hard black cover; it occupies a certain region of space, into which it was recently moved; and so on. But it is scattered, for volume 1 is in Cambridge and volume 2 is in Boston. Each volume occupies, or at least to the ordinary eye appears to occupy, a connected open domain; but these regions are separated, and hence their union is disconnected. This example will bring to mind hosts of similar ones. Let me mention two others of a somewhat different kind. There is at the moment a pipe on my desk. Its stem has been removed, but it remains a pipe for all that; otherwise no pipe could survive a thorough cleaning. So at the moment the pipe occupies a disconnected region of space, a region which appears to common sense to be the disconnected open domain that is the union of the connected open domains occupied by the two parts. Consider, finally, some printed inscription: the token of 'existence' on the title page of my copy of McTaggart's *The Nature of Existence*, for example. Presumably it is a material object—a "mound of ink," as some say. But evidently it occupies a disconnected region of space.

If there are scattered objects, then some disconnected open domains are receptacles. It does not follow that all are. Still, once some have been admitted, it seems arbitrary to exclude any—just as it seems arbitrary to impose limits on the size or shape of receptacles. And it should be remembered that to call a region a receptacle is not to say that some object is in fact coincident or coextended with it but only to say that this is not impossible. All this inclines me to identify receptacles with non-null open domains.[7]

An interesting question remains, however. To introduce it, let me mention an objection that is apt to be brought against the contention that my copy of *The Nature of Existence* is a scattered material object. Some will be inclined to say, with Leibniz, that my copy of *The Nature of Existence* is a "being by aggregation," not a "true unity."[8] Leibniz would not himself have taken this to imply that it is not a material object—only that it is not what he called an "individual substance." His notion of individual substance aside, however, some will still be inclined to say that my copy of *The Nature of Existence* is a mere 'plurality' or 'aggregate' or 'assemblage' of material objects and not properly speaking a single material object in its own right. It is no more correct, they will say, to suppose there is one thing composed or made up of my copy of volume 1 and my copy of volume 2 than to suppose there is one thing composed or made up of, say, the Eiffel Tower and Old North Church. We do speak of my copy of *The Nature of Existence* as if it were a single thing, and there is no parallel to this in the case of the Eiffel Tower and Old North Church. But it will be claimed that this is reflective merely of our special human interests, not of the metaphysical status of the entities involved. The two volumes are a mere assemblage, just as are the tower and the church.

The obscurity of the objection makes a direct response difficult. What exactly is meant by "a mere plurality or aggregate or assemblage"? And what sense is to be made of the claim that my copy of *The Nature of Existence*—or anything else, for that matter—is not 'one' thing? Furthermore, one wonders how far the objection is to be carried. The alleged defect in my copy of *The Nature of Existence* is surely not simply that the region occupied by volume 1 is at some distance from that occupied by volume 2. Even were the two volumes side by side, separated only by a plane, they would presumably still be said not to constitute or compose a single material object. The interior of the closure of the union of the region occupied by the one volume with that occupied by the other would be a receptacle, but an unoccupied one. But then why not argue, as Leibniz did, that *no* material thing is properly speaking *one* thing? Any connected open domain can be cut by a plane in such a way as to leave two open domains whose union is disconnected. Therefore, Leibniz reasoned, every corporeal object is in theory divisible and what is in theory divisible is only a being by aggregation.[9]

In spite of its obscurity and the uncertainty of its extent of applicability, the objection brings to the surface a question of some interest. *Is* there a material object composed of the Eiffel Tower and Old North Church? In general, is it the case that for each non-null set of material objects there is a material object composed of the members of the set? The question needs sharper formulation, and for that some additional technical terminology is required.

A set M of material objects will be said to *cover* a region A if and only if A is included in the union of the receptacles occupied by members of M. If A simply is that union, then obviously M covers A. For example, the set the members of which are the Eiffel Tower and Old North Church covers the region which is the union of the receptacle occupied by the Eiffel Tower and the receptacle occupied by Old North Church. In particular, if x is any material object, the set having x as sole member covers the region occupied by x. Clearly, if M covers A, then M covers any region included in A. Hence a given region may be covered by more than one set. The region occupied by Old North Church, for example, is covered by the set having Old North Church as sole member and also by the set the members of which are the Eiffel Tower and Old North Church. If M covers A, then A is included in the interior of the closure of the union of the receptacles occupied by members of M. But notice that M may cover A and yet fail to cover the interior of the closure of A. Thus, although a set the members of which are two books situated side by side covers the union of the receptacles occupied by the books, it does not cover the interior of the closure of that union.

If and only if a set covers a region, the region itself will be said to be *covered*. It should be noticed that if each member of a collection of regions is covered, so is the union of the collection. Indeed, so is any region included in the union of the collection.

Given the notion of a covered region, a proposition I shall call the Covering Principle can be formulated: *If A is any non-null covered open region, there exists exactly one material object x such that the region occupied by x is the interior of the closure of A.* Our question is whether this principle, or more especially a certain consequence of it, is true.

A preliminary word of explanation. Given a non-null covered open region A, the Covering Principle guarantees that A is the region occupied by a unique material object if and only if A is the interior of its closure, that is, if and only if A is an open domain. This accords with our requirement that only open domains be counted receptacles. It is in fact easily shown that the Covering Principle runs no risk of violating that requirement; for the interior of the closure of any set is an open domain. But then, it may be asked, why limit the principle to non-null covered *open* regions? The answer is that otherwise there would be a conflict with the requirement that receptacles be non-null; for the interior of the closure of a non-open region may well be the null set.[10]

Notice now the power of the principle. To use a familiar and convenient metaphor, it provides for the generation by composition of new objects from old in somewhat the fashion of the Power Set Axiom in Set Theory. Given three objects in separated receptacles A, B, and C, there will exist four others. For if A, B, and C are covered, so are each of $A \cup B$, $A \cup C$, $B \cup C$, and $A \cup B \cup C$; and if A, B, and C are separated, these unions are distinct from one another and from each of A, B, and C. In general, given a set M of n objects situated in pairwise separated receptacles, there will exist $2^n - (n + 1)$ further objects, each compounded of members of m. A dozen dollar bills in your wallet makes for 4,083 additional objects in your wallet—none of them dollar bills, however. And this is by no means the end. For the Covering Principle provides for generation of objects by division as well as by composition. Let A be a covered receptacle, and for purposes of simplification suppose it connected. Then A is the interior of the closure of the union of two connected and separated receptacles B and C, so situated that B lies on one side of a plane that intersects A while C lies on the other. Clearly, the same is in turn true of B and C, and of the receptacles into which they are thus divided, and so on without end. So there corresponds to A an infinity of connected and pairwise separated receptacles each of which is covered. The Covering Principle provides that each of these receptacles is the region of space occupied by a unique material object. Now, it is easily seen that if any region is covered, at least one connected receptacle is covered. Hence, by the Covering Principle, if there is one material object, there are infinitely many.[11]

Our present concern is less with division than composition. It will therefore be of use to extract from the Covering Principle an appropriately weaker principle, one directed squarely at the issue of scattered objects. First a definition. A material object x will be said to *fuse* a set M of material objects just in case the receptacle occupied by x meets two conditions: (i) it includes the receptacles occupied by members of M, and (ii) it is included in every receptacle that includes the receptacles occupied by members of M. More simply, x fuses M if and only if the region occupied by x is the smallest receptacle that includes the receptacles occupied by members of M. In the case of any collection of receptacles, there is always a smallest receptacle that includes each member of the collection—namely, the interior of the closure of the union of the collection. So we might as well have said: x fuses M if and only if the region occupied by x is precisely the interior of the closure of the union of the receptacles occupied by members of M. My copy of *The Nature of Existence*, for example, fuses the set whose members are my copy of volume 1 and my copy of volume 2; and the object, if such there be, composed of the Eiffel Tower and Old North Church fuses the set whose members are the Eiffel Tower and Old North Church. Notice that any material object fuses the set having that object as sole member. And notice also a sort of transitivity: if x fuses a set the members of which in turn fuse other sets, x fuses the union of those other sets.

Can distinct objects fuse the same set? Not if the Covering Principle is true. If x and y fuse M, the receptacle occupied by x is the very same as that occupied by y; and the Covering Principle tells us that no receptacle is the region occupied by more than one object. Can there be a non-null set of material objects which no material object fuses? Again, not if the Covering Principle is true. For the union of the receptacles occupied by members of the set is a covered non-null open region the interior of the closure of which is the smallest receptacle that includes the receptacles occupied by members of the set. Thus the Covering Principle entails what I shall call the Fusion Principle: *If M is any non-null set of material objects, there is exactly one material object x such that x fuses M.* According to this principle, each non-null set of material objects has a unique *fusion*: a material object so situated that its receptacle is the interior of the closure of the union of the receptacles occupied by members of the set. If the Fusion Principle is true, there really is a material object—exactly one, in fact—composed of the Eiffel Tower and Old North Church. It is composed of them in the sense that the region it covers is the union of the regions they cover.

I have taken the word 'fusion' from the exposition given by Leonard and Goodman of the so-called calculus of individuals.[12] And it may be instructive at this point to digress briefly from our main concerns in order to make contact with the principal ideas of that calculus.

Let E be a non-empty set, and let R be a relation that is reflexive in E, antisymmetric in E, and transitive in E. (We are to think of R as a part-whole relation among elements of E, though of course that plays no role in the abstract development.) Two elements of E are said to *overlap* just in case they have a part in common; that is, if x and y are in E, x overlaps y if and only if some element of E bears R to both x and y. Now, the ordered pair (R, E) is a *mereology* just in case two further conditions are satisfied: (i) if x and y are members of E such that every member of E that overlaps x also overlaps y, then x is part of y; (ii) there exists a function f from the collection of non-empty subsets of E into E such that, for each non-empty subset A of E, a member of E overlaps $f(A)$ if and only if it overlaps some member of A.[13] As thus defined, mereologies are natural models of the Leonard-Goodman calculus.

Examples of mereologies are readily available. In fact, if B is the set of non-zero elements of a complete Boolean algebra and R is the inclusion relation among elements of B, (B, R) is a mereology in which the Boolean join plays the part of the mereological function f.[14] More pertinent examples are provided by the following small theorem:

> Let N be a non-empty family of non-empty open domains of a topological space. And suppose N is such that (i) the interior of the closure of the union of each non-empty subset of N is itself in N; (ii) if A and B are members of N such that $A - B$ is non-empty, then the interior of the closure of $A - B$ is in N. Then $(N, \subseteq)$ is a mereology with respect to which the mereological function f is the function that assigns to each non-empty subset of N the interior of the closure of its union.

Notice that the theorem holds for any topological space—that is, for any space defined simply via a specification of the subsets that are to count as open, where the notion of an open set is subject only to the usual condition that among the open sets are to be found all unions of collections of open sets and all intersections of finite collections of open sets. Of greater interest for our purposes is the following corollary. Assume the Covering Principle; and assume that each material object occupies a unique receptacle, where receptacles are non-empty open domains of a topological space. Let M be a non-empty set of material objects that satisfies two closure conditions: (i) the fusion of each non-empty subset of M is itself in M; (ii) if x and y are elements of M such that the receptacle of x minus the receptacle of y is non-empty, then the material object that occupies the interior of the closure of the receptacle of x minus the receptacle of y is in M. (Note that the existence of this object is a consequence of the Covering

Principle.) Then, if P is the relation that an element x of M bears to an element y of M just in case the receptacle of x is included in the receptacle of y, (M, P) is a mereology with respect to which the mereological function f is the function that assigns to each non-empty subset of M its fusion.

So much for connections with the calculus of individuals. Let us return to our main themes.

As already noticed, every material object is the fusion of at least one set, namely, the set having that object as sole member. Commonly, an object will be the fusion of other sets as well. A scattered object, for example, will be the fusion of the set having itself as sole member; but it will also be the fusion of the set of those objects that occupy maximal connected receptacles included in the receptacle of the scattered object. Indeed, if the Covering Principle is true, every object will be the fusion of endlessly many sets. The Covering Principle provides for fission as well as fusion, and what is obtained at any stage by fission is a set of which the original object is the fusion. Any given object occupies a receptacle; and covered receptacles are, as we have seen, endlessly divisible into further covered receptacles. The given object will be the fusion of the set of objects occupying the subreceptacles obtained at any stage of the division—provided, of course, the division is exhaustive, in the sense that the receptacle occupied by the object is the interior of the closure of the union of those subreceptacles. To think of an object in this way will seem more or less natural depending on our willingness to count as genuine the alleged occupants of the various subreceptacles. Two halves of an intact baseball will perhaps seem material objects only in some contrived sense, and the baseball itself will then not naturally be thought of as the fusion of a set the members of which are the two halves. Similarly with bottles, doughnuts, and sheets of paper. But it is otherwise with automobiles, books of matches, and salami sandwiches. In these cases we take rather easily to the idea that the object is the fusion of a set of other objects—not just any set of alleged objects yielded by the Covering Principle, of course, but a set consisting of what are in the natural way thought of as parts of the object.

To become quite specific, consider some particular book of matches, and for ease of reference call it 'Charlie'. It is altogether natural to think of Charlie as consisting of twenty matches, a paper base to which they are attached, a surrounding paper cover, and an appropriately placed metal staple. That is to say, Charlie is quite naturally thought of as the fusion of the set that has these various objects as members. Thus, calling the set in question 'A', we are inclined to assert

(1)   Charlie = the fusion of A.

Of course, we are not prepared to regard every set the members of which are twenty matches, a paper cover, and so on as having a book of matches as its fusion. The objects in the set must be properly put together. But the objects in A are properly put together. And the region of space Charlie occupies is the interior of the closure of the union of the receptacles occupied by members of A.

But now let us remove a single match from Charlie and place it some distance from him, while putting him back where he was—that is, putting him in a receptacle properly included in the receptacle he earlier occupied. Charlie, we should all agree, has undergone a change. He has lost a part, as material objects often do. He now consists of the various objects he consisted of before, save for the removed match. The receptacle he now occupies is the interior of the closure of the union of the receptacles occupied by members of $A - \{z\}$, where z is the match that has been removed. Just as we were earlier inclined to assert (1), so we are now inclined to assert

(2)   Charlie = the fusion of $(A - \{z\})$.

But we can hardly deny

(3)   The fusion of $A \neq$ the fusion of $(A - \{z\})$.

And so we seem to be in violation of the principle that no one thing is identical with diverse things.

It will no doubt be suggested at once that the appearance of paradox is removed once time is properly taken into account. Charlie *was* identical with the fusion of A but is *now* identical with the fusion of $(A - \{z\})$; or, avoiding tensed verbs:

(4)   At t, Charlie = the fusion of A

whereas

(5)   At t', Charlie = the fusion of $(A - \{z\})$,

where it is to be understood that t' is appropriately later than t. If it is pointed out that (3), (4), and (5) together entail

(6)   At t', Charlie $\neq$ the fusion of A,

the response will be that this is no cause for alarm, since (4) and (6) are perfectly compatible.

But is it really possible for both (4) and (6) to be true? Their conjunction appears to imply that there is a certain object—namely, the fusion of A—with which Charlie is identical at t but not at t'. And this surely is impossible. It is impossible for Charlie to have been identical with one object, the fusion of A, and then to have become identical with another object, the fusion of $(A - \{z\})$. No object can be identical with something for a while and then become identical with something else. Once identical with one thing, never identical with another.[15]

It will be pointed out that the conjunction of (4) and (6) does not imply that there is an object with which Charlie is identical at t but not at t'. According to (4), Charlie has at t the property of being sole fuser of A; and according to (6), he lacks that property at t'. But this no more requires Charlie to have been temporarily identical with the fusion of A than the fact that Lyndon Johnson had and then lost the property of being president of the United States requires him to have been temporarily identical with a certain object with which Richard Nixon became identical. Thus (4) amounts to

(7) (x) (x fuses A at t iff x = Charlie),

(5) amounts to

(8) (x) (x fuses $(A - \{z\})$ at t' iff x = Charlie),

and (6) amounts to

(9) $\sim (x)$ (x fuses A at t' iff x = Charlie).

And it is evidently quite possible that all these should be true.

There is reason to doubt, however, whether this ends the matter. If the Fusion Principle is true, some object is the fusion of A at t', a certain scattered object we may call 'Harry'. Now why should we not say that Harry fused A at t? We have treated Charlie as a continuant, an object that endures for a period of time during which it undergoes change. It would seem only fair to treat Harry in the same way. Like Charlie, Harry underwent a certain change. He occupied a connected receptacle at t and a disconnected one at t'. Harry became a scattered object.

It would appear, then, that Harry has as good a claim to having been sole fuser of A at t as does Charlie. If (7) is true, so, it would appear, is

(10) (x) (x fuses A at t iff x = Harry).

Now, from (7) and (10) it presumably follows that at t Charlie and Harry were identical. But they are not identical now. And so once more we seem to have on our hands a temporary identity.

And another is in the offing. For consider Sam, the object which at t occupied the receptacle now occupied by Charlie. Sam is right where he was at t. He has of course undergone a change: at t he and z were in contact, the boundaries of their receptacles intersected; and this is no longer the case. But his position has not changed. The receptacle he now occupies is the one he occupied at t—namely, the interior of the closure of the union of the receptacles occupied by members of $A - \{z\}$. In short, Sam is at t' the fusion of $(A - \{z\})$. Or, to adopt the preferred form,

(11) (x) $(x$ fuses $(A - \{z\})$ at t' iff $x =$ Sam).

But from (8) and (11) it presumably follows that at t' Charlie and Sam are identical, which they certainly were not at t. Though now identical, Charlie and Sam were once diverse. Or so it seems.

How are these temproary identities to be avoided? Perhaps some will say that there really is no such object as Harry: Charlie exists and so does the removed match, but those two objects do not compose or make up a single scattered object. But if there are scattered objects at all—and I have urged that there are—why object to Harry? There would appear to be no difference in principle between Harry, on the one hand, and my copy of *The Nature of Existence*, on the other. It has to be conceded that there is no readily available response to a request to say what sort or kind of object Harry is. But it is not clear to me that this is indicative of anything more than a paucity of readily available schemes of classification, a paucity resulting from quite parochial concerns of human beings. It is not out of the question that objects composed in the way Harry is should come to be of some interest; we should not then be at a loss to find an appropriate kind or sort.

Short of denying outright the existence of Harry, it might be contended that he begins to exist only at t', that he starts his career with Charlie's loss of z. This suggestion does have the merit of preserving the Fusion Principle while removing the necessity to puzzle over the apparent temporary identity of Charlie with Harry. But I see nothing else to be said for it. Bodies do from time to time become scattered. What reason is there to suppose this is not the situation with Harry? And in any case, what is to be done about Sam? There is no plausibility at all in an outright denial of his existence, and it seems obvious enough that his duration coincides with Charlie's. To deny the existence of Harry or to claim that he begins to exist only upon z's removal from Charlie simply leaves the problem of Sam untouched.

An alternative suggestion, one that not only preserves the Fusion Principle but also has the required generality, is that Charlie is really identical with Harry. On this view, Charlie fuses A at t and also at t'. He does not lose a part; he becomes scattered. As for Sam, well, once Charlie is thought of as scattered at t', we are free to think of Sam as fusing $A - \{z\}$ at t' without thereby implying a temporary identity of Sam with Charlie. There is simply no time at which Charlie and Sam occupy the same receptacle.

In spite of its neatness, I think this view will seem less than wholly satisfactory. We are all, I believe, inclined to think that after the removal of z Charlie survives as a nonscattered object. If asked to give his present location, we should indicate a certain connected receptacle, the one occupied by Sam. Perhaps our stake in Charlie's nonscattered persistence is not especially great, but it is there all the same; and certainly in other, analogous cases the view under discussion would seem quite unacceptable. If a branch falls from a tree, the tree does not thereby become scattered; and a human body does not become scattered upon loss of a bit of fingernail.

At this point some will despair of preserving the Fusion Principle. They will see no alternative to saying that Charlie and Harry, though distinct, nevertheless occupy the same receptacle at t and that Charlie and Sam, though again distinct objects, share a receptacle at t'. To take this position is to sacrifice the Fusion Principle by denying that exactly *one* thing fuses a given non-empty set of material objects. Both Charlie and Harry, according to this view, fuse A at t; neither has the property of being *sole* fuser of A at t. Similarly, neither Charlie nor Sam is sole fuser of $A - \{z\}$ at t; for at t' Charlie and Sam are spatially coincident.

This view seems to me to put undue strain on one's metaphysical imagination. Locke wrote: ". . . never finding, nor conceiving it possible, that two things of the same kind should exist in the same place at the same time, we rightly conclude, that, whatever exists anywhere at any time, excludes all of the same kind, and is there itself alone."[16] Are not Charlie and Harry two things of some one appropriate kind? Notice, furthermore, that it is not that just *two* material objects will, on this view, occupy the same receptacle at the same time; for it takes only a little ingenuity to find material objects other than Charlie and Harry with an equal claim to occupancy of that receptacle at t. To give some indication of the procedure involved, let us remove a second match from Charlie, place it some distance from z and from Charlie, and again put Charlie back where he was. Charlie has lost another part. In thus putting Charlie back where he was while leaving the position of z unchanged, we have also put Harry back where *he* was; he now occupies a receptacle properly included in the receptacle he occupied at t'. Harry too has lost a part. As a result, he has lost the property, which he had at t', of being sole fuser of A. But something now has that property, a certain scattered object whose receptacle is the union of two receptacles: the one occupied by Harry and the one occupied by the second removed match. Let us call that object 'Bill'. Now, there is no more reason to suppose that Bill just now came into existence than there is to suppose that Harry came into existence at t'. Indeed, there is no reason to deny that there is a material object which occupied a connected receptacle at t, became somewhat scattered at t', and has just now had its degree of scatter increased. Bill has as good a claim to occupancy of Charlie's receptacle at t as do Charlie and Harry. So, if Charlie and Harry shared a receptacle at t, they shared it with Bill.

If the Fusion Principle is to be retained, is there an alternative to acquiescence in the view that Charlie fails to survive in nonscattered form? I think there is. The view I have in mind involves recourse to what are sometimes called 'temporal parts' or 'stages' of objects. In the case at hand the suggestion would be that although Charlie and Harry are distinct objects, as is revealed by their divergent careers, a certain temporal part of Charlie is identical with a certain temporal part of Harry: Charlie's t-stage, as we might call it, is identical with Harry's t-stage. Similarly, although Charlie and Sam are distinct objects, Charlie's t'-stage is identical with Sam's t'-stage. No stage of Sam is identical with any stage of Harry, though it happens that each stage of Harry has some stage of Sam as a spatial part. What was loosely spoken of earlier as the fusion of A at t is now to be thought of as the fusion of the set of t-stages of members of A; and this object is simply Charlie's t-stage—that is, Harry's t-stage. Similarly, Harry's t'-stage is the fusion of the set of t'-stages of members of A; and Sam's t'-stage—that is, Charlie's t'-stage—is the fusion of the set of t'-stages of members of $A - \{z\}$. Charlie, Harry, and Sam thus come to be conceived as distinct four-dimensional objects, which happen on occasion to share a common temporal part.

Philosophers as divergent in their outlooks as McTaggart and Quine have found the doctrine of temporal parts congenial or even obviously true.[17] But there are others who exhibit something less than overwhelming enthusiasm for it.[18] To these latter I can say only that if they are drawn to the Fusion Principle and are at the same time reluctant to think that Charlie fails to survive in nonscattered form, they had better learn to live with temporal parts.

Notes

This essay was first published in Keith Lehrer, ed., *Analysis and Metaphysics* (Dordrecht: D. Reidel, 1975), pp. 153–171. Reprinted by permission of D. Reidel Publishing Company.

1. *De corpore*, 2.8.1.

2. Georg Cantor, "Ein Beitrag zur Mannigfaltigkeitslehre," *Journal für die reine und angewandte Mathematik* 84 (1878): 242–258.

3. The phrase, though not the view, is J. L. Austin's. See *Sense and Sensibilia* (Oxford: Clarendon Press, 1962), p. 8.

4. *Principles of Philosophy*, part 2, principle 15. (Trans. Elizabeth S. Haldane and G. R. T. Ross, Cambridge: Cambridge University Press, 1967.)

5. K. Kuratowski, *Topology*, vol. 1 (New York: Academic Press, 1966), p. 75. A common alternative is 'regular open set'.

6. Compare Paul R. Halmos, *Lectures on Boolean Algebras* (Princeton, N.J.: Van Nostrand, 1963), p. 14.

7. The identification of receptacles with non-null open domains was suggested to me by remarks made by Alfred Tarski in "Foundations of the Geometry of Solids," included in his *Logic, Semantics, and Metamathematics* (Oxford: Clarendon Press, 1956), pp. 24–29.

8. See, for example, his letter to Arnauld, 30 April 1687, in George R. Montgomery, trans., *Leibniz: Discourse on Metaphysics, Correspondence with Arnauld, and Monadology* (La Salle, Ill.: Open Court, 1945), esp. pp. 189–191.

9. "Every extended mass may be considered as a composite of two or of a thousand others, and the only extension there is, is that by contact. Consequently, we shall never find a body of which we can say that it is really one substance; it will always be an aggregate of several." Leibniz, draft of the letter of 28 November–8 December 1686 to Arnauld, in Montgomery, *Leibniz*, pp. 149–157. The quotation is from pp. 154–155.

10. For instance, the interior of the closure of a region containing a single point. Any set the interior of the closure of which is null is called *nowhere dense*.

11. "The least corpuscle is actually subdivided *in infinitum* and contains a world of other creatures which would be wanting in the universe if that corpuscle was an atom, that is, a body of one entire piece without subdivision." Leibniz, fourth letter to Clarke, in Leroy E. Loemker, trans. and ed., *Leibniz: Philosophical Papers and Letters*, 2d ed. (Dordrecht: Reidel, 1970), pp. 687–691. The quotation is from p. 691.

12. Henry S. Leonard and Nelson Goodman, "The Calculus of Individuals and Its Uses," *Journal of Symbolic Logic* 5 (1940): 45–55. I have not had access to the earlier expositions given by Lesniewski, for references to which see the bibliography in Eugene C. Luschei, *The Logical Systems of Lesniewski* (Amsterdam: North-Holland, 1962).

13. More economical characterizations are known. See, for instance, Tarski's "Foundations of the Geometry of Solids."

14. See Tarski, *Logic, Semantics, and Metamathematics*, p. 333n.

15. Compare David Wiggins, *Identity and Spatio-Temporal Continuity* (Oxford: Blackwell, 1967), p. 68.

16. *Essay Concerning Human Understanding*, bk. 2, chap. 27, section 1. And compare Aquinas: "nec est possibile, secundum naturam, duo corpora esse simul in eodem loco, qualiacumque corpora sint." (*Summa theologiae*, I, q. 67, a. 2, *in corpore*.) See also Aristotle, *Physics*, 209a6.

17. See J. M. E. McTaggart, *The Nature of Existence*, vol. 1 (Cambridge: Cambridge University Press, 1921), p. 176; W. V. Quine, *From a Logical Point of View*, 2d ed., rev. (New York: Harper and Row, 1963), pp. 65–79.

18. Thus C. D. Broad: "It is plainly contrary to common sense to say that the phases in the history of a thing are parts of the thing." (*Examination of McTaggart's Philosophy*, vol. 1, Cambridge: Cambridge University Press, 1933, pp. 349–350.)

On the Logical Problem of the Trinity

Early on in his treatise on the Trinity, Augustine remarks that "in no other subject is error more dangerous, or inquiry more laborious, or the discovery of truth more rewarding."[1] Augustine is right about the difficulty of the subject; and I too think, though for reasons that would not in the first instance have been his, that the subject is one in which it is especially important to distinguish truth from falsity. Augustine's primary concern was religious: on the matter of the Trinity, the difference between true belief and false belief was all the difference between spiritual life and spiritual death. It is clear, however, that much of the laborious inquiry to which Augustine refers is philosophical. His own treatise testifies to his recognition that those who accept the doctrine of the Trinity must face fundamental and difficult problems of philosophical logic.[2] My aim here is to explain these problems. I hope to make clear how, though seemingly remote and arid, they bear directly on a matter that to many people has been of the utmost practical importance.

We shall need a preliminary account of what the doctrine of the Trinity is; I cannot assume general familiarity with it, even less can I assume its general acceptance. It is a doctrine about God the Father, God the Son, and God the Holy Spirit that achieved the status of dogma in the fourth century. It persists today, of course; but in seeking its definition I think we cannot do better than look to its patristic and medieval formulations. Here one naturally turns first to the creeds—especially to those that have, through continued liturgical use, become authoritative. Of these the most informative on Trinitarian matters is the Athanasian Creed, and I shall therefore take it as my point of departure.

The Athanasian Creed is of uncertain date and origin.[3] Indeed, scholars like to say that only two things are known with certainty about it: that it is not a creed, and that it was not composed by Athanasius. Throughout the Middle Ages it was attributed to Athanasius, whence its name; but the attribution is now known to have been incorrect, and perhaps the likeliest hypothesis is that it originated in southern France in the late fifth or early sixth century. Aquinas rightly observed that it is less a creed than an exposition of doctrine.[4] It is an exposition in particular of the doctrines of the Trinity and the Incarnation, and its Trinitarian portion reads as follows:

> Now this is the Catholic faith: that we worship one God in Trinity, and Trinity in unity, neither confusing the persons nor separating the substance; for one is the person of the Father, another of the Son, another of the Holy Spirit; but the divinity of the Father and of the Son and of the Holy Spirit is one, the glory equal, and the majesty coeternal. What the Father is, such is the Son and such the Holy Spirit: the Father is uncreated, the Son is uncreated, the Holy Spirit is uncreated; the Father is immense, the Son is immense, the Holy Spirit is immense; the Father is eternal, the Son is eternal, and the Holy Spirit is eternal; and nevertheless there are not three eternals but one eternal, just as there are not three uncreateds or three that are immense, but one uncreated and one that is immense. Similarly, the Father is omnipotent, the Son is omnipotent, the Holy Spirit is omnipotent; nevertheless there are not three omnipotents but one omnipotent. So also the Father is Lord, the Son is Lord, the Holy Spirit is Lord; and nevertheless there are not three Lords but one Lord: because, just as we are compelled by Christian truth to confess that each person is individually both God and Lord, so we are forbidden by the Catholic religion to say that there are three Gods or Lords. The Father is made by no one, neither created nor begotten; the Son is from the Father alone, neither made nor created but begotten; the Holy Spirit is from the Father and the Son, neither made nor created nor begotten, but proceeding. Therefore, there is one Father, not three Fathers; there is one Son, not three Sons; there is one Holy Spirit, not three Holy Spirits. And in the Trinity there is nothing prior or posterior, nothing greater or less, but all three persons are coeternal and coequal. So in every way, as was said above, unity must be worshiped in Trinity and Trinity in unity. He who wants to be saved must believe this about the Trinity.

The creed would evidently have us take the following seven sentences as formulating propositions belief in which is required for salvation:

(1)   The Father is God

(2)   The Son is God

(3)   The Holy Spirit is God

(4)   The Father is not the Son

(5)   The Father is not the Holy Spirit

(6)   The Son is not the Holy Spirit

(7)   There is exactly one God.

Thus we read in the text: "The Father is Lord, the Son is Lord, the Holy Spirit is Lord" and "we are compelled by Christian truth to confess that each person is individually . . . God." Hence sentences (1), (2), and (3). Sentences (4), (5), and (6) are sanctioned by the words "for one is the person of the Father, another of the Son, another of the Holy Spirit," together with the injunction against "confusing the persons." And (7) pretty clearly gives the intent of the words "we worship one God" and "we are forbidden by the Catholic religion to say that there are three Gods."

Narrowly understood, the doctrine of the Trinity is the doctrine formulated in sentences (1) through (7). In a somewhat wider sense, it includes as well the propositions expressed by the sentences

(8)   The Father is neither made, nor created, nor begotten

(9)   The Son is from the Father alone, neither made nor created, but begotten

(10)   The Holy Spirit is from the Father and the Son, neither made nor created nor begotten, but proceeding.

Moreover, the sentence

(11)   What the Father is, such is the Son and such the Holy Spirit

enjoys a prominent place in the creed and, as we shall see, cannot be ignored in a treatment of the logical problem of the Trinity. On the other hand, it would be pointless to include within Trinitarian doctrine propositions to the effect that the Father, the Son, and the Holy Spirit are eternal, omnipotent, and the like; for such propositions can reasonably be taken to be consequences of (1) through (11) together with orthodox doctrines about the divine attributes. And we do well to ignore such catchphrases as "unity in Trinity and Trinity in unity." Whatever content they have appears already in (1) through (7).

A virtue of sentences (1) through (7), and of (11) as well, is that in them theological jargon is kept to a minimum. The *doctrine* of the Trinity ought not to be confused with this or that *theology* of the Trinity. Even in theory, however, the line between the two is not sharp, and in practice the distinction is one that Christians have found hard to observe. In the face of what were seen as distortions of or deviations from true doctrine, church councils from time to time felt compelled to incorporate technical terminology into the formulation of doctrine.

A notable instance occurred at the First Ecumenical Council, held at Nicaea in 325. It is preserved in what is popularly, but inaccurately, known as the Nicene Creed.[5] Those who eventually prevailed at the council aimed to put down the teaching of Arius, a presbyter of Alexandria, who preached that the Son was "not equal to" the Father, nor "of the same

substance," and that "the substances of the Father and of the Son are
different and have no share in each other." His main point appears to have
been that the Son is a creature, hence not truly God.[6] The council might
therefore have responded with a firm enunciation of (2). But it chose
instead to adopt Arius's own terminology—in the words of Ambrose, "to
sever the head of the foul heresy with the very sword which [its advocates]
had themselves unleashed."[7] The resulting creed read in part as follows:

> We believe in one God, the Father almighty, creator of all things both
> visible and invisible. And in one Lord Jesus Christ, the Son of God,
> the only-begotten born of the Father, that is, of the substance of the
> Father; God from God, light from light, true God from true God;
> begotten, not created, of the same substance as the Father. . . .[8]

In view of the obscurities and ambiguities of the word 'substance' (*ousia*),
to affirm that the Son is "of the same substance" (*homoousion*) as the Father
hardly contributes to clarification of doctrine.[9] Our (2) is at least as clear.
And (2) might also have been a better weapon with which to combat the
heretic; for the language employed in the Creed of Nicaea aroused opposition even among the orthodox,[10] and contributed to a temporary ascen-
dancy of Arianism, or at least of "Semi-Arianism," in the late 350s.[11] But
for our purposes the important point is that to affirm the consubstantiality
of Father, Son, and Holy Spirit is so far to say something that needs
explanation; and the explanation had better not jeopardize (1) through (7).
When it comes to orthodoxy on the matter of the Trinity, they are
inviolable.

Not only the Athanasian Creed testifies to this, but also numerous
conciliar pronouncements. I cite just one, issued in 1442 at Florence by the
Seventeenth Ecumenical Council:

> The Holy Roman Church firmly believes, professes, and teaches [that
> there is] one true God omnipotent, unchangeable, and eternal, Father
> and Son and Holy Spirit, one in essence, three in persons: the Father
> unbegotten, the Son begotten of the Father, the Holy Spirit proceed-
> ing from the Father and the Son. The Father is not the Son or the Holy
> Spirit; the Son is not the Father or the Holy Spirit; the Holy Spirit is
> not the Father or the Son: but the Father is only the Father, the Son
> is only the Son, the Holy Spirit is only the Holy Spirit. The Father
> alone begot the Son from his substance, the Son alone was begotten
> from the Father alone, the Holy Spirit alone proceeds from both
> Father and Son. Thus these three persons are one God and not three
> gods: for the three are one substance, one nature, one divinity, one
> immensity, one eternity, and are one in all ways, where this is not
> impeded by the opposition of relation.[12]

This pronouncement suggests somewhat crisper sentences than our (8), (9), and (10); and its final clause appears to contemplate some qualification of (11), about which I shall have something to say later on. But the pronouncement leaves no doubt as to the orthodoxy of (1) through (7). Of course, metaphysical jargon intrudes, especially in the words "for the three are one substance, one nature," "one in essence." But evidently such talk is to be understood consistently with the truth of what is said in (1) through (7).

Of course, it is one thing to know that the doctrine of the Trinity is formulated in a certain set of sentences and another to know what the doctrine is. Someone might know that the first proposition of Wittgenstein's *Tractatus* is the proposition formulated in the sentence 'Die Welt ist alles was der Fall ist', and yet in a plain sense not know what the proposition is: to take the worst case, he might have no idea what the German sentence means. We are not, I think, in that position with respect to our seven Trinitarian sentences. They are not sentences of an unfamiliar language, conveying no more to us than would some string of nonsense syllables. On the other hand, mere competence in English is insufficient to ensure understanding. Obviously enough, to understand the seven sentences one must understand the theological expressions contained in them; and it is at least open to question whether mastery of English suffices for that. But another barrier to understanding is perhaps less obvious. It has to do with what philosophers have come to call "logical form."

Consider for the moment just the first six of our sentences. A natural thought is to take the theological terms contained in them as in effect proper names and to understand the verb 'is' to have the sense of 'is identical with', or 'is the very same thing as'—as when we say that Samuel Clemens is Mark Twain, that Tully is Cicero, that Venus is the Morning Star. Thus construed, the six sentences come to formulate propositions that might better be put this way:

(1a)   The Father is identical with God

(2a)   The Son is identical with God

(3a)   The Holy Spirit is identical with God

(4a)   The Father is not identical with the Son

(5a)   The Father is not identical with the Holy Spirit

(6a)   The Son is not identical with the Holy Spirit.

But obviously this will not do. No one thing can literally be the very same thing as each of two things; or, better, if something x is identical with y and with z, then y must be identical with z. If Venus is the Morning Star and

Venus is the Evening Star, it follows that the Morning Star is the Evening Star.

The inconsistency is plain, and I take it to show that we have not yet discovered the logical forms of sentences (1) through (6). But of course an alternative interpretation immediately suggests itself: construe the word 'God' in (1), (2), and (3) as a common noun, or general term, and supply the indefinite article. Thus:

(1b)   The Father is a God

(2b)   The Son is a God

(3b)   The Holy Spirit is a God

(4b)   The Father is not identical with the Son

(5b)   The Father is not identical with the Holy Spirit

(6b)   The Son is not identical with the Holy Spirit.

The result is a consistent set. The Cappadocian Fathers saw this and appear to have suggested that consubstantiality of Father, Son, and Holy Spirit could be understood accordingly. Thus Basil wrote that

> when a name is sought for two or more similar objects, as, for example, Paul, Silvanus, and Timothy, which will indicate the substance of these men, you will not apply one term to the substance of Paul, but a different one to that of Silvanus, and still another to that of Timothy; but whatever terms indicate the substance of Paul will apply to the two others as well; and those who are described with reference to their substance by the same terms are consubstantial with one another.[13]

It seems to have been left to Gregory of Nyssa, Basil's younger brother, to notice that, thus understood, consubstantiality of the Father, the Son, and the Holy Spirit appears to license saying that there are three Gods. Gregory himself rather desperately suggested that strictly speaking there is only one man.[14] But besides being itself heretical, the suggestion is of no help: if (1b) through (6b) are true, (7) must be false.

I have singled out the Cappadocians, and this is somewhat unfair. After all, their explanation of consubstantiality is close to the surface in a pronouncement of the Council of Chalcedon (451) according to which the Son is "consubstantial with the Father in respect of deity and consubstantial with us in respect of humanity"[15]—a phraseology apparently lifted from the earlier Formula of Union (433).[16] Moreover, it is quite common to be told that there are three divine Persons but only one divine substance or essence or nature. Some such is present in the Athanasian Creed and is explicit in the pronouncement of the Seventeenth Ecumenical Council quoted above. But the whole question concerns the relation of the Persons to the essence. If each Person is identical with the essence, there cannot be more than one Person. And if, on the other hand, the Persons are to be thought of as sharing a common nature, in the manner of Paul, Silvanus, and Timothy, there cannot be fewer than three Gods. How, in short, can there be three divine Persons and yet only one God?

At this point I need to anticipate an objection. It will be said that a philosopher is trespassing on the territory of the theologian: the doctrine of the Trinity is a mystery, beyond the capacities of human reason, and hence the tools of logic are irrelevant to it. The objection is based on a misunderstanding. The doctrine of the Trinity is indeed supposed to be a mystery. That simply means, however, that assurance of its truth cannot be provided by human reason but only by divine revelation. It is to be believed "not because of the natural light of reason, but because of the authority of God who reveals it."[17] But a mystery is not supposed to be refutable by human reason, as if a truth of reason could somehow contradict a revealed truth; on the contrary, putative refutations are supposed themselves to be refutable. Nor is a mystery supposed to be unintelligible, in the sense that the words in which it is expressed simply cannot be understood. After all, we are asked to believe the propositions expressed by the words, not simply that the words express some true propositions or other, we know not which.[18]

In any case, we have not yet exhausted the resources of logical theory. One suggestion in particular will probably have occurred to some of you already. I do not know its origin. I think I detect it in a letter written by Anselm of Canterbury to Urban II in 1094,[19] and it is perhaps justifiably read into a creed adopted at the Eleventh Council of Toledo in 675.[20] Peter Geach attributes it to Aquinas[21]—presumably with approval, for the philosophical theory on which it rests is one that Geach himself has vigorously defended on a number of occasions.[22]

The Trinitarian sentence (7) can be taken as an answer to the question, How many God are there? Now, I have so far implicitly assumed that if that answer is correct, then, if x is a God and y is a God, x must be identical with y. The assumption is natural enough; indeed, (7) is naturally understood as saying neither more nor less than

(7b)   Something is a God, and anything that is a God is identical with it.

But on Geach's view, the view he attributes to Aquinas, (7b) is at best incomplete, through presence in it of the unqualified phrase 'is identical with'. According to that view it makes no sense to say something of the form 'x is identical with y', or 'x is the same as y', unless the context makes clear that this is short for 'x is the same such-and-such as y', where 'such-and-such' stands in for a common noun of restricted applicability—'man' or 'planet', say, but not 'thing' or 'object' or 'entity'.[23] Thus it would be said to make no sense to ask whether what we heard at today's concert is unqualifiedly identical with what we heard at yesterday's: we may have heard the same motet, but of course we did not hear the same performance; it makes no sense to ask whether you and I are reading the very same thing: we may be reading the same novel, but no doubt different copies; it makes no sense to ask whether 2/3 is identical with 4/6: 2/3 is the same rational number as 4/6, but not the same ordered pair of integers. Identity is accordingly said to be "relative," in the sense that x and y may be the same such-and-such but different so-and-so's.[24]

How, then, is (7) to be understood? Well, think of counting the novels on a shelf. We assign the number 1 to some novel on the shelf and to whatever on the shelf is the same novel; if, after this, no novel on the shelf remains unnumbered, there is exactly one novel on the shelf. Thus, there is exactly one novel on the shelf if and only if something is a novel on the shelf and is the same novel as anything that is a novel on the shelf. Similarly with (7). On Geach's view it is equivalent to

(7c)   Something is a God, and anything that is a God is the same God as it,

which differs from (7b) only in that 'is identical with' has been relativized to 'is the same God as'.

Now from (7c) together with

(1c)   The Father is a God,

(2c)   The Son is a God,

and

(3c)   The Holy Spirit is a God

it follows that the Father is the same God as the Son and the same God as the Holy Spirit, and that the Son is the same God as the Holy Spirit. But Geach contends that consistently with this the Father, the Son, and the Holy Spirit may be different Divine Persons. Thus (4), (5), and (6) are to be understood in the sense of, respectively,

(4c)   The Father is a different Divine Person from the Son,

(5c)   The Father is a different Divine Person from the Holy Spirit,

and

(6c)   The Son is a different Divine Person from the Holy Spirit.

Now, I shall want to argue that it is at least open to question whether Geach's interpretation of (1) through (7) successfully avoids tritheism. But

before going into that it will be instructive to consider how his interpretation bears on (11), a sentence I promised some time back to give some
attention to. I did not include that sentence within Trinitarian doctrine,
narrowly understood. This was in part because of the exclusionary clause
added to it at the Council of Florence. But only in part. I was concerned
more with the fact that the content of (11) seems to be at odds with
orthodoxy. In (11) we appear to be authorized to affirm each of an entire
class of propositions—all those, namely, that can be expressed in sentences
of the forms

(A)   If the Father is . . . then the Son is . . .

and

(B)   If the Father is . . . then the Holy Spirit is . . . .

But some sentences of these forms appear to express propositions that are
not only heretical but also inconsistent with Trinitarian, or near-Trinitarian,
doctrine. Consider, for example, the sentence 'If the Father is unbegotten
then the Son is unbegotten'. This is of form (A), but surely expresses a
proposition inconsistent with the content of (8) and (9); for according to
(8) the Father is unbegotten, whereas according to (9) the Son is not
unbegotten. Or consider 'If the Father is one from whom the Holy Spirit
proceeds then the Holy Spirit is one from whom the Holy Spirit proceeds'.
This is of form (B), but the proposition it expresses presumably conflicts
with the content of (9) and (10). Even worse from the point of view of
Trinitarian orthodoxy, it would seem that the sentence 'If the Father is not
the Son then the Son is not the Son', which is of form (A), expresses
a proposition that yields a contradiction when conjoined with the
proposition expressed by (4).

It is thus understandable that the delegates to the Council of Florence
should have felt a need to restrict the scope of (11). On pain of heterodoxy,
it must be held that not all sentences of forms (A) and (B) express truths.
But some do: if the Father is eternal then the Son is eternal and the Holy
Spirit is eternal; if the Father is omnipotent then the Son is omnipotent and
the Holy Spirit is omnipotent; and so on. Whether the Florentine formula
("where this is not impeded by the opposition of relation") successfully
explains the 'and so on' is a question for another occasion. My point here
is that an assertion of *relative* identity of the Father with the Son and with
the Holy Spirit does not imply, as would the corresponding assertion of
absolute identity, that all sentences of forms (A) and (B) express true
propositions. If the Father is absolutely identical with the Son and with the
Holy Spirit, then surely all sentences of forms (A) and (B) do express true
propositions.[25] If, however, the Father is the same God as the Son but not
the same Person as the Son, it follows at once that at least one sentence of

form (A) expresses a false proposition: the Father is surely the same Person as the Father, and therefore 'If the Father is the same Person as the Father then the Son is the same Person as the Father' must express a false proposition. Similarly, if the Father is the same God as the Holy Spirit but not the same Person, then the sentence 'If the Father is the same Person as the Father then the Holy Spirit is the same Person as the Father' must express a false proposition.

Let me turn now to the question of orthodoxy, especially to the question whether Geach's interpretation of (1) through (6) avoids tritheism. I shall argue that it does not. My argument is very simple: every Divine Person is a God; there are at least three Divine Persons; therefore, there are at least three Gods. The first premise is a trivial truth. The second follows from the conjunction of (4c), (5c), and (6c). The heretical conclusion follows, by the general principle that if every A is a B then there cannot be fewer B's than A's. This principle, I claim, is evident to the natural light of reason. Thus, if every cat is an animal, there cannot be fewer animals than cats; if every senator from Massachusetts is a Democrat, there cannot be fewer Democrats than senators from Massachusetts. Just so, if every Divine Person is a God, there cannot be fewer Gods than Divine Persons.

As you might expect, Geach contests the general principle.[26] He cites cases in which, allegedly, every A is a B and yet there are fewer B's than A's. A favorite, typical of the lot, requires two definitions. Let us say, first, that something, x, *is the same surman as* something, y, if and only if x is a man and y is a man and x and y have the same surname. John Adams is thus the same surman as Henry Adams, William James is the same surman as Henry James, etc. Second, let us say that a *surman* is anything that is the same surman as something. Consider, now, men in the city of Leeds. If we make the reasonable assumption that each man in Leeds has one and only one surname, then every man in Leeds is a surman: each is the same surman as something, for each has the same surname as some man in Leeds—himself, if no one else. Yet, Geach claims, there are likely to be fewer surmen in Leeds than men. For suppose we were to count the surmen in Leeds. Geach says we ought to proceed by assigning numbers, beginning with 1, to the surmen in Leeds, taking care to assign the same number to x and y if and only if x is the same surman as y. Thus, if the number n is assigned to Samuel Jones, n should be assigned as well to Howard Jones but not to Edward Smith: Howard is the same surman as Samuel, but Edward is not. If we count this way and if, as seems altogether likely, at least two men in Leeds have the same surname, we shall obtain a number smaller than the number of men in Leeds.

Applied to the Trinity, the thing goes as follows. To count the number of Divine Persons, we assign 1 to the Father and then 2 to the Son, since He is not the same Divine Person as the Father, and we assign 3 to the

Holy Spirit, for He is a Divine Person different from both the Father and the Son. But to count Gods, we assign the number 1 to the Father and to the Son and to the Holy Spirit as well, for each is the same God as the Father. Thus three Persons, one God. Trinity in unity.

So Geach would have it. But let us look again at the matter of surmen in Leeds. Are there really fewer surmen in Leeds than men? I think it can be shown that there are not. What, after all, is a surman? According to the second of Geach's definitions, a surman is anything that is the same surman as something; hence, going by the first definition, a surman is a man who has the same surname as some man. Briefly, a surman is a man who has a surname—that is, a surnamed man. So to ask how many surmen there are in Leeds is to ask how many surnamed men there are in Leeds. But then, on the assumption that every man in Leeds has a surname, the number of surmen in Leeds is evidently the same as the number of men in Leeds. The correct way to count the number of surmen in Leeds is to count the men.

Geach's definitions invite confusion. One naturally expects that in the phrase 'is the same surman as' the word 'surman' will have the sense given it in Geach's second definition. But it does not—it does not, at any rate, if one goes by his first definition. We have just seen that the word 'surman' means *surnamed man*. But 'is the same surman as' does not, according to Geach's first definition, mean *is the same surnamed man as*. Samuel Jones is the same surman as Howard Jones, by the first definition; but Samuel is not the same surnamed man as Howard, for he is not the same man. Geach's definitions in fact generate two senses for the phrase 'is the same surman as'. One is that given in his first definition, the sense in which 'is the same surman as' amounts to 'has the same surname as'; the other is the sense derived from his second definition, the sense in which 'is the same surman as' amounts to 'is the same surnamed man as'. Failure to notice the ambiguity leads one to the false conclusion that although every man in Leeds is a surman, in Leeds men outnumber surmen.

Using Geach's definitions as models, one might say: Something, x, *is the same God as* something, y, if and only if x is a Person and y is a Person and x has the same Divine Nature as y; and x is a *God* if and only if x is the same God as something. Would (7c) then serve as an interpretation of (7)? Surely not. What is a God? By the second definition, a God is anything that is the same God as something; and by the first definition, this means that a God is a Person that has the same Divine Nature as something—that is, a Divine Person. If the word 'God' is thus understood and if the phrase 'is the same God as' is taken in the sense of the first definition, (7c) ensures only that there is at least one Divine Person and that any two Divine Persons have a common nature. Now, of course, our definitions generate an additional sense for the phrase 'is the same God as', just as Geach's definitions generated an additional sense for the phrase 'is the same surman as'. In this sense, 'is the same God as' means *is the same Divine Person as*. But if the phrase is thus understood and if we continue to use the word 'God' in the sense of the second definition, (7c) comes to formulate the proposition that there is exactly one Divine Person, a heretical proposition inconsistent with the propositions expressed by (4c) through (6c).

We have come no farther than the Cappadocian Fathers. Either we divide the substance, or we confound the Persons. But then, we have only scratched the surface of the logical problem of the Trinity. The verb 'to be' is remarkably versatile. We say such things as: 'that speck on the horizon is a destroyer'; 'the sound you hear is a jet'; 'that's burley'; 'the desk is walnut'; 'Gielgud is Hamlet'; 'the Apostles are twelve'; 'the population of Boston is decreasing'; 'that is Descartes' (pointing to a picture); 'that is the Sonesta Hotel' (pointing to a reflection in the water); 'that is the Fuller Brush man' (pointing to a foot in the doorway). Each of these suggests a possible construal of our Trinitarian sentences, and a full treatment would take account of them all. But perhaps I have said enough to convince you of the difficulty of the subject; and, if I have not exhibited the rewards of truth, I hope I have demonstrated the dangers of error.

Notes

This is a slightly revised version of a lecture delivered at North Carolina State University at Raleigh in 1978 to an audience consisting largely of nonphilosophers. I have not altered its lecture style.

1. *De Trinitate*, bk. 1, chap. 3.

2. See especially bks. 5–7.

3. For a thorough discussion, see J. N. D. Kelly, *The Athanasian Creed* (New York: Harper and Row, 1964), on which I have relied in the brief remarks that follow.

4. *Summa theologiae*, II-II, q. 1, a. 10, ad 3.

5. The origin of what is popularly referred to as the Nicene Creed is a matter of scholarly controversy. For a discussion of the issues, see J. N. D. Kelly, *Early Christian Creeds*, 3d ed. (New York: David McKay, 1972).

6. The quotations are from Kelly's *Early Christian Creeds*, p. 236. For fuller accounts of Arian theology, see, e.g., J. N. D. Kelly, *Early Christian Doctrines*, 2d ed. (New York: Harper and Row, 1960), pp. 226–231, and Jaroslav Pelikan, *The Christian Tradition*, vol. 1 (Chicago: University of Chicago Press, 1971), pp. 191–200.

7. I take the quotation from Kelly, *Early Christian Creeds*, p. 253.

8. For the Greek text, see H. Denzinger and A. Schönmetzer, eds., *Enchiridion symbolorum*, editio 35 emendata (Freiburg: Herder, 1965), 125.

9. And the apparent equation of *ousia* with *hypostasis*, which occurs in the anathemas appended to the creed, only serves to cloud matters further.

10. "The victory over Arianism achieved at the Council was really a victory snatched by the superior energy and decision of a small minority with the aid of half-hearted allies. The

majority did not like the business at all, and strongly disapproved of the introduction into the Creed . . . of new and untraditional and unscriptural terms." (J. F. Bethune-Baker, *An Introduction to the Early History of Christian Doctrine*, 8th ed. (London: Methuen, 1949, p. 171.)

11. The culmination took place on the last day of 359, when the delegates to a council at Seleucia explicitly condemned the *homoousion* formula and adopted 'like the Father' (*homoion to patri*) in its stead. "The whole world groaned and wondered to find itself Arian," Jerome wrote. (Quoted from Kelly's *Early Christian Creeds*, p. 293. The preceding ten pages contain a detailed account of the events that occasioned Jerome's remark.)

12. Denzinger and Schönmetzer, *Enchiridion symbolorum*, 1330. The final clause appears to originate with Anselm. See his *De processione Spiritus Sancti*, in F. S. Schmitt, ed., *S. Anselmi opera omnia* (Stuttgart: Friedrich Frommann, 1968), vol. 2, pp. 177–219. An English translation is contained in J. Hopkins and H. Richardson, eds. and trans., *Anselm of Canterbury: Trinity, Incarnation, and Redemption* (New York: Harper and Row, 1970).

13. Epistle 38. See also epistle 236. The translation is that of Roy J. Deferrari in *St. Basil: The Letters* (Cambridge, Mass.: Harvard University Press, 1926).

14. See Bethune-Baker, *Early History of Christian Doctrine*, p. 220; Kelly, *Early Christian Doctrines*, p. 267; Pelikan, *Christian Tradition*, p. 221.

15. Denzinger and Schönmetzer, *Enchiridion symbolorum*, 301.

16. Denzinger and Schönmetzer, *Enchiridion symbolorum*, 272.

17. First Vatican Council, Denzinger and Schönmetzer, *Enchiridion symbolorum*, 3008.

18. It may therefore be a little troubling to find Aquinas saying that the mysteries "are so revealed to man as not to be understood (*intelligantur*), but only to be believed as heard." (*Summa contra gentiles*, 4.1.) But the intended contrast, as Aquinas proceeds to explain, is not that between sense and nonsense, but that between something seen to be true (*demonstrata ad videndum*) and something put in words to be believed (*sermone prolata ad credendum*).

19. *Epistola de incarnatione verbi*, in Schmitt, ed., *Opera omnia*, vol. 2, pp. 3–41. English translation in Hopkins and Richardson, eds. *Anselm of Canterbury*, pp. 5–36.

20. Denzinger and Schönmetzer, *Enchiridion symbolorum*, 525–532.

21. In G. E. M. Anscombe and P. T. Geach, *Three Philosophers* (Ithaca, N.Y.: Cornell University Press, 1961). See p. 118.

22. The theory is stated, briefly, in *Mental Acts* (London: Routledge and Kegan Paul, 1957), p. 69. Fuller exposition and defense are to be found in "Identity," *Review of Metaphysics* 21 (1967): 3–12, which is reprinted as pp. 238–247 of Geach's *Logic Matters* (Berkeley: University of California Press, 1972), and in "Ontological Relativity and Relative Identity," in Milton K. Munitz, ed., *Logic and Ontology* (New York: New York University Press, 1973), pp. 287–302.

23. I write with deliberate vagueness here, through uncertainty as to what precisely Geach's view is. In "Identity" he requires that 'such-and-such' be replaced by a "count noun"; in "Identity—A Reply" (*Review of Metaphysics*, 22 [1968]: 556–559; *Logic Matters*, pp. 247–249) the implied exclusion of "mass nouns" is said to have been a slip; in "Ontological Relativity and Relative Identity" mass nouns once more appear to be excluded. Perhaps of greater importance is the fact that 'restricted applicability' invites questions which, I think, Geach has never satisfactorily addressed. Still, I think the vagueness is of no consequence to what follows.

24. 'May be' is apparently much too weak. In "Identity—A Reply" (*Logic Matters*, p. 249) Geach says that "any equivalence relation . . . can be used to specify a criterion of relative identity." This has the consequence that if 'A' is a count noun (of limited applicability) that correctly applies to both a and b, there is a criterion of relative identity on which a is the same as b. For the relation that x bears to y if and only if both x and y are A's is an equivalence relation.

25. For a defense of the general point involved, see "Indiscernibility Principles," in this volume.

26. See "Ontological Relativity and Relative Identity," pp. 293–295.

Indiscernibility Principles

If α and α' are distinct variables and ϕ and ϕ' are open sentences alike save that ϕ' has α' free at one or more places at which ϕ has α free, then a universal closure of $\ulcorner(\alpha)(\alpha')(\alpha = \alpha' \rightarrow (\phi \rightarrow \phi'))\urcorner$ is an *indiscernibility principle*.[1] In certain recent discussions[2] of identity and substitutivity, and of such related matters as essentialism, special attention is given to a particular indiscernibility principle, namely,

(1) $(z)(x)(y)(x = y \rightarrow (z$ is a property of $x \rightarrow z$ is a property of $y))$.

Others tend to be ignored. It is of some interest, I think, to ask why (1) is thus singled out. Why not instead

(2) $(z)(x)(y)(x = y \rightarrow (z$ is a friend of $x \rightarrow z$ is a friend of $y))$,

or for that matter any number of other indiscernibility principles that are like (1) not only in point of a certain logical form but also in truth value and degree of certitude? According to (1), nothing is identical with a given thing unless it shares all the properties of that thing; according to (2), nothing is identical with a given thing unless it shares all the friends of that thing. Why the stress on properties rather than friends?

1

The idea that (1) has a special position among indiscernibility principles may sometimes originate in confusion over

(3) $(x)(y)(x = y \rightarrow (Fx \rightarrow Fy))$.

If this is not a closed sentence of some first-order language, it is naturally understood to be a schema, one that might have been used in characterizing indiscernibility principles: a sentence is an indiscernibility principle just in case it or some alphabetic variant of it is a universal closure of an instance of (3). But (3) may also be viewed as an open sentence in which 'F', in spite of its typography, is a variable on all fours with 'x' and 'y' and in which concatenation of α with β abbreviates $\ulcorner\alpha$ is a property of $\beta\urcorner$. The result of prefixing '(F)' to (3), so understood, is simply a notational variant of (1). If these distinct construals of (3) are not kept apart, it can seem that (1) stands to other indiscernibility principles as axiom to theorems. To see the confusion, notice that prefixing '(F)' to (3) can as well be viewed as resulting in a notational variant of (2).[3]

The thought is nevertheless apt to persist that (1) stands in some asymmetric deductive relation to other indiscernibility principles. Thus we are inclined to say that if every property of x is a property of y, then every friend of x is a friend of y and hence that if (1) is true, so is (2). But there is no inclination to turn the thing around: we are not inclined to say that x and y share all their friends only if they share all their properties. Now, it is true that (2) is quantificationally implied by the conjunction of (1) with

(4) $(x)(y)((z)(z$ is a property of $x \to z$ is a property of $y) \to$
       $(z)(z$ is a friend of $x \to z$ is a friend of $y))$;

and although, similarly, (1) is quantificationally implied by the conjunction of (2) with

(5) $(x)(y)((z)(z$ is.a friend of $x \to z$ is a friend of $y) \to$
       $(z)(z$ is a property of $x \to z$ is a property of $y))$,

(5) will no doubt be thought false. But why is (4) thought to be true? Presumably, there is thought to be some property, or collection of properties, possession of which by x and y guarantees that every friend of x is a friend of y. The guarantee must, of course, be independent of (2). It would not do to appeal, say, to

(6) $(x)(\exists z)(y)(z$ is a property of $y \leftrightarrow y = x)$,

for this provides such properties only via (2). What is wanted is, rather,

(7) $(w)(\exists z)(x)(z$ is a property of $x \leftrightarrow w$ is a friend of $x)$,

which affirms, for any given thing w, the existence of a property present in precisely those things of which w is a friend. And if (7) is at hand, (4) may be skipped: (7) quantificationally implies (4), and hence the conjunction of (1) with (7) quantificationally implies (2). Of course, it is also true that (1) is quantificationally implied by the conjunction of (2) with

(8) $(w)(\exists z)(x)(z$ is a friend of $x \leftrightarrow w$ is a property of $x)$.

But it will be said that whereas (8) is false, (7) is true, Indeed, (7) is apt to seem sufficiently trivial or obvious or otherwise incontestable that it may go unmentioned, allowing one to say simply that (2) follows from (1).

If α, α', ϕ and ϕ' are as above, if ψ is like ϕ save for having free occurrences of a variable β at precisely those positions of α in ϕ at which ϕ' has α', and if γ is a variable other than β and not free in ψ, then a universal closure of $\ulcorner(\exists \gamma)(\beta)(\gamma$ is a property of $\beta \leftrightarrow \psi)\urcorner$ is a *comprehension principle corresponding to* indiscernibility principles that are universal closures of $\ulcorner(\alpha)(\alpha')(\alpha = \alpha' \rightarrow (\phi \rightarrow \phi'))\urcorner$; and since comprehension principles corresponding to an indiscernibility principle differ only in choice of variables or in order of initial universal quantifiers, there is no harm in speaking of *the* comprehension principle corresponding to a given indiscernibility principle. Thus (7) is the comprehension principle corresponding to (2), and (6) is the comprehension principle corresponding to

(9) $(x)(y)(x = y \rightarrow (x = x \rightarrow y = x))$.

Just as the conjunction of (1) with (7) quantificationally implies (2), so the conjunction of (1) with (6) quantificationally implies (9). In general, an indiscernibility principle is quantificationally implied by the conjunction of its corresponding comprehension principle with (1). And since the truth of the comprehension principle tends to be taken for granted, the indiscernibility principle tends to be thought of as following simply from (1). Thus (1) comes to be seen as the general truth of which other indiscernibility principles are special cases.

Some will propose an amendment: *true* indiscernibility principles one and all follow from (1). Anyone who accepts (1), and who thinks all other indiscernibility principles are special cases of it, will accept the amendment, seeing it as having no effect. But the view is abroad that some indiscernibility principles are false, and those who hold it do not see it as detracting from the importance of (1); on the contrary, they are apt to see in it further indication of the fundamental position of (1) among indiscernibility principles.

The view that some indiscernibility principles are false originates in reflection on certain counterexamples to the principle of substitutivity, the principle that the terms of a true identity sentence may be substituted one for another in any true sentence *salva veritate*. To have at hand a typical instance, let 'astro' abbreviate 'it is a truth of astronomy that' and consider

(10)   astro Hesperus = Phosphorous,

(11)   Hesperus = Phosphorus,

and

(12)   astro Phosphorus = Phosphorus.

Here (12) results from (10) by substitution on the basis of the true identity (11). Yet (10) is true and (12) is false. It is tempting to infer that

(13) $(x)(y)(x = y \rightarrow (\text{astro } x = \text{Phosphorus} \rightarrow \text{astro } y = \text{Phosphorus}))$

is a false indiscernibility principle; for it appears to conform to the above definition and yet to have the false substitution-instance obtained by putting 'Hesperus' for 'x' and 'Phosphorus' for 'y' in '$x = y \rightarrow$ (astro x = Phosphorus $\rightarrow$ astro y = Phosphorus)'.

The example is not seen as threatening (1). We can put 'Hesperus' for 'x' and 'Phosphorus' for 'y' in the open sentence that follows the quantifiers of (1), but what is to be put for 'z'? An answer would be forthcoming if we could discern a property rightly attributed to Hesperus in (10) and then wrongly attributed to Phosphorus in (12). But (1) is sufficiently compelling that we are apt, rather, to see the failure of substitutivity as ground for denying that there is any such property. It would, in any case, be incoherent to suppose there to be a property z which, by virtue of the truth of (10), is present in Hesperus but which, by virtue of the falsity of (12), is not present in Phosphorus. Both

(14) $(y)(y = \text{Hesperus} \leftrightarrow y = \text{Hesperus})$. z is a property of Hesperus

and

(15) $(y)(y = \text{Hesperus} \leftrightarrow y = \text{Phosphorus})$. $\sim z$ is a property of Phosphorus

would have to be judged true. Hence also

(16) $(\exists x)((y)(y = \text{Hesperus} \leftrightarrow y = x)$. z is a property of $x)$

and

(17) $(\exists x)((y)(y = \text{Hesperus} \leftrightarrow y = x)$. $\sim z$ is a property of $x)$.

What, then, of the thing that is Hesperus? Would *it* have z? Evidently there would be no saying.[4]

There can seem to be here not only a defense of (1) but also an explanation of what is wrong with (13): it is false, and false precisely because of what we just now appear to have shown, namely, the falsity of

(18) $(\exists z)(x)(z$ is a property of $x \leftrightarrow$ astro x = Phosphorus).

Now, if (13) is an indiscernibility principle, (18) is its corresponding comprehension principle. So the defect in (13), on this view of the matter, is its failure to satisfy a condition necessary for the truth of any indiscernibility principle, namely, that the corresponding comprehension principle be true. True indiscernibility principles are those that are special cases of (1); but an indiscernibility principle qualifies as such only if its corresponding comprehension principle is true.

2

If the views I have been describing are nowhere explicitly affirmed, there are, nevertheless, signs of them here and there. A paper of my own[5] defended (1) against critics[6] who argued to its falsity from failures of substitutivity. I would have done as much for (2) had there been the occasion. Still, my reference to (1) as "the principle of identity," and my concern to distinguish it from the principle of substitutivity, suggest that I took (1) to be somehow fundamental among indiscernibility principles. I would not have called (2) "the principle of identity," nor would I have cautioned against confusing it with the principle of substitutivity. There is an echo of this in Wiggins. "It is not true," he writes, "that designations of the same thing are *everywhere* intersubstitutible. . . . What really is true is that *if x = y, then every property of x is a property of y*."[7] In a similar vein, Linsky[8] and Plantinga[9] call (1) "the principle of the indiscernibility of identicals" and contrast it in point of truth value with the principle of substitutivity. There is a hint, too, in Linsky's explanation of certain failures of substitutivity, of the view that an indiscernibility principle is true only if its corresponding comprehension principle is true: not every open sentence, he says, "expresses a property," And perhaps that view lies behind Plantinga's insistence that essentialist claims involve property attributions. He wants it understood, for example, that 9 is essentially composite only if anything identical with 9 is essentially composite; and he sees a guarantee in (1) together with the alleged equivalence of '9 is essentially composite' and '9 has the property of being essentially composite'.

That (1) has some distinguished position among indiscernibility principles is implied also in some recent discussions of the doctrine that if x is identical with y, then necessarily x is identical with y. A standard argument for the doctrine proceeds simply from the premises

(19) $(x)(y)(x = y \rightarrow (\Box x = x \rightarrow \Box x = y))$

and

(20) $(x)\Box(x = x)$

to the conclusion

(21) $(x)(y)(x = y \rightarrow \Box x = y)$.

Here (19) is looked upon as an indiscernibility principle, in need of no special defense. But in Kripke's presentation[10] (19) appears as second line of a derivation having (3) as first line. Now, as already noticed, (3) is subject to more than one interpretation: if, as we may safely assume in the present context, it is not intended as a closed sentence of some first-order language, it may be understood either as a schema or as tantamount to (1). Kripke seems to intend the latter. True, he calls (19) a "substitution instance" of (3), a phrase some will think better suited for the relation of instance to schema than for any relation (19) bears to (1); and he calls (3) "the law of substitutivity of identity," a description that can perhaps be taken to reflect confidence that (3) is a valid schema but that seems inappropriate to an instance of the schema: '$2 + 3 = 5$ or $2 + 3 \neq 5$' is not the law of excluded middle. Still, there is the fact that (3) appears as a line in the argument, seemingly on a par with (19), (20), and (21). And if this does not settle the matter, there is Kripke's comment that (3) "says that, for any objects x and y, if x is identical to y, then if x has a certain property F, so does y."

But if (3) is to be understood as a notational variant of (1), its presence in the argument might seem hard to explain. Evidently it is not designed to enhance the power of (19) and (20), so far at least as concerns the deduction of (21). And if intended as a premise to (19), it can seem insufficient: there is in (19) no talk of properties. What, then, is its function? Perhaps the following passage gives an answer: "Where [F] is any property at all, including a property involving modal operators, and if x and y are the same object and x [has] F, then y has to have the same property F. And this is so even if the property F is itself of the form of necessarily having some other property G, in particular that of necessarily being identical to a certain object."[11] Here we seem invited to regard (19) as a particular case of (1), as following from (1) in the sense of being a consequence of (1) in conjunction with

(22) $(x)(\exists z)(y)(z$ is a property of $y \leftrightarrow \Box x = y)$,

which is the comprehension principle corresponding to (19) and the truth of which is taken for granted.

I have no desire to press too hard a few sentences from a transcription of a tape of a lecture delivered without a written text. And even if Kripke's remarks about (19) suggest the view that (1) stands to other indiscernibility principles as general truth to particular instances, there is no indication in anything he says of the doctrine that some indiscernibility principles are false. This doctrine is strongly suggested, however, in Wiggin's commentaries[12] on Kripke's argument.

Wiggins reads Kripke's argument much as I do: he takes Kripke's (3) to be a formulation of the principle that if x is identical with y then every property of x is a property of y, and he sees the argument as involving a "transition" from (3), so understood, to (19). It is, in fact, doubt about the legitimacy of this transition that makes him suspect the argument fails as convincing proof of (21). Specifically, Wiggins has doubts about (22), the comprehension principle that mediates the transition to (19). What reason, he asks, is there to think it true? His question is not intended to voice some general skepticism of comprehension principles. On the contrary, Wiggins thinks that if '$\Box x = y$' could be shown to be an "extensional" open sentence, an open sentence substitution instances of which do not generate failures of substitutivity, (22) would be in good standing. But he thinks there is a "real *prima facie* possibility" that '$\Box x = y$' is a non-extensional open sentence, like 'Philip believes that x denounced y' or 'probably x denounced y', and that therefore (22) may be no better off than (18).[13]

It would be somewhat tangential to our main concerns to try to do justice to the subtle considerations that lead Wiggins thus to suspect '$\Box x = y$'. Suffice it to say that, finding "possible worlds . . . an algebraic device . . . or nothing,"[14] he sees no explanation of '$\Box$' that will accommodate its use as a sentence operator and at the same time enable us to see (21), for example, as thoroughly *de re*—"as simply saying of anything x and anything y, however described, that if x is y then x necessarily is y."[15] What must be noticed, however, is that Wiggins's doubts about the transition from (1) to (19) must carry over to (19) itself. Otherwise he would see a sound argument for (21) based simply on the premises (19) and (20). Indeed, if '$\Box x = y$' *is* an open sentence that is not extensional, (19) is surely false. Non-extensionality of '$\Box x = y$' would mean the existence of names α, β, and β' such that $\ulcorner \beta = \beta' \urcorner$ and $\ulcorner \Box \alpha = \beta \urcorner$ are true and yet $\ulcorner \Box \alpha = \beta' \urcorner$ is false. But then $\ulcorner \beta = \beta' \rightarrow (\Box \alpha = \beta \rightarrow \Box \alpha = \beta') \urcorner$ would falsify (19).

My account of Wiggins takes certain liberties with his text—partly for the sake of brevity and uniformity in approach, partly because I have not hesitated to resolve without argument questions of interpretation that are disputable. Wiggins does not, for example, separate as sharply as I have the schematic and nonschematic readings of (3). Neither does he explicitly formulate (22), and it would in fact be closer to his own way to represent him as questioning rather

(23) $(x)(\exists z)(z = (\lambda y)(\Box x = y))$.

I would say this is his way were it not for uncertainty on my part as to how to understand his use of lambda-notation. In (23) it must be understood as a device whereby singular terms (open or closed) are formed from open sentences. Although much that Wiggins says points in this direction,[16] there is more that points, rather, to taking his lambda-expressions as complex predicates,[17] so that $\ulcorner (\lambda \alpha)\phi \urcorner$ has roughly the sense of $\ulcorner$is something such that $\phi \urcorner$. Thus understood, he should be represented as questioning

(24) $(x)(\exists z)(y)(z$ is a property of $y \leftrightarrow (\lambda w)(\Box x = w)y)$.

Notice that (23) implies (22) but goes farther in purporting actually to mention, for a given thing x, the property of being something with which it is necessary that x is identical. On the other hand, (24) is equivalent to (22), since '$(\lambda w)(\Box x = w)y$' amounts simply to '$\Box x = y$'.

My account also omits mention of Wiggins's attempt to refurbish Kripke's argument. Very roughly, the idea is to use '$\Box$'—or 'nec', for purposes of distinguishing—as a modifier of lambda-expressions rather than a sentential connective. The advantage claimed is that essentialist doctrines—in particular, the doctrine that x is necessarily identical with anything with which it is identical at all—can thereby be more accurately represented. Thus '$(\lambda w)(nec(\lambda r)(\lambda s)(r = s)xw)$' is alleged to be superior to '$(\lambda w)(\Box x = w)$' in point of being constructible without suspicion of recourse to non-extensional open sentences, so that

(25) $(x)(\exists z)(y)(z$ is a property of $y \leftrightarrow ((\lambda w)(nec(\lambda r)(\lambda s)(r = s)xw)y)$

is free from the alleged defect of (24). But discussion of the refurbishing is best left to another occasion. Our present concern is with the views about indiscernibility principles that seem to Wiggins to make them desirable.

3

These views, as some will have long since anticipated, run afoul of Russell's paradox.[18] Surely

(26) $(x)(y)(x = y \rightarrow (\sim x$ is a property of $x \rightarrow \sim y$ is a property of $y))$

is a true indiscernibility principle. But its corresponding comprehension principle is

(27) $(\exists z)(x)(z$ is a property of $x \leftrightarrow \sim x$ is a property of $x)$,

which is demonstrably false. In order for an indiscernibility principle to be true, it is therefore not necessary that its corresponding comprehension principle be true. Of course, (26) is quantificationally implied by the conjunction of (1) with (27). But that is hardly ground for seeing (26) as standing to (1) in the manner of special case to general principle: recall the deductive powers of (2) when conjoined with false principles of friendship.

The instance is not, in Hume's phrase, "particular and singular." Another is

(28) $(x)(y)(x = y \rightarrow ((w) \sim (x$ is a property of $w . w$ is a property of $x) \rightarrow$
        $(w) \sim (y$ is a property of $w . w$ is a property of $y)))$.

Moreover, (26) and (28) are only first and second in an infinite sequence of like cases.[19] And there are infinitely many others. One such is

(29) $(x)(y)(x = y \rightarrow (x = x . \sim x$ is a property of $x \rightarrow$
        $y = y . \sim y$ is a property of $y))$;

for its corresponding comprehension principle is

(30) $(\exists z)(x)(z$ is a property of $x \leftrightarrow x = x . \sim x$ is a property of $x)$,

which has the false consequence

(31) $\sim (x)(x = x)$.

Others can be obtained by altering (29) only to the extent of replacing '$x = x$' with open sentences like it in having just 'x' free and in having true universal closures. We may, in fact, simply replace '$x = x$' with one or another arbitrarily chosen true sentence; for an instance of the schema

(32) $(\exists z)(x)(z$ is a property of $x \leftrightarrow p$. $\sim x$ is a property of $x)$

is true or false according as the sentence put for 'p' is false or true (assuming, as I suppose is fair in the present context, that there is at least one unexemplified property). This shows, by the way, that judgment as to the truth value of a comprehension principle may have to await the outcome of extensive scientific inquiry—or, for that matter, the outcome of next year's World Series.

If these examples seem to diminish the importance of (1), that is as it should be. Once they are recognized, it becomes difficult to see the point of singling out (1) as "the principle of the indiscernibility of identicals" or, as I unfortunately called it, "the principle of identity." It is a true indiscernibility principle, one among others; but it is not a general truth of which the rest are special cases. And to claim that it is a general truth of which *some* of the rest are special cases strikes me as at best a not very happy way of asserting that some indiscernibility principles are quantificationally implied by the conjunction of (1) with true comprehension principles. If we are to say that

(33) $(x)(y)(x = y \rightarrow$ (Boston will win next year's World Series .
        $\sim x$ is a property of $x \rightarrow$ Boston will win next year's World Series .
        $\sim y$ is a property of $y)$

is or is not a special case of (1) depending upon the course of next year's season, then we might as well say that

(34) $(x)(y)(x = y \rightarrow (x$ is a resident of Darrtown $\rightarrow$
        y is a resident of Darrtown))

is or is not a special case of (2) depending upon whether

(35) $(\exists z)(x)(z$ is a friend of $x \leftrightarrow x$ is a resident of Darrtown)

happens to be true. There are, after all, *some* true friendship principles.

It should not be thought that the incapacity of (1) to serve as an all-purpose indiscernibility principle results from peculiarities of 'is a property of'. So far at least as the considerations just now adduced are concerned, no other predicate fares any better. No doubt 'is a member of' is clearer: sets are superior to properties with respect to individuation[20] and perhaps also with respect to conditions of existence.[21] But as a candidate for the principle of the indiscernibility of identicals

(36) $(z)(x)(y)(x = y \rightarrow (x \in z \rightarrow y \in z))$

exhibits deficiencies like those of (1). And we may say, if we choose, that x is identical with y only if everything true of x is true of y. But if this is taken as equivalent to a universal closure of an instance of the schema (3), it serves no better than (1) or (36). There is no indiscernibility principle that stands to the others, or to the others that are true, as general truth to particular cases. It should not be thought, either, that this circumstance is peculiar to indiscernibility principles. It is ubiquitous. Thus, among universal closures of instances of the schema

(37) $(x)(Fx \vee \sim Fx)$.

there is no one that generalizes on the rest. In particular,

(38) $(z)(x)(z$ is a property of $x \vee \sim z$ is a property of $x)$

does not—and for reasons like those brought to bear in the case of indiscernibility principles.

4

If the comprehension principle corresponding to a given indiscernibility principle is true, then certainly the indiscernibility principle itself is true: it is quantificationally implied by (1) together with the comprehension principle. Hence, if an indiscernibility principle is false, so is its corresponding comprehension principle. There may thus seem to be a point after all in emphasizing the truth of (1). It may seem that (1) is a peg on which to hang explanations of such anomalous cases as (13).

Now there is a step here that might well be questioned. It is indeed true that an indiscernibility principle is false only if its corresponding comprehension principle is false. But it is also true that an indiscernibility principle is false only if its corresponding friendship principle is false: the indiscernibility principle is quantificationally implied by (2) together with that friendship principle. So why not emphasize the truth of (2) and use *it* as a peg on which to hang explanations of cases like (13)? Whatever perplexity this question occasions would be serious were it not that the project of explaining the *falsity* of one or another indiscernibility principle is in any case wrongheaded. The reason is that there are no false indiscernibility principles.

This is not to say that there is nothing to be explained: (13) has the look of an indiscernibility principle and yet

(39)   Hesperus = Phosphorus → (astro Hesperus = Phosphorus →
         astro Phosphorus = Phosphorus)

is false. The explanation has, in effect, been given by Quine. The defect in (13) is not falsity but unintelligibility. Falsity of (39) demonstrates the opacity of the 'astro'-construction, the function that assigns $\ulcorner$astro $\phi\urcorner$ to a given sentence ϕ. That construction transforms a referential position, one subject to the substitutivity of identity, into a nonreferential one. Thus (13) violates Quine's law that *"no variable inside an opaque construction is bound by an operator outside."*[22] The point is, of course, not that 'astro x = Phosphorus' is an open sentence whose free variable mysteriously resists binding from outside. Rather, it is not properly an open sentence at all.

Quine's own way has been to use his law in direct support of the validity of the schema (3):

> . . . one feels that any interpretation of 'Fx' violating (3) would be simply a distortion of the manifest intent of 'Fx' and 'Fy'. Anyway I hope one feels this, for there is good reason to. Since there is no quantifying into an opaque construction, the positions of 'x' and 'y' in 'Fx' and 'Fy' must be referential if 'x' and 'y' in those positions are to be bound by the initial '(x)' and '(y)' of (3) at all. Since the notation of (3) manifestly intends the quantifiers to bind 'x' and 'y' in all four shown places, any interpretation of 'Fx' violating (3) would be a distortion.[23]

Briefly, the validity of (3) "rests on the incoherence of bound variables in any but referential position."[24] Although it is not my intention to disagree, I think it worthwhile to inquire into the credentials of the law. Why is there no quantifying into an opaque construction?

Quine has more than once argued substantially as follows.[25] Let us try to apply existential generalization to (10), thereby obtaining the apparent consequence

(40) $(\exists x)(\text{astro } x = \text{Phosphorus})$.

What is this object which, according to (40), is such that it is a truth of astronomy that it is identical with Phosphorus? According to (10), from which (40) was inferred, it is Hesperus, that is, Phosphorus; but to suppose this would conflict with the fact that (12) is false. Now, it is not altogether clear, I think, what the conflict alluded to is supposed to be. Quine has sometimes been understood as arguing simply that a double application of existential generalization to the conjunction of (10), (11), and (12) would result in

(41) $(\exists x)(\exists y)(x = y \, . \, \text{astro } x = y \, . \, {\sim}\text{astro } y = y)$,

which would conflict with the validity of (3); that, in general, quantification into opaque constructions would yield results incompatible with the validity of that schema.[26] For anyone already prepared to accept the validity of the schema, this is good enough. But validity of the schema was just now made to rest on the incoherence of quantification into an opaque construction. There appears to be a circle.

Perhaps Quine is to be understood, rather, as follows. It would be counter to astronomy to deny

(42) $(y)(y = \text{Phosphorus} \leftrightarrow y = \text{Hesperus})$,

and an application of existential generalization to the conjunction of (42) with (10) would yield

(43) $(\exists x)((y)(y = \text{Phosphorus} \leftrightarrow y = x) . \text{astro } x = \text{Phosphorus})$.

Again, no one could reasonably deny

(44) $(y)(y = \text{Phosphorus} \leftrightarrow y = \text{Phosphorus})$,

and an application of existential generalization to the conjunction of (44) with (12) would yield

(45) $(\exists x)((y)(y = \text{Phosphorus} \leftrightarrow y = x) . \sim \text{astro } x = \text{Phosphorus})$.

Consider, then, the thing identical with Phosphorus. Is *it* a thing such that it is a truth of astronomy that *it* is identical with Phosphorus? In view of (43) and (45), no answer could be given. There is some one thing identical with Phosphorus. But there is no settling the question whether it satisfies 'astro $x = \text{Phosphorus}$'. To permit quantification into opaque constructions is thus at odds with the fundamental intent of objectual quantification.

Whether or not this reasoning is Quine's, it does provide a way out of the circle. It can be put to use in direct support of any indiscernibility principle. Consider just one example. If it is suggested that, although x is identical with y, something z is a friend of x but not of y, then x, y, and z will be such that

(46) $(w)(w = y \leftrightarrow w = x) . z$ is a friend of x

and

(47) $(w)(w = y \leftrightarrow w = y) . \sim z$ is a friend of y.

Hence y and z will be such that

(48) $(\exists u)((w)(w = y \leftrightarrow w = u) . z$ is a friend of u)

and

(49) $(\exists u)((w)(w = y \leftrightarrow w = u) . \sim z$ is a friend of u).

But then consider the thing that is y. Is z a friend of *it*? There will be no saying.

It is no accident that this reasoning parallels that given early on in defense of there being no property of Hesperus that is not also a property of Phosphorus. There the names 'Hesperus' and 'Phosphorus' occurred vacuously, of course; so, we now see, did 'is a property of'. Indeed, any indiscernibility principle can be defended in the same manner. Here, then, is added reason for refusing (1) a special place among indiscernibility principles.

5

I have come down firmly on the side of opacity of the 'astro'-construction. There is no alternative if the only available rule is that $\ulcorner$astro $\phi\urcorner$ counts as true if and only if ϕ itself is a truth of astronomy. It might be suggested, however, that a sentence such as (10) can be taken another way: as saying that Hesperus is a thing x and Phosphorus a thing y such that it is a truth of astronomy that x is identical with y. If (12) were read similarly, (10) and (12) would not diverge in truth value. This is not to say that their truth value would thereby be fixed. The task would remain of settling, somehow, which pairs of things satisfy 'astro $x = y$'. Here a fundamental constraint, consequent upon the intended interpretation of ' $=$ ' and of devices of quantification, would be that

(50) $(x)(y)(x = y \rightarrow (\text{astro } x = y \rightarrow \text{astro } y = y))$

come out true. But the question of the truth value of

(51) $(y)(\exists z)(x)(z$ is a property of $x \leftrightarrow$ astro $x = y)$

need not arise.

These remarks carry over to '$\Box$'. That symbol is sometimes so used that $\ulcorner\Box\phi\urcorner$ counts as true if and only if ϕ itself is necessary. If that is all there is to go on, we have no option but to count the '$\Box$'-construction opaque and hence (19) unintelligible. But (19), (20), and (21) are witnesses to a contemplated transparent '$\Box$'-construction. Now, the intelligibility of such a construction is not guaranteed simply by an antecedent understanding of quantification and of the opaque '$\Box$'-construction.[27] The problem remains of settling, somehow, which sequences of objects satisfy $\ulcorner\Box\phi\urcorner$ where ϕ is an open sentence. And a fundamental constraint on a solution to the problem is that indiscernibility principles involving '$\Box$' come out true. That their corresponding comprehension principles come out true is neither here nor there.

Notes

This essay was first published in *Midwest Studies in Philosophy* 4 (1979): 293–306.

1. Strictly speaking, it is only with respect to one or another interpretation that a sentence is, or is not, an indiscernibility principle. I follow the common practice of suppressing reference to the intended interpretation where there seems no risk of confusion. But to guard against certain misunderstandings it must be said at once that I count a sentence an indiscernibility principle only if its variables are objectual and unrestricted in range. The second of these requirements could be relaxed in various ways, but I have not seen the point of doing so: variables unrestricted in range are unavoidable if justice is to be done to the views I intend to discuss, and restricted variables serve no theoretical purpose once unrestricted variables are at hand. I am aware of the view that unrestricted quantification is somehow illegitimate; but the arguments given in support of it, insofar as I understand them, are unpersuasive, resting as they do on the gratuitous assumption that the various objects over which a variable ranges must belong to or comprise or be in some one object, the domain of values of the variable.

I take for granted throughout the (total) reflexivity, symmetry, and transitivity of ' = '. Given just symmetry, $\ulcorner(\alpha)(\alpha')(\alpha = \alpha' \to (\phi \to \phi'))\urcorner$ is equivalent to $\ulcorner(\alpha)(\alpha')(\alpha = \alpha' \to (\phi \leftrightarrow \phi'))\urcorner$.

2. See, for example, my "Identity and Substitutivity," in this volume; Saul Kripke, "Identity and Necessity," in Milton K. Munitz, ed., *Identity and Individuation* (New York: New York University Press, 1971), pp. 135–164; Leonard Linsky, "Substitutivity and Descriptions," *Journal of Philosophy* 63 (1966): 673–683, and *Referring* (New York: Humanities Press, 1967), especially chap. 5; Alvin Plantinga, "De Re et De Dicto," *Noûs* 3 (1969): 235–258, and *The Nature of Necessity* (Oxford: Clarendon Press, 1974), especially chap. 2 and appendix; David Wiggins, "Essentialism, Continuity, and Identity," *Synthese* 23 (1974): 321–359, "Identity, Necessity, and Physicalism," in Stephan Körner, ed., *Philosophy of Logic* (Berkeley: University of California Press, 1976), pp. 96–132, and "Reply to Comments," same volume, pp. 159–182.

3. The interpretation of '$(F)(x)(y)(x = y \to (Fx \to Fy))$' according to which it is a rather curious notational variant of (1), is *not* any of its various second-order interpretations—if for no other reason than that on such interpretations the so-called individual variables must be restricted in range. (See George Boolos, "On Second-Order Logic," *Journal of Philosophy* 72 (1975): 509–526.) No sentence, on a second-order interpretation, says that, whatever x and y may be, x is identical with y only if every property of x is a property of y.

4. This reasoning is set forth more fully, but with respect to another example, in my "Identity and Substitutivity," pp. 141–145.

5. "Identity and Substitutivity."

6. Such as E. J. Lemmon. See his "A Theory of Attributes Based on Modal Logic," *Acta Philosophica Fennica* (1963): 95–122.

7. "Essentialism, Continuity, and Identity," p. 343, and "Identity, Necessity, and Physicalism," p. 109.

8. "Substitutivity and Descriptions," p. 681, and *Referring*, p. 79.

9. "De Re et De Dicto," p. 239, and *The Nature of Necessity*, p. 15. In the former the principle is put thus: "Where P is any property and x and y are individuals, x is identical with y only if x has P if and only if y has P." In the latter 'individuals' is replaced by 'objects'.

10. "Identity and Necessity," p. 136.

11. "Identity and Necessity," p. 137.

12. For which see "Essentialism, Continuity, and Identity"; "Identity, Necessity, and Physicalism"; and "The *De Re* 'must': A Note on the Logical Form of Essentialist Claims," in Gareth Evans and John McDowell, eds., *Truth and Meaning* (Oxford: Clarendon Press, 1976), pp. 285–312.

13. See especially "Reply to Comments," pp. 169–170, 174.

14. "Identity, Necessity, and Physicalism," p. 105.

15. "Essentialism, Continuity, and Identity," p. 329, and "Identity, Necessity, and Physicalism," p. 103.

16. Thus Wiggins does not hesitate to use lambda-expressions as objects of the verb 'to have': "Identity, Necessity, and Physicalism," p. 112; "Essentialism, Continuity, and Identity," pp. 346 and 348; "The *De Re* 'Must'," p. 293. And $(\lambda x)(\lambda y)(x = y)$ is said to be "the relation of identity"; similarly $nec(\lambda x)(\lambda y)(x = y)$ is said to be "that relation which any r and s have if they are necessarily identical" ("The *De Re* 'Must'," p. 293).

17. We are told repeatedly that 'nec' is a modifier of *predicates*, or a predicate (as opposed to a sentential) operator. See "Essentialism, Continuity, and Identity," p. 345; "Identity, Necessity, and Physicalism," p. 112; "Reply to Comments," p. 174. That lambda-expressions are complex predicates seems virtually required by their treatment in "The *De Re* 'Must'." See also Christopher Peacocke, "An Appendix to David Wiggins' 'Note'," in Evans and McDowell, *Truth and Meaning*, pp. 313–324.

18. This is pointed out, though not altogether satisfactorily, in my "Substitutivity" (abstract), *Journal of Philosophy* 63 (1966): 684–685. It is also noticed by W. V. Quine, Review of Munitz, ed., *Identity and Individuation*, *Journal of Philosophy* 69 (1972): 488–497, see especially p. 490.

19. To see how to construct the sequence, consult W. V Quine, *Mathematical Logic*, rev. ed. (Cambridge, Mass.: Harvard University Press, 1951), p. 130.

20. As Quine has repeatedly pointed out. See, for example, *Word and Object* (Cambridge, Mass.: MIT Press, 1960), pp. 209ff, and *Set Theory and Its Logic*, rev. ed. (Cambridge, Mass.: Harvard University Press, 1969), p. 2.

21. I have in mind those who see in the cumulative type structure an articulation of the intuitive concept of set.

22. *Word and Object*, p. 166.

23. *Word and Object*, pp. 167–168. Notation and numbering have been altered to conform with mine.

24. Review of Munitz, p. 490.

25. See, for example, *From a Logical Point of View*, 2d ed., rev. (New York: Harper and Row, 1963), p. 148.

26. See Robert C. Sleigh, Jr., "On Quantifying into Epistemic Contexts," *Noûs* 1 (1967): 23–31, especially pp. 25–26.

27. Cf. Quine, *From a Logical Point of View*, p. 150.

Propositions of Pure Logic

The phrase 'propositions of pure logic' occurs in the second of Russell's Lowell Lectures of 1914;[1] Russell had already used it, or rather its French equivalent, three years earlier in a lecture at the Ecole des Hautes Etudes Sociales;[2] and it appears four years later, in the singular, in the fifth of the lectures called "The Philosophy of Logical Atomism."[3] I have taken it for a title because it suggests a question which Russell addressed in those lectures, and in other writings as well, and which I intend to discuss here: the question, Of what sort is a proposition of logic? Save indirectly as I proceed, I cannot do much by way of clarifying the question. I had better say at once, however, that it is not the boundaries of logic that are here at issue but the nature of the truths found or sought within territory indisputably logical. First-order logic is logic if anything is; whether logic glimpses beyond is a question I shall not discuss.

I

As text for much of the discussion that follows I take four passages that occur close upon one another in the second Lowell Lecture:

> In all inference, form alone is essential: the particular subject-matter is irrelevant except as securing the truth of the premises. This is one reason for the great importance of logical form. When I say, "Socrates was a man, all men are mortal, therefore Socrates was mortal," the connection of premises and conclusion does not in any way depend upon its being Socrates and man and mortality that I am mentioning. The general form of the inference may be expressed in some such words as, "If a thing has a certain property, and whatever has this property has a certain other property, then the thing in question also has that other property." Here no particular things or properties are mentioned: the proposition is absolutely general. All inferences, when fully stated, are instances of propositions having this kind of generality. . . . In logic it is a waste of time to deal with inferences concerning particular cases: we deal throughout with completely general and purely formal implications. (pp. 53–54)

It will be remembered that we excluded from pure logic such propositions as, "Socrates is a man, all men are mortal, therefore Socrates is
mortal," because *Socrates* and *man* and *mortal* are empirical terms, only
to be understood through particular experience. The corresponding
proposition in pure logic is: "If anything has a certain property, and
whatever has this property has a certain other property, then the
thing in question has the other property." This proposition is absolutely general: it applies to all things and all properties. And it is quite
self-evident. Thus in such propositions of pure logic we have the
self-evident general propositions of which we were in search. (p. 66)

A proposition such as "If Socrates is a man, and all men are mortal,
then Socrates is mortal," is true in virtue of its *form* alone. . . . The
general truth of which it is an instance is purely formal, and belongs
to logic. (p. 67)

Logic, we may say, consists of two parts. The first part investigates
what propositions are and what forms they may have; this part
enumerates the different kinds of atomic propositions, of molecular
propositions, of general propositions, and so on. The second part
consists of certain supremely general propositions, which assert the
truth of all propositions of certain forms. (p. 67)

The first two of these passages contain certain confusions that I want
quickly to mention only to set aside as peripheral to my main concerns.
Inference from the propositions that Socrates is a man and that all men are
mortal to the proposition that Socrates is mortal is confused with the
argument which has the first two propositions as premises and the third as
conclusion; this argument is in turn confused with its corresponding conditional, the conditional which has the conjunction of the premises of the
argument as antecedent and the conclusion as consequent; and the conditional itself is confused with the proposition that the conjuncts of its
antecedent together imply its consequent. It is unfortunate, I think, that
these confusions permit Russell in effect to ignore the argument, or the
associated assertion of implication, in favor of the conditional proposition
and thereby to focus attention on logical truth rather than the more general
notion of logical consequence. But I shall not pursue that matter here.
There are grounds even so for dissatisfaction with Russell's views about
propositions of pure logic.

As an example of such a proposition Russell offers

(1)   If a thing has a certain property, and whatever has this property has
a certain other property, then the thing in question also has that other
property.

His point is not, or is not simply, that this proposition is logically true. So are, for example,

(2)   If Socrates is a man, and all men are mortal, then Socrates is mortal

and

(3)   If a thing is a man, and whatever is a man is mortal, then the thing in question is mortal.

Yet we are specifically told that (2) is not a proposition of logic, and I think it is clear that Russell would have said the same of (3). One reason he gives for excluding (2), a reason that would apply to (3) as well, is that it contains "empirical terms": *Socrates, man,* and *mortal*. I shall have nothing to say about this. I want to concentrate instead on another respect in which (1) and (2) are said to differ, a point of contrast on which Russell himself lays greater stress. He says that (1), in contrast with (2), is absolutely, completely, supremely general; it "applies to all things and all properties." Now I suppose we are ready to agree that (1) does differ from (2) in point of generality. But we might wonder whether (3) does not differ from (2) in the same way; and if it is said, as there is some reason to think Russell would have said, that in (3) there is mention of the particular properties of being a man and being mortal, then it might be wondered why we should not equally say that in (1) there is mention of a particular relation, the relation things bear to their properties. Let me try to circumvent these worries, temporarily at least, by bringing to bear another remark Russell makes about (1), namely, that it is "the general truth of which [(2)] is an instance." The definite article is unjustified, of course: (3), for example, is also *a* general truth of which (2) is an instance. But I take Russell to have meant that (1) is the general truth the instances of which include not only (2), and other instances of (3), but also all propositions of the form

(4) $(Fa \ \& \ (y)(Fy \rightarrow Gy)) \rightarrow Ga$.

Proposition (3) generalizes over some propositions of this form; (1) generalizes over them all. It is by virtue of being a general truth the instances of which are precisely the propositions of a certain logical form that (1), in contrast with (2) and (3), qualifies as a proposition of pure logic.

By way of an example of a proposition of pure logic, Russell sometimes offers not (1) but a close relative:

(5)   If all the members of any class α are members of a class β, and if x is a member of the class α, then x is a member of the class β.

And what he says of (5) is similar to what he says of (1):

Take for example the classical argument: All men are mortal, Socrates is a man, therefore Socrates is mortal. Here it is evident that what is said remains true if Plato or Aristotle or anybody else is substituted for Socrates. We can, then, say: If all men are mortal, and if x is a man, then x is mortal. This is a first generalization of the proposition from which we set out. But it is easy to go farther. In the deduction which has been stated, nothing depends on the fact that it is men and mortals which occupy our attention. If all the members of any class α are members of a class β, and if x is a member of the class α, then x is a member of the class β. In this statement, we have the pure logical form which underlies all the deductions of the same logical form as that which proves that Socrates is mortal.

One naturally assumes that (5) "underlies" deductions of the form in question in the sense that it is the generalization of which their corresponding conditionals are the instances. But these conditionals are propositions of the form (4), and one therefore wonders whether it is (1) or (5) that is *the* generalization of which the instances are precisely the propositions of the form (4). In light of Russell's view that classes are logical fictions, I think we are best advised to take it to be (1). So at any rate I shall assume. In any case, what Russell immediately goes on to say, in the passage from which I just quoted, presumably applies to (1) as well as (5):

> To obtain a proposition of pure mathematics (or of mathematical logic, which is the same thing), we must submit a deduction of any kind to a process analogous to that which we have just performed, that is to say, when an argument remains valid if one of its terms is changed, this term must be replaced by a variable, i.e., by an indeterminate object. In this way we finally reach a proposition of pure logic, that is to say a proposition which does not contain any other constant than logical constants.[4]

We are thus to see (1) as the result of generalizing on the three nonlogical constants of (2), just as (3) results from generalizing on the single nonlogical constant 'Socrates'—where in both cases generalization consists in replacing constants with variables and supplying devices of universal quantification sufficient to effect closure.[5]

2

I intend to argue against this account of (1) later on. I shall argue that neither it nor any other proposition is a general truth having as its instances all propositions of the form (4), and, indeed, that (1) no more merits the name 'proposition of pure logic' than does (2) or (3). But first let me call attention to another view about propositions of logic to which Russell inclined, a view which makes its appearance in the Lowell Lectures when he comes to describe what he calls "the second part of logic." This part of logic consists, he says, of "certain supremely general propositions, *which assert the truth of all propositions of certain forms.*" I have referred to this as "another view," but the words just quoted, and the context in which they occur, strongly suggest that Russell regarded it rather as an elaboration or elucidation of the alleged supreme generality of a proposition such as (1). Apparently he took that proposition to be a proposition to the effect that every proposition of a certain logical form is true. And the form in question is presumably (4), so that (1) comes to be identified with

(6)   Every proposition of the form
       $(Fa$ & $(y)(Fy \rightarrow Gy)) \rightarrow Ga$
       is true.

Now this really is another view, however Russell may have intended it; for it is incompatible with the first view. No doubt (6) is a general truth; and, if we are willing to exempt the form (4), we can perhaps agree that in (6) no particular things or properties are mentioned. But (6) is not a general truth of which (2) and other propositions of the form (4) are the instances. An instance of (6) is a proposition, with respect to some proposition, that it is true if of the form (4); and evidently no proposition of the form (4) is itself such a proposition. A proposition to the effect that every proposition of a certain logical form is true is not a general truth of which propositions of that form are the instances.

Russell gives distinct and incompatible accounts of (1): on the one hand, it is said to be a general truth of which propositions of a certain logical form are the instances; on the other hand, it is said to be the proposition that every proposition of that form is true. What is more, though neither account seems to me to be right, the second is utterly implausible. Surely (1) is not a proposition about a propositional form.

One wonders how Russell could have come to think otherwise. How could he have come to think, or even to be inclined to think, that (1) is the very same proposition as (6)? And how could he have failed to notice the incompatibility of this with the view that (1) is a general truth of which propositions of the form (4) are the instances? I think the explanation is to be found in part in a certain view he took of universal quantification and in part in a confusion of propositional forms with propositional functions.

Russell took (1) to be the proposition that the propositional function

(7) $(x$ has A & $(y)(y$ has $A \rightarrow y$ has $B)) \rightarrow x$ has B

is "always true." In *Principia Mathematica* 'always true' is officially undefined; but informally, there and elsewhere, two explanations are given of its sense.[6] According to one of these, to say that (7), for example, is always true is to assert, in one fell swoop, each value of (7)—each instance of (1), as we might say were we not engaged in giving Russell's account of universal propositions. Taken at face value, this explanation has the consequence that there is, strictly speaking, no such proposition as (1). We may assertively utter the sentence 'If a thing has a certain property, and whatever has this property has a certain other property, then the thing in question has that other property'; or, what is supposed to come to the same thing, we may assertively utter '(7) is always true'. But to do so is to assert many propositions, no one of which is *the* proposition formulated in the sentence uttered. No doubt this has consequences for Russell's views about propositions of logic. But I shall not pause over them, for it is the second explanation of 'always true' that I see at work in his inclination to identify (1) with (6). According to that explanation, to say that (7) is always true is to assert that every value of (7) is true. This is at odds with the first explanation, since to assert that every value of (7) is true is not to assert every value of (7); it is not, in fact, to assert any value of (7). And whatever we may think of the first explanation, the second results in a mistaken account of universal propositions. If (1) were the proposition that every value of (7) is true, it would be the proposition that a proposition is a value of (7) only if true. An instance of it would accordingly be a proposition, with respect to some given proposition, that it is a value of (7) only if true. But evidently no instance of (1) is such a proposition.

But suppose this mistaken account of universal propositions to be combined with the further mistake of confusing the propositional form (4) with the propositional function (7). Then *value of* (7) will be confused with *proposition of form* (4). And (1), already mistakenly identified with the proposition that every value of (7) is true, will come to be thought of as the proposition that every proposition of the form (4) is true. Thus I see the generation of the idea that (1) is the same proposition as (6). And once the idea has taken hold, it is easy enough not to notice that instances of (6) are not propositions of the form (4); for, again, *proposition of form* (4) has been confused with *value of* (7), and values of (7) are in any case instances of (1).

Now, the view that (6) is a proposition of pure logic is a plausible one; hence to associate with it the implausible identification of (6) with (1) is unfortunate. So let me set (6) to one side for the time being and concentrate on the contention that (1) is a general truth of which propositions of the form (4) are the instances. I can thereby set aside, also, Russell's mistaken account of universal propositions; for, in order to arrive at the view that (1) is a general truth of which propositions of the form (4) are the instances, it suffices to confuse the propositional form (4) with the propositional function (7).

That Russell did confuse form with function is suggested by the frequency with which, in "The Philosophy of Logical Atomism" and in *Introduction to Mathematical Philosophy*, the expression 'always true', originally intended for application to propositional functions, is applied to what are ostensibly propositional forms. And the suggestion is strengthened when we juxtapose two remarks from the second of these works. Logic, we are first told, "is concerned only with *forms*, and is concerned with them only in the way of stating that they are always or sometimes true" (p. 199). Then, five pages on, we read that "propositions of logic will always be such as affirm that some propositional function is *always* true" (p. 204). Since it is intended to express Russell's conviction that the truth of a proposition of logic "is independent of the existence of the universe" (p. 202), the second remark omits 'sometimes true' and stresses 'always'. But the attentive reader will notice the switch from 'form' to 'function'.

It may nevertheless be wondered how he *could* have confused (4) with (7). And, using the notation I have adopted, it is a little difficult. It would be even more difficult were the relevant form of (2) represented this way:

(8)   (. . . so-and-so . . . & $(y)(\ldots y \ldots \rightarrow \underline{\quad} y \underline{\quad})) \rightarrow$
       $\underline{\quad}$ so-and-so $\underline{\quad}$.

Dots and dashes, even 'so-and-so', are unlikely candidates for variables; hence there is little temptation to take (8) to be an open sentence. But Russell's own notation invites confusion. He suppresses 'has', letting concatenation, with the order of the variables reversed, take over its role. And he lets 'x' do double duty: sometimes it is a variable, sometimes it is schematic for proper names. It is thus easy for him to see in

(9) $(Ax$ & $(y)(Ay \rightarrow By)) \rightarrow Bx$

a representation of both (4) and (7). Remembering the suppression of 'has', the letters 'A' and 'B'—and then 'x' as well—will be seen as variables, and the whole as an alternative formulation of (7). Forgetting the suppression of 'has', 'A' and 'B' will be seen as schematic letters; if in addition 'x' is given its schematic role, the result is an alternative representation of (4). The danger is that one will forget the suppression of 'has' and also forget to adjust accordingly the status of 'A', 'B', and 'x'. Then (9) will seem to express a propositional function the values of which are propositions of the form (4).

To see the confusion at work, consider the following passage from *Introduction to Mathematical Philosophy*:

> Take (say) the proposition "Socrates was before Aristotle." Here it seems obvious that we have a relation between two terms, and that the constituents of the proposition . . . are simply the two terms and the relation, *i.e.* Socrates, Aristotle, and *before*. . . . We may represent

the general form of such propositions by "xRy," which may be read "x has the relation R to y." This general form may occur in logical propositions, but no particular instance of it can occur. (p. 198)

If 'xRy' is an open sentence, and if it is to be understood in accordance with a convention whereby concatenation does the job of the three-place predicate 'has the relation . . . to', then it may indeed be read 'x has the relation R to y': we may straightforwardly utter it in the course of formulating a proposition. But if, as Russell tells us, it represents a form, it cannot in the relevant sense be read at all, any more than (8) can. We can talk about it, as I am doing; and of course we can use it to talk about the form it represents. We can pronounce it. But we cannot use it as a subformula of a formulation of a proposition.

In the last sentence of the passage just quoted, Russell uses 'instance of' for the relation a proposition of a certain form bears to that form—a standard usage, but one I have avoided, wanting 'instance of' rather for the relation borne by one proposition to another when the other is a universal proposition from which the one results by instantiation. But if Russell is right, the distinction in sense is idle in the case of (1) and (4). If (1) is a general truth from which all and only propositions of the form (4) result by instantiation, the instances (my sense) of (1) are the instances (his sense) of (4). The question whether he is right needs to be addressed independently of the confusion of propositional form with propositional function.

3

Every instance of (1) is a proposition of the form (4). The question is whether every proposition of the form (4) is an instance of (1). Now, it seems clear that (2), for example, is an instance of (1) only if it is the same proposition as

(10)   If Socrates has the property of being a man, and whatever has the property of being a man has the property of being mortal, then Socrates has the property of being mortal.

Let me further abuse an already abused adjective by calling (10) the *Platonic counterpart* of (2). Similarly in the case of other propositions of the form (4), but with this reservation: the Platonic counterpart of the Platonic counterpart of a proposition is simply the Platonic counterpart of that proposition. Thus (10) is its own Platonic counterpart; no need, then, to ascend to the proposition that if Socrates bears *has* to the property of being a man and whatever bears *has* to the property of being a man bears *has* to the property of being mortal, then Socrates bears *has* to the property of being mortal. And thus a necessary condition for a proposition of the form (4) to be an instance of (1) is that it be identical with its Platonic counterpart.

Deflationists will say that every proposition of the form (4) satisfies this condition. They will say that 'has the property of being' is mere puffery, amounting to no more than 'is'. And it has to be conceded, I think, that a good deal of property-talk is as they describe it: no content is lost by paraphrase downward. But the sticky point has to do with (1) itself. No doubt 'has the property of being a man' and 'has the property of being mortal' often come to no more than, respectively, 'is a man' and 'is mortal'. But what is to be said of 'has a certain property'? Here no comparable device of paraphrase seems available. But if property-talk is indispensable when we go to formulate (1), it is perplexing to be told that it is mere puffery in formulations of instances of (1). How can instantiation effect such a semantic reduction? Instances of (1) are values of (7); their formulations call for names to flank the two-place predicate 'has'. But if 'has the property of being' is only puffery for 'is', then 'has the property of being a man' and 'has the property of being mortal' lack the structure required to formulate a value of (7): 'has' does not occur in them as a two-place predicate, and the contained phrases 'the property of being a man' and 'the property of being mortal' do not there function as singular terms. If on deflationist grounds (10) is the same proposition as (2), then on the same grounds it appears not to be an instance of (1).

Some deflationists will respond that it is wrong, or anyhow misleading, to formulate (1) by prefixing universal quantifiers to an open sentence such as that used above to express (7). It is rightly, or preferably, formulated in

(11) $(A)(B)(x)((Ax \ \& \ (y)(Ay \to By)) \to Bx)$,

for then no mystery attaches to its having (2) and the like as instances. True, when we go to read (11), what Russell called "the habit of using ordinary language"[7] makes us want a verb to link juxtaposed variables; so we dub in 'has' or 'is a property of', according as we reverse or leave unchanged the order of the variables. But we need not be slaves to our linguistic habits. If an aseptic reading of (11) is wanted, or for some reason thought necessary, we may read 'Ax' as '$x \ A$'s' or 'x is an Aer'. The import of (11) is clear in any case: it is simply a compendious way of recording that every proposition of the form (4) is true.

But if the proposed reading of 'Ax' does not give the game away, this last remark surely does. Thus explained, (11) is not a general truth of which propositions of the form (4) are the instances. It is rather what Quine calls an "oblique generalization"[8] over propositions of the form (4). It is (6) in a new formulation. And it would have been better to stay with the old. Since 'true' serves the purpose of oblique generalization, there is no need to prefix quantifiers to the hybrid (9), thereby making schematic letters appear to be variables and again risking confusion of propositional forms with propositional functions. No need, in fact, for deflationary tactics—not, that is, if all that is wanted is a formulation of (6).

Looked at from the other side, identification of propositions of the form (4) with their Platonic counterparts amounts to adoption of an inflationist theory of 'is'. If (10) is really only (2), then (2) really is (10). Inflationists detect in (2) reference to the property of being a man and the property of being mortal. For them (2) is a proposition about those properties. It is the proposition that the property of being a man and the property of being mortal are such that if Socrates has the one and whatever has the one has the other, then Socrates has the other. It is genuinely a value of (7), and hence an instance of (1).

One welcomes the inflationist's recognition of what it is for a proposition to be an instance of (1). But a consequence seems sometimes to go unrecognized. If (2) is an instance of (1), then it is true only if there is such a thing as the property of being a man and such a thing as the property of being mortal. In general, if a proposition of the form (4) is identical with its Platonic counterpart and if its Platonic counterpart is an instance of (1), then it is true only if certain *comprehension principles* are true, propositions of the form

(12) $(\exists A)(x)(x$ has $A \leftrightarrow Fx)$.

Comprehension principles are sometimes casually presupposed, as if not seriously open to question; and perhaps over some range of cases this attitude is justified. But it cannot be sustained over all cases, for some propositions of the form (12) are false. There is no property A such that, for every x, x has A if and only if x does not have x; there is no property A such that, for every x, x has A just in case x has x only if the Earth is flat; and so on, through a host of more or less familiar cases. But propositions of the form (4) are one and all true. It is therefore not true that every proposition of the form (4) is identical with its Platonic counterpart—not true, that is, if the Platonic counterpart of a proposition of the form (4) is always genuinely an instance of (1). And it is therefore not true that (1) is a general truth of which every proposition of the form (4) is an instance.

Russell made the discovery that some propositions of the form (12) are demonstrably false. But of course he would not have put the thing this way. His view was that what were just now alleged to be false comprehension principles are in reality no propositions at all.[9] The sentences that purport to formulate them are meaningless, violating as they do the rule of the theory of types that $\ulcorner \alpha \in \beta \urcorner$ is meaningful only if β is one type higher than α. But Russell seems not to have noticed that the theory of types is incompatible with his view that the propositions of logic are supremely general—incompatible, in particular, with the view that (1) is a general truth having as instances all propositions of the form (4). The authors of

Principia Mathematica recognized that formal similarities among propositions cut across differences of type; indeed, they took this to justify their use throughout that work of "typically ambiguous" notation. Thus they write that

> in almost all the reasonings which constitute mathematics and mathematical logic, we are using ideas which may receive any one of an infinite number of different typical determinations, any one of which leaves the reasoning valid. Thus by employing typically ambiguous words and symbols, we are able to make one chain of reasoning applicable to any one of an infinite number of different cases, which would not be possible were we to forego the use of typically ambiguous words and symbols. (Vol. 1, p. 67)

Propositions of the form (4) are accordingly not to be thought of as confined to some one order in the hierarchy of propositions; the schema used to represent that form is typically ambiguous, susceptible of "any one of an infinite number of different typical determinations." But not so the open sentence used to express (7). Its variables must, according to the theory of types, be fixed as to type; for (7) is not a propositional form but a propositional function of some definite order in the hierarchy of propositional functions. Hence the values of (7) hardly begin to exhaust propositions of the form (4). But the values of (7) are the instances of (1), and therefore (1) is not a general truth which has as instances all propositions of the form (4). On the theory of types there can be no such proposition.

4

If, as I have been arguing, (1) is not a general truth the instances of which are the propositions of a certain logical form, what reason is there to say that it belongs to pure logic? It is logically true, but then so are (2) and (3). And perhaps it is a general truth formulable without recourse to nonlogical constants. But how does that qualify it as a truth of the science which sets forth "the principles by which conclusions are inferred from premises"[10]— or, for that matter, of the science which codifies logical truths?

In his *Philosophy of Logic*,[11] Hilary Putnam appears to offer answers to these questions. Not that he discusses (1); but he seems to argue with respect to a proposition apparently not far removed from (1) that it deserves to be called a proposition of logic. I should say at once that I am uncertain which proposition this is. Early on it appears to be the proposition, in Putnam's words, "that if a class S is a subclass of a class M, and M is in turn a subclass of a class P, then S is a subclass of P" (p. 5). Expanding 'is a subclass of' in the usual way, we obtain

(13) $(S)(M)(P)(((x)(x \in S \rightarrow x \in M) \ \& \ (x)(x \in M \rightarrow x \in P)) \rightarrow (x)(x \in S \rightarrow x \in P))$.

But later it appears to be a proposition that Putnam would have us formulate this way:

(14) $(S)(M)(P)(((x)(Sx \rightarrow Mx) \ \& \ (x)(Mx \rightarrow Px)) \rightarrow (x)(Sx \rightarrow Px))$.

And it is at least doubtful that he takes the proposition thus formulated to be the same proposition as (13). I shall have something to say subsequently about the identity of the proposition formulated in (14) and about its relation to (13). In the meantime it will be instructive to consider, as if it is directed to (13), Putnam's argument that his proposition is a proposition that belongs to logic.

The argument is simply this: logicians assert the validity of the schema

(15) $((x)(Fx \rightarrow Gx) \ \& \ (x)(Gx \rightarrow Hx)) \rightarrow (x)(Fx \rightarrow Hx)$;

but to assert the validity of (15) is just to assert (13). More fully, and in Putnam's words:

> when a logician builds a system which contains such theorems as [(15)], *what does he mean to be asserting*? He may, of course, not mean to be asserting anything; he may just be constructing an uninterpreted formal system, but then he is certainly not doing logic. The simple fact is that the great majority of logicians would understand the intention to be this: the theorems of the system are intended to be valid formulas. Implicitly, if not explicitly, the logician is concerned to make assertions of the form "such-and-such is *valid*"; that is, assertions of the kind [(13)]. (p. 31)

(Here I have dubbed in at the end a reference to (13) where Putnam refers to another formulation of the proposition he also formulates in (14). But remember: I am considering his argument as if it is directed to (13).) Now, we can concede that logicians do, if only implicitly, assert the validity of such schemata as (15). But the proposition that (15) is valid is a proposition about (15), whereas (13) is not. So the proposition that (15) is valid cannot be the very same proposition as (13), and therefore it cannot be quite right to say that to assert the validity of (15) is to make an assertion of the kind (13). But then how *are* (13) and the proposition that (15) is valid supposed to be related?

Notice that the sentence used to formulate (13) is the universal closure of what Quine would call the *set-theoretic analogue* of (15);[12] it is the universal closure of the open sentence that results when the atomic schemata 'Fx', 'Gx', and 'Hx' of (15) are replaced by the atomic open sentences

'$x \in S$', '$x \in M$', and '$x \in P$', respectively. And of course (13) is true. It is perhaps tempting in light of this to think that validity of (15) is simply truth of the proposition expressed by the universal closure of its set-theoretic analogue; that, in general, a schema is valid if and only if the universal closure of its set-theoretic analogue is true. And tempting then to think that (13) enters logic, not by being itself the proposition that (15) is valid, but by being a proposition truth of which is, by definition of validity, a necessary and sufficient condition for a certain schema to be valid.

But this will not do. It is not the case that a sufficient condition for a schema to be valid is that the universal closure of its set-theoretic analogue express a true proposition. Given a schema ϕ, the universal closure of the set-theoretic analogue of ϕ expresses a proposition of set theory; and truth of that proposition is no guarantee that ϕ is valid. For example,

(16) $(\exists x) \sim Fx$

is evidently not valid; but

(17) $(S)(\exists x)(\sim x \in S)$,

the universal closure of the set-theoretic analogue of (16), formulates a true proposition. What faults (16) is that (17), though it expresses a truth, does not do so on all *relativizations*—that is, all results of restricting its variable 'x' to members of a non-empty set U and its variable 'S' to subsets of U. In fact, (17) expresses a truth on no relativization—an interesting circumstance, but more than enough for invalidity of (16). In general: a schema is valid if and only if the universal closure of its set-theoretic analogue expresses none but true propositions on all relativizations—that is, all results of restricting its variables 'x', 'y', 'z', and so on to members of a non-empty set U and its set variables to subsets of U, or sets of ordered pairs of members of U, or sets of ordered triples of members of U, and so on, as increasing polyadicity requires.[13]

These considerations will suffice to convince some that (13) is not the proposition with respect to which Putnam conducts his argument. But let me add to the evidence by quoting the remainder of the passage which I interrupted, somewhat abruptly, above. It continues:

> Thus even first-order logic would normally be thought of as a "metatheory"; insofar as he is making assertions at all in writing down such schemata as [(15)], the logician is making assertions of validity, and that means he is implicitly making second-order assertions: for to assert the validity of the first-order schema [(15)] is just to assert [(14)]—and this is a second-order assertion.
>
> In sum, I believe that (a) it is rather arbitrary to say that "second-order" logic is not "logic"; and (b) even if we do say this, the natural

understanding of first-order logic is that in writing down first-order schemata we are implicitly asserting their validity, that is, making second-order assertions. (pp. 31–32)

One might think that for Putnam 'second-order' and 'metatheoretical' are synonyms, were it not for notational features of (14) and his remarks about first-order and second-order logic. These suggest that (14) is to be taken as a sentence of some second-order language. And that does suffice to distinguish whatever proposition it expresses from (13). For (13) speaks of *all* sets—or classes, there being no need at this point for a distinction. Using again Putnam's formulation, (13) is the proposition "that if a class *S* is a subclass of a class *M*, and *M* is in turn a subclass of a class *P*, then *S* is a subclass of *P*"; and here the indefinite article indicates that *S*, *M*, and *P* are any classes whatever. But if (14) is a sentence of some second-order language, whatever proposition it expresses speaks only of subsets of some fixed set of values of the variable '*x*'.[14] If the proposition expressed by (14) is a "second-order assertion," it is a proposition expressed on some relativization by the sentence used to formulate (13). But (13) is not itself such a proposition.

If, however, we thus conclude that (13) is not the proposition expressed by (14), two problems arise. One is of a kind already familiar: if the proposition expressed by (14) is a proposition expressed on some relativization by the sentence used to formulate (13), it is surely not identical with the proposition that (15) is valid. The propositions expressed by relativizing the sentence used to formulate (13) are no more about (15) than is (13) itself. Hence it cannot be quite right to say that to assert that (15) is valid is just to assert the proposition expressed by (14). But how then are the proposition that (15) is valid and the proposition expressed by (14) supposed to be related?

An answer of the sort tried in the case of (13) might work in the present case if a second problem can be solved, namely, the problem of determining which proposition *is* the proposition expressed by (14). We are apparently to understand that it is expressed by a certain second-order sentence; and from our knowledge of that sentence together with our grasp of second-order notation, we can infer that it is also expressed by some relativization of the sentence used to formulate (13). But which relativization? Of the many propositions that (14) can, without abuse of notation, be used to express, which is the proposition that Putnam takes to be asserted, at least implicitly, by the logician who says that the first-order schema (15) is valid?

It would be a mistake to think that the logician who pronounces (15) valid already answers the question by taking the variable '*x*' to range over antecedently specified "individuals." If we insist on calling '*x*' an "individual" variable, we must be ready to count everything an individual; for, again, a first-order schema is valid if and only if the universal closure of its set-theoretic analogue expresses a true proposition on *every* relativization. We may also say, however, that a first-order schema is valid if and only if the universal closure of its set-theoretic analogue comes to express a true proposition when relativized to the set of natural numbers. That in effect is Löwenheim's Theorem. Suppose we were willing to convert the theorem into a definition. Then we could say, given a schema ϕ, that the universal closure of its set-theoretic analogue, on relativization to the set of natural numbers, expresses a proposition which is not identical with the proposition that ϕ is valid but truth of which is, by definition of validity, necessary and sufficient for ϕ to be valid. Here, it might be suggested, is a way of accommodating the claim that to assert of a first-order schema that it is valid is implicitly to make a second-order assertion.

I doubt that Putnam would welcome the suggestion. Had he intended some such thing, I think he would have said so. Anyhow, he rejects a definition of validity close to the one just now derived from Löwenheim's Theorem on the ground that it "completely fails to capture the intuitive notion even if it is coextensive with the intuitive notion" (p. 17). But then I see no solution to the problem of identifying, with respect to a given first-order schema, the second-order assertion made by the logician who asserts that the schema is valid. The candidates are too numerous, the conditions imposed too demanding.

It might be thought that the problem has been misconceived; that Putnam takes (14) to be, not a sentence of a specific second-order *language*, but a formula of second-order *logic*. It might be thought that this is how to understand his reference to second-order logic in the passage under discussion and how to understand, also, his description[15] of (14) as the result of prefixing '$(S)(M)(P)$' to a *schema*; his (14) is only a notational variant of

(18) $(F)(G)(H)(((x)(Fx \to Gx)$ & $(x)(Gx \to Hx)) \to (x)(Fx \to Hx)$.

But I cannot see that this helps: (18) formulates no proposition at all. My point is not that (18) is a hybrid, nor am I ready to say that prefixing quantifiers to a schema inevitably produces nonsense. That practice results in formulas of second-order logic, which can no more be cast aside as nonsense than can the schemata of first-order logic. But, like the schemata of first-order logic, the formulas of second-order logic do not express propositions. The second-order logician who enters some of them in his book does indeed thereby make assertions, just as does the first-order logician who enters selected schemata in his book. But, as Putnam says, the assertions are metatheoretical: the propositions asserted are about the formulas, not expressed by the formulas. The assertions made, if only implicitly, are assertions of validity.

The situation is a little tricky, and I think confusing. The move from (15) to (18) is in a certain respect like the move from the induction *schema*

(19) $(\ldots0\ldots \ \& \ (n)(\ldots n\ldots \rightarrow \ldots n+1\ldots)) \rightarrow (n)(\ldots n\ldots)$

of first-order arithmetic to the induction *axiom*

(20) $(P)((P0 \ \& \ (n)(Pn \rightarrow Pn+1)) \rightarrow (n)(Pn))$

of second-order arithmetic. In the move to (20), atomic schemata of (19) are replaced by open sentences, and a quantifier is prefixed so as to effect closure. Similarly, in the move to (18) the schema (15) is promoted to the status of open sentence and universal quantifiers are prefixed. Since (20) formulates a proposition of second-order arithmetic, we are tempted by the similarity to say that (18) formulates a proposition of second-order logic. But there is a crucial difference between the two cases. The variable 'n' of (19) already has a range; this remains fixed in the move to (20), and a range is thereby determined for the dependent variable 'P'. But 'x' in (15) has no range, and it does not acquire one in the move to (18). Hence there is no saying what is the range of 'F', 'G', and 'H' in (18); it waits upon assignment, for one or another purpose, of a range to 'x', and that may be any non-empty set that suits the purpose. In the sense in which there are propositions of second-order arithmetic, there are no propositions of second-order logic; and none either of first-order logic.

5

It does not follow that there are no propositions of logic. Indeed, in the proposition that (15) is valid we seem to have one; and with it come others, one for each valid first-order schema. We seem to have an abundance.

But is it really an abundance of propositions of *logic*? The question may seem perverse. Surely logicians do say, or imply by saying what they say, that (15) is valid. But in what sense of 'valid'? That word entered my vocabulary as an adjective applicable to arguments in which the conclusion follows from the premises. The possibility of demonstrating invalidity of an argument by exhibiting another of the same form having true premises and a false conclusion eased the way to application of 'valid' to the argument-forms themselves, those no specimens of which have true premises and a false conclusion. Somehow I came to acquiesce in still another usage, according to which a *propositional* form—a schema, at the linguistic level—is valid just in case all propositions of that form are true. Probably the idea was that an argument-form is valid if and only if a certain corresponding conditional propositional form is a form of none but true propositions. In any case, the basic notion was that a schema is valid if and only if the form it represents is a form only of true propositions. In *that* sense of 'valid', I suppose I would have been ready to say that the proposition that (15) is valid is a proposition of logic. But given some other sense, I should have wanted assurance that it was coextensive with mine.

My own history may be peculiar. And no doubt it is in certain ways philosophically naive. But there is this much to be said for it: a schema deserves to be called valid only if it is a form of none but true propositions. Surely this is a condition of adequacy on any proposed definition of validity of schemata. Hence, using 'valid' in the sense of 'such that the universal closure of its set-theoretic analogue is true on every relativization', we may ask: Do valid schemata represent forms only of true propositions?

A natural thought is to argue for the affirmative as follows: given a valid schema ϕ and a proposition p of the form represented by ϕ, p will be an instance of the proposition expressed, on some relativization, by the universal closure of the set-theoretic analogue of ϕ; but, since ϕ is valid, p will then be an instance of a true proposition and hence itself true. Consider, for instance, (15). One proposition of the form it represents is the proposition that if every consistent schema is satisfiable and every satisfiable schema is satisfiable in a countable domain, then every consistent schema is satisfiable in a countable domain. This proposition, so the argument would have it, is an instance of the proposition expressed, on a certain relativization, by the sentence (13)—that is, the sentence which is the universal closure of the set-theoretic analogue of (15). The relativization results by restricting 'x' to first-order schemata and 'S', 'M', and 'P' to sets of first-order schemata. And a formulation of the desired instance results by the further step of instantiating 'S', 'M', and 'P' to, respectively, the set of consistent schemata, the set of satisfiable schemata, and the set of schemata satisfiable in a countable domain. But since (15) is valid, the proposition expressed by (13) on this relativization is true, and therefore so is the instance.

But the argument fails at its first step. Even if, in spite of the inflation involved, we accept the example, it is nevertheless not always the case that a proposition of the form represented by a valid schema is an instance of the proposition expressed, on some relativization, by the universal closure of the set-theoretic analogue of the schema. More generally, propositions of the form represented by a schema outrun instances of propositions that can be expressed by relativizing the universal closure of the set-theoretic analogue of the schema; in fact, to anticipate a possible amendment of the argument, they outrun instances even of the proposition expressed by the universal closure of the set-theoretic analogue of the schema. Consider the proposition formulated in (17). It is the proposition that there is no universal set; the proposition that *no* set has *everything* as a member. The variable 'x' of (17) is thus unrestricted. 'S' is indeed restricted to sets; but it ranges over all of them, and there is no set to which they all belong. Anyhow, use of a restricted variable is there unnecessary. The proposition expressed by

(17) is also expressed by

(21) $(x)(\text{Set } x \to (\exists y)(\sim y \in x))$.

This formulation makes it clear that the proposition that there is no universal set is a proposition of the form represented by

(22) $(x)Fx$.

And the universal closure of the set-theoretic analogue of (22) is

(23) $(S)(x)(x \in S)$.

But on every relativization of (23) the variable 'x' is restricted to members of some non-empty set, and the restriction will carry over to instances of whatever proposition is expressed. Hence no instance of a proposition expressed, on relativization, by (23) is the proposition expressed by (21). Nor is the proposition expressed by (21) an instance of the proposition expressed by (23) itself. There is no universal set, and therefore no appropriate instantiation. Of course (22) is invalid. But the point carries over to valid schemata. Put the matrix of (21) for each of 'Fx', 'Gx' and 'Hx' in (15), keep 'x' unrestricted in range, and the result will be a formulation of a proposition the generality of which prevents its being an instance of the proposition expressed, on some relativization, by the sentence used to formulate (13). Nor will the result be a formulation of an instance of (13) itself, for the matrix of (21) determines no set.

Some philosophers of logic protest the use of variables unrestricted in range. Their view, on a strong version, requires that the objects over which a variable ranges be members of some one set; a weaker version demands only a class—a set or a so-called "proper," or "ultimate," class. The idea in either case is that the many objects over which a variable ranges must constitute or compose or be in some *one* object, the range of values of the variable. Because I have yet to understand the arguments for the view, I remain unconvinced that irremediably plural specifications of values of variables are illegitimate. But consider for a moment the consequences of the view for the matter here under discussion. Evidently (21) and its like would have to go. But notice that on the strong version so also would purported assertions of validity. To call a schema valid is to speak, or purport to speak, of all non-empty sets, and there is no set of such. A weaker version of the view admits a (proper) class of all sets, hence a class of all non-empty sets, and thus authorizes us to take the variables of (21) to range over all sets. And that is enough to ensure that the proposition expressed has a generality that prevents its being an instance of the proposition expressed by (23) or an instance of a proposition that can be expressed by relativizing (23). Again, there is no set of all sets. Of course, once proper classes are on the scene, we may adjust validity accordingly, so that it becomes, roughly, truth of proposition expressed on all relativizations to any non-empty *class* of the universal closure of the *class*-theoretic analogue. But if it is legitimate to speak thus of all classes, we may take the variables of (21) to range over them. And then the same difficulties recur, at a higher level. For even if there is a class of all sets, there is no class of all classes.

Relative to one or another of various familiar proof-procedures, every valid first-order schema is provable. That in effect is Gödel's completeness theorem, and it is the first step of a standard solution to the question posed above.[16] It links validity to provability. To link provability in turn to the notion of representing a form of none but true propositions, one argues as follows. Among complete proof-procedures some have two features: each "axiom" obviously has the property of representing none but true propositions, and the "rules of inference" obviously preserve this property. It follows that such procedures generate only schemata that represent forms of none but true propositions.

Especially noteworthy here is the role played by provability. It is sometimes said that validity is in a certain respect prior to provability: a soundness proof, linking provability to validity, is said to provide a justification for the proof-procedure. The above solution reverses the situation, for it is by being linked to provability that validity is shown to deserve its name. This should encourage the view that not only assertions of validity but also assertions of provability are propositions of pure logic.

Notes

Versions of this essay were presented in 1982 to the Cambridge Moral Science Club, the Oxford Philosophical Society, and the American Philosophical Association (Eastern Division). In connection with the last of these, an abstract appeared in *The Journal of Philosophy* 79 (1982): 689–692. I am grateful for the comments of Timothy Smiley at Cambridge, Christopher Peacocke at Oxford, and Warren Goldfarb at the meeting of the APA.

1. Bertrand Russell, *Our Knowledge of the External World* (London: Allen and Unwin, 1961). Delivered as Lowell Lectures in Boston, March and April 1914. First published in 1914.

2. Bertrand Russell, "The Philosophical Implications of Mathematical Logic," in Douglas Lackey, ed., *Essays in Analysis* (New York: Braziller, 1973), pp. 284–294. First published in French in *Revue de Métaphysique et de Morale* 19 (1911): 281–291. English translation by P. E. B. Jourdain, with revisions by Russell, in *The Monist* 22 (1913): 481–493.

3. Bertrand Russell, "The Philosophy of Logical Atomism," in R. C. Marsh, ed., *Logic and Knowledge* (London: Allen and Unwin, 1956), pp. 177–281. Original publication: *The Monist* 28 (1918): 495–527; 29 (1919): 33–63, 190–222, 344–380.

4. "The Philosophical Implications of Mathematical Logic," pp. 287–288.

5. The idea that the mark of a proposition of pure logic is complete generality appears in Russell's writings as early as 1901. See his "Recent Work on the Principles of Mathematics,"

International Monthly 4 (1901): 83–101; reprinted as "Mathematics and the Metaphysicians," in *Mysticism and Logic* (New York: Norton, 1929), pp. 74–96. And its equation with the idea that a proposition of pure logic is one in whose formulation there occur no constants save logical constants appears two years later. See *The Principles of Mathematics*, 1st ed. (London: Cambridge University Press, 1903), pp. 7–9. Under the influence of Wittgenstein, Russell came later to think that a proposition may fail to be a proposition of pure logic even though formulable in a sentence containing no nonlogical constants: witness, he remarks, the proposition that there is at least one thing in the world, or the axiom of infinity, or (very probably) the axiom of choice. To belong to pure logic a proposition must in addition be "in some sense or other like a tautology" ("The Philosophy of Logical Atomism," p. 240). And in the concluding chapter of *Introduction to Mathematical Philosophy* (London: Allen and Unwin, 1920) Russell seems ready to pull apart the two ideas he had earlier equated: a proposition may be formulable in a sentence containing no nonlogical constants and yet not be completely general, through failure to hold in all possible universes (of which one is the empty universe).

6. Alfred North Whitehead and Bertrand Russell, *Principia Mathematica*, 2d ed., 3 vols. (Cambridge: Cambridge University Press, 1925). For informal accounts of 'always true' see vol. 1, pp. 14–17, 41, 127. See also Russell's "Mathematical Logic as Based on the Theory of Types," in Marsh, *Logic and Knowledge*, pp. 59–102, especially p. 72.

7. Marsh, *Logic and Knowledge*, p. 239.

8. W. V. Quine, *Philosophy of Logic* (Englewood Cliffs, N.J.: Prentice-Hall, 1970), p. 11.

9. Strictly, it *became* his view. For his earlier descriptions of and responses to the discovery see, for example, *The Principles of Mathematics*, chap. 10, and "On Some Difficulties in the Theory of Transfinite Numbers and Order Types," *Proceedings of the London Mathematical Society* 4 (1906): 29–53 (the latter reprinted in Lackey, *Essays in Analysis*, pp. 135–164).

10. *Principia Mathematica*, vol. 1, p. 90.

11. New York: Harper and Row, 1971.

12. *Philosophy of Logic*, pp. 51–52.

13. For convenience, I consider as schemata only 'Fx', 'Gx', 'Hyz', and the like, together with such further ones as can be obtained from them by truth-functional composition and quantification, in the usual ways.

14. See George S. Boolos, "On Second-Order Logic," *Journal of Philosophy* 72 (1975): 509–527.

15. *Philosophy of Logic*, p. 32.

16. See G. Kreisel, "Informal Rigour and Completeness Proofs," in I. Lakatos, ed., *Problems in the Philosophy of Mathematics* (Amsterdam: North Holland, 1967), p. 153; J. L. Bell and A. B. Slomson, *Models and Ultraproducts: An Introduction* (Amsterdam: North-Holland, 1969), p. 65; Quine, *Philosophy of Logic*, pp. 54–55.

Implications and Entailments

In this essay I am concerned with the problem of marking off, within a class of relations I call "implications," those that are "entailments." It is an old problem, and what I have to offer by way of a solution is hardly new. But, since they are often neglected, I have thought it worthwhile to deal mainly with preliminaries; paraphrasing Locke, to clear Ground a little and perhaps even remove some Rubbish.

1

Protologic studies relations of logical consequence for sets of sentences, in abstraction from any special properties the sentences themselves may have. Perhaps because of its generality, it is seldom featured in texts and treatises on logic. A quick look at some of its basic concepts and laws may thus be of some interest, and will in any case provide background for the discussion that follows.[1]

By an *implication* for a set S of sentences I shall mean a relation $\vdash$ that takes subsets of S to members of S in such a way that, for all subsets X and Y of S and for any member p of S, the following conditions are satisfied:

> *Reflexivity*: $p \vdash p$
> *Dilution*: If $X \vdash p$ then $X, Y \vdash p$
> *Cut*: If $X \vdash q$, for every q in Y, and $Y \vdash p$ then $X \vdash p$.

(Here I follow common conventions in suppressing set-theoretic braces to the left of '$\vdash$', in allowing the comma to serve as a symbol for set-theoretic union, and in abusing the word 'reflexivity'.) Obviously, not every implication, in this sense, deserves the name. But no relation that deserves the name is excluded,[2] and for purposes of protologic no reasonable narrowing seems possible.

In essays of more than half a century ago, Tarski pursued protologic under the name "methodology of the deductive sciences."[3] He took as central not the concept of an implication but that of what has come to be called a *consequence operation* on a set of sentences, i.e., a function Cn that takes subsets of S to subsets of S in such a way that, for all subsets X and

Y of S, the following conditions are satisfied:

(i) X is included in $Cn(X)$

(ii)   If X is included in Y then $Cn(X)$ is included in $Cn(Y)$

(iii) $Cn(Cn(X))$ is included in $Cn(X)$.[4]

The theory of consequence operations and the theory of implications come to the same thing, as the following theorem shows:

(1.1)   Associated with each consequence operation Cn for S is a unique implication for S, according to the equation

(i) $\vdash = \{\langle X, p \rangle : p \in Cn(X)\}$.

Conversely, each implication $\vdash$ for S determines a unique consequence operation for S, according to the equation

(ii) $Cn = \{\langle X, Y \rangle : Y = \{p : X \vdash p\}\}$.

Moreover, $\vdash$ is the implication associated with Cn if and only if Cn is the consequence operation determined by $\vdash$.

Proof: It is obvious that not more than one implication is associated with Cn. Hence, for the first part, it is enough to show that $\vdash$, as defined in (i), is an implication. Since $X \in Cn(X)$, $\vdash$ satisfies Reflexivity. To show that it satisfies Dilution, assume $X \vdash p$. Since $X \subseteq X \cup Y$, for any Y, $Cn(x) \subseteq Cn(X \cup Y)$. But p is in $Cn(X)$, and hence in $Cn(X \cup Y)$. Thus $X \cup Y \vdash p$. To prove that Cut is satisfied, suppose $X \vdash q$, for every q in Y, and $Y \vdash p$. Then $Y \subseteq Cn(X)$ and p is in $Cn(Y)$. But then $Cn(Y) \subseteq Cn(Cn(X))$, and in any case $Cn(Cn(X)) \subseteq Cn(X)$. So p is in $Cn(X)$, and hence $X \vdash p$. For the second part, it is again obvious that not more than one consequence operation is determined by $\vdash$. So it suffices to show that Cn, as specified in (ii), is a consequence operation. By Reflexivity and Dilution, $X \subseteq Cn(X)$. If $X \subseteq Y$, so that $X \cup Y = Y$, then by Dilution $X \vdash p$ only if $Y \vdash p$—i.e., $Cn(X) \subseteq Cn(Y)$. Assume p is in $Cn(Cn(X))$. Then $Cn(Cn(X)) \vdash p$, and plainly $X \vdash q$ for every q in $Cn(X)$. So by Cut $X \vdash p$, i.e., p is in $Cn(X)$. Hence $Cn(Cn(X))$ is included in $Cn(X)$. Thus Cn is a consequence operation on S. For the last part, if $\vdash_{Cn}$ is the implication associated with Cn and Cn' the consequence operation determined by $\vdash_{Cn}$, then, $X \vdash_{Cn} p$ if and only if p is in $Cn(X)$, and p is in $Cn'(X)$ if and only if $X \vdash_{Cn} p$; hence $Cn = Cn'$. Similarly, if $Cn_\vdash$ is the consequence operation determined by $\vdash$ and $\vdash'$ the implication associated with $Cn_\vdash$, then, $X \vdash p$ if and only if p is in $Cn_\vdash(X)$, and p is in $Cn_\vdash(X)$ if and only if $X \vdash' p$; hence $\vdash = \vdash'$.

The set of implications for a set S of sentences is of course partially ordered by inclusion. But more can be said. With respect to the ordering by inclusion, the set of implications for S has a unique maximum, namely, the relation that X bears to p just in case X is included in S and p is a member of S; all subsets of S bear the relation to all members of S. In addition, it is routine to show

(1.2)   The intersection of any non-empty set of implications for S is an implication for S.

The intersection of a non-empty set of implications is of course the greatest lower bound of the set, with respect to inclusion. From this, together with the existence of the maximum, it follows that every set of implications for S has both a greatest lower bound and a least upper bound, with respect to the ordering by inclusion. For let I be a set of implications for S. Since each member of I is included in the maximum implication for S, the set of upper bounds of I is non-empty and hence has a greatest lower bound. Evidently this is the least upper bound of I. (If I is empty, its greatest lower bound is the maximum implication for S.) Summing up, in the terminology of algebra:

(1.3)   The set of implications for S is a complete lattice with respect to inclusion.

Some caution is necessary, however. Although the greatest lower bound of a non-empty set of implications for S is its intersection, its least upper bound is not in general its union. Indeed, the union of a set of implications for S is not in general an implication for S: although it always satisfies Reflexivity and Dilution, it does not always satisfy Cut. If, however, a set of implications for S is a chain (i.e., if of any two members one is included in the other), then the union of the set satisfies Cut. In fact:

(1.4)   With respect to inclusion, the union of a chain of implications of S is the least upper bound of the chain in the set of implications for S.

I leave the proof to the reader.

If it seems odd that the greatest lower bound of the empty set is the maximum implication for S, it is in keeping with expectations that the least upper bound of the empty set is the minimum implication for S, i.e., the intersection of the set of all implications for S. It may also be described as the relation that a subset X of S bears to a member p of S if and only if p is a member of X.

It is worth noticing that (1.3) can be seen as a corollary of a more general theorem:

(1.5)   If $\vdash$ is an implication for S, the set of implications included in $\vdash$ is a complete lattice with respect to its ordering by inclusion.

The proof is essentially the same: The intersection of any non-empty set of implications for S included in $\vdash$ is by (1.2) an implication for S, is the greatest lower bound of the set with respect to inclusion, and is itself included in $\vdash$. And $\vdash$ is evidently the maximum with respect to inclusion of the implications for S included in $\vdash$. It follows that, with respect to inclusion, each set of implications for S included in $\vdash$ has a greatest lower bound and a least upper bound in the set of all implications for S included in $\vdash$.

In the essays referred to above, Tarski took consequence operations to be defined in terms of rules of inference.

> Let A be an arbitrary set of sentences of a particular discipline. With the help of certain operations, the so-called *rules of inference*, new sentences are derived from the set A, called the *consequences of the set A*. To establish these rules of inference, and with their help to define exactly the concept of consequence, is . . . a task of special metadisciplines; in the usual terminology of set theory the schema of such a definition can be formulated as follows:

>> The set of all *consequences of the set A* is the intersection of all sets which contain the set A and are closed under the given rules of inference.[5]

Tarski's 'schema' can be converted into a characterization of an important class of implications, along the following lines.

To cover such wanted cases as disjunction introduction, in which some latitude exists as to choice of conclusion, Tarksi's 'operation' must be replaced by 'relation'. Let us say accordingly that a *rule of inference*, or simply a *rule*, for a set S of sentences is a relation the domain of which consists entirely of finite subsets of S and the range of which consists entirely of members of S. Exclusion of infinitary rules means a loss in generality; but it simplifies exposition, and the loss in generality will not seriously affect the discussion which is to follow. Like the definition of implications, the definition of rules of inference will no doubt seem to take in too much; but again, in a general setting no alternative is altogether satisfactory. Notice that a rule, in the present sense, need not be effectively decidable; that the union of any number of rules is a rule, and hence that a set of rules may be regarded as a single rule; and that a rule may have only the empty set in its domain, so that so-called axioms, or axiomatic rules, are accommodated.

Let S be a set of sentences, and let R be a rule for S. A subset X of S will be said to be *closed under R* if and only if q is a member of X whenever Y is included in X and $\langle Y, q \rangle$ is in R. Let $\vdash_R$ be the relation that a subset X of S bears to a member p of S just in case p belongs to every set that includes X and is closed under R. It is easy to prove

(1.6) $\vdash_R$ is the least implication for S that includes R.

I shall call $\vdash_R$ the implication *based on* R. It is the ancestral of R, and hence

(1.7) $X \vdash_R p$ if and only if there is a finite sequence of members of S of which p is the last term and of which each term q is a member of S or is such that, for some set Y of terms that precede q in the sequence, $\langle Y, q \rangle$ is a member of R.

In a standard terminology, $X \vdash_R p$ if and only if there is a *derivation of p from X by R*. We thus make contact, however tenuous, with the familiar idea that a sentence is a consequence of others, relative to certain rules of inference, if and only if it can be deduced from those sentences by means of the rules.

We also need to make such contact as is possible at this level of generality with model-theoretic, or so-called semantic, concepts of consequence. Given a set of sentences, the model theorist typically specifies, first, a class of "structures" ("models") for S, and, second, a function that assigns to each structure a *valuation* on S, i.e., a function from S into the set $\{T, F\}$ of truth values. Where V is the set of valuations so obtained, a subset X of S is said to bear the (purported consequence) relation $\vdash$ to a member p of S just in case, for every v in V, if $v[X] = T$ then $v(p) = T$. (I use the notation '$v[X] = T$' as short for '$v(p) = T$ for every p in X'.) Now, for my purposes it is the valuations that matter, not the way in which they are generated. So, where V is any set of valuations on a set S and $\vdash$ any relation that takes subsets of S to members of S, I say that V *induces* $\vdash$ just in case the following condition obtains: for every subset X of S and for every p in S, $X \vdash p$ if and only if, for every v in V, if $v[X] = T$ then $v(p) = T$. The following theorem then provides an alternative characterization of the set of implications for a set:

(1.8)   Every set of valuations on S induces an implication for S, and every implication for S is induced by some set of valuations on S.

Proof: Where V is a set of valuations on S, let $\vdash$ be the set of ordered pairs $\langle X, p \rangle$ such that, for every v in V, $v[X] = T$ only if $v(p) = T$. It is then easy to show that $\vdash$ is an implication for S. For the second part, let $\vdash$ be an implication for S, and let V be the set of valuations on S that respect $\vdash$, where a valuation v *respects* $\vdash$ just in case $v(p) = T$ whenever $X \vdash p$ and $v[X] = T$. It is to be shown that V induces $\vdash$. It is completely trivial that if $X \vdash p$ and v is in V then $v[X] = T$ only if $v(p) = T$. So let X be any subset of S and p be any member of S, and suppose that, for each v in V, if $v[X] = T$ then $v(p) = T$. To show that under these circumstances $X \vdash p$, let u be the valuation on S such that, for every q in S, $u(q) = T$ if and only if $X \vdash q$.

Then u is in V. For suppose $Y \vdash q$ and $u[Y] = T$. Then $X \vdash r$, for each r in Y. But then $X \vdash q$ by Cut, and hence $u(q) = T$. So if $u[X] = T$ then $u(p) = T$. But by Reflexivity and Dilution, $X \vdash q$ for each q in X. Hence $u[X] = T$, and therefore $u(p) = T$. It follows that $X \vdash p$, which was to be shown.

No implication is induced by exactly one set of valuations. For if v is the valuation on S that assigns T to every member of S, $V - \{v\}$ and $V \cup \{v\}$ induce the same implication for S. For a somewhat less trivial exception, note that if S is a pair $\{p, q\}$, the set of (two) valuations that assign opposite truth values to p and q induces the minimum implication for S; but that implication is also induced by the set of all valuations on S. More interesting cases are common, but their description falls outside protologic. In the absence of a one-one correspondence, the "best" result appears to be

(1.9)   If U and V are sets of valuations on S, and U is included in V, then $\vdash_V$ is included in $\vdash_U$.

The easy proof is left to the reader.

For implications of the form $\vdash_R$, (1.8) can be strengthened:

(1.10)   If R is a rule for S, the set of valuations that respect R induces $\vdash_R$,

where, of course, a valuation v *respects* R just in case $v(p) = T$ whenever $\langle X, p \rangle$ is in R and $v[X] = T$. *Proof*: Let V be the set of valuations on S that respect R, and let $\vdash_V$ be the implication induced by V. To prove the theorem it suffices to show that $\vdash_V = \vdash_R$. If U is the set of valuations that respect $\vdash_R$, so that $\vdash_R = \vdash_U$, then evidently U is included in V. But then $\vdash_V$ is included in $\vdash_R$, by (1.9). For the reverse inclusion, we may take advantage of (1.7), and proceed by induction. Call a positive integer n *favorable* just in case, for every X and p, if $p_1, \ldots, p_n$ is a derivation of p from X by R, then, for every v that respects R, $v[X] = T$ only if $v(p) = T$. To prove the desired inclusion it is enough to show that every positive integer is favorable. So suppose that every positive integer less than k is favorable, let $p_1, \ldots, p_k$ be a derivation of p from X by R, and let v be a valuation that respects R and is such that $v[X] = T$. Then p_k is in X or else $\langle Y, p_k \rangle$ is in R, for some Y the membership of which is drawn exclusively from terms of the sequence $p_1, \ldots, p_{k-1}$. If the former, then obviously $v(p_k) = v(p) = T$. Suppose the latter, and let q be an arbitrary member of Y. Then $q = p_i$ for some i less than k. But, as is easily enough shown, $p_1, \ldots, p_i$ is a derivation of p_i from X by R, and by supposition i is favorable. Hence $v(p_i) = v(q) = T$. Hence $v[Y] = T$. But v respects R, and therefore $v(p_k) = v(p) = T$. So k is favorable. Hence every positive integer is favorable, and the desired inclusion follows.

A rule R for S is *sound* with respect to a set V of valuations for S just in case every member of V respects R—just in case, that is, $\vdash_R$ is included in $\vdash_V$. And R is *complete* with respect to V if and only if $\vdash_V$ is included in $\vdash_R$. In these terms (1.10) says that every rule is sound and complete with respect to the set of valuations that respect it. It thus points up the fact that the signficance of a soundness or completeness theorem depends upon the makeup of the set of valuations the theorem invokes.

2

With certain misgivings, I shall say that an *entailment* for a set of S of sentences is an implication $\vdash$ for S with the property that, for every subset X of S and every member p of S, if $X \vdash p$ then p follows from the members of X taken together. Moore introduced the term, or rather the verb from which it derives, in the following well-known passage:

> We require . . . some term to express the *converse* of that relation which we assert to hold between a particular proposition q and a particular proposition p, when we assert that q *follows from* or *is deducible from* p. Let us use the term "entails" to express the converse of this relation. We shall then be able to say truly that "p entails q," when and only when we are able to say truly that "q follows from p" or "is deducible from p," in the sense in which the conclusion of a syllogism in Barbara follows from the two premises, taken as one conjunctive proposition; or in which the proposition "This is coloured" follows from "This is red."[6]

But my usage departs from Moore's in ways that need to be made explicit.

First, where Moore speaks of propositions, I speak instead of sentences. I suspect he would have censured my usage. But perhaps some rapprochement is possible, for my "sentences" are Quine's "eternal sentences."[7] Each is thus free of all features that would prevent its expressing a unique proposition, and hence to say of one that it follows from others is at least as clear as to say of one proposition that it follows from others. *Second*, whereas Moore speaks of entailment, I speak of entailments. The departure need represent no substantive disagreement; for I do not thereby deny the existence of Moore's single relation, and, if it does exist, each of my many relations is included in it. My usage has the advantage that it easily accommodates talk of truth-functional entailment, first-order entailment, and the like. *Third*, while Moore's entailment is a homogeneous relation, taking propositions to propositions, my entailments are inhomogeneous relations, taking *sets* of sentences to sentences. He would try to accommodate my cases by taking the conjunction of the members of the set. But the device fails if, as often happens, the set is infinite. Neither does it work across the board for finite sets, as Shoesmith and Smiley neatly demonstrate:

> It is true that any finite set of premises is equivalent to a single conjunctive one, $A_1, \ldots, A_m$ having the same joint force as $A_1 \,\&\, \ldots \,\&\, A_m$. But this equivalence is only established by appealing to the workings of the rule 'from A, B infer $A \,\&\, B$', understood as involving two separate premises (not one conjunctive one), and it would be circular to appeal to the equivalence to establish the dispensability of the rule.[8]

In ordinary usage 'follows from' is homogeneous alright, but it is also multigrade: the conclusion, we say, follows from the premises, and these may be of any number. Readers who prefer the ordinary usage may rectify mine by replacing any offending singular reference to a set with an essentially plural reference instead to the members of the set. *Fourth*, the range of entailment (Moore's sense) is the class of all propositions, but the range of an entailment (my sense) is always some *set* of sentences. Unless there is a set of all sentences, none of my entailments approximates Moore's in size. I see no disadvantage in the limitation, and I see advantages in adjusting usage to fit the common practice of logicians.

The above definition simply introduces a technical term. Can anything more illuminating be said as to the circumstances under which an implication is an entailment?

Entailments are at the least *truth-preserving*: if $\vdash$ is an entailment for a set S of sentences, then, for every p in S and every X included in S, p is true if every member of X is true and $X \vdash p$. If every member of S is either true or false, an implication for S is truth-preserving just in case the *correct* valuation on S, the one that assigns to each member of S its actual truth value, is among the valuations that respect the implication. In view of (1.9), this comes to saying that a set S of true or false sentences is truth-preserving just in case it is included in $\vdash_{\{t\}}$, where t is the correct valuation on S. Notice that $\vdash_{\{t\}}$ is Russell's "material implication" restricted to S. In a more general sense, a *material* implication is one induced by the singleton of a valuation. Such relations give rise to familiar "paradoxes": if v is any valuation on S, then

$$\text{if } v(q) = T \text{ then } X \vdash_{\{v\}} q$$

and

$$\text{if } v(p) = F, \text{ for some } p \text{ in } X, \text{ then } X \vdash_{\{v\}} q.$$

These and other oddities have convinced most philosophers that not all truth-preserving implications are entailments. Seeming statements to the contrary come, I suspect, from failure to observe, in exposition anyhow, the distinction between *true* and *true on*. It is customary to say that a member *p* of a set *S* of sentences is *true on* a valuation *v* on *S* if and only if $v(p) = T$. If each member of a set *V* of valuations on *S* respects an implication ⊢ for *S*, then ⊢ might be said to preserve truth-on relative to *V*. But it is at least misleading to put this by saying that ⊢ preserves truth. For a sentence true on some *v* in *V* may be false, and a sentence false on some *v* in *V* may be true. So ⊢ may in fact lead from truths to falsehoods, even though every member of *V* respects it. And even if *V* contains the correct valuation on *S*, it will typically understate matters to say of an implication respected by every member of *V* that it preserves truth.

An implication ⊢ for a set *S* of sentences is *strict* just in case, for every subset *X* of *S* and every member *p* of *S*, if *X* ⊢ *p* then it is impossible that every member of *X* be true and yet that *p* be false. To put the idea in terms of valuations, call a valuation *v* on *S* *admissible* just in case it represents a possible distribution of truth values to the members of *S*—possible, not in some combinatorial sense, but in the sense that the distribution is one that might have obtained, even if in fact it does not. We may then say that strict implications for *S* are those that every admissible valuation respects— equivalently, those induced by some set of valuations that includes the set of all admissible valuations.

One naturally associates with C. I. Lewis, among recent philosophers, the idea that the entailments for a set of sentences are precisely its strict implications.[9] Not that he said so, however; for he tended to speak of a single relation of strict implication, and to confuse it with an operation which, applied to a pair $\langle p, q \rangle$ of sentences, yields a sentence which is true just in case *p* bears the relation to *q*. Moreover, had he talked in such terms, he would perhaps have taken an admissible valuation to be any that represents a "logical" possibility, and thus have allowed as admissible a valuation that assigns, say, *T* to '2 + 3 = 6' or *F* to 'no bachelor is married'.[10] But if the idea that entailments coincide with strict implications is not precisely Lewis's, he can in retrospect be seen as its champion in the battle against those who seemed to favor certain material implications.

Although implicit in the seeming platitude that a conclusion follows from premises just in case it is impossible that they be true and yet it false, the idea has not met with universal acceptance. In particular, some logicians and philosophers charge that certain strict implications are subject to "para- doxes" not unlike those to which material implications are subject. I do not know how to describe in precise terms the class of strict implications against which this objection is brought. But perhaps the following remarks will serve to indicate it roughly.

Relative to a set *V* of valuations on a set *S* of sentences, a member *p* of *S* is *valid* if and only if $v(p) = T$ for every *v* in *V*, and *invalid* if and only if $v(p) = F$ for every *v* in *V*. Equivalently, valid sentences relative to *V* are those to which the empty set bears $\vdash_V$, or, in view of Dilution, those to which every subset of S bears $\vdash_V$; and the sentences invalid relative to V are those that bear $\vdash_V$ to every member of S. Invalidity can be seen as a special case of a more general notion: a subset X of S is *unsatisfiable* relative to V if and only if $v[X] = F$ for every v in V. Suppose, now, that every admissible valuation is in V and, in addition, that V satisfies at least one of these conditions: (i) some member of S is valid relative to V; (ii) some subset of S is unsatisfiable relative to V. Then $\vdash_V$ is strict, but either there is a member of S to which every subset of S bears $\vdash_V$ or there is a subset of S which bears $\vdash_V$ to every member of S. I say "but" because the clause that follows is taken to show that unless S is exceptionally impoverished, $\vdash_V$ is not an entailment.

The contention is that an implication $\vdash$ is an entailment only if, whenever $X \vdash p$, some member or members of X are "relevant" to p; and strict implications, it is said, often fail to satisfy this condition. By way of a simple illustration, consider a set $\{\perp, q\}$, where $\perp$ is some absurdity—'0 = 1', say—and q is 'there are subways in Boston'. It seems evident to advocates of relevance that the only entailment for $\{\perp, q\}$ is the minimum implication. Although every admissible valuation assigns F to $\perp$, and therefore never assigns T to $\perp$ while assigning F to q, there is no "connection of meaning" between $\perp$ and q.

It will not do, borrowing a phrase from Quine, to *give* these philosophers the word 'entails'. There is the good old-fashioned 'follows from', but of course their point is that X may bear a strict implication to p even though p does not follow from X. And there is no hope of *demonstrating* that strict implications are always entailments.

Lewis thought he could disarm the opposition by proving that if X is unsatisfiable relative to the set of admissible valuations on S, then every sentence in X follows from X.[11] But his proof works only if X and S are specially constituted, and it appeals to rules of inference and to laws of protologic none of which is acceptable to all philosophers among the opposition. Specifically, if X contains p and the negation of p and if S is closed under the formation of disjunctions, then every member of S can be derived from X by the rules of disjunction introduction and disjunctive syllogism. Some opponents of Lewis reject disjunction introduction.[12] Others reject disjunctive syllogism.[13] Still others accept both rules but deny that implications based on valid rules are always entailments; in view of (1.6), they must deny that entailments always satisfy each of Reflexivity, Dilution, and Cut.[14]

But in support of such deviations Lewis's opponents seem unable to appeal at bottom to anything save the alleged paradoxes to which strict implications lead. By my lights anyhow, nothing but avoidance of the paradoxes recommends their rejection of classical rules of inference or laws of protologic.

Since the match appears to end in a draw, it is fortunate that I need not here take a stand. In what follows I urge only that implications must be strict to qualify as entailments. If that satisfies neither side, at least it does not block the path of inquiry.

3

Not infrequently, textbooks of logic begin with a statement to the effect that a conclusion p follows from a set X of premises if and only if it is impossible that all the members of X be true and yet that p be false. It is striking, however, that the official definitions of relations of logical conse- quence given in these same texts make no use of modalities. In others modalities simply do not appear, even informally. It is of interest to inquire how the avoidance of modalities comes about and whether it comes off.

As to how it comes about, no doubt part of the explanation lies in there being a distinction between two projects. One is that of characterizing in general terms those implications that are entailments. Presumably this is the project undertaken in introductory chapters. Another is that of specify- ing one or another particular entailment, or class of entailments thought to be importantly similar. But the whole explanation cannot lie here. If only strict implications are entailments, one needs assurance that the officially specified implications are indeed strict; but the question whether they are is typically not addressed. And when modalities are altogether eschewed, one may well be left wondering what recommends the particular implications singled out. After all, implications are cheap.

Let us not eschew modalities; not yet anyhow, for we need to see how things stand if entailments are required to be strict implications.

By a *sentential language* I shall understand a quadruple $\langle S, P, C, N \rangle$ such that P is a non-empty set of sentences (the *atomic* sentences of the lan- guage) from which S is freely generated by the binary sentential operation C together with the singularly sentential operation N. (An *n-ary sentential* operation O takes n-tuples of sentences to sentences in such a way that each of $p_1, \ldots, p_n$ is a component of $Op_1 \ldots p_n$; thus, in a particular case, Np and Cpq might be $\ulcorner -p \urcorner$ and $\ulcorner p \to q \urcorner$, respectively. The set S is *gener- ated from* P by C and N in the sense that it is the least set that includes P and is closed under the operations C and N; and *freely* so in the sense that P, the range of C, and the range of N are pairwise disjoint.)

A valuation v on the set S of sentences of a sentential language is called *Boolean* just in case, for every p and q in S, (i) $v(Np) = T$ if and only if $v(p) = F$ and (ii) $v(Cpq) = T$ if and only if $v(p) = F$ or $v(q) = T$. The implication induced by the set $B(S)$ of Boolean valuations on S will also be called *Boolean*.

I hope it is obvious that there is no saying at this point whether the Boolean implication for a given sentential language is strict: as yet nothing has been said as to what sentences of the forms Cpq and Np mean. And if, as I am supposing, sentences of those forms are meaningful, it is not open to us to stipulate that Boolean implications are strict, any more than it is open to us to stipulate that the Continuum Hypothesis is a consequence of the axioms of Zermelo-Fraenkel set theory. If, on the other hand, we somehow have the information that Np always has the sense of ⌜it is not the case that p⌝ and Cpq the sense of ⌜it is not the case that (p and it is not the case that q)⌝, then it seems an easy matter to show that $\vdash_{B(S)}$ is strict. For if u is a non-Boolean valuation on S, then either $u(p) = u(Np)$, for some p in S, or $u(Cpq) = u(p) = T$ while $u(q) = F$, for some p and q in S. But in view of the information we have about the meanings of Np and Cpq it is manifestly impossible that Np and p have the same truth value, and that Cpq and p be true and yet q false. Hence u is not admissible. Thus every admissible valuation is in $B(S)$, and $\vdash_{B(S)}$ is therefore strict. (Notice that it has not been shown that every Boolean valuation is admissible. Indeed, there is no reason to think that every Boolean valuation *is* admissible: nothing bars the presence, among the atomic sentences of a sentential language, of the premises and conclusion of a syllogism in Barbara or of a pair of sentences 'a is red' and 'a is colored'.)

The result is nevertheless not likely to be counted a theorem of mathematical logic, because of the appeal made in its proof to "impossibility in the light of meaning." Is there an improvement? I think not; but the question deserves more than a quick answer.[15]

Setting aside matters of meaning, or touching on them only minimally, let us consider *classical* sentential languages, i.e., sentential languages that satisfy three condition: (i) every member of S is either true or false, (ii) for every p in S, Np is true if and only if p is false, and (iii) for every p and q in S, Cpq is true if and only if p is false or q is true. These conditions are together equivalent to the single condition that the correct valuation on S is in $B(S)$. It follows at once that Boolean implications for classical sentential languages are truth-preserving. It does not follow that they are strict. But this might be thought to follow from a stronger result, for which certain technical preliminaries are necessary.

A *homomorphism* of a sentential language $\langle S, P, C, N \rangle$ into a sentential language $\langle S', P', C', N' \rangle$ is a function h from S into S' which "preserves" the sentence-forming operations, in the sense that $h(Np) = N'h(p)$ and $h(Cpq) = C'h(p)h(q)$, for every p and q in S. Where $h''X$ is the homomorphic image of X, i.e., the set of values of h for members of X as arguments, we have

(3.1)   If h is a homomorphism of $\langle S, P, C, N \rangle$ into $\langle S', P', C', N' \rangle$, then $h''X \vdash_{B(S')} h(p)$ whenever $X \vdash_{B(S)} p$.

(*Proof sketch*: Suppose it is not the case that $h''X \vdash_{B(S')} h(p)$. Then, for some Boolean v' on S', $v'(h(p)) = F$ and $v'[h''q] = T$. Let v_0 be a valuation on P such that, for every q in P, $v_0(q) = v'(h(q))$; and let v be the Boolean extension on S of v_0.[16] It follows, by induction on the complexity of sentences in S, that $v(q) = v'(h(q))$ for every q in S. Hence it is not the case that $X \vdash_{B(S)} p$.) Note that the theorem holds in particular where $\langle S, P, C, N \rangle = \langle S', P', C', N' \rangle$. In such a case the homomorphism is called an *endomorphism*, or a *substitution*; and, by virtue of (3.1), $\vdash_{B(S)}$ is then said to be *structural*, or *closed under substitutions*.

An easy consequence of (3.1) is the stronger result mentioned above:

(3.2)   If $\langle S, P, C, N \rangle$ is classical and h is a homomorphism of $\langle S, P, C, N \rangle$ into a classical sentential language $\langle S', P', C', N' \rangle$, then $h(p)$ is true whenever every member of $h''X$ is true and $X \vdash_{B(S)} p$.

Let me put the content of (3.2) another way. An *argument* in a sentential language L is an ordered pair $\langle X, p \rangle$ such that X is a set of sentences of L (the *premises* of the argument) and p is a sentence of L (the *conclusion* of the argument); and a *counterexample* to an argument $\langle X, p \rangle$ in L is an argument $\langle X', p' \rangle$, in a sentential language L', which has true premises and a false conclusion, but which is nevertheless a homomorphic image of $\langle X, p \rangle$ in the sense that $h''X = X'$ and $h(p) = p'$ for some homomorphism h of L into L'. (Assurance that counterexamples, so defined, take in all wanted cases is provided by the fact that any mapping of atomic sentences of L to sentences of L' is included in a unique homomorphism of L into L'.[17]) In these terms, (3.2) comes to this: if an argument in a classical sentential language belongs to the Boolean implication for the set of sentences of the language, then no counterexample to it exists in any classical sentential language.

The result is not an unlikely candidate for a theorem of mathematical logic. But from it one cannot conclude that Boolean implications for sets of sentences of classical sentential languages are strict. The reason is not, as some might think, that there *could* have been classical sentential languages other than those there *are*. Assume, as is commonly done in such abstract discussions, that actual classical sentential languages exhaust possible ones: that it is not possible that there should have existed a classical sentential language other than those that do in fact exist. From this assumption, together with (3.2), we can indeed conclude that if an argument in a classical sentential language belongs to the Boolean implication for the set of sentences of that language, then no counterexample to the argument exists in any possible classical sentential language. But we cannot go on to conclude that it is impossible that there should have been a counterexample to the argument. For thus far nothing excludes the possibility, with respect to some homomorphic image of the argument in some classical sentential language, that its premises should have been true and yet its conclusion false. In fact, thus far nothing excludes the possibility that the argument itself should have had true premises and a false conclusion.

The gap between (3.2), on the one hand, and the proposition that Boolean implications for classical sentential languages are strict, on the other, seems often to go unrecognized, even by those one would expect to be most sensitive to it. Let me paraphrase a passage from a recent exposition of first-order logic:[18]

> If we asked a Proof Theorist to explain what it means to say
>
> (1) X logically implies p
>
> where p and the members of X are sentences of a classical sentential language, he would say that it means this: there is a proof of p from X in one of the standard proof calculi. A Model Theorist would prefer to say that (1) means: whenever every member of X is true on a Boolean valuation on the set of sentences of the language, p is true on that valuation too. The Traditional Logician for his part would explain it thus: every argument that has the form of $\langle X, p \rangle$ is valid. There need be no fight between these three honest scholars, because it is elementary to show that (1) is true under any one of the definitions if and only if it is true under any other.

The suggestion is that, if L is any classical sentential language, two propositions with respect to L are on the same footing: one is a proposition to the effect that, where R is the union of some standard set of rules for sentential languages, $\vdash_R$ is sound and complete with respect to Boolean valuations on the sentences of L; the other is a proposition to the effect that X bears to p the Boolean implication for L if and only if every homomorphic image of $\langle X, p \rangle$ is valid. Now, the first of these propositions belongs to pure mathematics. Its proof need not invoke even the concept of truth, let alone that of impossibility, nor need $B(S)$ and R have any recognizable connection with the meanings of sentences of the forms Np and Cpq. But the second is not a proposition of pure mathematics. It is not, at least, if we can take the author at his word when he defines 'valid': "An argument is called *valid* when its premises *entail* its conclusion, in other words, if the premises can't be true without the conclusion also being true."[19] The second proposition is thus to the effect that X bears to p the Boolean implication for L just in case every homomorphic image of $\langle X, p \rangle$ has the property that it is impossible for its premises to be true and yet its conclusion false. I do not know what elementary demonstration of this proposition the author would produce; perhaps it is something in the neighborhood of the "proof" given above that every admissible valuation on the sentences of L is Boolean. But whatever it is, it must call upon more than the resources of pure mathematics.

The authors of another text begin their first chapter by asking the reader to consider the "inference"

(1)   Every tove is slithy

(2)   Alice is not slithy

---

(3)   Alice is not a tove.

After remarking that "statement (3) is correctly inferred from statements (1) and (2)," the authors offer an explanation: "What makes (3) a logical consequence of (1) and (2) is the fact that *if* (1) and (2) are true *then* (3) must be true as well. *Any* interpretation of 'tove', 'slithy', and 'Alice' under which (1) and (2) come out true will make (3) true also".[20] But how are the two sentences in the explanation related? I suspect the authors think they come to the same thing, or at any rate that the first follows from the second. Either way, I am perplexed. Let us agree that (3) comes out true under any interpretation of 'tove', 'slithy', and 'Alice' under which (1) and (2) come out true. How is it supposed to follow that if (1) and (2) are true, (3) *must* be true? If 'any interpretation' means *any possible interpretation*, as I suppose it does, then perhaps it follows that, whatever 'tove', 'slithy', and 'Alice' were to mean, (3) would be true if (1) and (2) were. And from that in turn it follows that, given the actual meanings of 'tove', and 'Alice', (3) is true if (1) and (2) are. But how does it follow that, given the actual meanings of the words, (1) and (2) *cannot* be true unless (3) is also true? My point is not that 'tove' and 'slithy' are nonsense words. Assume them to have certain meanings, and assume 'Alice' denotes some one person. What is wanted is the conclusion that, so understood, it is impossible that (1) and (2) should be true and yet (3) false. And I do not see how that conclusion is to be obtained from the proposition that, under any and all reinterpretations of the words, (3) is in fact true if (1) and (2) are. One might as well argue that '$2 + 3 = 5$' is not a necessary truth, on the ground that '5' might have denoted 6.

The point carries over to classical sentential languages. An *interpretation* (*structure*, *model*) for such a language is commonly taken to be a valuation on the set of atomic sentences of the language, and a sentence of the language is *true on* an interpretation v_0 if and only if it is true on the Boolean extension of v_0. But an interpretation of a classical sentential language L might just as well be a function that assigns to the atomic sentences of L sentences of some classical sentential language L'. Any such function extends to a unique homomorphism of L into L', and the homomorphic image in L' of a sentence p of L can be thought of as actually having a meaning p might have had. If, as our liberal ontology of classical sentential languages presumably guarantees, every meaning p might have had is the meaning of some sentence in some classical sentential language, the possible reinterpretations of an argument $\langle X, p \rangle$ in L come to be represented by the images of $\langle X, p \rangle$ under all homomorphisms of L into other classical languages. Arguments in L which, under all intrepretations, have true conclusions if they have true premises are thus precisely those to which there are no counterexamples. And we have already seen that absence of counterexamples to an argument is not enough to ensure that its conclusion must be true if its premises are.

4

The gap will not disconcert those philosophers who, as a matter of principle, shun modalities. They will be content with (3.2) itself, or something to the same effect. Their idea is that nonexistence of counterexamples is good enough: if an analogue of (3.2) holds for an implication for the set of sentences of a sentential language, the implication is a relation of logical consequence.

The trouble with the idea is not that it gives unwanted results for classical sentential languages but that it does not easily generalize. If the idea is to be brought to bear on the question, When is an implication an entailment? some general notion of a counterexample must be at hand. But what we have so far is a notion specific to sentential languages, and from it alone one cannot gather how to go on.

Let me illustrate the difficulty by calling attention to a class of languages, each of which harbors a classical sentential language. These are languages of the form $\langle S, P, C, N, p^* \rangle$, where $\langle S, P, C, N \rangle$ is a classical sentential language and p^* is a member of P which is true if and only if there are subways in Boston. Let $Z(S)$ be the set of Boolean valuations on S that assign T to p^*. And let a *homomorphism* of $\langle S, P, C, N, p^* \rangle$ into $\langle S', P', C', N', q^* \rangle$ be a function from S into S' that not only preserves the sentence-forming operations but also assigns q^* to p^*. By modifying the proof of (3.1) so as to accommodate the validity of p^* and q^* relative to, respectively, $Z(S)$ and $Z(S')$, one obtains a proof of

(4.1)   If h is a homomorphism of $\langle S, P, C, N, p^* \rangle$ into
$\langle S', P', C', N', q^* \rangle$, then $h''X \vdash_{Z(S')} h(p)$ whenever $X \vdash_{Z(S)} p$.

Taking advantage of the fact that there are subways in Boston, it is then easy to obtain an analogue of (3.2):

(4.2)   If h is a homomorphism of $\langle S, P, C, N, p^* \rangle$ into $\langle S', P', C', N', p^* \rangle$, $h(p)$ is true whenever every member of $h''X$ is true and $X \vdash_{Z(S)} p$.

In an appropriately adjusted sense of 'counterexample', if $X \vdash_{Z(S)} p$ then there are no counterexamples to $\langle X, p \rangle$. But, bearing in mind that the distinguished atomic sentence p^* of many languages of the kind in question is the very sentence 'there are subways in Boston', we naturally resist the conclusion that the implication is always an entailment. Absence of counterexamples appears not to be enough.

Perhaps it will be objected that, in contrast with (3.2), (4.2) is not a theorem of mathematical logic, since its proof appeals to the extralogical fact that there are subways in Boston; or, in the same vein, it may be objected that (4.2) is not knowable a priori, again in contrast with (3.2). I am ready to agree that proof of (4.2) invokes an empirical (and hence, I suppose, an extralogical) fact. But that supports the idea that absence of counterexamples is enough only on the assumption that counterexamples must meet an epistemological condition heretofore unmentioned. And it is a condition not likely to be imposed by those with whom modalities are in disfavor: the distinction between the a priori and the empirical is no clearer than that between the necessary and the contingent.

A more serious objection is that the new, and narrower, notion of a homomorphism is deliberately contrived to yield unacceptable results. Of course it is. But it is deliberately contrived also to force an opponent of modalities to show his hand. What are the limits on acceptable homomorphisms? Some philosophers will invoke the notion of a logical constant: homomorphisms should preserve operations associated with logical constants, and p^* is not, or is not always, a logical constant.

The objection raises the question, What is a logical constant? and thereby entangles the question, When is an implication an entailment? with what are to my mind bootless controversies about the boundaries of logic. A distinguished logician once said to me (a) that the Axiom of Choice does not follow from the (other) axioms of Zermelo-Fraenkel set theory, and, after a decent interval, (b) that 'the set of points on a straight line is ordinary infinite' follows from 'the set of points on a straight line is Dedekind infinite'. In response to his (b), I said that the proof requires the Axiom of Choice—to which he replied that of course it does, but the Axiom of Choice is *true*. Well, it was a conversation over dinner, and there was wine. But a moral can be drawn. What counts as a logical constant, and hence what counts as part of "the underlying logic," varies from context to context. A certain well-known implication will not take one from the axioms of ZF to the Axiom of Choice; neither will it take one from 'the set of points on a straight line is Dedekind infinite' to 'the set of points on a straight line is ordinary infinite'. Another implication will do both. The two have equally good claims to be called entailments, and the relevant constants have equally good claims to be called logical.

Perhaps Tarski would take the conversation as evidence for what he said in remarks prefatory to his definition of logical consequence:

> With respect to the clarity of its content the common concept of consequence is in no way superior to other concepts of everyday language. Its extention is not sharply bounded and its usage fluctuates. Any attempt to bring into harmony all possible vague, sometimes contradictory, tendencies which are connected with the use of this concept, is certainly doomed to failure. We must reconcile ourselves from the start to the fact that every precise definition of this concept will show arbitrary features to a greater or less degree.[21]

The paper concludes on a similar note: it is "quite possible," Tarski says, "that we shall be compelled to regard such concepts as 'logical consequence' . . . and 'tautology' as relative concepts which must, on each occasion, be related to a definite, although in greater or less degree arbitrary, division of terms into logical and extra-logical."[22]

I prefer to say that, even in relatively sophisticated discourse, no one implication is inevitably associated with 'follows from' and like expressions. From this point of view, what appears as a definition of logical consequence is at best a specification of some one implication, or class of implications, thought for one or another reason to be of interest and importance. It is not a sweeping claim about the meaning of 'follows from', nor a decision, in some respects arbitrary, as to what the phrase is henceforth to mean.

When we say that p follows, or does not follow, from X, we allude—often vaguely—to an implication, relying on the context to steer the audience to the one intended. Thus it was when I said above that from (3.2) it does not follow that Boolean implications are strict; for I do not deny that (3.2) bears *some* implication, even some entailment, to that proposition. When push comes to shove, we try to specify the implication exactly, if we can. In so doing we engage ourselves in the business of logic.

But are there no limits? Are we free to take even 'there are subways in Boston' as a logical constant and thereby to count $\vdash_{Z(S)}$ an entailment? Tarski hints that we are not when, in support of his own defintion of logical consequence, he says that "it can be proved, on the basis of this definition, that every consequence of true sentences must be true."[23] Friends of modalities will see here a suggestion that any reasonable selection of logical constants must be responsible to the fact that implications are entailments only if strict. But enemies of modalities are without a principle to stand on. They can dismiss implications of the form $\vdash_{Z(S)}$ as uninteresting for systematic purposes, and they can point out that to call them all entailments accords ill with logical practice. But beyond considerations of truth value, in the home language and in structurally similar languages, there is for them no firm ground on which to address the question, When is an implication an entailment?

Notes

1. I have drawn on D. J. Shoesmith and T. J. Smiley, *Multiple-Conclusion Logic* (Cambridge: Cambridge University Press, 1978), especially chap. 1. Although the rest of the book deals mainly with multiple-conclusion logic, it contains much information about protologic as well.

2. But see n. 13.

3. Alfred Tarski, "On Some Fundamental Concepts of Metamathematics" and "Fundamental Concepts of the Methodology of the Deductive Sciences," pp. 30–37 and 60–109, respectively, of *Logic, Semantics, and Metamathematics*, 2d ed. (Indianapolis: Hackett, 1983), edited and introduced by John Corcoran and translated by J. H. Woodger. Each appeared originally in 1930. Full bibliographical information is contained in notes to each article.

4. Tarski required in addition that consequence operations be *compact*, i.e., that $Cn(X) = Cn(Y)$ for some finite subset Y of X. I see no good reason for imposing the requirement, especially since, as Shoesmith and Smiley remark (*Multiple-Conclusion Logic*, p. 21), "the classical logic of second- and higher-order quantification, which has as good a claim as any to represent the underlying logic of the working mathematician, is not compact." For the use of 'consequence operation' see, e.g., R. Wojcicki, "Matrix Approach in Methodology of Sentential Calculi," *Studia Logica* 32 (1973): 7–37, and the bibliography therein. Save for the requirement that consequence operations have sets of sentences as arguments and values, they are indistinguishable from what are called in algebra *closure operations*. See, e.g., G. Birkhoff, *Lattice Theory*, 3d ed. (Providence: American Mathematical Society, 1967), p. 111.

5. *Logic, Semantics, and Metamathematics*, p. 63.

6. G. E. Moore, *Philosophical Studies* (London: Routledge and Kegan Paul, 1922), p. 291.

7. W. V. Quine, *Word and Object* (Cambridge, Mass.: MIT Press, 1960), pp. 193–194.

8. *Multiple-Conclusion Logic*, p. 2.

9. See especially *A Survey of Symbolic Logic* (Berkeley: University of California Press, 1918) and, with C. H. Langford, *Symbolic Logic* (New York: Century, 1932).

10. "Necessary truths . . . coincide with the class of tautologies, or truths which can be certified by logic alone; and impossible propositions coincide with the class of those which deny some tautology." (Lewis and Langford, *Symbolic Logic*, pp. 248–249.)

11. See Lewis and Langford, *Symbolic Logic*, p. 250, where Lewis purports to show that "from a proposition whose truth is impossible, anything whatever may be deduced." Supposing p and q to be any propositions, the deduction is the following sequence: $KpNp$, p, Apq, Np, q. (Here $KpNp$ is the conjunction of p with Np, and Apq is the disjunction of p with q.) Lewis also claimed to have a proof that "from every proposition whatever . . . every proposition of the form $[ApNp]$ may be deduced" (p. 251), but it has attracted less attention. The explanation may be that, as Casimir Lewy remarks, it "seems at first sight more 'fishy'"

than the proof that from a contradiction everything follows. See his *Meaning and Modality* (Cambridge: Cambridge University Press, 1976), p. 111.

12. See W. T. Parry, "Ein Axiomensystem für eine neue Art von Implikation (Analytische Implikation)," *Ergebnisse eines mathematischen Kolloquiums* 4 (1933): 5–6.

13. See A. R. Anderson and N. D. Belnap, Jr., *Entailment* (Princeton: Princeton University Press, 1975). The authors follow Lewis in focusing on strong conditional operations, rather than implications in the sense of this essay. But see chap. 3, wherein "the reader is entitled to interpret [the conditional sign] as signifying a metalinguistic relation of logical consequence standing between truth functional expressions" (p. 150).

14. E. J. Nelson objected to conjunction elimination, which was used by Lewis in his original derivation: see Nelson's "Intensional Relations." *Mind*, n.s. 39 (1930): 440–453. But that rule need not be invoked, once it is agreed that derivations proceed from *sets* of sentences to sentences; and misgivings about the rule presumably carry over to Dilution, for Nelson's objection to conjunction elimination is that not the whole of the premise need be relevant to the conclusion. G. H. von Wright ("The Concept of Entailment," in his *Logical Studies* [London: Routledge and Kegan Paul, 1957]) and P. T. Geach ("Entailment," in *Logic Matters* [Berkeley: University of California Press, 1972], pp. 174–186) have proposed definitions that seem to restrict the transitivity of "entailment" and hence on which Cut would apparently fail. For an effort to apply their ideas with precision at the level of propositional logic, see T. J. Smiley, "Entailment and Deducibility," *Proceedings of the Aristotelian Society*, n.s. 59 (1959): 233–254. Finally, G. E. Moore appears to have denied that "entailment" is reflexive: see "Russell's 'Theory of Descriptions,'" in his *Philosophical Papers*, especially p. 180.

15. John Etchemendy is the only philosopher I know of who has considered the question at any length. See his "Tarski, Model Theory, and Logical Truth" (Ph.D. dissertation, Stanford University, 1982) and "Models, Semantics and Logical Truth" (1985, unpublished). I have benefited from his discussion in ways that go well beyond the limits of this essay.

16. I here assume the theorem that every valuation on the set of atomic sentences of a sentential language is included in a unique valuation on the entire set of sentences of the language. For a proof, see, e.g., R. M. Smullyan, *First-Order Logic* (New York: Springer-Verlag, 1968), pp. 10–11.

17. For an outline of a proof, see, e.g., H. B. Enderton, *A Mathematical Introduction to Logic* (New York: Academic Press, 1972), pp. 27–29.

18. Wilfrid Hodges, "Elementary Predicate Logic," chap. 1, vol. 1 of D. Gabbay and F. Guenther, eds., *Handbook of Philosophical Logic* (Dordrecht: Reidel, 1983). See p. 33 for the passage here paraphrased. I apologize to Hodges for any misrepresentation.

19. Hodges, "Elementary Predicate Logic," p. 2.

20. J. Bell and M. Machover, *A Course in Mathematical Logic* (Amsterdam: North-Holland, 1977), pp. 5–6.

21. "On the Concept of Logical Consequence," in *Logic, Semantics, and Metamathematics*, pp. 409–420. The quotation is from p. 409.

22. *Logic, Semantics, and Metamathematics*, p. 420.

23. *Logic, Semantics, and Metamathematics*, p. 417.

Appendix: Two Problem Sets

1

In the case of any of the following that is as it stands false or senseless, remedy matters (if possible) by supplying quotes and/or corners in accordance with customary conventions. Look for "best" solutions, i.e., solutions that involve as few additional symbols as possible.

1. Boston is north of Providence, but Providence is not south of Boston.

2. The last word of a "best" solution for # 1 is Boston.

3. The quotation-name of the last word of a "best" solution for # 2 is Boston.

4. For every sentence ϕ, the last word of the last word of ϕ is polysyllabic is polysyllabic.

5. Moore's wife called Moore Moore.

6. It is not the case that Moore's wife called Moore Moore's surname.

7. The last word of # 7 is obscene.

8. The last word of # 7 is obscene.

9. The first letter of the Greek alphabet is α is satisfied by an object β only if β is identical with α.

10. For every sentence ϕ, ϕ implies not-ϕ implies ϕ implies ϕ and not-ϕ.

2

Let us say that an entry in problem set 1 is *incorrigible* just in case there is no way of supplying quotes and/or corners such that the result is neither false nor senseless. It would appear that

(1)   # 7 is incorrigible

(2)   # 8 is not incorrigible

and yet that

(3)   #7 is identical with #8.

But at least one of (1), (2), and (3) must be false. Otherwise we should have a violation of the principle that x is identical with y only if everything true of x is true of y. Which is false? Why?

Index